Site Planning

Site Planning

Third Edition

Kevin Lynch   Gary Hack

The MIT Press
Cambridge, Massachusetts, and London, England

Seventh Printing, 1990

© 1984 by Gary Hack, Catherine Lynch,
David Lynch, Laura Lynch, and Peter Lynch

Printed and bound in the United States
of America by Maple-Vail, Inc.

Library of Congress Cataloging in
Publication Data

Lynch, Kevin.
  Site planning.

  Bibliography: p.
  Includes index.
  1. Building sites—Planning.
 I. Hack, Gary.
 II. Title.
NA2540.5.L9 1984 720 83-26742
ISBN 0-262-12106-9

Contents

Preface   vi

1   The Art of Site Planning   1
2   The Site   29
3   The User   67
4   The Program   107
5   Design   127
6   The Sensed Landscape and Its Materials   153
7   Access   193
8   Earthwork and Utilities   223
9   Housing   251
10   Other Uses   295
11   Weak Controls, Built Places, Few Resources   333
12   Strategies   369

Appendixes
A   Soils   379
B   Field Surveys   385
C   Reading Aerial Photographs   392
D   Regional Climate   402
E   Sun Angles   407
F   Noise   412
G   A Site and Impact Checklist   420
H   Costing   426
I   Trees, Hedges, Ground Covers   431
J   Intersections   444
K   Earthwork Computations   448
L   Numbers   455

Bibliography   471
List of Illustrations   483
List of Tables   486
Credits   487
Index   491

Preface to the Third Edition

This is an introduction to the art of site planning, an exposition of its principles, and a condensed technical reference. It is meant for students and for practicing professionals. But those who simply enjoy the urban landscape, or who are concerned with the social issues it generates, will also find pleasure in it.

In 1971, the second edition responded to basic changes in the principles of the art. This edition responds to the recent marked expansion of the field, in such areas as programming, participation, user analysis, development economics, impact analysis, design strategies, housing tenure, and the characteristics of work in built places or in developing countries. At the urging of its users, it has been completely reorganized and rewritten to follow the normal sequence of professional work. The first chapter summarizes this process, and an illustrated case example follows. Eleven chapters discuss the principal activities and concerns of site planning, while eleven appendixes cover special techniques. A final appendix compiles the numerical standards for quick reference.

Since this is an introduction to an old and well-developed art, there is not much here that is original. These ideas come from many sources and have been so condensed, reordered, and interpreted that they can hardly be attributed to any single origin. Frank Lloyd Wright opened our eyes to architecture and its roots in the land; the ideas of Gyorgy Kepes have been fundamental. Wittingly or unwittingly, many skilled teachers and professionals have made their contributions: Lawrence Anderson, Tridib Banerjee, Paul Buckhurst, Stephen Carr, David Crinion, Ralph Eberlin, Robert Kennedy, Tunney Lee, Lionel Loshak, John Mason, John Myer, Jack Nasar, Laurie Olin, William Porter, Robert Rau, Hideo Sasaki, Tomasz Sudra. Teachers and students who have used past editions made useful suggestions for reworking it. Pam Wesling, Caryn Summer, and Tertia Perkins helped gather the new illustrations, and Anne

Simunovic managed our enterprise. Ron Reid helped in the production of the illustrations, while Susan Sklar and Dianne Pansen aided in the many revisions of the text.

We hope that the book will continue its usefulness.

Kevin Lynch
Gary Hack

Cambridge, Massachusetts
October, 1983

Chapter *1*

The Art of Site Planning

Site planning is the art of arranging structures on the land and shaping the spaces between, an art linked to architecture, engineering, landscape architecture, and city planning. Site plans locate objects and activities in space and time. These plans may concern a small cluster of houses, a single building and its grounds, or something as extensive as a small community built in a single operation.

Site planning is more than a practical art, however complex its technical apparatus. Its aim is moral and esthetic: to make places which enhance everyday life—which liberate their inhabitants and give them a sense of the world they live in. Professional skill—that easy familiarity with behavior settings, grading, planting, drainage, circulation, microclimates, or survey—is only a path to that result.

Roads and buildings, even gardens, do not grow by themselves. They are shaped by someone's decision, however limited or careless. The economic and technical advantages of large-scale development incline us to organize sites in a more comprehensive and convulsive way than when there was time for the gradual adjustment of use and structure. But regardless of scale or the degree of deliberation, any human site is somehow planned, whether piecemeal or at one sweep, whether by convention or by conscious choice.

Site planning has a new importance, but it is an old art. One thinks of such magnificent places as the Katsura Palace, the Italian squares and hilltowns, the crescents of

Reference 44

1

Bath, Wright's Taliesin, or the New England town green. By contrast, most site planning in our country today is shallow, careless, and ugly. This reflects a lack of skill, but also the stubborn structural problems of our society, which are political, economic, and institutional. Place making is divided from place using; purposes change, conflict, and are not well understood. Site planning may be a hurried layout, in which details are left to chance; or a cursory subdivision, to which buildings will be added later; or a last-minute effort to fit a previously designed building onto some available piece of land. Site plans are seen as minor adjuncts to the dominant decisions of developers, engineers, architects, and builders. At the same time, they are the subject of significant public regulations.

This neglect is a dangerous error, since the site is a crucial aspect of environment. It has a biological, social, and psychological impact that goes far beyond its more obvious influence on cost and technical function. It limits what people can do, and yet also opens new opportunities to them. For some groups—small children, for example—it can be the dominant feature of their world. Its influence outlives that of most buildings, since site organization persists for generations. What we do to our habitat has an enduring effect on our lives.

Normal process

Site planning is usually accomplished in a regular sequence, a sequence around which we organize this text. This typical process has its flaws and admits of variations, as we will explain. But we begin by mapping that normal stream, and comment later on its inadequacies (in Chapter 12).

In the most common case, a site plan is made by a professional for some paying client, who has the power to carry it out. The development is to consist of a collection of buildings, which will be built on some largely open piece of ground, already chosen for the purpose. In a project of moderate size, site planning and the design of the buildings will be done simultaneously, preferably in a single office. Development will be completed in a few year's time. Once occupied, the site will continue to be used in the same way, as far as can be foreseen. For a larger and more complex work to be created over a longer period of time, the site plan may be prepared first and the building designs later.

What is the problem?

Let this stand as the normal case. The first step—the most difficult and most often bungled step—is to ask what

FIGURE 1 *The towering Potiala at Lhasa: the expression of site and of political domination.*

the problem is. Defining the problem means making a whole cluster of decisions: for whom is the place being made? for what purpose? who will decide what the form is to be? what resources can be used? what type of solution is expected? in what location will it be built? These decisions set the stage for the entire process to come. Although they will to some extent be modified as the process develops—and should be modified more frequently than they are—later changes are painful and confusing.

The purpose of the development depends on the situation and on the values of the influential clients. But some of those who will be affected by the plans are absent, or uninformed, or voiceless. There usually are conflicts among the various clients. There may be sharp distinctions between the future users and those who pay for the professional services. In this touchy situation, the designer (if he has the opportunity) has the responsibility to clarify the given objectives, raise hidden ones for debate, reveal new possibilities and unexpected costs, and even speak for absent or voiceless clients. More often, however, designers will simply speak for their own values—an aggravated error, since most of them are members of a particular social class.

The decisions which define the problem are so closely interrelated as to be circular: the clients determine the pur-

FIGURE 2
*Frank Lloyd
Wright's Millard
House: the
intimate relation
of a building's
form and texture
to its unusual
site at the bottom
of a ravine.*

poses, and yet the purposes indicate the proper clients; the probable solution determines the resources required, and yet the resources available limit the possible solutions. This ring of decisions is fashioned according to the limits and the possibilities which the initiator of the project sees before her, but the designer can also enter this ring and affect its shape. More often, he fails to do so, and the ring is forged by customary solutions and by the prevailing distribution of power.

In embryo, the problem statement contains the final design, and any alert designer is anxious to play a role in making it: to comment on site, purpose, and user, to consider the type of solution required, and whether the resources are sufficient to accomplish it. Commonly, however, the problem is determined by the client before the site designer is brought in. As a minimum, in that case, the latter is responsible for seeing that the problem has been explicitly set out, that its parts are internally consistent (sufficient resources, solution appropriate to purpose, adequate site, etc.), and that he can in conscience work for the clients and purposes given. To do that, he must run through the entire site planning process in his mind, using his experience and judgment to guess at its outcome.

Assume that the problem is properly set out and the site planner is willing to begin. The principal objectives of the work are stated, as well as the expected users and their needs. The site is chosen, and so is the type of development and activity intended to occupy it. The basic character of the new environment has been proposed. A budget has been provided to carry it out, including the time and resources necessary to make the plan. The planner begins by analyzing the future use and users, on the one hand, and the given site, on the other.

Every site, natural or man-made, is to some degree unique, a connected web of things and activities. That web imposes limitations and offers possibilities. Any plan, however radical, maintains some continuity with the preexisting locale. Understanding a locality demands time and effort. The skilled site planner suffers a constant anxiety about the "spirit of place."

Analysis of the site begins with a personal reconnaissance, which permits a grasp of the essential chraracter of the place and allows the planner to become familiar with its features. Later, then, she can recall mental images of those features as she manipulates them. Analysis proceeds

Site and user analysis

5

FIGURE 3
*The sense of
sacred place: the
Isono-kami Shrine
on a rainy
morning.*

FIGURE 3
*The sense of
sacred place: the
Isono-kami Shrine
on a rainy
morning.*

FIGURE 4
*Salem, Mass.: a
harmonious set-
ting produced by a
homogeneous,
confident culture.*

to a more systematic data collection, which may follow some standard list, but lists are treacherous. Certain information, such as a topographic base map, is almost always required. Other data are special to particular places. Some data are best gathered early, and some later. No data should be gathered unless they will have a significant influence on the design. New and unforeseen information will be needed as the design progresses.

The site is analyzed for its fitness for the purpose of the plan, and so it will be seen differently by people who are considering different uses for it. But the designer must also look at the site in its own right, as a living community of plants and animals (including human animals)—a community with its own interests that may, if ignored, respond in unsettling ways to any reorganization.

Through her analysis, the designer looks for patterns and essences to guide her plan, as well as simply for facts that she must take into account. She ends with a graphic summary, which communicates the fundamental character of the place, as well as how it will most likely respond to the proposed intervention. The study concludes with a statement of problems and potentials. The techniques of site analysis are discussed in Chapter 2.

How future users will act in the new configuration is the second pillar of knowledge. Frequently ignored, or simply drawn from intuition or personal experience, an understanding of future behavior is critical. When he can, the designer observes, and talks directly with, the actual people who will use the new place. Even better, these people may themselves participate in the design. This is the most straightforward way of making an effective plan.

At other times, future users will be dispersed, or unknown, or transient, complex, or conflicting, and indirect methods of study must be employed. Requirements may be taken from the literature, which is now becoming extensive. The functioning of analogous places may be studied. Surrogate users may be analyzed or simulated environments presented for discussion. But people can be unaware of their own purposes and problems or be unable to predict how they would act under different circumstances. Behavioral studies can also be misused in attempts to control other people. How people use their physical environment is a new field of study. The site designer must be familiar with the methods of that field and be able to employ them. The issues and techniques of user analysis are discussed in Chapter 3.

Program   When the problem has been set and site and users analyzed, then a detailed program can be made out. Traditionally
this has been a perfunctory affair: no more than a list of the
number and size of required spaces and structures ("twelve
one-bedroom apartments, a common laundry room, a tot
lot, parking for twenty cars, and a management office of
200 square feet"). The paying client presents this to the
designer, who fits it onto the site. The quality of those spaces,
the behavior expected to occur in them, and how they will
match the purposes of their users, are not mentioned. This
quantitative schedule is confined to routine categories of
form and neglects much that will make for success or failure
of the plan. Unwittingly, the site has been predesigned by
a narrow set of financial and administrative considerations.
Important purposes are not served; trivia are overemphas-
ized. Freedom of solution is restricted, and unforeseen consequences develop.

Properly prepared, on the other hand, the program will
play a central and decisive role in the design. It explicitly
connects the designer to objectives and to behavioral information. It begins with the actions that are expected to
take place, by whom, and with what purpose. It then proposes a schedule of "behavior settings," or places where
physical form and human activity are repeatedly associated
("a compact cooking place," "a mysterious place for exploration," "a dust-free space for assembling electronic parts").
The program gives the required character and equipment
for each setting and specifies how form should connect with
action and purpose. But it does not fix concrete shape or
exact size. It may also specify the intensity and timing of
use, the desirable connections between settings, and the expected management and service support. However detailed
or generalized, the program expresses environment, management, and behavior as one connected whole and also
describes how the attainment of that whole will be organized,
including its timing and financing.

This program is the first act of design. It is built in a
dialogue between client and designer, based on the knowledge of site and user, and expressed in diagrams and verbal
statements. It is the proposed outcome, a hypothesis of how
the design will work when finally occupied, an understanding
of what the client will receive for his outlay and what the
designer promises to deliver. The program changes as design
proceeds, since design is a process of learning about possibilities, but the changes can then be made explicitly. Chapter 4 elaborates on program preparation.

Once the program has been defined, designing in the conventional sense begins, although images of form have been latent in all the preceding stages, and program and design interact continuously throughout the remaining process. Here we are at the creative center. It is a mystery, like all human thought, and yet it is something that everyone does to some degree, and its techniques can be taught, again to some degree.

Schematic plan

Design is the imaginative creation of possible form and is done in many ways. It develops clouds of possibilities, both fragments and whole systems, in places vague, in others precise, in a state of mind which alternates between childish suggestibility and stern criticism. It is a dialogue between the designer and the growing, shifting forms that she is developing—not a determinate, logical process but an irrational search over a ground prepared by a knowledge of principles, of prototypes and the characteristics of site and users.

In our case, design consists of imagining patterns of activity, circulation, and physical form, as they will occur in some particular place. It is expressed in freely drawn plans, sections, and activity diagrams, and perhaps also in sketch views and rough models. As these possibilities drift and accumulate, the program is redefined and the site and its users are reanalyzed. There are various strategies for entering and then mastering this play with complexity. See Chapter 5.

At the end of this phase, the designer has developed one or more complete schematic plans, showing building form and location, outdoor activity, surface circulation, ground form, and general landscaping. The quality of this landscape is discussed in Chapter 6. Rough cost estimates are made for each plan. (See Appendix H.) Plans and costs are linked to a revised program.

Reference 80

This material is now presented to the paying client for her review and decision. She may choose one alternative; she may reject them all; she may direct that one of them be modified; or she may revise her program or her financial plan. At this point, the whole project may be recycled back to programming or design or even be abandoned. If it goes forward, it is on the basis of one schematic plan, chosen by the client, together with its program and its estimated cost. This choice is founded on a prediction of future behavior and performance, a prediction that will be confirmed only when the project is occupied.

Given that choice, the designer now proceeds to a detailed development of the plan, which will allow more exact cost estimates and final client approval. Plan development produces an accurate site plan, showing the location of all buildings, roads, and paved surfaces; the planted areas by type; the existing and proposed ground contours; the location and capacity of utilities; and the location and nature of site details. These plan drawings will be accompanied by sections, studies of detailed areas, typical views, and outline specifications. Any detailed tests of the plan—such as of wind effect—are made, and any formal impact analyses are prepared. An accurate cost estimate is drawn up, covering both construction and maintenance. Program and construction schedule are adjusted to fit this detailed plan.

Once the detailed plan is approved, the site planner goes on to make the contract documents, on which bids can be based. These usually consist of a precise layout of roads and structures, sufficient for their location by survey on the site; a complete grading plan and earthwork computation, with spot elevations for all major features; a utility layout and road and utility profiles; a planting plan; and plans and sections of site details and site furniture. Chapters 7 and 8 discuss these elements of site engineering. Complete specifications are drawn up, as well as the conditions of work and bid procedures. The documents distinguish the "add-ons"—features that may or may not be part of the final contract and should be priced separately to allow a last-minute adjustment between budget and contract price. These contract documents may be incorporated in the architectural or engineering documents or be independent, in the form of land development plans, landscape plans, or urban designs.

The client now asks for bids by contractors, based on these drawings and specifications. If there is an acceptable bid, the drawings and specifications become the contract documents, and construction begins. If the bids are not acceptable, plan and program must be revised once more. Careful planning and accurate costing help to avert this painful outcome, but not always.

Normally, the last professional step is to supervise construction on the ground, in order to ensure compliance, but also to make detailed adjustments as unexpected problems and opportunities arise. If properly made, the plans were based on a thorough knowledge of construction procedure and equipment, and so they allowed for the movement of machinery, the storage of material, the succession of site operations, and similar events. The inevitable disruptions of the construction period have already been discounted and provided for.

But the designer is also responsible for helping to make a smooth transition between construction and management of the site. Management support should have been part of the program from the beginning and is just as essential to success as the form itself. Ideally, the future managers of the site have already been involved in the creation of its form, and, at the latter end of the sequence, the site designer should continue to consult with management as use of the site builds up a pattern and momentum of its own. By watching how people use the place he has imagined, the designer learns something for his next endeavor. He compares the predictions of the program with actual events, and his inevitable mistakes are powerful lessons. In the typical case, unfortunately, designers rarely have a systematic opportunity to learn from their mistakes, and managers are rarely involved in the early stages of design. The transition to use is abrupt, and little information flows across the break.

To summarize, there are eight stages in the typical site planning cycle in which the designer is properly involved. (But often, alas, the designer has little to do with the first and the last.) Beyond this cycle of events, of course, other actors are engaged in other actions: the consideration and approval of plans, for example, or the securing of financing. Nevertheless the stages of site planning proper are:

1. defining the problem;
2. programming and the analysis of site and user;
3. schematic design and the preliminary cost estimate;
4. developed design and detailed costing;
5. contract documents;
6. bidding and contracting;
7. construction; and
8. occupation and management.

Reciting these stages makes them sound logical and linear, but the recital is only conventional; the real process is looping and cyclical. Knowledge of a later phase influences conduct of an earlier one, and early decisions are later reworked. Site design is a process of learning in which a coherent system of form, client, program, and site gradually emerges. Even after decisions are made and building begins—even after the site is occupied—the feedback from experience continues to modify the plan. These issues are reviewed again in Chapter 12. The designer thinks that her organization will have an absolute, permanent influence on all later occupants. In reality, this is only partly so, since whatever she does will soon undergo some modification. Every site has a long history that bears on its present. Every site will have a long future, over which the designer exerts only partial control. The new site form is one episode in a continuous interplay of space and people. Sooner or later, it will be succceeded by another cycle of adaptation.

Environment
and quality of
life

References 31, 86

Some critics assert that our physical settings determine the quality of our lives. That view collapses under careful scrutiny, and then it is a natural reaction to say that the spatial environment has no critical bearing on human satisfaction. Each extreme view rests on the fallacies of the other. Organism and environment interact, and environment is both social and physical. You cannot predict the happiness of anyone from the landscape he lives in (although you might predict his unhappiness), but neither can you predict what he will do or feel without knowing his landscape and others he has experienced. People and their habitat coexist. As humans multiply and their technology comes to dominate the earth, the conscious organization of the land becomes more important to the quality of life. Pollution impairs the living system, and some of our technical feats threaten all life. Careless disturbance of the landscape harms us; skilled siting enhances us. Well-organized, productive living space is a resource for humanity, just as are energy, air, and water.

Site planning, then, is the organization of the external physical environment to accommodate human behavior. It deals with the qualities and locations of structures, land, activities, and living things. It creates a pattern of those elements in space and time, which will be subject to continuous future management and change. The technical output—the grading plans, utility layouts, survey locations, planting plans, sketches, diagrams, and specifications—are simply a conventional way of specifying this complex organization.

One Example of the Site Planning Process

The best site plans are a unique response to the land and the program. This being so, no one example can be a prototype for every occasion but much can be learned by reconstructing a particular process. It will serve as a concrete example to which our subsequent discussion can refer.

Here we examine how a work environment became a sensitive addition to a memorable landscape. Our example is the product of a team effort by planners, architects, landscape architects, engineers, and many others.* Their client asked them to locate two large laboratories (one for polymer research, the other for chemical research), along with their associated facilities, on a 125 hectare (312 acre) site in a suburb of a large metropolitan area. Everyone agreed that buildings, roads, and parking should fit into the site with as little disruption as possible, capitalizing on the beauty of the existing site to create an imageable campus. At the same time, it would be necessary to provide for future expansion.

At the beginning, the program was sketchy, and site capabilities and the requirements of the local government were unknown. The illustrations that follow are traces of the site planning process.

*ARCO Research and Engineering Center, Newtown Square Pennsylvania. Architects and planners: Davis, Brody & Assoc. and Llewelyn-Davies Assoc. Landscape architects: Hanna/Olin. Engineers: Wiesenfeld & Leon; Robert Rosenwasser; Cosentini Assoc.; Syska & Hennessy; Day & Zimmerman.

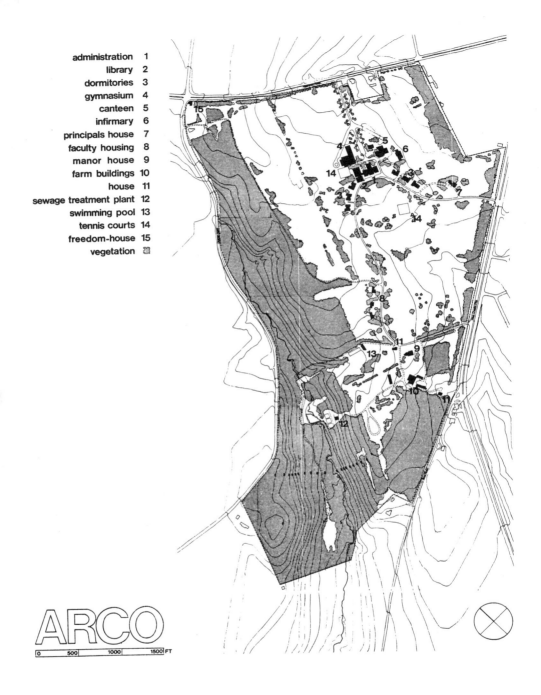

administration 1
library 2
dormitories 3
gymnasium 4
canteen 5
infirmary 6
principals house 7
faculty housing 8
manor house 9
farm buildings 10
house 11
sewage treatment plant 12
swimming pool 13
tennis courts 14
freedom-house 15
vegetation

0   500   1000   1500 FT

FIGURE 5   *A base map was prepared and existing features were plotted from aerial photographs and an initial field survey.*

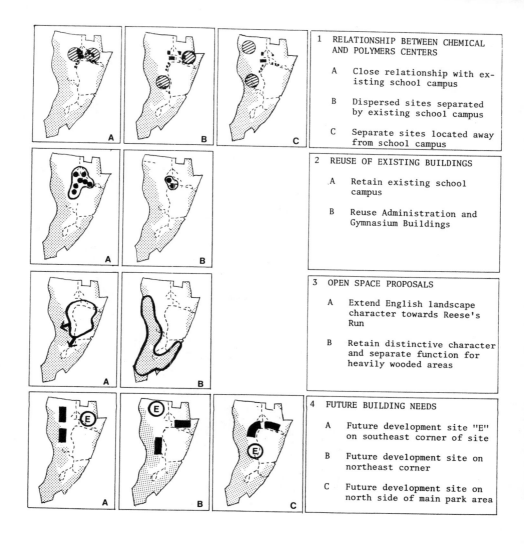

1   RELATIONSHIP BETWEEN CHEMICAL AND POLYMERS CENTERS

    A   Close relationship with existing school campus

    B   Dispersed sites separated by existing school campus

    C   Separate sites located away from school campus

2   REUSE OF EXISTING BUILDINGS

    A   Retain existing school campus

    B   Reuse Administration and Gymnasium Buildings

3   OPEN SPACE PROPOSALS

    A   Extend English landscape character towards Reese's Run

    B   Retain distinctive character and separate function for heavily wooded areas

4   FUTURE BUILDING NEEDS

    A   Future development site "E" on southeast corner of site

    B   Future development site on northeast corner

    C   Future development site on north side of main park area

FIGURE 6   *Four main planning issues were singled out for attention: the siting and relationship of the two laboratories; which of the existing small structures on the site should be saved; the character and use of wooded areas; the location of future development. A series of alternatives were weighed for each.*

15

FIGURE 7 *After selecting the most promising options, an initial site scheme was prepared for discussion and criticism. But much more needed to be known about site capacity, program, community attitudes, and client preferences before detailed design was possible.*

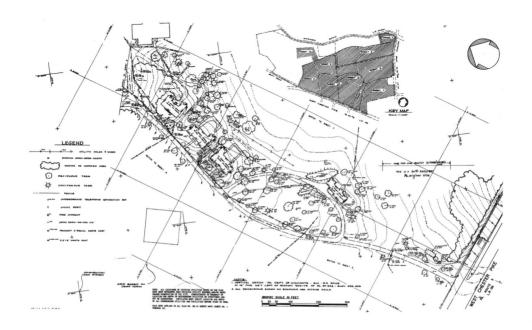

FIGURE 8   *A careful field survey was prepared, plotting the correct locations of all site elements, spot elevations and contours, the alignments of underground utilities, and the species and caliper of principal vegetation. A small section of the survey is reproduced here.*

17

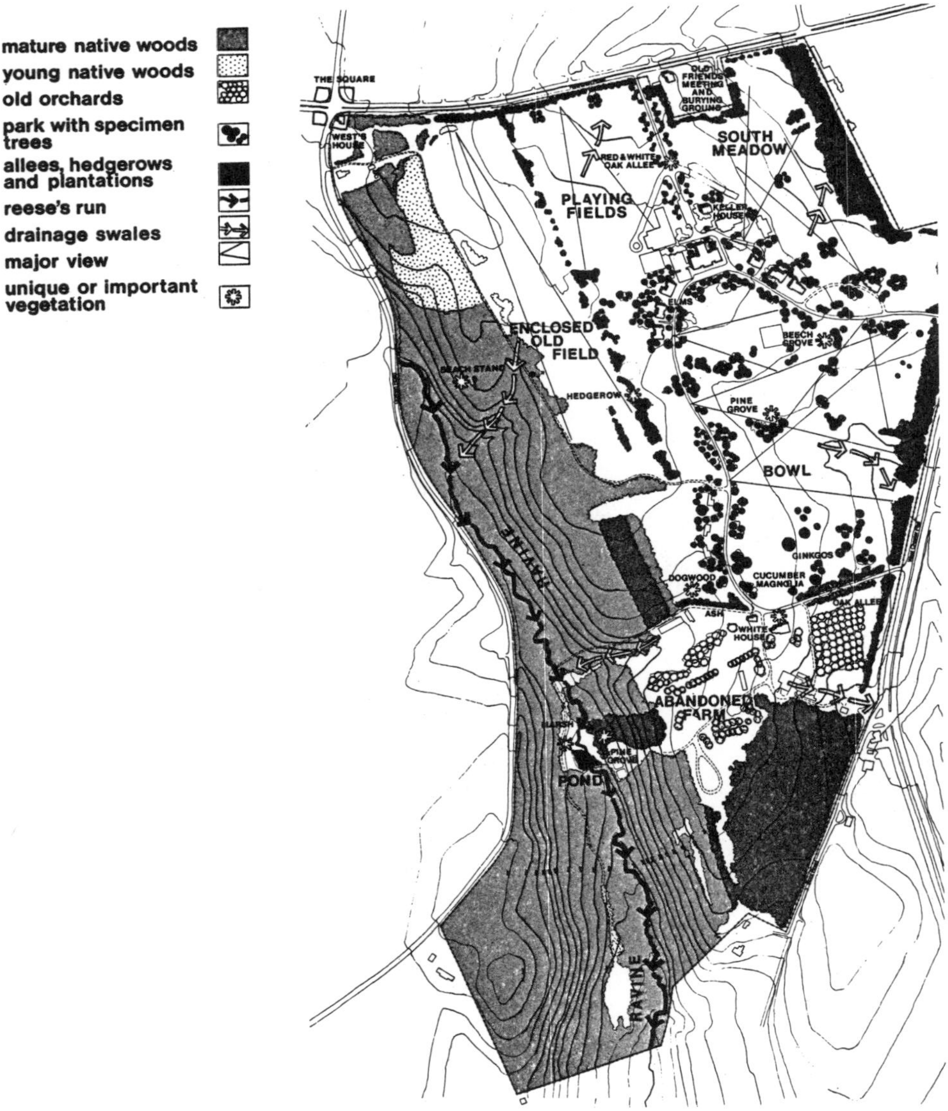

Legend:
- mature native woods
- young native woods
- old orchards
- park with specimen trees
- allees, hedgerows and plantations
- reese's run
- drainage swales
- major view
- unique or important vegetation

Map labels: THE SQUARE, WEST HOUSE, OLD FRIENDS MEETING AND BURYING GROUND, SOUTH MEADOW, RED & WHITE OAK ALLEE, PLAYING FIELDS, KELLER HOUSE, ENCLOSED OLD FIELD, BEECH STAND, HEDGEROW, BEECH GROVE, PINE GROVE, BOWL, PATH, GINKGOS, DOGWOOD, CUCUMBER MAGNOLIA, ASH, WHITE HOUSE, OAK ALLEE, ABANDONED FARM, POND, RAVINE

FIGURE 9 *The character and origin of the existing landscape was analyzed, along with the drainage courses essential to its preservation.*

18

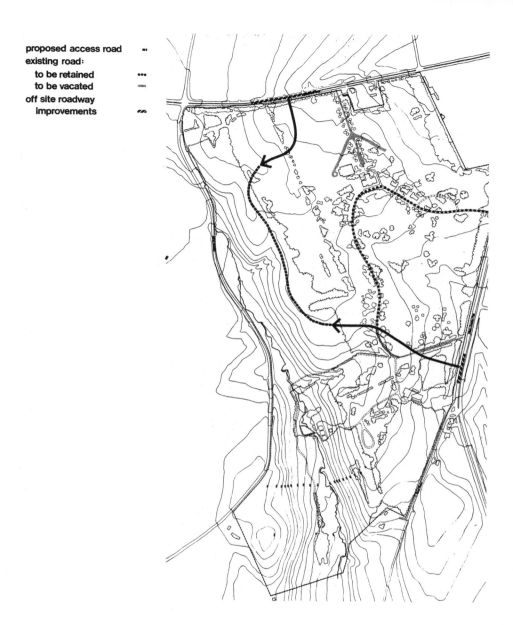

proposed access road ··
existing road:
   to be retained ···
   to be vacated =
off site roadway
   improvements ⌒

FIGURE 10 *Access demands and possibilities were considered in greater detail and discussed with local authorities. It was decided that two new access points would be necessary, and the most promising locations were identified. An indirect connection across the site was thought desirable. Several of the smaller roads could be retained for limited purposes. Similar investigations were made of utility needs, setback requirements, soils, and other issues.*

19

FIGURE 11 *Site sketches were made to discover and convey the character of each area, hoping to evoke images of how structures and roads might be fitted to the landscape.*

FIGURE 12 *More detailed programming exposed a large amount of overlap in common uses and therefore the first schematic architectural sketches suggested a change in direction: create a single linked set of stuctures, zoned by type of activity, rather than two separate groups for the two company divisions. A hedgerow on the site seemed to provide a logical break between office structures and industrial buildings.*

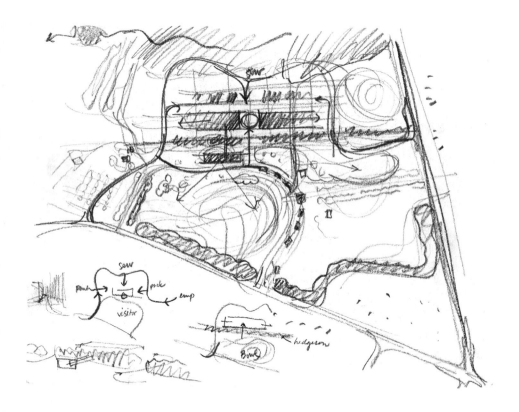

FIGURE 13 *The new concept for activities, location and access was summarized in this diagram, which became the guide for the design of buildings, site works and landscape additions.*

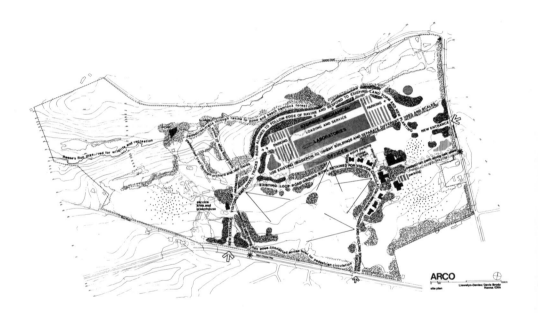

FIGURE 14 *Once preliminary designs for the buildings had been made, a site plan was prepared in sufficient detail to allow design development of parking areas, landscaping, road and walkways. A first approximation of the necessary site grading was made.*

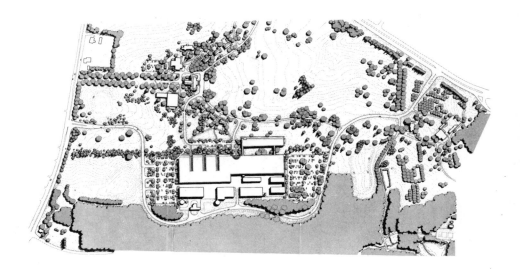

FIGURE 15 *The detailed grading plan adjacent to the structure was overlaid with a plan of the walkways and the areas to be seeded and sodded.*

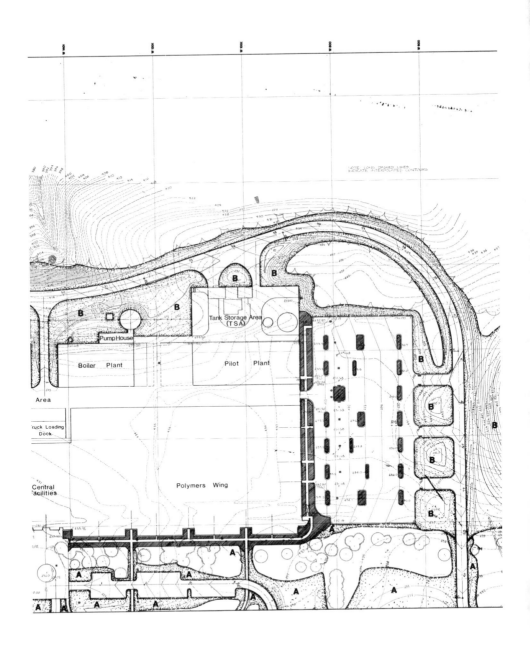

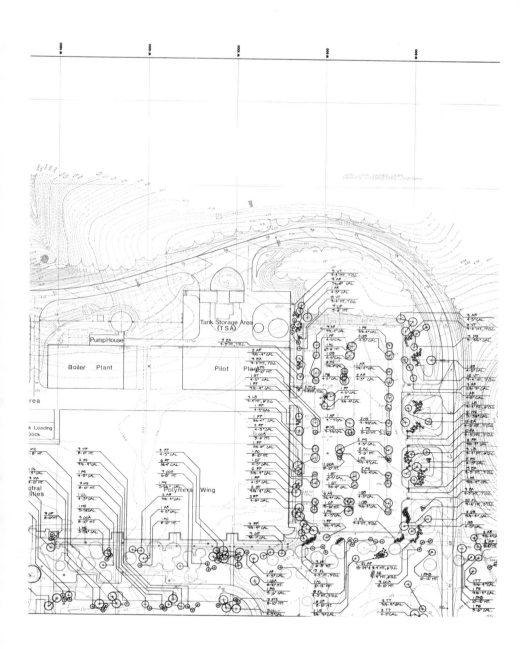

FIGURE 17   *Construction drawings with plans and sections were made for the site works that needed to be detailed in a form beyond what could be indicated on large site plans. Shown here is the ceremonial turnaround at the main public entrance.*

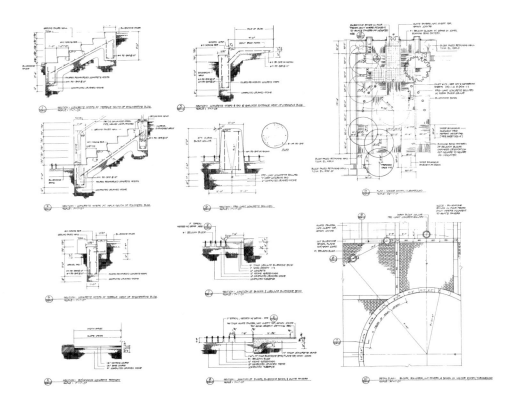

FIGURE 18 *Construction drawings were prepared for all utilities, roads, parkways and paths. The storm drainage plans shown here prescribe the location and dimensions of all drainage elements.*

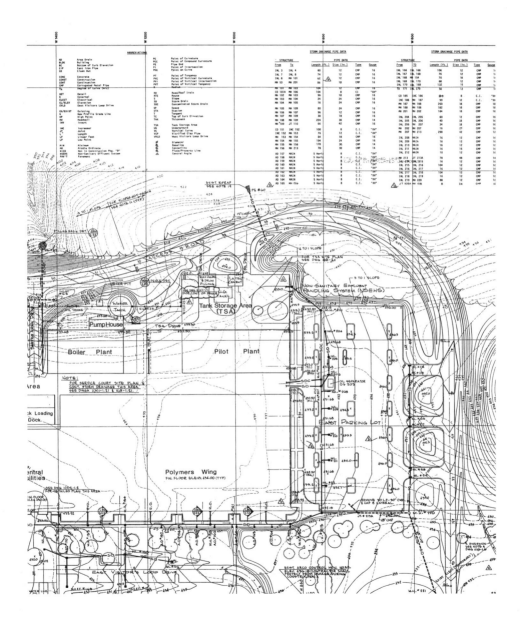

FIGURE 19
The photograph illustrates the industrial wing of the completed buildings, near its connection to the offices and the main entrance. The hedgerow has been retained to mask the large dimensions of the whole. In the middle ground is the ceremonial entrance with its deliberately over-scaled bollards.

FIGURE 20
The complex is hardly visible in the distance— which is what its planners intended. The rolling site dotted with spreading trees remains the dominant image.

Chapter 2

The Site

The site and the purpose for which it will be used—
the two sources of site design—are curiously interrelated.
Purpose depends on the limitations of the site, and site analysis depends on purpose. The same piece of ground will be
seen quite differently by a fortifications engineer or a farmer
or even by builders using different technologies and serving
different markets. Each view is correct.

The site is analyzed for fitness to purpose but also in
its own right as a living, changing community of plants and
animals. Such a community has its own interests. We expect
our interests to prevail, yet we must at least consider those
of the existing occupants. This is vital even in selfish terms,
since if we know the interconnections of the existing system,
we are less likely to set off some inadvertent disaster: severe
erosion, an explosive invasion of weeds, or a drop in the
water table. Thus site analysis has two branches—the one
oriented to our particular purpose and the other to the site
itself.

Experience allows us to set realistic purposes before a
particular site has been fully analyzed and to judge a site
before detailed purposes are known. Some site factors are
influential in almost all building development, but an unusual
purpose may make them irrelevant. No site can be studied
pedantically, by describing all the factors in some standard
list.

Since preindustrial people had little power to change a place in the short run, they were keenly aware of the limitations it imposed. Magical beliefs had an added influence. If a locality is the home of a local spirit, one avoids disturbing that home without due precaution, without a careful study of local configurations. The land is sacred, not to be violated. It is enduring, powerful, extensive, the home of spirits and the dead, the productive mother on whom human life depends. As we discard these religious ideas and as our power to impose change increases, we lose those restraining attitudes. We no longer unconsciously achieve harmony with setting or structures expressive of locality.

We now dominate the earth. In history men could burn a forest, wash away a field, foul a river, exhaust a mine, or extinguish a local species. Today we can pollute great lakes or the ocean, dirty the global air, and diffuse a chemical throughout the living world. Even if we walk softly we mark the land, and the quality of that man-marked surface comes to be one of the critical resources for our continued existence.

Site identity and change

Because of the complexity of its parts and their patterning, we find that each site is unique in some measure. The words *site* and *locality* should convey the same sense that the word *person* does: a complexity so closely knit as to have a distinct character worthy of our interest, concern, and even our affection. No one should engage in site design who does not have a passion for the land, who is not as fascinated by the variations of site character as a teacher is fascinated by the marvelous variations of the human personality. And so a site of uncertain form should disturb us as much as a person of disordered character.

Although the completely harmonious and mature site is unusual (and had best be left alone), the completely chaotic and meaningless one does not exist. Every site, however disturbed, has had some time to experience the mutual adjustment of its elements. The flow of water has created a drainage pattern, plant and animal life is linked in an ecology, neighboring structures lean against each other, shops have arranged themselves in relation to the resident population, and climate has weathered all. A site is composed of many factors—above, below, and on the ground—but these factors are interrelated. They have achieved some approximate balance, whether static or moving toward a new equilibrium. These interrelations indicate the designer's limits and point out the damage that he may inflict, since site development can have unexpected effects that pass along the whole chain

30

FIGURE 21
A fine rural land-
scape has an
obvious harmony
and character.

FIGURE 22
But urban land-
scapes also have
their own special
qualities.

31

of living things. Analysis also reveals hidden potentialities: where a design can clarify character, build new connections, and develop deeper meanings. Site analysis is a basis for conservation and also a prelude to successful revolution.

Fearful critics deplore new development: they wish that the land might be as it was. But how was it? Certainly never long the same. Environment changes steadily, even without our interference: new species crowd out the old, climates shift, geological processes continue. Decay, waste, entropy, and change are all part of the natural order. The past cannot be regained or the present fixed.

Ecology

References 24, 66, 84

The diverse living species, which capture the energy of the sun, or prey and are preyed upon, live in close relation with their immediate setting of water, earth, and air. Self-reproducing, evolving organisms interact with their changing spatial environment and create a persisting community. Individuals come and go; the forest remains, itself slowly shifting. If men cut the forest, new species colonize the cutlands. The new community is less stable and less diverse than before, and tends toward the forest once more. But if in the interval the soil is washed away, the forest may not return. In the absence of such external disturbance, the ecosystem moves toward a mature, steady state in which the diversity of species and the standing crop, or biomass, are at a maximum. Characteristic mature associations are formed—rain forest, grassland, salt marsh, tundra—whose form largely depends on the available light, warmth, moisture, and mineral elements. These living communities in turn regulate their habitat: the soil and the climate are modified by the plant cover. Exotic intrusions into a mature association—a new species, a fire, a volcanic eruption—cause violent oscillations. An increased volume of waste may overload the processes of decomposition or be of a kind for which no effective decomposing process exists. Saving such intrusions, populations are kept at stable numbers and in specific locations by competition, predation, natural barriers, and such self-regulating processes as territoriality.

Maximum organic production occurs in mature communities such as coral reefs or marine estuaries, but in those conditions net or surplus production is very close to zero. The optimum net production for human consumption occurs in communities that are continually upset, to keep them biologically young and poor. A lovely meadow, an orchard, a clean pond, or a field of wheat are all maintained by human interference. Many cultures prefer a particular land-

FIGURE 23 *Under a young stand of pitch pine, an understory of oak and sassafras is rising to succeed it.*

scape, especially the mix of forest and open land, the savanna or forest edge. So we make further disturbances, planting trees on the plains and opening clearings in the woods.

Typically, then, there is a conflict between human action and the tendency for a habitat to reach maturity. Stable, man-made landscapes are relatively rare. Certain rural areas of central France, of Moorish Spain, Japan, or eighteenth-century England come to mind. These stable, productive regions exact unremitting human effort. With good management, men can sustain intermediate states that are appropriate to their purposes. Species and habitat diversity, and basic resources such as soil, air, and water, can be conserved. It is even conceivable that the cycling of scarce nutrients and the efficiency of energy utilization might be improved by human interference without losing the fit to human preferences. But that will require inventive management.

An ecosystem is not moral. A stable one may appear ugly, wasteful, and uncomfortable to us. Ecology describes the limits and conditions of human intervention. It implies certain values—diversity, approximate stability, conservation—but these are neither ultimate nor comprehensive. Scientific and design criteria coincide only partially. Absolute preservation conflicts with human purpose, and we have little to guide us in resolving that conflict. With a better understanding of our values as well as of our condition, we may create a more consistent ethic that embraces all living organisms. Meanwhile, when we favor our own ends, we must at least remember that human purpose excludes making the world uninhabitable.

Behavior

Reference 7

How human beings are acting is usually, for us, the more critical aspect of any place. This can be described in terms of *behavior settings* or small localities, bounded in time and space, within which there is some stable pattern of purposeful human behavior, interacting with some particular physical setting. A teen-age hangout, a hunt, a church service, and an operating repair garage are examples of behavior settings. These settings are subsets of the more general ecological system. Both are organized complexities. Normally both change slowly, but they can shift in unexpected ways if disturbed. They are in part self-regulating, changing their surroundings to maintain themselves, while also adapting to their surroundings. Changes are propagated throughout the system, sometimes causing catastrophes but normally damping out. How the ecology and in particular the behavior setting are working and how they may be modified to our advantage are the key site questions. Watching truck movements or the walk to work, spotting the local hangout or the sled run, will be more informative than pages of statistics.

Preventing the loss of rare habitats or the extinction of species makes sense in selfish human terms, since diversity of place and gene may have unknown potentialities for the future, and we depend for our survival on the total web of living things. We have learned to reverse our judgment about wetlands, for example. Once fit only for dumping or for conversion into usable firm ground, they now appear as regulators of the water regimen and habitats for living creatures that are important to us.

Out of these new understandings there has arisen a new doctrine of site determinism: a place has an inherent right to its proper form, a "carrying capacity," a "best use." If that were true, then the analysis of existing interrelations would by itself indicate what the future use should be. But carrying capacity is indeterminate until we know what is to be carried, in what manner, and for what purpose. Best use depends on how we value uses. Site and purpose together are the arbiters of the plan, and not either one alone. However, we might broaden our purposes to embrace longer spans of time and more inclusive communities.

In order to understand the ecological and behavioral system as a whole, we must have some knowledge of its parts. We must disentangle the knot in order to retie it. We leave perception and behavior, issues most directly linked to ourselves, to the following chapter and focus here on the fundamental physical and biological aspects of the site. We begin underground and work up.

Beneath the surface, our first consideration is the soil, the pulverized mantle formed from rock and plant remains by the action of weather and organisms. On the same parent rock, grassland and forest produce very different soils. Soil is not static, but is continually developing and wasting. Beneath the organic litter of decomposing material, it is divided into conventional layers. First is the topsoil, a mixture of mineral and organic components, some of whose minerals have leached down to lower levels. The topsoil has direct organic functions. Then comes the soil, which is largely mineral and is below most plant roots, but which has some organic function. Finally, there is the fractured and weathered parent material of the soil above, which has little or no biological activity and lies directly over bedrock.

The particles of any soil are classified by their size— from visible stones to fine invisible grains. Soils are extremely variable mixtures of these particles, and these variable mixtures have many distinct implications for site development. Soil mixtures are classified in two different ways: by the soil scientists who were interested in the relation between soils and agriculture and wanted to learn how soils came to be, and by the engineers who were interested in the usefulness of soils for roads and foundations.

In the agricultural classification, the whole mantle of soil in one place, to depths of 2 m (6 ft) or more, is characterized as a unit. There are generic soil types that result from the basic climate, geology, and plant cover under whose influence that soil was formed. These great soil orders are further broken down into suborders, great groups, subgroups, families, and series. Each series has an identifying place

Soil

References 26, 53

35

See Figure 104,
Appendix A

name and is further divided according to the texture of the surface soil: "Merrimac sandy loam," for example. The textural names refer to the relative percentages of sand, silt, and clay in the surface layers.

The series name groups soils of similar history, constituents, depth, and structure. Therefore they have roughly similar characteristics as to bearing capacity, drainage, and agricultural value. Most of the United States has been mapped by those soil classes, down to areas as small as a few acres, and this work continues. Over 70,000 soil series have been identified. Originally made for agriculture, these maps are now regularly used in planning and have value for site design. We learn about potential water, sand, and gravel supply, about probable drainage, run-off, and erosion, about suitability for earth moving, foundations, and plant cover. Soil maps are especially useful in initial site reconnaissance.

Engineering class of soil

The engineering classification, on the other hand, refers to the exact composition of a particular soil body, wherever it occurs, as it is determined by laboratory tests on field specimens. It allows accurate predictions of bearing capacity, for example, or the optimum percentage of some additive that will improve the soil's performance for some engineering use. To a degree, it is possible to identify the engineering class of soil in the field, and rough field estimates may be all that is needed for siting light structures. There are ten broad classes of soil that can be identified in the field; these act very differently under loads or in the presence of water. Appendix A and Figure 105 define these ten types and summarize their site planning implications. The definitions reveal the crucial factors of difference: whether gravel, sand, silt, or clay predominates; whether the mix is well or poorly graded; the liquid limit; and the presence of organic matter. The site designer should be able to recognize those broad classes and know what they mean for her plans. Appendix A describes the procedures by which these classes can be identified in the field.

Soil as plant medium

The topsoil is the critical medium for plants. In this case, its important features are its drainage, its content of humus, its relative acidity (pH), and the presence of available nutrients, particularly potassium, phosphorus, and nitrogen. Any one of the latter may be deficient, owing to leaching down below the roots of plants. Phosphorus may be in an insoluble form and thus unavailable, or waterlogging may have discouraged the nitrifying bacteria that replenish the

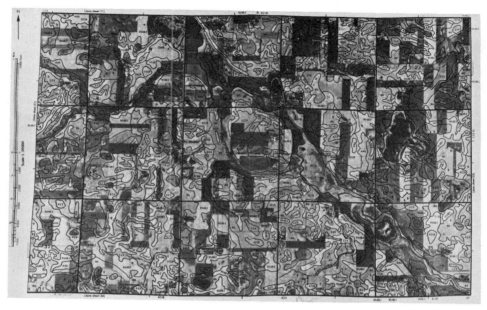

FIGURE 24 *A typical soil survey, overlaid on an aerial photo of the ground to which it refers. Note how these fourteen soil types conform to the natural features, if not to the field patterns. Each type has its particular consequences for engineering or agriculture.*

nitrogen supply. Impervious layers may impede drainage. High acidity (high pH) is particulary difficult for most plants, since available ions have largely been taken up by hydrogen. An abundant supply of earthworms is a reliable index of fertile soil of low acidity.

To learn what plants are best suited to a place, as well as what measures must be taken to improve the soil, there are simple tests for acidity and for available potassium, phosphorus, and nitrogen. Chemical deficiencies can be remedied, acidity can be modified to some degree, at least temporarily, and drainage can be improved. A compacted subsoil can be broken up before respreading the topsoil. Sandy soil is easily improved by adding peat or compost and by adjusting the pH with lime. Alkaline chalky soil can be improved with acid fertilizers. A heavy clay is more difficult, but sharp sand can be added to it, or perhaps it is easier simply to cover it with imported topsoil. Even slag heaps and similar wastes can be brought back to usefulness by pulverizing and fertilizing them and by planting pioneer plant species to begin soil regeneration. The limits to these procedures are economic rather than technical.

For engineering purposes, however, the topsoil is disregarded. It will be stripped off during construction and then respread. Soil samples are taken from small pits or by earth augers or boring tubes. But soils may change within a short distance and must be checked at many points where construction will occur. If different types are intimately mixed, assume the characteristics of the worst. Soil structure, or the layering or clustering of particles and the presence of holes or slippage planes, will also affect bearing strength and drainage.

The distribution of boulders and the depth to bedrock are important features. Driving a pointed rod into the ground tests soil density and depth and checks for boulders and ledges. If bedrock, large boulders, or ledges are encountered, the critical distinction is whether they are hard, and must be blasted out, or are sufficiently soft or loose for excavation by power equipment. Some shales, weak conglomerates, and highly weathered rocks are of this latter kind. The presence of numerous large boulders and ledges obviously adds appreciably to site costs.

For heavy construction or in dubious ground, one cannot rely on a simple field inspection. Systematic borings must be taken, and the soil and rock samples must be tested in specialized laboratories. Borings are usually taken at 15 m (50 ft) intervals to depths at least 6 m (20 ft) below the bottom of the eventual foundations, or to bedrock. Subsurface characteristics are also gleaned from examining previous structures and excavations, from looking at the sides of cuts, or from studying old records, aerial photographs, and geological reports.

Perhaps the most important subsurface variable of all is the presence or absence of water: the moisture content of the soil, its internal and surface drainage, and the location of the water table. The water table is that underground surface below which the interstices of the soil grains are filled with water. Normally, this is a sloping, flowing surface, which roughly follows the ground surface above and intersects with the ground at ponds, lakes, streams, seeps, or springs. Its depth can vary remarkably, however, and can fluctuate seasonally or over longer periods. Impervious layers of rock or soil will modify its location by trapping water above or below themselves or by guiding it through seams. Pumping from a well, or introducing such deep-rooted plants

as the Lombardy poplar, the tamarisk, or the cottonwood, will draw it down.

Clearly, a low water table is a problem for water supply and for vegetation. A fluctuating water table will cause a heavy clay soil alternatively to shrink and to swell, disturbing foundations just as a periodic frost will do. A high water table, on the other hand, makes for difficulties in excavation, as well as causing flooded basements, flooded utilities, and unstable foundations. A high table is indicated by the levels in existing wells and diggings, by seeps and springs, by a mottled soil, and by the presence of such water-loving plants as willows, alders, and reeds. A 2 m (6 ft) test pit in the wet season will reveal the presence of a table high enough to cause trouble in an ordinary residential development.

It is also possible that the ground may be subject to periodic floods. In a floodplain, the soil is likely to be rather deep and uniform, perhaps with alternating layers of fine and coarse material. Banks, stones, and tree trunks show the marks of previous flood crests. The presence of an underground water course is particularly critical, and no structure should be sited over them. Blocking or filling in existing surface drainage should be avoided; culverts must always be inserted to allow continued flow.

In summary, then, the most critical subsurface problems—the danger flags that call for a detailed investigation— are as follows: a high or fluctuating water table; the presence of peat or other organic soils, or of soft plastic clay, loose silt, or a fine water-bearing sand; rock close to the surface; new, unconsolidated fill or land previously used as a dump, especially if any toxic material may be present; or any evidence of slides, floods, or subsidence. Total site improvement costs may increase 25% in rocky land and 85% in peat or muck. The latter will also substantially increase foundation costs. In areas of permafrost, the erection of heated buildings on the frozen ground, or even the heat generated by compressing the earth under the foundations, may bring on all the problems of a saturated soil.

The topographic surface, the boundary between earth and air, is the the zone rich in living things. In itself, topography sometimes determines a plan. The gradient of paths, the flow of utilities, the use of areas, the disposition of buildings, and the visual form are all dependent on it. The designer must grasp the landform as a whole and identify its key points. He must sense its scale, the meaning of its

Subsurface problems

Reference 82

Landforms

slopes, the relation of its plan shape to its perspective appearance. In most cases, the topography has an underlying order brought about by the flow of surface water. Thus the basic modeling of the ground can be analyzed by locating the ridge and drainage lines.

Use and maintenance are dependent on the slope of the ground. Slopes under 4% (gradients which rise less than 4 m in every 100 m of horizontal distance) seem flat, and are usable for all kinds of intense activity. Slopes between 4% and 10% are easy grades, suitable for movement and informal activity. Slopes over 10% seem steep and can be actively used only for hill sports or free play. They require a noticeable effort to climb or descend. It is more expensive to erect a building on them, since more complicated foundations and more difficult utility connections are required. But they also offer certain advantages to structures expressly designed for them: fine views, privacy, terraced grounds or roof terraces, or perhaps separate ground-level entrances to units stacked one above the other. Slopes under 1%, on the other hand, do not drain well unless they are paved and carefully finished.

The steeper the land, and the more impervious its soil, the more quickly rain runs off its surface instead of seeping into the ground. This means erosion, a loss of groundwater, and the flooding of surface channels. Open slopes over 50 or 60% cannot be protected against erosion in a humid climate, except by terracing or by cribbing (reinforcing the surface by imbedding concrete or wooden beams in it). Different materials have a characteristic angle of repose—that limiting slope above which the material begins to slump downhill. These angles range from 30% for loose wet clay or silt to 100% for compact dry clay or forested land. The degree and orientation of slope also determines the sunlight incident upon it, for any given latitude and climate. Since the slope of the ground is so critical, it is common to analyze a site by marking off areas by their class of slope: steep, moderate, or flat. Variations of slope can easily be read from a contour map, by using a graduated scale that shows the separation between contour lines at the various critical slopes, for that scale of map at the contour interval given.

Ground form limits circulation along the roads and along the gravity-powered utilities, such as the sewers. This is not only an effect of local slope, but of the way in which the total system of slopes allows continuous lines of suitable grade to be constructed. Sewerage and surface drainage are difficult when large areas of a site have grades under 1%, while small patches of such ground can easily be dealt with. On consistently steep ground, on the other hand, sewer pipes and surface channels will have to be specially designed, to prevent rapid, scouring flows, and it will be difficult to install drain fields. The gradient of roads is preferably kept within 1 and 10%. A 17% slope approaches the limit that an ordinary loaded vehicle can climb, for any sustained period. The normal limit of climb for pedestrians is 20 to 25%, without resorting to stairs. But road and walkway grades can be manipulated by cut and fill and by drawing them across or parallel to the slope of the ground.

The experienced designer looks at ground with an eye to how it can be connected into a whole system of acceptable character. There may be "passes," or restricted localities that offer the best opportunity to cross some rough terrain, or lines along which an approach would develop an interesting visual sequence, or key points to which a connection must be made. Her eye moves across the land. She decides whether to follow ridge and stream lines or to cross them—whether to work with the land or in opposition to it. She considers what the principal alternatives for connection may be, and so analyzes for circulation capability, even at an early stage.

Another topographic characteristic is its visual form. In the mechanical sense, this simply refers to visibility, that is, what terrain can be seen from what locality. Computer programs are available that can construct and display diagrams of visibility, or bird's eye views of a piece of terrain, given sufficient data on ground elevations. But visual form is also a more subtle quality, rising from the total context of land, cover, atmosphere and activity. We treat these topics in Chapter 6.

The plant cover is a useful sign of soil and weather conditions. Red maple, alder, tupelo, hemlock, and willow indicate wet ground that is poorly drained. The oak and hickory association grows on warm, dry land; spruce and fir in cold, moist places. Pitch pine and scrub oak are signs of very dry land and good drainage. Red cedars mark poor soil. This list can easily be extended, and it is a list worth learning for your locality. Watch for the order in which similar plants bud out in spring: it is a delicate index of small microclimatic variations. The suitability of particular plants for any position depends on drainage, acidity, and humus, as well as on temperature, sunlight, moisture, and wind. Well-adapted local flora may be best for new plantings, or they

Plant cover

References 10, 36, 59

are a guide to selecting new species of similar habit. Some sites are particularly difficult for plants. The inner city is especially hard for them, due to the lack of water, light, and humus, as well as the air pollution, the heat reflected from the pavements, and the poisonous chemicals we use. There are also special difficulties in floodplains and wetlands, at seashores where plants are exposed to salt winds, on dry barren ground, and so on. Any new planting must respect these limitations.

The existing plant cover is very likely undergoing succession and so will not endure in its present form. Certainly it will change as human use puts new pressures on it. Feet and wheels will destroy the native ground cover and compact the earth above the feeding roots, if nothing else. The water table is likely to fall, pollution to appear, the climate to change. Thus it is rarely possible to preserve the native flora intact. At least in part, it must be replaced or modified.

Even if the plant association will be stable, the individual specimens will grow and die. It is a mistake to preserve large but ancient or decayed trees, while cutting out the young plants that would normally succeed them. New plantations will seem skimpy at first, and overcrowded later. They must then be ruthlessly thinned. Plantings of mixed age are advantageous, since they are constantly growing their own replacements. Quick-growing trees can be planted for immediate effect, and slow-growing trees, such as beech or white oak, be put in for the future. New plants are therefore chosen with two criteria in mind: their ecological harmony with the site and its intended use, and their fitness for a planned program of continuous management.

Site character The local association of plants, persons, and other animals, all dependent on one another, together with the surfaces and structures they inhabit, give the site its essential character. There are landscape families that have a common pattern and a common history: the bushy pasture of New England, the North American ribbon shopping street, the coastal mangrove swamp, or the intricate farming pattern of Tuscany. Tough, resilient communities can be distinguished from delicate ones, which could easily be destroyed. One looks for the signs of change: erosion, muddy water, empty stores, dying trees. What further changes will occur as the site is developed? Any site is an equilibrium of surface, use, and cover. In geologic time, all surfaces change, but within a human generation, these natural shifts are usually slow. Wherever the ground is disturbed by man or the intensity of its use is changed, the plant cover and surface form must be modified to attain a new balance.

Most data about surface form are conveniently recorded on a map. There are many types of available maps: the familiar road map with its compressed symbols about connections between settlements; the outline map of city streets; the assessor's map of lots and ownerships; the engineer's plat of rights-of-way road structures and utilities; the U.S. Geologic Survey contour map, packed with accurate data on the landscape at a small scale; the urban Sanborn maps for fire underwriters, displaying the use, size, and construction of each building. Each map serves its particular purpose and can furnish useful information for site planning. But making a plan always requires a base map fitted to its own purpose, which will serve not only for site analysis but also for design and construction. Its preparation justifies substantial expense. The typical base map scale in the metric system is 1:500 for sites of moderate size, but this may range from 1:200 for small sites to 1:1000 for large ones. In foot measure, the counterparts are one inch equals forty feet, twenty feet, or one hundred feet, respectively. The base map shows legal lines, such as boundaries and easements; the location of existing utilities, roads, and buildings; the presence of swamps, streams, and other water bodies; the general vegetative cover and the location of large trees; rock outcrops and other geological features; contours and spot elevations. It will show the compass directions, have a graphic scale, and may be annotated to indicate activity, soil character, views, the character of the environs, and other information.

By necessity, a site planner is at ease in reading such a map. She knows how to orient it, how to interpret its scale and its symbols, how to correlate the perspective view on the ground with this abstract projection on a horizontal plane, how to allow for the selection and compression of map data—in short, how mentally to enter into a map, on the one hand, and, on the other, how to recognize map features in the confusion of the actual scene. She can imagine a whole landscape by looking at its map and see the patterns of roads and buildings that might fit into it.

The form of the ground surface is usually indicated by *contours*, or imaginary lines which connect all points of equal elevation on the ground, separated vertically by some regular interval depending on the scale of the map. Since the ground

Maps

Contours

43

is continuous, these lines are continuous within the space of the map and cannot merge or cross, except at vertical or overhanging surfaces. By definition, the contours run at right angles to the rise and fall of the ground. The closer they lie to each other, the steeper the ground. The more nearly parallel they are to each other, the smoother and more regular that surface. In rolling land, they take on flowing curves; in broken land, they wriggle; over plane surfaces they run in straight lines. If any small contoured region is looked at "downhill" (that is, with the lower contours lying away from the observer), the shape of those lines is a (usually exaggerated) representation of the land seen in section. (Appendixes B and C describe some of the ways in which contour maps are prepared.)

One soon learns the contour patterns of typical terrain features: stream valley, ridge, bowl, mesa, depression, flat grade, escarpment, barrow, pass, or peak. But one must keep in mind which contour lines are lower, and which are higher, or the terrain will be read in reverse. The contour interval must be compared to the horizontal scale of the map, to grasp the relative steepness of the different spacings. Incomprehensible at first, the swirling patterns become eloquent. One has a synoptic view of an extensive area, and yet can read the elevation of some particular place, or the slope at that point. A continuous profile of the ground can be drawn along any line. Contours can also be sketched out to describe some proposed ground form.

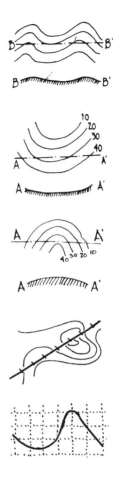

Even the most accurate map has a margin of error. Furthermore, the map represents only a few elements, puts them in arbitrary classes, and locates them by symbols that may have little relation to their actual size or nature: a dot for a tree, a sharp line for the blurred edge of a gravel road, a bold dashed line for an invisible boundary. The map reader must allow for these abstractions, omissions, and distortions, or he may be seduced into thinking that the map world is really there.

The graphic record of a precise land surveying operation is even more abstract than the common map, and it puzzles the ordinary reader. By its abstraction, it deals directly with the question of accuracy, since distances and directions are given in mathematical form, and the degree of error can be explicitly stated. While some detail can also be sketched in, these survey drawings are essentially a record of the invisible survey lines measured in the field, with their lengths and their azimuths (that is, their directions relative to north). The end points of these lines are carefully described so that

Record of survey

See Figure 106, Appendix B

Reference 40

45

they can be rediscovered in the field, and the lines are related to preestablished horizontal and vertical control points of greater accuracy. Many of the lines shown are not actually present on the ground, being legal boundaries, road centerlines, lines of sight, or the like. The result is a drawing that to the casual observer is crowded with minutiae and yet empty of reference to any real place. Surveys are essential for accurate record and measurement; they are key documents for legal or construction purposes.

Aerial photographs

See Figure 107, Appendix C

References 6, 93

Vertical aerial photographs, in contrast, are more immediate representations of reality. They are an excellent source of detailed, renewable site data. Yet many designers are put off by their ambiguous shadings, their doubtful scale, the tiny images, and the fact that photographs come in small pieces, no one of which covers the area of interest. The designer is much happier with the clear, stable map, which has exact boundaries, a fixed scale, and well-selected detail.

With a little practice, however, aerial photos can be read for such things as soil type, the health and species of plants, building repair, activity traces, traffic flow, erosion, old lot lines, or even things underwater, underground, or otherwise invisible. All these conditions are evidenced by slight variations of tone, pattern, and context. Pairs of photographs can be read for detailed topography, for lines of sight, or the relative elevation of given points. Successive photographs reveal changes in the landscape. Because of this wealth of data, a site planner should use aerial photos habitually. Sets of photographs can be converted by specialists into contoured maps of great accuracy and detail. Supplemented by ground control, they are now the preferred means for mapping extended areas.

Site reconnaissance

Photo interpretation includes the ability to recognize various features, how to orient and match the prints, how to determine scale and correct for distortion, and how to use stereopairs for reading the landscape in three dimensions. Using a simple pocket instrument, or even the naked eye, one can see a marvelously detailed, three-dimensional, miniature model of the ground below. It is an easily-acquired skill, one well worth cultivating. See Appendix C.

Reference 92

One makes a habit of taking a map or photo into the field and covering it with illegible notes as to character, views, salient points, unique locations, problems, and potential paths and sites. These notes are then recorded in legible form in the office. The very act of notation fixes them in the memory. Similarly, a quick sketch of some fragment of the landscape forces one to observe it more carefully and to remember it more sharply. If no base map is available, one can make a sketch map in the field or even conduct a rough field survey. See Appendix B.

A camera accompanies the first reconnaissance, to photograph things that strike the eye. For each photo, the observer notes its viewpoint and sector of view on his map. Later, these field photos reveal things that never struck the eye at the time. Inevitably some important feature or problem will escape the photographer, and a resurvey will prove necessary. Thus a more systematic camera coverage of all the major terrain features, views, and paths may be attempted from the first. In the office, perspective views can be built up from these shots, or new structures and landscape modifications can be drawn upon them. When the area is large and its future use not clearly foreseen, it may be worthwhile to make a "photogrid." In this procedure, a regular square grid of convenient scale is drawn on the base map, and photographs looking to the four cardinal directions are taken from each grid point. There will be redundant shots, and yet a useful image of almost any terrain feature can be retrieved in the office, and the material is at hand for simulating any journey across the site, or for making a "mosaic" of the whole that conveys its varied landscape character. On a more developed site with fixed routes, one might record the views in both directions at some regular interval along those routes, or at each intersection and mid-block.

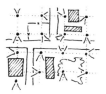

Lacking existing aerial photography, or the means for having it flown, it is possible to make one's own aerial obliques, using an ordinary camera taken up in a light airplane or helicopter. In good, slanting light, the site is caught from various angles, and its environmental context is shown. When enlarged, these photos make an excellent office record. They are especially useful when discussing the site with clients and other nonprofessionals since they show the whole in a form easy to understand. All of these photographic records are later invaluable as a base for representing the site in its proposed, developed form.

Standing on the ground, we are subject to the ocean of air, to its varying temperature, humidity, and purity, and to the light and sound transmitted through it. We prefer certain ranges and rhythms of these things. Natural climates can be erratic and violent; men add noise and airborne impurities. We defend ourselves by physiological adaptation and with

Climate

clothing and shelter. But it is also possible to manipulate the climate by the arrangement and choice of site.

The general climate of a region sets the stage and is expressed in data on temperature, humidity, precipitation, cloudiness, wind speed, wind direction, and sun path. These are the constraints within which the site planner operates. Simplified data are desirable, but averages will not suffice, since it is the extremes that are uncomfortable. Normal maximums and minimums are therefore used. What is the intensity of precipitation that must be drained away? What are the favorable and unfavorable winds? At what hour or season should solar radiation be avoided or invited, and from what direction? When does the effective temperature move outside the comfort zone?

Bodily comfort

References 39, 70

Effective temperature is the sensation produced by the combination of radiation, ambient temperature, relative humidity, and air movement. Outdoor cold can be mitigated by clothing, wind shelters, radiant collectors, and heating devices, but outdoor heat is more trying. If a person's body temperature varies even slightly, he will be uncomfortable. If it rises 4°C (10°F), he will die or suffer serious damage. Thus one limit is the maximum outdoor temperature in which a person can do extended work without raising his body temperature significantly (it is about 65°C or 150°F in completely dry air and near 32°C or 90°F in completely humid air). But comfort is more often the issue than extreme tolerance. Most people in the temperate zone, sitting indoors in the shade in light clothing, will feel tolerably comfortable at temperature ranges between 18° and 26°C (65° and 80°F), as long as the relative humidity lies between 20 and 50%. As humidity increases, the same people will begin to feel uncomfortable at lower temperatures, while, in a draft, the range of tolerable temperature shifts upward, and if one is receiving radiation from the sun or from some warm surface nearby, then one is comfortable in cooler air. But these sensations of comfort are also affected by previous experience, by cultural background, by age, and by the degree of activity. In the United States, 22°C (72°F) had been considered the "ideal" indoor temperature, but this is falling to 20°C (68°F) and even 18°C (65°F) as fuel costs rise. Elderly people may risk hypothermia in rooms less than 18°C (65°F), while active persons will be comfortable at still cooler temperatures.

A general analysis of the prevailing local climate furnishes important clues in arranging the site. See Appendix D for two comparative examples of such data and their im-

25°
20°

20% 50% 80%

plications. Whenever a designer works in a new region, he must study this information and look at the way in which local people deal with their weather. Traditional buildings and their siting represent accumulated experience.

But the designer is particularly interested in the micro-climate—that detailed modification of the general climate which is brought about by topography, cover, ground surface, and structural form. This is the climate with which people are in contact, and it is the one that the designer can actually modify. Microclimates may change within distances of a few meters or less. The significant variations are confined to a shallow zone no more than a few stories high. The constant commerce of heat and water vapor, between the different surfaces and media, produces small climates that fluctuate markedly, especially at the interface between earth and air.

Reference 89

Heat is exchanged by radiation, conduction and con-vection. There are three corresponding physical character-istics that must be taken into account: albedo, conductivity, and turbulence. *Albedo* is a surface characteristic, defined as that fraction of the total radiant energy of a given wavelength incident on a surface that is reflected back instead of being absorbed. A surface with an albedo of 1.0 is a perfect mirror, reflecting back everything that shines on it, without itself receiving any heat or light. A surface whose albedo is zero is a perfect matte black surface, reflecting nothing and soaking up all the radiation that falls on it. These same properties hold when the flow of radiation reverses: a hot surface of low albedo radiates rapidly. Albedo may therefore be imag-ined as the relative permeability of a surface to radiant energy flowing in either direction. High albedos resist this flow, and low albedos facilitate it.

Albedo

The albedos of natural surfaces vary markedly for ra-diation within the visible spectrum. Thus, on an aerial pho-tograph, the snow looks white, and forest and the sea look dark. In the visible spectrum, the albedos of wet or dark-colored surfaces are lower than those of dry or light-colored surfaces. They may vary from as much as 0.9 for fresh snow, through 0.4 or 0.5 for bare dry sand, 0.2 or 0.3 for dry clay soil, 0.1 or 0.2 for meadows and fields, and 0.1 for forests or dark cultivated soil, to as low as 0.05 for black asphalt or a calm water surface. But the albedo of a surface may be quite different at different wavelengths. For infrared radia-tion, the albedo of most natural materials is rather low.

Conductivity refers to the speed with which heat or sound passes through a given material, once having penetrated its

Conduction

surface. Heat flows rapidly through substances of high conductivity and slowly through those of low. The variations in the conductivity of materials control the rate with which reservoirs of heat, in the earth or in the sea, can be built up and released. Commercial insulation is a material of very low conductivity. Warm metal feels hotter than wood of the same temperature because the highly conductive metal releases its heat more rapidly to the hand. In general, the conductivity of natural materials decreases as they are drier and less dense. For example, thermal conductivities decrease in the following order: wet sand, ice, concrete, asphalt, still water, dry sand or clay, wet peat, fresh snow, still air. The decrease in conductivity across this range is approximately in the proportion of 1 to 100. Still air is an excellent insulator, and so is fresh snow.

Convection

Heat and sound are also distributed by fluid movement, or *convection*. Here the significant factors are speed and turbulence, or the degree to which movement occurs as random eddies rather than as steady, directed flow. Turbulence disperses heat, sound, and impurities, while steady flow may contain them and preserve contrasts. Air turbulence may increase with height and then decrease again at upper levels. Wind direction can shift with height, while wind speed tends to increase with height as it is freed from the surface friction at the ground. Wind speed 6 inches off the ground may be only half of the velocity 6 feet up. Lie down, if you wish to avoid the wind. Wind speed, by its rate of transport of heat, has a marked effect on cooling. A 50 kilometer per hour (30 mph) wind, with the air at 0°C (32°F), has six times the cooling effect of still air at −12°C (10°F), as a frostbitten nose will testify. When a 20 km/hr (12 mph) wind, at 0°C (32°F), is reduced in speed to 5 km/hr (3 mph) before it strikes a house, then fuel consumption in that house may be halved.

Specific heat

We must also consider the ability of an object to store the heat it receives, an ability that is the product of its total mass times its *specific heat*, or the amount of heat energy absorbed by a unit mass of that substance, for each unit rise in temperature. A cool object of high specific heat and large mass, whose interior is easily accessible to heat flow by convection or high conductivity, will absorb large amounts of heat over long periods. When exterior temperatures drop, it can then return that energy over an equally long period. A house with thick masonry walls will be cooler in the heat of the day, and warmer at night, than a more lightly built

50

structure. Large water bodies, with their high specific heat, internal convection, moderate conductivity, and low surface albedo, act like climatic flywheels, evening out the daily and seasonal swings of temperature. So an island in the temperate zone has a late spring, a cool summer, an extended autumn, and a warm winter. In contrast to water, the earth has a lower conductivity and little convection, so that continental temperatures above ground range more widely, while those below ground reduce, and lag behind, the aerial fluctuations. At a depth of only 500 mm (15 in), the diurnal range is no longer apparent, while even the seasonal range is damped out below 3 m (10 ft). Cellars have stable climates.

But if the ground has a low albedo and high conductivity, then it produces a mild and stable microclimate. Excess heat is quickly absorbed and stored, and as quickly released when the temperature drops. Ground of high albedo and low conductivity, which retard the exchange of heat, make for a microclimate of extremes, since they do not help to balance the swings of the general climate. Thus the sea, or grass, or wet ground, tend to even out the climate above them, while the weather over sand or snow or pavement is more violent: hot in the sun and cold at night. On a day when the general temperature is 25°C (77°F), the surface of a concrete walk in the sun may be 35°C (95°F).

The drainage of wet land increases albedo and decreases conductivity and so makes the local climate more unstable. A water surface usually has a low albedo, but not for light striking it at a low angle of incidence, when the water suddenly begins to act as a mirror. Now heat and light may be directed twice at waterside objects, directly from the sun and then as a reflection from the water. The effect will be unpleasant in a house facing the late afternoon sun across a lake but desirable for crops. A high density of artificial structures, or a substantial area of paving, increases the albedo, and this results in higher summer temperatures. Moreover, since the land drains more quickly, the general humidity tends to fall. A deep fall of fresh snow will raise daytime temperatures by reflection, while insulating the surface it covers.

The slope of the ground has an added climatic effect. **Slope and** (In fact, the word *climate* derives from the Greek for "slope.") **climate** The orientation of the ground with respect to the sun, and the way in which the topography affects air movement, are the principal influences here. Orientation is most critical in the middle latitudes, since in the far north much radiation

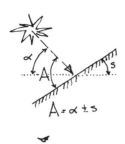

$A = \alpha \pm s$

Shading

is diffuse, coming from a cloudy sky and illuminating north slopes as much as southerly ones. In the tropics, the high angle of the sun tends to minimize differences between slope orientations. Maximum radiation is received by a surface that is perpendicular to the direction of the sun. When sunlight strikes the ground at any other angle, the radiation received is equal to that maximum perpendicular radiation times the sine of the angle between the sun's rays and the ground. The angle between sunlight and ground is determined by the altitude and azimuth of the sun, at that latitude, season, and hour, and the ground slope and direction. For ground sloping south at noon, this ground sunlight angle is equal to the altitude of the sun *plus* the ground slope in degrees; for ground sloping due north, it is that altitude *minus* the ground slope. A 10% slope to the south receives as much direct radiation (and to that extent has the same climate) as flat land 6 degrees closer to the equator—or the difference in latitude between Portland, Maine, and Richmond, Virginia. Yet at middle latitudes, slope orientation affects radiation rather little in midsummer, when the sun is high. It is far more critical in midwinter, when a moderate north slope may receive only half the radiation of a south-facing one. In midsummer, a northwest facing wall will be warmer than a south wall, while that south wall receives more radiation in winter than in summer, since in these situations the sun's rays strike those walls at a more nearly perpendicular angle.

Plants and structures modify these effects by blocking the direct sun radiation. The designer arranges shadows to avoid radiation when it is hot and to receive it when it is cold. Deciduous trees are ideal since they will cut off the summer sun and allow some winter sunlight through. But not all: bare-branch penetration through a dormant deciduous tree may range from 80% in the case of a honey locust to only 30% for an elm. Louvers and overhangs can be designed to exclude radiation from the high sun of summer and admit the low rays of winter. Where shading cannot be manipulated easily, it is wise to provide a variety of sun and shade, so that users may choose the climate they prefer. So the shadows cast by structures, particularly by tall ones, are studied to see how they affect neighboring structures and the ground about their base.

In order to study the system of moving shadows, the designer must understand how the apparent path of the sun varies with hour, date, and latitude. At the vernal and autumnal equinox, the sun appears to rise due east at 6 a.m., sets due west at 6 p.m., and swings through an arc that is at its highest point due south at local noon. Its angular height above the southern horizon then equals 90 degrees less the latitude of the place. In midwinter, the day is shorter. The sun rises and sets well to the south of east and west, and its elevation at noon is 23.5 degrees below that at the equinox. In midsummer, just the opposite occurs: the day is longer; the sun rises and sets well to the north of east and west; and the noon elevation is 23.5 degrees above equinoctial noon. In 40 degree latitudes, for example, the midwinter rising is about 30 degrees south of east, and an hour and a half later, while sunset is 30 degrees south of west, and an hour and a half earlier, than they are at the equinox. This reverses at midsummer. Between these dates, there is a reasonably regular transition.

This crude description will give some sense of the shadow patterns that arise from a given site design. But more exact studies are required. For this purpose, tables are available that give sun direction and altitude for different hours and seasons at the various latitudes. A sample table for 42 degrees north latitude is given in Appendix E, along with a procedure for computing such a table when none is available. A sun table, constructed or acquired, is of permanent value for any design in that latitude, anywhere on the globe. Using these data, the designer can draw shadow contours on her plan to show all the ground that will be shaded on a given day or even throughout the year. She can compute the relative intensity of solar radiation on any wall or piece of sloping ground facing in any direction or can design a sundial for a garden. Or, using sun direction and altitude at the turning points of the year, she may analyze, in section, the relations between buildings or areas and the objects that shade them. Thus she can proportion overhangs and try out different facade orientations or window sizes.

See Table 7

One of the more comprehensive and graphic devices for doing this is to simulate the casting of shadows on a model. Make a small cardboard sundial, marking it with the shadow path of its pointer's tip, for the different hours and seasons at the given latitude, according to the instructions in Appendix E. Attach this sundial to a three-dimensional model of the site and its proposed structures, placing the dial so that its meridian is oriented to model north. Out in the sunlight (or in bright artificial light whose source is over ten feet away), tip and tilt the model until the shadow of

See Figure 109

the sundial's pointer falls on the correct hour and season. The light is now falling on the model as it will fall on the real object at that time and place, and the pattern of shadows is accurate to the model scale. Even the effect of overhangs and the interior sunlighting of the rooms may be studied, if overhangs, rooms, and window openings have all been made to scale.

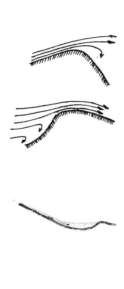

Topography and air movement

Topography affects climate by its influence on air movement, as well as by its orientation to the sun. Wind speeds on a crest may be 20% greater than those on flat ground, and the wind is generally quieter on the lee side of a hill than on its weather side. But the latter condition may be reversed if the lee slope is gentle and the weather side steep.

Cold air floods are a nocturnal phenomenon of open slopes. The layer of air near the ground is cooled by the earth beneath it, which is losing its heat by radiation to the night sky. This film of heavy cold air flows downhill as a shallow sheet, gathering into a still pool in open valleys, or where it is blocked by some "dam" of topography or cover. Thus positions at the foot of long open slopes are notoriously cold, and hollows are frost pockets. Cold air floods can be diverted by uphill barriers or prevented from pooling by breaching the downhill dam. Frost pockets may persist the next day if they are large enough, especially if fog or haze has formed, which prevents the sun from warming the ground surface. In this case, the air is coldest at the ground and warmer higher up—a situation termed an "inversion" because it is the reverse of the normal daytime condition. Since cold air is heavier than warm air, the formation is stable and will persist. There is no customary upwelling of warm, light, surface air. If the day should also be windless, then fog or smoke will not be dissipated, and smog will collect over inhabited areas.

On the shores of seas or large lakes, on an otherwise windless day, there will typically be an afternoon breeze blowing in from the sea and a night breeze off the land. This is due to the warm air rising, now from the land, and now from the water, as the relative warmth of each reverses from day to night. The resulting inflow of surface air, from the cooler surface to the base of the rising warm air column, creates the surface breeze.

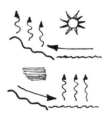

Windbreaks and wind tunnels

These topographic effects are in their turn modified by structures and plant cover. Plants alter the surface form, increase the area of radiation and transpiration, shade the ground, brake and trap the moving air. A cooler, more humid, more stable microclimate is the result. Plants will also trap some smoke and dust, but this is more likely to affect their own health than it is to purify the air in any marked way. Belts of shrubs and trees are effective windbreaks, however. They reduce wind velocities by up to 50% for a distance downwind of ten to twenty times their height. For this purpose, the belt should rise gradually in height on the windward side and should be somewhat open in its upper levels to reduce air turbulence in its lee. Use a diversity of species, with a dense understory of shrubs and a medium density of larger trees overhead. Evergreen plants, especially at the shrub level, are more effective in winter. Shelterbelts can also be planted on windward crests, or on artificial berms, to reinforce their effect.

Structures block and divert winds, or channel them at increased speed through narrow openings. The latter may be desirable along a street in summer, or quite disagreeable underneath a large building on stilts, in a winter storm. Long straight streets are wind channels. Structures can invite a summer breeze, and yet divert the winter wind if the prevailing wind direction shifts with season, as it often does. Plants and buildings have their most significant effects when the general wind is light and steady. In a strong, turbulent wind, their influence is more erratic. Smoke will disperse rapidly in turbulent air, for example, even downwind of a source.

In general, the taller and the longer a building or other barrier, the more extensive is the eddy on the downwind side. The eddy is a zone of low pressure, where the air is relatively quiet and is moving erratically, or even in a direction contrary to the prevailing flow. But the thicker such a building is in the direction of flow, the smaller the extent of the eddy, or at least up to a point. Thus a tall, thin, long wall is the most effective windbreak. Surprisingly, it will be even more effective if it is not completely impenetrable, so that air pressure in the lee is not lowered so far that it causes strong turbulence.

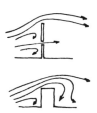

Air movements between groups of buildings are so complex that it may sometimes be desirable to bring a low building close up behind a tall one in order to improve the ventilation of the lower structure! Therefore it is useful to study air movement on the site by means of a scale model. Such studies are best made with technical apparatus by trained personnel, in a low-speed wind tunnel. This is the only way to get quantitative data on predicted wind speed

FIGURE 26
*A plume of smoke
in a wind tunnel
reveals the wind
patterns that will
develop around a
tall building.*

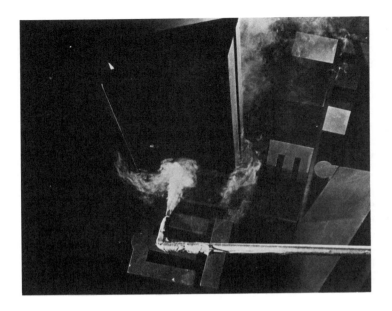

Reference 5

and pressure. Without such an apparatus, however, it is still possible to make rough predictions of wind direction, and the regions of calm and turbulence, by testing a site model with smoke in an amateur wind tunnel or even by blowing a fine powder through a section or a plan of a structure if that section or plan is a solid layer set between two panes of glass.

Wind speeds affect human beings as given in Table 1. But winds are normally variable and often gusty, which is more difficult for us. Wind standards are therefore given in terms of the "equivalent speed" that should not be exceeded more than a certain percent of the time. Equivalent speed equals the average speed (taken perhaps over five-minute periods) times $(1 + 3T)$. T, or the degree of turbulence, is the root mean square of the instantaneous deviations from the average speed divided by the average speed. Lacking other data, assume that the equivalent speed is 1.5 times the average speed. For comfort in outdoor sitting areas, the equivalent wind speed should not exceed 4 m/sec (9 mph) more than 20% of the time. For ease of walking in streets, parks, and plazas, it should not exceed 12 m/sec (27 mph) more than 5% of the time. For safety in any area where there are people outdoors, it should not exceed 16 m/sec (36 mph) more than 0.1% of the time (or about 10 hours per year).

TABLE 1. WIND EFFECTS

Wind speed in m/sec (mph)	Effects
2 (4.5)	wind felt on face
4 (9)	newspaper reading difficult; dust and paper raised; hair disarranged
6 (13)	begins to affect control of walking
8 (18)	clothing flaps; progress into wind slowed
10 (22)	difficult to use umbrella
12 (27)	difficult to walk steadily; unpleasant noise on ears
14 (31)	almost halted into wind; tottering downwind
16 (36)	difficulty with balance
18 (40)	grabbing at supports
20 (45)	people blown over
22 (50)	cannot stand

Man has changed the microclimate over much of the earth. He has reduced its contrasts by his drainage, clearances, plowing, and the planting of standard crops. He has invented the urban microclimate as a result of his extensive paving, dense structures, and the emission of heat, noise, and impurities. By the year 2000 the average man-engendered heat output per unit area within the Boston-Washington urban strip may attain 50% of the incoming solar radiation in the winter. Thus a "heat island" is formed over a city, and the upward convection within this island generates clouds and draws land breezes in from the surrounding countryside. Rainfall increases; clouds and haze reduce the sunshine. Happily, these effects are reversible. In London, when open fires were banned for heating buildings, winter sunshine increased by 70%, and ground visibiity increased by a factor of three. The romantic fogs of the past are now almost forgotten.

City climate

Reference 52

Extensive city paving causes rapid runoff, with a loss of local humidity and cooling, the depletion of groundwater, and more frequent and more disastrous floods downstream. The multitude of structures check the wind, so that at street level velocities may be 25% less than in a nearby rural area. Cities are warmer, dustier, drier, and yet have more rain, cloud, and fog than their rural counterparts. The level of noise and air pollution is higher; there is more glare and less sunlight. Upper-story urban living quarters may enjoy a better microclimate since there the winds sweep away more of the heat, noise, and air pollution.

57

This is the city climate that we so frequently criticize and that restricts the plant species that may be grown there (but also advances and lengthens their growing season). These defects are not due to the crowding of people but to the nature of city structures, their mechanical emissions, and the substances we choose to consume. Healthy bodies give off no aerial poisons. For house-bound modern man, indoor air pollution is now more critical than pollution outdoors. Tobacco smoke, airborne viruses, and the carbon monoxide and nitrous oxides emitted by open combustion are the principal dangers here. Otherwise, the atmospheric ill effects of large numbers of people in confined spaces are primarily due to the resulting heat and humidity and to the psychological effects of body odors. Outdoors, at least, it should be possible to make the city climate more comfortable than the rural one, rather than the reverse.

The site planner uses many sources to evaluate the microclimate of a locality: the weathering of older buildings, the knowledge of old residents, the appearance of existing plants. He will avoid certain site situations or make special provision for them: steep north slopes, west slopes facing water, hilltops, frost pockets, positions at the foot of long open slopes, bare dry ground, or nearby sources of noise and pollution. Other situations attract him: middle slopes facing southeast to southwest, water and forest edges, the military crest, open rolling land with groves of trees. He uses his skill to improve the local weather: orients his structures to take advantage of the sun, produces shade in the right spots, channels the wind, chooses surface materials for their albedo. The heating and cooling of buildings consumes more than 20% of the nation's energy. Until we learn to harness solar power more efficiently, we shall see no more of cheap power. Our lavish use of fossil and nuclear energy imposes global heat and carbon dioxide pollution, and this may cause a shift in world climate. The avoidance of unwanted heat loss or gain, and the positive use of sun energy for heating and cooling, while by no means new considerations, have become compelling principles of site design.

Building orientation

References 48, 60

In temperate latitudes, the favorable orientation for the principal facade of a building is south or southeast. Then the winter sun can flood the interior or be received by solar panels on the roof. The hot summer rays, high above at midday, are more easily warded off. Window openings are reduced on the northern and western facades, or these walls may even be sunk into the ground to retard the flow of heat.

Large glass areas, at least, should not face the low western sun of summer, and yet most rooms should get some sun on a winter's day.

Tall buildings are sun snatchers, and public regulation may be necessary to prevent the theft of sunlight. In hot climates, on the contrary, buildings clad in reflective surfaces redouble the radiation on people nearby and deny them the comfort of any shade. In low-rise development, streets can be oriented to increase the number of building sites with a favorable solar outlook. If one assumes a conventional disposition of the principal facade—either toward the street or the back garden—then the houses will be placed along access roads running east to west or east-northeast to west-southwest. Siting and building design can reduce energy consumption substantially.

But we will not argue for some ideal layout. Each climatic region, each way of life, each site, has its own requirements. There are many techniques for shielding or inviting the sun, much radiation is diffuse or directionless, and a variety of outlook is also desirable. Windows to the north will look on a landscape flooded with sun. Wind patterns vary. Developing technologies may liberate us from strict dependence on ideal orientations. Rather than relying on a standard orientation, a whole system of measures must be taken. Nor should energy conservation be the dominant objective. We are prone to follow a disconnected trail of temporary concerns, to leap from crisis to crisis. Energy is only one cost of operating a site, whose principal aim is the well-being of its inhabitants. Huge solar panels and buildings that sink into the earth or display blank north walls raise new problems for those who must look at them or out of them. Architects have rarely yet been able to manage these new features. Site planners sensitive to the natural context have been more successful.

It remains true, however, that there is much to learn about the climate of the site. The original studies of microclimate were concerned with agriculture. There are not yet many quantitative data on the outdoor effects of man-made structures and materials. Nor is there any large-scale, systematic recording of the microclimate in any urban or suburban area. Because of its importance for comfort, health, and conservation, a site designer could make as good a use of a mapping of the microclimate as of information on topography, subsoil, and utilities.

Noise

References 21, 54, 79

The control of outdoor noise is a subject in its own right. Although an environment with too little noise is conceivable, the usual problem is to reduce either the level of the noise, its pitch, or its information content. Sound sources are increasingly ubiquitous and powerful, as we expand our consumption of energy, since most modern noise is a form of wasted energy.

Noise levels are measured in *decibels*, a logarithmic scale that is 0 at the threshold of hearing and 140 at the threshold of pain. Each interval of 10 decibels indicates a level of sound energy ten times greater than before, an increase that the human ear will usually distinguish as being roughly twice as loud. Thus a noise that is 20 decibels higher than another has 100 times the energy of the latter and is perceived as being four times as loud.

In most locations, we like to keep noise levels down below 55 decibels in any outdoor area, 40 decibels indoors (which is the maximum that will not impair sustained conversation in a normal tone), and 35 decibels in rooms devoted to study or to sleep. In the normal building, indoor noise levels can be up to 20dB less than those just outdoors, if windows are closed, and perhaps a maximum of l5dB less, if windows are partly open for ventilation. But noises are annoying or noticeable as much because of their frequency (their pitch) as because of their loudness. High-pitched noises, or those that interfere with the frequencies of human speech, will be particularly obnoxious. Sounds whose pitch contrasts with that of the background noise will be picked up even if they are relatively soft. A measure of loudness (dBA) is often used that weights those sounds more heavily which are in the frequencies to which the human ear is more sensitive.

We are more aware of sudden noises, that occur at unpredictable times, or those at night, when we hope to sleep, or those that are full of information, the human voice in particular. Thus we are upset by a sudden backfire, a distant, high-pitched scream, or the soft murmur of talk next door, while far louder and more continuous sounds, such as of the sea, the wind, or heavy street traffic, may be ignored. It is sometimes useful to make a site survey of existing noise whenever the issue is controversial. The survey records the actual variation of sound level over some chosen period of time, using standard recording devices. But these extended recordings, varying constantly by loudness and pitch, must then be converted into some index that corresponds to a common level of annoyance. This is difficult to do. Site designers should be able to interpret surveys and indexes of this kind, and so their conduct and construction is laid out in Appendix F, as well as accepted techniques for predicting sound levels from expected use and location.

Outdoor sounds can be attenuated in many ways. Most useful to the site planner is sheer distance, since the energy level necessarily "thins out" while spreading from its source. For example, opening windows in different rooms should not be closer than 9 to 12 m (30 to 40 ft) if face to face, in order to prevent the transmission of speech from one room to the other. Each doubling of the distance between source and receiver causes sound levels to drop by approximately 6dB. In addition to the effect of distance, sound is dispersed by turbulence and gusty winds. Barriers will also reduce sound transmission. Belts of trees are scarcely useful, being most efficient against noise of high frequency, whose wavelengths are not much greater than the average size of leaves and other obstacles they meet, that is, high-pitched sounds above 10,000 cycles per second. Sound and sight, however, are connected senses. One hears more keenly if one sees the source, more poorly if one does not. Thus, at relatively low sound levels, trees and hedges may be useful as a means of disconnecting sound and sight. Solid barriers—walls, buildings, earth berms—are much more effective. If the barrier is impenetrable to sound, then the noise reaching the receiver is what has passed around it. Thus the effectiveness of the barrier increases as its height increases and as it is moved closer to either source or receiver. A high wall, close to the source, will cause a marked reduction, and a low wall, halfway between source and receiver, very little. A formula for computing this reduction is given in Appendix F.

$$D = a + b - c$$

Sound is reflected by surrounding objects and hard surfaces and so can be intensified. To some extent, it is absorbed by fine-grained, "soft" ground and wall surfaces, and so the use of nonreflecting textures will have a quieting effect. But it is difficult to make artificial surfaces that are both weatherproof and also sufficiently fine-textured to be efficient sound absorbers. Snow and small-leaved vegetative cover plants are of some value. If noise cannot be brought down to an acceptable level by any of these devices—or by reducing the output at its source, which is the most efficient means— it is sometimes possible to mask unwanted sound by adding desirable or random noise: the play of water, the rustle of leaves, or a shapeless stream of "white noise."

Site acoustics, in contrast to architectural acoustics, has focused on the suppression of unwanted sound. Rarely is any design concerned with enhancing the transmission of sound or with producing pleasant or informative sound. Yet the acoustic environment is a chief attraction of many fine rural settings. There is no reason that a site plan might not deal with audial quality as well as with visual quality. In the normal, defensive mode, however, the site planner will mainly rely on suppressing the noise source or on putting distance between it and his active locations. His next defense is to use buildings, walls, or berms as partial barriers and to arrange his openings to repel the assault. Next, he may use the "backfire" technique, deliberately introducing background noise in order to mask the annoying intrusion or to reduce its information content. For his last stand, he dons ear muffs, seals his buildings, and abandons the out of doors.

Site analysis

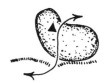

All of the factors we have recited in this chapter—the conditions below ground, the surface form, activity and life, the structures and utilities, the ocean of light and air that envelops them, and the human meanings, rights, and regulations—make up the nature of a site. The picture is always complex and often confusing. The designer sifts through the data to find what is decisive for her purpose and tries to fit this selected information into some pattern on which she can base her design. She separates transitory or fading features from permanent or emergent ones: discounts the fine old trees in favor of the new growth or distinguishes basic hill forms from the scars of a recent excavation. A convincing site pattern appears only after repeated analysis and trial of possibilities. It is the essence of the place for the purpose in mind. Yet the designer must not be so strongly directed toward her purpose, or so intent on finding a coherent pattern, that she misses the misfit facts that might change that purpose.

Therefore it is advisable to study a site in several ways. One begins by searching aimlessly, forgetting the use to which the area is to be put, looking intently at the site itself, watching for interesting features and revealing clues. The Chinese garden designers sat quietly for days in the location of a proposed garden, meditating on its character, before they began to consider its possibilities. One visits a place on different occasions, under varied circumstances of weather, light, and activity. This unsystematic, almost subconscious, reconnaissance produces information that would otherwise be missed. It often sows the seed of the eventual design and will at least serve as an introductory orientation.

Next, it is useful to look to the history of the site: its natural evolution, its former use and association. Inquire into its image in the minds of users and decision makers: how they characterize it, how they feel about it, what they expect of it. Much of the flavor of a place, and its present direction of change, is thereby revealed. Finally, look at the place as an ongoing ecological system, including its present human use: how it maintains itself and where the vulnerable points may be. Understanding site history, ecology, and image are always fundamental.

At this point, a more systematic and detailed survey can be undertaken, guided by the purpose to be served and a desire to predict how the site will react to the proposed disturbance. Some types of information, such as a topographic map, climatic data, or a mapping of activity and circulation, are almost always required, but there is a continuing temptation to gather too much. No information should be sought unless it will influence the design in some important way. Knowledge of the site is essential to design, but information is expensive to gather and expensive to use. A complete set of site data is an infinite set; a thorough survey can paralyze design. One plans data gathering carefully, estimating the time and resources needed to acquire and use each item at the specified level of detail. Will knowing this affect our decision enough to justify the cost of learning it? Can it be gotten in time to be useful? It is usually more efficient to confine initial data to bare essentials, and to gather special data later, as new questions arise. The data store must therefore be organized to receive new information. Too much data should not be gathered at first, not only to save energy for later investigations but also to prevent being drowned in irrelevant material.

However, some standard data continue to be useful during construction and subsequent operation, and they require substantial time to prepare. So they justify an early start and considerable expense. One example is a complete and accurate base map. The designer takes such a map into the field for personal annotation, as she gets a feel for the site. Later, it is the base for the design, then for construction drawings, and finally for record and management.

Before the systematic survey begins, it is useful to prepare a complete schedule of the data to be gathered. A typical, but overlong, checklist, from which the data actually sought

Systematic surveys

in any particular case would be selected, is given in Appendix H. Any standard schedule must be viewed with suspicion; there is no universal list. The data gathered and the form into which they are put depend on the purpose of the development, the nature of the place, and the resources available to make the survey. An adequate survey may consist of a single freehand sketch made on the site, or it might require an elaborate technical organization. Elaborate or simple, the survey is as succinct as possible and flexible enough to receive new information. It must always contain personal observation. Making a personal survey—as opposed to receiving a competent one from someone else—means direct learning, recording in memory as well as on paper, making unconscious connections, modeling the place in a form that can be designed.

Synthesis

Once assembled, the survey must be put into concise and usable form, a brief graphic and written statement that describes the essential nature of the site for the purpose at hand, and how it is changing. Major constraints, problems, and potentialities are indicated. This concept of the site will be modified as the design unfolds, as further information is stumbled upon, or must be sought out: site analysis is not self-contained. First thoughts on design guide the original reconnaissance, and analysis continues as long as the design is being created.

The image of the site guides the design. It does not create the design, however, nor is there a unique solution latent in a site, waiting to be uncovered. The plan develops from the creative effort of the designer. But it must respond to the site, not ignore it. Most often, the designer will be working with the grain of the locality, emphasizing its strong points and teasing out its potentialities. Sometimes he will dramatically oppose its nature. This, too, will succeed only if the site is thoroughly understood.

Site selection

Reference 43

It sometimes happens, and should happen more often, that the site is not yet selected before a designer is called in. He is given the objectives of the client and asked to search for a site. This may mean the weighing of a few alternatives, or a search over a broad area. The search begins by reducing possible sites to a manageable set of alternatives. In some cases, where very large regions and complex factors are involved, a massive, area-wide collection and comparative weighting of information may be attempted, using a computer to store and combine the data. More often, a reductive search is done by a simple screening based on judgments of thresholds: that is, by piling up a series of overlays that block off those regions unacceptable for reasons such as excessive grade or cost, special habitats that should be preserved, extreme vulnerability, difficulty of acquisition, small size, poor ground, incompatible development, pollution, lack of access, and so on.

The remaining lands not so blocked off are personally reconnoitered to eliminate unacceptable localities. The surviving plots are then analyzed in some depth as alternative sites. Crucial factors are arranged comparatively, and preliminary layouts are made on each, since nothing illustrates the character of an area quite so well as an attempt to make use of it. An informed choice can then be made from this comparative display.

Occasionally, a designer is called on to make the contrary analysis: given some site, what is its best use? This is a vaguer and more difficult question. It demands an especially careful analysis of the place as an ongoing social and ecological system, since the values internal to the site may be expected to have greater weight in this case. The context of the locality must also be examined with equal care: ecology, circulation, behavior, structures, and associated images. Possible markets will be explored. A broad framework of objectives is established and, within that, more specific objectives that might govern the use of that piece of land. The possible uses that arise from this are then reduced to the most feasible ones, and a comparative analysis is made for each set of use and purpose, including sketch layouts, market analyses, and a schedule of probable costs and benefits. A choice can be made among these alternatives, using qualitative judgments that balance ecology, market, and social purpose. The judgment will help to set the price of the land, which in its turn tends to set the eventual site plan, in a circular process.

Although site selection and "best use" analysis are somewhat less common than the analysis of a given site for a given purpose, site designers always engage to some degree in both of these modes of thinking, or at least they should do so. That is, they must be prepared to advise a client that his chosen site is inadequate for his purpose and that he must seek a new one; or that his purpose, in the designer's judgment, is incoherent or mistaken; or that the chosen site has a better use than the one proposed. While advice of this kind may terminate the designer's employment, still it is his responsibility.

Best use

65

Permanence
and relevance
of data

Most site analyses are conducted for a single purpose and lose their utility once a development has been carried through. Planners' files are full of outmoded information. Even documents intended for lasting use—such as the topographic maps of the U.S. Geological Survey, the base maps of the city engineer, and the land use records of a planning agency—can only record the landscape at some one point in time. They are not easily kept up. Long-lived data are relatively stable (geologic form or general climate), organized in some abstract, neutral form that allows easy future modification (elevations from an arbitrary base, population per square mile), and kept as disaggregated as possible, for recombination according to need. Sites have long futures, and site planning must increasingly be seen as a continuous stream of modifications applied to a changing landscape rather than as a convulsive creation imposed on a static world. Site analysis should then be a continuing process, on which continuing design can be based. Eternal surveys founder when conditions and purposes change.

Degree of permanence does not equate with degree of relevance. A shifting market, an ecology in transition, or a fluctuating behavior setting may be crucial factors. Some framework that can accept and correlate changing data is therefore useful, such as a situation map, a grid system, or a computer. (Beware, of course, that this fixed framework does not, like the blinkers of a horse, shut off the view of sideward things.) One begins to rely on such quasi-continuous sources as aerial photographs, social and economic accounts, and periodic censuses.

We have had little opportunity to practice continuous site analysis. The grounds of large institutions could be exceptions, or those of other agencies that control an area for long periods and for stable purposes. Here we would be justified in maintaining a continuing record of behavior settings, communications, ecology, microclimate, visual form, the repair and capacity of structures, and the conditions and use of roads and utilities. Periodic designs could be based on this ever-renewing bank of information. Continuous site analysis would be the spatial and local analogue of the economic and population data now continuously gathered at the national scale.

Chapter 3

The User

Making places that fit human purposes is the task of site planning. Two things must then be understood: the nature of the site, on the one hand, and how its users will act in it and value it, on the other. By "users" we mean all those who interact with the place in any way: live in it, work in it, pass through it, repair it, control it, profit from it, suffer from it, even dream about it. The study of environmental behavior and meaning has been systematically pursued for less then twenty years, while the human experience of place is ancient. The latter material is rich and unreliable; the former still lies at some distance from the felt experience of place, which is the designer's chief concern. The air is thick with texts, techniques, research proposals, and reports. This *References 71, 73, 95* chapter does not pretend to be a condensation of that literature; it refers to it. Where the previous chapter could summarize a body of established information, this one lays out issues, some principles, and the various methods that a site planner can use in coming to understand his own particular puzzle.

A few generalizations about the interaction of man and place can be made. But most findings are partial or refer to specific situations. Time and again, the designer must learn in the very process of designing, and so he is particularly interested in the methods he himself can use. Time and again, and to his peril, he is thrown back on his own experience and his sympathetic insight. There are things that we are unlikely to learn from systematic studies, such as the very personal environmental experience. There are things that we should not wish to learn, such as how to make people act against their will. But there is much that we would like to know. Small, conventional designs, rapidly executed with scarce resources, can use very simple analyses. Large-scale, innovative site plans justify extended, sophisticated studies. But some analysis of the response of those who will inhabit the place is essential to even the simplest task.

Which user?

Analysis stumbles immediately on the vexing question: *which* user? Only in the rare case, such as when designing a private garden for a single person, is the user easily identified, present, articulate about his values, and identical with the paying client. Even then, one can wonder about those who may see the garden from the street, or about the gardener, or about someone who will live in the house next. Nevertheless, the addition of a limited number of users—as long as they are present, articulate, and possessed of equal power—does not seriously complicate the situation. Using simple dialogue and observation, the site planner can perform rather well.

Troubles multiply when the users have different values and purposes and when the paying client becomes distinct from the actual user. A way must now be found to identify and satisfy diverse, conflicting requirements. This is inevitable in large site plans and in those for public areas. Where the interests of client and users diverge, as they so often do, shall the designer work conscientiously for the one who pays him, or shall he attempt to modify or enlarge that client's interests? Or should he subvert them? The designer is now involved in politics.

The user may not only be complex, and distinct from the client, but may have no direct voice in the proceedings. Students do not design schools, nor children homes, patients hospitals, prisoners jails, nor employees offices. The user may have a strong indirect influence, as when shoppers affect store layout by their propensity to buy. But wherever there is neither an effective market nor a responsive political mechanism, there are likely to be users of whom the designer is unaware and with whom she cannot easily communicate. Even if she can, she may be unable to influence the design in their favor. Moreover, how do we rank users in terms of their importance: those who have the greatest stake in it? those who maintain it? those who suffer most from it? those who use it most often? These are political decisions.

If the users are not present on the site, they will not have that concrete experience with the actual place that is a firm basis for design. But they may still influence the outcome if they can be reached. They might be the members of a future housing cooperative or the truck drivers for a future warehouse. The difficulties mount when the users cannot be reached, even though their type may be known. Shoppers, house buyers, or laborers in a new factory, they will assemble only after the site is organized. They can still exert some influence, by votes or markets, but more often they are silent. Analysis must now fall back on surrogate users, or on findings from previous developments, unless there is some way of converting absent users into reachable ones, as by organizing future house buyers before planning begins, or by leaving some decisions open, to be made after the users are on the site. As plans increase in scale, the problem of the absent client looms ever larger.

Worst of all, the user may simply be unknown, whether because he is unpredictable or is not yet alive. Any site plan imposes limits on people yet to be born, and even the near-future use of some places is doubtful. The designer makes guesses and tries to make her forms adaptable. It is when considering the voiceless or unknown user that her responsibilities are the most difficult to bear.

Thus the first step in user analysis is a demographic analysis: who will use this site, and how are they distributed among what classes of people? Significant differences of effect may be expected if users differ in culture or in socio-economic class. Generalizations made across such fundamental social divisions are always suspect. Further differences may appear between people of different age, sex, personal history, life style, or ethnicity. Variations in the environmental role of users will surely vary their response to it; it matters whether they own it or not, use it frequently or are tourists, or depend on it for their livelihood. All these variations can produce a bewildering array of classes of users in any large project: Lithuanian adult male home owners of long standing, unemployed Chicano adolescents recently arrived, and so on. The site planner has neither the time nor the resources to investigate them all, nor, more important, could he manage the political conflicts that would be generated by an active participation of all these groups.

He is therefore forced to make (or to accept, which is the same) a choice of the classes of users to whose requirements he will most closely attend while assuring the general

User groups

needs or minimal requirements of other groups. In part, this is a technical decision, based on past experience as to significant differences and critical groups in similar cases. But it is clearly a political and ethical decision. The initial demographic statement—which may be a simple checklist of the types of users or may be an elaborate population prediction—can be relatively neutral, although its manner of classification, and especially its failure to list a user group, can mask a hidden bias. But the next step—whom shall I focus on?—is the beginning of decision.

Clients

The designer has a set of nominal clients, who called in her services and who will pay her fee. Clearly, she must attend to their requirements. The very acceptance of work has therefore been a first decision as to user weighting. Next, the designer asks: who has a significant influence over the creation or maintenance of the site? It is a sufficiently common error to neglect some powerful user (a bank, a regulatory agency) until too late, only to have unwanted changes imposed at the last moment. It is a very common error to neglect the seemingly less powerful groups who will maintain the site: the janitors, managers, gardeners, and repairmen. Only if their needs are considered—indeed only if their active support is enlisted—will the site be successful in use.

But user analysis should go beyond those who have power, and here the designer faces difficult choices. Considering the limited resources that he may have for analysis, should he simply attend to well-known and rather general human requirements (body measurements, fire safety, preferred climates), and entrust particular needs to the market and to subsequent adjustment? Has he the means to investigate all the significant user groups, and, if so, how will their conflicting requirements be mediated? Or shall he focus on a strategic set?

Who is
consulted?

If a strategy of selection is chosen, then the usual procedure is to focus on those users who are most able to affect the satisfactions of the paying client: for example, those who will purchase the goods or the houses, those whose future votes will ensure the survival of the agency, or those whose vandalism or neglect can impose serious costs. In other words, the planner is simply extending the client's normal interests, and so he has a good chance of persuading that client to pay attention. When the designer goes beyond this, he takes on a more public, more consciously ethical, more problematic role.

The more neutral stance is to use the utilitarian rule: pay most attention to those who are most exposed to the environment, who use it most often, and are most intimately connected with it. Favor the long-term resident over the tourist or temporary sojourner; the housewife who spends her days there over the builder who moves on to other projects. The rule is easy to understand, but it may be resisted by the client. A more incisive strategy, with a stronger ethical bias, is to focus on those who are most vulnerable to that particular setting, the most likely to be harmed or supported by it. Give special attention to the blind, to people in wheelchairs, to the aged, to the children. The designer appeals to the sympathies of the client, looks for diffuse support among the general public, and uses research findings about the special difficulties of vulnerable groups.

Finally, the designer may use a rule of reform. On the assumption that it is right to broaden user participation, he will choose to focus on those groups which at present have little power over the environment but who could have a significant voice were they organized and aware of their interests. One studies the needs of some ethnic group in the hope that they will use this to assert themselves in the decision process, or looks at what teenage gangs do as a prelude to permitting them to plan and manage their own clubhouse. This focus must identify a user group whose requirements are distinct, who at present have no voice, but who are capable of raising their voice and of exercising responsible control. This is a touchy strategy, since it implies a redistribution of power. It involves a nice calculation of possibility and is bound to generate resistance.

Thus the very first step of user analysis (and in this it is less like the first steps of site analysis) is a strategic, value-laden decision. By accepting the work, the designer has decided to attend to the needs of the paying client. If he is wise, he will discover the requirements of the other powerful actors. But to what extent, and by what rule, he will further extend his analysis is an open question: whether he will rely on very general and well-known needs, or will look to the wants of those who can most directly affect his client's interests, or will use the utilitarian rule, or will employ the more compelling selective strategies of focusing either on those most vulnerable, or on those now powerless who have some chance of power. Planning the analysis of user needs becomes an anxious ethical and political calculation.

Beneath the underbrush of particular situations and special groups, we find some common ground—fundamental criteria shared by all human users. Our first concern is for our biological requirements, the *habitability* or vital support of a place. Any environment may be judged by the degree to which it supports human vital functions and matches the capabilities of our bodies. This is most easily defined in the negative, by the incidence of disease, polluted air, noise, poor climate, glare, dust, accidents, contaminated water, toxic wastes, or unnecessary stress. These evils are felt by all, although certain groups may be more vulnerable to them. We can cope with them but often neglect them. People suffer discomfort and ill health in silence, adapting as they can, often unaware of the load imposed. Our knowledge is particularly deficient in assessing the long-term, hidden costs of those environmental stresses to which we seem to adapt.

The nominal client may be concerned with no more than minimal standards of sanitation and structural safety. Other biological evils—such as polluted air and water, epidemic, or criminal or military attack—are beyond our province, being features of very large environments or having social causes at their root. Yet much stress and danger can be ameliorated by the site plan. Ergonomics and environmental medicine are our guides and are applicable with great generality.

A place must not only fit the structure of our bodies. It must fit the way in which our minds work: how we perceive and image and feel. This may be called the *sense* of a place, and while sense varies with culture and with personal temperament and experience, there are regularities in these perceptions due to the structure of our senses and our brains. We are all engaged in identifying the features that surround us, organizing them into images, and connecting those images to the other meanings we carry in our heads. Places should have a clear perceptual identity: be recognizable, memorable, vivid, engaging of our attention. It should be possible for the observer to relate the identifiable features one to another, making an understandable pattern of them in time and space. These sensuous characteristics, so often dismissed as "mere esthetics," are fundamental for executing practical tasks. They are a source of emotional security and can reinforce the sense of self. Psychological and environmental identity are

linked phenomena, and so a key function of a place may be its support of our inner feelings of coherence and continuity. Places play a part in the intellectual and emotional

FIGURE 27   Gaudí's Parc Guell in Barcelona: unique form and active use give it a special sense of place. The broad platform with its
curving mosaic benches sits on a forest of great slanting Doric columns, from which the stairs cascade down past fantastic rockeries.

development of the individual, particularly in childhood but also in later years. Visible clues must work for the anxious visitor, the old inhabitant intent on some task, and the casual stroller. They confer esthetic pleasure and are a means for extending one's knowledge of the world. Many devices for enhancing this "sense of place" are part of the intuitive, experiential lore of site design and will be developed in subsequent chapters.

Moreover, the place must be seen as meaningful, related to other aspects of life: to function, social structure, economic and political patterns, human values. Congruence between the spatial and the social world facilitates action and makes both comprehensible. Spatial identity can be an outward expression of personal or group identity. But we understand less about this symbolic role of landscape, and meanings and values differ widely among various groups. Spatial legibility is at least a common base around which groups can cohere and on which they can erect their own meanings. Temporal legibility is equally important. A setting orients its inhabitants to the past, to present rhythms, and to the future, with its hopes and dangers.

Fit

Third, a good environment supports purposeful behavior; it makes a good *fit* with user actions. Is there space to carry out that action? Is the site equipped and managed for it? Does the setting reinforce its mood and structure? Is there room to pile the snow, enough light to see by? In other

Reference 1

words, are the behavioral settings adequate for their purpose and free from internal conflict? To judge this, the designer must understand the prevailing manner of life. In his imagination, he goes through the actions. What will it be like to mail a letter, talk to a neighbor, display wealth, hang out, dispose of trash, sit out in the evening? One needs to know both what people actually do and also what they experience and plan. The users will often be diverse, and their ways of life strange. Empathy is the beginning of understanding, but it is better to rely on a systematic study of behavior or to bring the users themselves into the decision process.

Under this heading, one considers such familiar behavioral issues and form devices as territory, personal space and crowding, social interaction and withdrawal, segregation and clustering, compartments and edges, latent and manifest functions. The specification of desired behavior and its means of support are carried forward into the design by means of the program. Behavioral conflicts must be dealt with and adaptability must be provided since activities are certain to

FIGURE 28 *Neighborhood card players occupy a corner of the Paul Revere Mall in Boston.*

change. Clients are obsessed with present need, but the designer must also see that her plan will accommodate the future. Since prediction is a dubious art, she falls back on such general devices as excess capacity, good access, the independence of parts, ease of manipulation, resource conservation, and flexible planning procedures. Rather little is known about adaptability, and much buncombe proclaimed. Adaptability and fit are as much a result of how the site is managed as of how it is formed.

Fourth, any site is concerned with *access*, the degree to which users can reach other persons, services, resources, information, or places. This is a fundamental advantage of any organized site, a quality we are accustomed to when dealing with traffic circulation, but too often neglected in regard to other kinds of access. Variations in access between different groups—the elderly, the teenagers, the handicapped, the various socioeconomic classes—are basic indexes of social justice. Many of the recurrent considerations of site planning have to do with privacy, with social interaction, with the distance to shopping, jobs, or schools, with preferred linkages between various activities, as well as with provisions

Access

75

FIGURE 29
A street of stairs in the self-built settlement of El Agostino in Lima, Peru. The street is used for work, play, passage, and social contact.

FIGURE 30
Small groups of prisoners in the Clinton Prison, Dannemora, NY, are allowed to furnish and manage individual "courts" in the prison yard and to choose their group members. This decentralized landscape is a social outlet for the men and has resisted administrative attempts to reduce it to a more regular form.

for cars, transit, bicycles, and pedestrians. These are all questions of access. The various utilities are also access systems and will be treated at length in Chapters 7 and 8.

We may wish to encourage communication or only to permit it. We may want to decrease it, for the sake of privacy, safety, or the prevention of conflict. Given a homogeneous group and the desire to meet, a site can encourage communication through common entrances, increased visual contact, and focal points such as mailboxes, laundries, or churches. On the other hand, sharp boundaries, extended open spaces, and poor connections tend to divide people. A fine grain of land use *may* encourage communication between different kinds of people, while a coarse grain will more surely facilitate interactions between similar people. It is never our objective simply to maximize access, however. Extreme accessibility would be unbearable. One needs to know the access that users consider adequate or optimum, including what it is that they most want access to.

Finally, the *control* of the site is always at issue. However **Control** far from reality in our society, the ideal environment is one controlled in all its essential respects by those who use it, who thereby have the greatest stake in its quality and are most familiar with its requirements. This ideal must be qualified, however, not only by the realities of power but also in those cases where the users are transient, or incapable of control, or careless of the legitimate demands of others. In general, the site designer seeks to encourage responsible control by the actual user. All too often, he struggles against the current: against the actual distribution of social and economic power, against the incapacities of users or their disregard for the needs of others, and at times against the technically necessary scale of the environment itself.

These basic criteria of vital support, sense, fit, access, **Justice and cost** and control are the enduring objectives of any site design—continuous threads which run through all fabrics of place and people. Detailed specifications vary; the basic considerations are constant. They are the central values of the site designer, from which he faces outward to the reasons and goals of other domains. He will of course be concerned with *justice*, or how these environmental goods are distributed among those who will inhabit the site. And he will be concerned about *cost*, which is an accounting of what quantities of other benefits must be given up in order to achieve these environmental benefits. These costs may be charges against

FIGURE 31
*Neighborly talk
along a common
pathway in
Chatham Village
in Pittsburgh: one
of the most skill-
fully designed row
house develop-
ments in the
United States.*

one of his own five central values: what degree of automobile access must we give up to make the street safe for children? what sacrifice in memorable form is necessary to achieve this flexibility? Trade-offs are the stuff of design. Costs of this kind are measures of the distribution of benefits among the different values, just as justice refers to their distribution among persons.

More often, we think of costs as being charges against other goods external to the design: money in particular, our all-purpose measure. But costs include organizational effort and social and ecological disruption, as well as the dollar costs of labor and capital. Clearly, a development should minimize construction and maintenance costs, given the benefits to be achieved. But how benefits are to be traded against costs, and how maintenance costs should be traded against construction costs, is a complex decision, which begins with the setting of the program and continues throughout the design. One must analyze who will pay, since costs are usually unequally distributed. Costs cannot be measured in the same units.

While cost is usually uppermost in the minds of those who make development decisions, it is cost of a restricted type, and thus many decisions are larded with irrationality. Future maintenance is neglected; last-minute savings are made by cutting "luxuries" which will impose nondollar costs; immediate economies gained by rapid design and decision may impose heavy burdens later. A critical examination of the whole balance of continuing costs and benefits is rarely seen.

Money costs of construction are normally minimized by regularity of form, by compact arrangements at moderately high density, by the reduction of expensive features such as roads and sewers, and by lower standards. But lower standards as often mean higher maintenance costs, and discounted maintenance costs are typically higher than initial building costs. Thus maintenance costs should always be included in a program. They are minimized by simplicity of form but also by a self-regulating ecological system, durable materials, and institutional arrangements that encourage responsibility. The cost differential between a good site plan and a poor one may be no more than the additional design time needed to find a better solution. Design costs are small in proportion to total costs, and design time is brief in relation to project life. But immediate outlays and delays loom gigantic to a hard-pressed client.

Ethnocentrism

The above criteria are all man-centered. Costs and benefits are referred to ourselves, and arguments focus on who gets what. A broader view is possible, which includes thought for other living things. As yet this view has no legal, and very little professional, standing. It raises difficult questions about what other living things we deign to consider, how we weight their requirements, and how we presume to speak for them. But it is clear that this broader perspective begins to trouble our ethnocentricity. Until then, we can at least keep our minds open and be sure that any radical disruption of the web of life is unlikely to be in our own best interest, much less that of other species.

Techniques of analysis

Reference 64

Once the relevant users are identified, their requirements and desires for such qualities as vital support, sense, fit, access, and control can be investigated by any of an array of techniques. What follows is a glossary of the more familiar social and psychological methods of analysis, which are relevant to environmental behavior and useful to the site planner. We have excluded special research techniques, as well as others of great practical importance which do not bear directly on the man-environment relation: demographic studies, economic analyses, indexes of social function, and the like. We pass the latter by, not because they are not useful but because they are well covered in other sources. They are the necessary background on which the man-environment interaction can be understood.

This is a list of possibilities. Each method has its particular costs and benefits. Each can be relevant or irrelevant, practical or impractical. Each entails its own problems of ethics and power and is suited for this situation and not that. We comment on these characteristics without making a handbook of procedure or any summary of findings. References in the bibliography may be used to go into these techniques more thoroughly. They are classified here according to the means used for evoking information, in four broad groups: indirect observation, direct observation, direct communication, and participant analysis. Both the immediacy of connection between source and receiver, and the consequent contamination of information by analysis, increase as one travels down the list.

Indirect observation

In *indirect observation* we use some record of past behavior to explain the present and predict the future. Since the evidence has already been produced, the existing community is not disturbed by referring to it and can be left in ignorance of the investigation. This has advantages of simplicity, economy, and ease of surveillance, but the design implications of the data may be difficult to extract. These techniques are used where the user is unassembled, or the design center is remote, or when time and money do not permit a more direct approach. They are also useful for excluding the user from decisions.

One can analyze what locales have been used, or what behaviors have occurred, when some choice was available. This is the market approach: where did people move? what housing did they buy? where did they go for recreation? did they use the public garden? The information is reliable, since it reveals what people actually do rather than what they say they will do (which is often quite different). One must be certain that these people had real choices: that they live in old tenements because they love them and not because they cannot afford a suburban house. If the past choices were real, and similar to present choices, the information is useful. Many plans are wholly based on it. It has three difficulties. First, did these choices depend on the site characteristics we are dealing with or on other factors? Second, even where exogenous factors can be excluded, the implications for future behavior are only empirical. Without a firm theory of man and environment, we are unsure of how people will act the next time. Third, the investigation deals with existing choices. Everyone may be leaving center city for the suburbs, but it does not follow that the movement cannot be reversed, given a new center city. Only when we penetrate into *why* the exodus occurs can we predict its reversal.

One can study the form of stable and accepted existing places, or the environment of origin of some group, thinking that such places must have come to some fit with prevalent values and actions, and that any new place which follows these models will appear "right" to displaced people. This is the study of precedent, so familiar to designers. The environment of origin is studied, if for no other reason than to sense what will be novel and what familiar. Some continuity of form is surely desirable, particularly in traumatic moves. Where it is not provided, the residents themselves will often create it. But precedents are slippery fish: one is never quite sure what elements of the environment are working well or how they will operate in a new context.

Much information has already been recorded for other purposes and is available in compact form; tax records, water hook-ups; the incidence of disease, accident, and crime; the

Past choices

Precedents

Archives

records of local nurseries, movers, or telephone companies; the minutes of hearings; and the like. These data are objective and often enlightening about past or current site behavior. They are the data of the historian and the sociologist, and may require some ingenuity to discover and to interpret. Once found, how much of the recorded effect was due to the nature of the site? Was the tuberculosis due to bad housing, poor diet, despair, random infection, inadequate clothing, or all or none of those? Since the data were recorded and preserved for other purposes, they may distort past reality or be only partially relevant to site planning purposes.

Content analysis

Newspapers, radio, television, guidebooks, novels, paintings, popular songs, political speeches, advertisements—all contain references to the environment that record widely held images and opinions about it. One sees there the typical views of what urban areas and their problems are like, and the stereotypes about desirable or undesirable settings. One replays past conflicts to see what people cared enough about to fight for. These are openings into group attitudes and very useful on that account. But they tend to express stereotyped ideas, fixed and narrow. They reflect the views of whoever controls the particular medium.

Traces

Any environment is full of the traces left by the actions of its inhabitants, mute witness of what they have done: worn steps, paths in the dirt, streaks and scratches on the wall, furniture set out, symbols displayed, laundry on the line, new name cards at the doorbell, goods for sale, the content of garbage cans, treehouses and mud castles, big cars at the curb, abandoned toys, flowers at the doorstep— the "unobtrusive measures" of the social psychologist. The site designer learns to read these signs just as the tracker reads the spoor of forest animals. She looks for them whenever she passes through a setting. They are eloquent of what people attempt to do, often in contradiction to the environmental shell that they must live in. She knows to look at the front side of any place, where the important symbols are displayed, but also at the back, where "it all hangs out." Traces are an economical source of information, whose collection causes little disturbance. But the information may be fragmentary, hard to read unless one is familiar with the culture, and expressive more of behavior than of inner feeling.

Formal studies

Finally, one consults the professional literature of research and evaluation, dealing with situations similar to those being confronted. What analyses have already been made of such problems as the one I am facing? In some particular

FIGURE 32
The steps up to Whitby Abbey in England, like a frozen river, bear the trace of human passage.

areas a fair amount of research has been built up. In other areas, the studies are distressingly thin. Even in the well-studied areas, one frequently finds that the situations analyzed are unlike the one that the designer faces, in some important feature, or that his most urgent questions remain unanswered. A body of findings is emerging, where there was nothing a decade ago, and yet the findings are uneven. Thus the methods of investigation used in some similar circumstance may be more useful to the designer than the particular findings. Moreover, previous innovative designs have not often been analyzed for their performance. The account of a design still stops at that magic moment when the project was just completed. This is repetitive idiocy, since most site plans solve and re-solve the same problems. But the post-occupancy gap is built into our institutions. If we were to analyze the performance of projects in relation to their programs on any regular basis, we would soon build an impressive body of evidence.

Direct observation records what people actually do in a place. This is a rich source of objective data, and every setting is a place for gathering it. The behavior being observed is usually visible behavior, but one can record speech as well. Data can be recorded by an alert observer with a notebook, supplemented with a camera and perhaps a tape recorder. Behaviorists will say that these direct observations are the only proper data for science; nothing else is reliable. But they have two general limitations. First, we are presented

Direct observation

with a bewildering mass of observations, and recording is tedious. Without adequate theory, we are not sure what to look for. Much of the action has little to do with the spatial setting, or we cannot tell whether it does. The moments of obvious relevance may be infrequent. Second, even when we have extracted the relevant action, we are not informed about the inner experience: the feelings, images, attitudes, and values that accompany and motivate overt behavior and give it human character. When people are deflected by a wall, how can we judge that wall until we know where those people want to go and how they feel about being deflected? But when behavioral observation is supplemented by an inquiry into felt experience, the combination is the most reliable data we can get on how places are working. Designers are well advised to study places in this two-pronged way, although they may have to employ short-cut means.

Behavior
settings
Reference 7

The type of observation that most closely suits site planning purposes is Roger Barker's analysis of the "behavior setting," in which some standing pattern of behavior repeats itself at regular intervals in some bounded locality—the corner newsstand, the evening ball game, the front stoop on a weekend—and in which space and behavior can be considered as one whole. Any large environment can be divided into an array of those spatial and temporal units, which can be identified and distinguished by regular procedures. Since the behavior, and overt purpose, of the actors tend to be regularized in such settings, it is easier to record them and to understand their significance. A description of the quantity and type of the settings, their spatial and temporal boundaries, their physical character, their actors, and their associated actions, is a basic description of any general environment and a first step in programming a new one.

Reference 97

The designer may be unwilling to conduct such a thorough analysis, since any complex place, considered over a cycle of time, will contain numerous behavior settings. He may then content himself with recording the stream of activity in some limited space of particular interest to him: a street, street corner, park, or pedestrian plaza. The place is more limited and corresponds to what the designer can manipulate, but the behavior is less well organized, and extends over a cycle of time. Since to record what each individual was doing throughout that period would be exhausting, the observation is simplified by noting, at sample intervals of time, the presence and number of persons, grouped by their kind and by the activity in which they are engaged, in various

FIGURE 33
The diagram records the activity of horse, children, and adults on a working-class street in Melbourne, Australia. The photograph records the scene, and the legend indicates how the activities were classified.

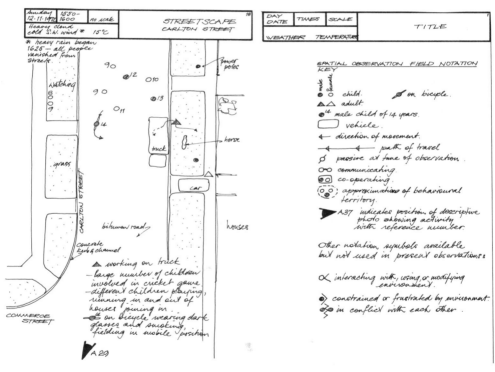

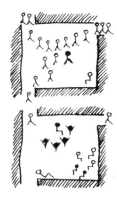

locations in the place. A graphic notation similar to dance notation is used, and automatic cameras can record the scene at regular intervals from some vantage point. Stop-frame motion pictures allow subsequent analysis, frame by frame, and will also give a compressed, high-speed display that dramatizes the tides of action in a very brief presentation. The resulting data bear on capacities, preferences, habitual actions, cyclic changes, and latent environmental problems or successes: unused places, crowded places, danger spots. Data analysis is tedious and can produce less than would be justified by the effort. The camera is a very useful record, but the experienced designer may do as much by sitting quietly at the scene, looking for something interesting and revealing. There is no substitute for this sympathetic experience of real places in action. Good designers do it habitually.

These techniques of observation are especially apt for designs that will adapt existing sites for present users, although studies can also be made of sites analogous to new designs. Direct observation can be done relatively unobtrusively, so that behavior is not distorted by the act of observation. But if people do not know that they are being studied, can this information be used to their disadvantage? Telephoto lenses, hidden cameras, and electronic eavesdroppers are invasions of privacy. Observations should never be done without the knowledge and consent of the observed (which means that one *has* disturbed how they normally act), unless the information will be made available to them for their use and censorship (a complicated procedure), or at least unless no information is gathered that might be detrimental to the welfare or dignity of the observed. That final rule excludes more than one might suppose but permits such studies as focus on helping people to do what they seek to do and do not identify individuals or small groups.

Movement patterns

The classic form of behavioral observation is the traffic count, in which we tally the number and perhaps the type of vehicles or persons passing or turning at some particular point, in some unit of time. We are usually interested in vehicles and in peak rates of flow but may also record flows along intensively used sidewalks or at major entrance gates. If counts at particular points are coordinated, the flows in an entire network may be determined. By manning all the crossings of some continuous cordon line, we determine the buildup and decline of vehicles or persons within the cordoned area. Sample persons or vehicles may be stopped and asked the origin and destination of their trip. In smaller areas, the motions of individual persons or vehicles may be tracked over a period of time to learn how the environment affects their motion. Such tracking may be done by hand, or more frequently by elevated cameras, taking pictures at standard intervals. The traffic flow count, at least, is almost always relevant, economical of effort, and raises no substantial ethical questions.

A more fundamental concept is the "behavior circuit," the twin of the behavior setting. Where the latter looks at a bounded unit of action and place, the former looks at the track of activity followed by an individual over a cycle of time—during a normal day, for example. It is the view of place as experienced by the person, who moves from location to location and engages in various roles. This is the insider's view and is best understood in dialogue with that person. But it is also possible to track him through a period of time, as a detective shadows his quarry. Thus Barker's team watched what a single boy did during one entire day and wrote a whole book about it. If the surveillance is without the knowledge of the subject, it is difficult to do and its ethics dubious. If known, behavior is inevitably distorted. But the idea that a place should be evaluated during the experience of a normal day remains important.

Behavior circuits

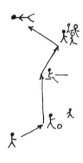

Observation becomes more efficient when we focus on particular behaviors that interest us. We may watch only the visible, material interactions with the setting: pushing doors open, walking up steps, sitting on seats, digging, climbing. Or we may look only for some evidence of difficulty: stumbling, falling, hesitation, collision, the retracing of steps or other evidence of being lost, squinting, seeking shelter from rain or wind, apparent anger, fear, or frustration. While not overt except in very unpleasant places, these signs are very revealing if detected. Or if we think that the key role of the environment is how it supports social interaction, then we focus on how and where people communicate with each other: the friendly wave or nod, the casual encounter, the rapt discussion on the brink of the traffic stream, the intimate meeting in some secluded corner. We might look just for the occasions in which users deliberately change their environment: reset the seating arrangements, draw shades over the picture window, climb the fence, park on the sidewalk. Selective observation is likely to be more directly relevant to site planning ends. It is also narrower than the holistic observation of the behavior setting and more

Selected behavior

FIGURE 34
People use street details in ways for which they were never designed.

FIGURE 35
*Children create
their own imagi-
nary worlds*

Experiments

dependent on previous theories and assumptions. It considers the physical setting primarily as something which blocks or facilitates intended human activities. It is rapid, powerful, and limited.

In all the preceding investigations, it is difficult to determine cause and effect since so many variables are involved. The classic means of uncovering causal links is the experiment, in which a single variable is changed, while all others are held constant, and the ensuing condition is then compared with the original condition. Following this model, our analyst would make a single modification in a setting and then see how behavior changes. The change might test some proposed design feature—a new color scheme, a street crossing, a new entrance, special seating—or it might test some hypothesis of environmental effect—such as the influence of seating location or of activity mix. But unless experiments make no more than minor changes in existing places, they will be expensive and time-consuming. We do not build a public space, much less an entire district, in order to test a theory. More important, contrived changes are a direct intrusion into the lives of users. They must not be critical intrusions. No one would remove a pedestrian crossing to see if traffic fatalities would rise (although we often do the opposite, when we wait for fatalities to "prove" the need of new crossing lights). Contrived changes must be kept small and benign.

Therefore the observer may resort to the "natural experiment," when some change has occurred for other reasons: a bridge has been closed for repair, a settlement is struck by disaster, or construction disrupts a street. The observer must have foreseen the event, so that he has been able to study previous behavior as a baseline for comparison, and the change must fit some featural change about which he desires to know. The most useful natural experiment, therefore, is the planned disruption itself—the site planning act. New developments, as will be explained in the following chapter, should be built according to a program that specifies the behavior to be attained. The design is then a hypothesis that this form will induce that behavior.

All experiments are complicated by the fact that behavioral effects develop over a substantial period of time. Immediate results may be striking but ephemeral as the novelty wears off and the users adapt to the new situation. The users themselves grow and change, in a long interplay between person and place. This may stabilize only much later, and by then it will have been contaminated by still other changes. Environmental change must therefore be evaluated by the resulting shape of behavior through time rather than the effect at any moment. So the longitudinal experiment is preferable to the simple comparative one. Since longitudinal experiments are usually beyond a designer's reach, this warning is properly directed at research. But it may suffice to alert the designer to the misleading temporary effects of change.

One is not confined to the external observation of behavior, despite the warnings of behaviorists. People can talk, draw, gesture, and so communicate with each other. *Direct communication* is therefore an important source of data, not only as to what people do but also as to what they feel, conceive, and value. Now, however, we face some familiar difficulties more directly. First, it is hard to "get inside" someone else's head, to externalize their feelings, images,

Direct communication

91

and experience. The uncertainties of the attempt require us to use a combination of methods so that cross-checking will improve reliability. Second, the investigation itself disturbs the phenomenon under study, as it only occasionally does in behavioral observation. The person interviewed responds to the interviewer, hides certain things—consciously or unconsciously—flaunts others, and revises his memories to accord with proper attitudes. Luckily, the analysis of environmental feelings is less difficult than the analysis of interpersonal relations, since the former are not so highly charged with emotion. If done with sympathy and tact and if cross-checked by several different approaches to internal reality, direct communication is a rich source of information that one can gain in no other way. Moreover, the very contamination of the findings by the act of communication gives the user an active, creative role in programming and design.

Interviews   In conducting interviews, be careful not to determine the answers by the way in which the questions are asked, and be sure that the questions are clear to the respondent. There is a general technique of interview, with which any questioner should be familiar: how to maintain a nonjudgmental but interested tone; how to avoid questions that lead to or preclude a specific answer; how to make sure that questions are understood; how to set the tone of the interview and explain its purpose when introducing it; how to make sure that the data will be relevant and analyzable. Since one can interview all users only in the rare case, there are statistical considerations in choosing the sample. How big must it be? what classes of persons should it represent? how will it be chosen? Shall we interview a large number of people, to enhance statistical validity, and so confine ourselves to those few simple questions that can be asked and analyzed in quantity? Or shall we talk to a few people and make a subtle, in-depth inquiry? Shall questions be factual, permitting simple answers on definite subjects set out by the interviewer, or should the interview be open-ended, allowing the respondent to explore the subject in his own terms? We will express three general preferences here. First, many of the issues of greatest interest to the site designer are complex and subtle and so are most effectively covered in the small, in-depth interview, despite its lack of statistical weight. Second, the large-scale, structured interview, designed for quantitative analysis, is most effective once the issues are clear. Therefore, it is often best to begin with a small, exploratory, open-ended survey and follow it with a large, structured one that focuses on the crucial items uncovered in the preliminary exploration. Third, since it is so easy to impose an alien point of view on the respondent, the open-ended interview, which allows the person to express himself in his own way, is almost always preferable, despite the difficulties it raises for precise analysis.

The respondent can be asked to describe her own behavior circuit in detail: what did she do yesterday, at what time, why and where? Based on recent memory, the account is likely to be fairly accurate, unless the person has something to hide. It gives us a solid picture of how people use their world and time and how they interact with others. We can make diagrams of social and geographical range from it, and comprehensive time budgets. The data can be extended by asking people to keep diaries of their daily actions over longer periods of time, although this requires that they be motivated to do so, and the thought of recording may affect how one spends the day. Descriptions of daily life are relatively accurate and useful behavioral accounts. They are person-centered, and expressed in terms of purpose, as the visual observation of behavior can rarely be. | Activity logs

Respondents are asked to identify the problems that they have with their environment and then their satisfactions. The questions are direct, and the answers equally so. Problems are easier to perceive than satisfactions, and so the former will be emphasized. Both are likely to be expressed in stereotyped ways picked up from the mass media and thus somewhat removed from actual experience. People can be unconscious of their real problems, in part because they are unaware of environmental possibilities. They may be silent about other problems because they seem foolish or improper. To avoid this, we can ask them about the difficulties that *other* people have. To go beyond generalities, we ask them to describe the specific frustrations, however trivial, that they encountered yesterday. This type of questioning directly supplements the visual observation of frustrated behavior. | Naming problems

It is revealing to ask the respondent for an open-ended description of a place in order to evoke their perception, feelings, and knowledge of it. This can be done on the site itself, but more frequently in retrospect, so that the person's way of storing these images is brought into play. The inverview is open-ended but is guided by leading questions such as "what first comes to your mind about this place?" "describe it to me as if I were a stranger and you wanted | Images to explain its most important features to me" "How do I get from x to y, and what would I see along the way?" "What are the outstanding features here? What do they look like? And how do you feel about them?" "Do you feel as if you belong in this place; have any control over it, or feel responsible for it?" "What kind of people live here, and what do they do?" "Do you like it? Would you grieve for its loss?" and so on. Respondents may be asked to respond graphically as well as verbally, as by drawing a map or making a sketch of the place. Although many people feel apologetic about their drawing (strangely enough, they never apologize for their words), yet the elements drawn, the order of drawing, and their style and juxtaposition can be very revealing. The basic content of the verbal answers can be noted on the spot, or immediately afterward, but it is useful to tape the interview, with the consent of the interviewee. Taping is not done to make a complete transcription but to preserve vocal inflections and to recover selected details. Since this is such an open-ended, subjective discourse, the circumstances of the interview, the set of the questions, the personal relationship, the ease with which the interviewer accepts and follows the thoughts of the speaker, and yet picks up and pursues some unexpected revelation, all affect the quality of the results.

Free descriptions produce a rich body of information, not easy to compare or to quantify. Since this is the natural way in which we communicate to each other about places, it is useful in the exploratory stage when we want to identify principal issues. We gain a rapid impression of the human impact of an environment. We evoke the spatial image: how the place and its features are recognized and mentally organized, the sense of territory and structure, and its relation to the sense of self. The interview can be supplemented by asking the person if they recognize selected photographs of the setting, explaining how they recognize them, and how they fit together. The interview may pursue the sense of time embodied in the environment. How is the place changing, how has it changed or will it change, how does it evoke past or future events, how does it vary with season and time of day?

Preferences A number of techniques have been developed to extract a more precise sense of internal values and images. Like all sharp-edged things, what they gain in precision they lose in broader connections. The responses are made to simulations of the environment, so that the stimuli are kept in-

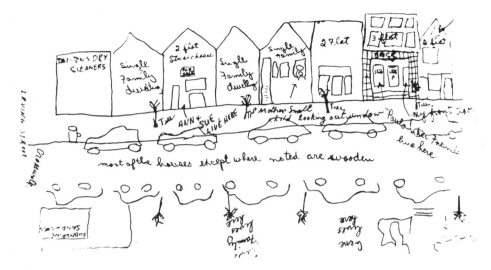

FIGURE 36 *The sketch of a neighborhood street by a resident of San
Francisco. Corner stores, trees, parked cars, the different entrances
and the families that live behind them are the principal features of
the drawing. The neighborhood is very local: "I've drawn the part of
the block where I live . . . the rest of the people, I have found, are dif-
ficut to meet on the street." She notes details like stained glass windows and brightly painted stucco, and still: "None of the houses
have peaked roofs, but my memory of how they do look is very limited." Yet the peaked-roof convention rules the drawing.*

variant from one person to another. These simulations may
be photographs of the place, drawings, models, motion pictures, or videotapes. There is a substantial literature on the
types of simulation that give the most reliable results. The
simulations may be altered by adding or subtracting some
feature, in order to study how changes affect value or classification. Thus one can add the image of a low-status person
to a photograph or delete signs or telephone poles.

One analysis consists of asking the respondent to sort
the simulations into as many piles as he may wish, putting
like with like as he sees it. He reveals his way of classifying
the world and can discuss what those classes mean to him.
Or ask him to indicate his relative preference for these places,
on some scale from one to ten or five, where one is worst
and five or ten is best. Environmental preference is of direct
interest, but its causes can be obscure. It is unreliable for
places that the respondent has not personally experienced.
The scalings will often bunch at "moderately poor" and

95

"moderately good"—the threes and sevens—since most people avoid harsh judgments.

Semantic differential
The semantic differential is a developed technique for probing the meaning of places. A long list of polar pairs of adjectives used to describe places is constructed: "good-bad," "cold-warm," "rough-smooth," "safe-dangerous," and so on. Tested lists of this kind are available. As each simulation is presented to the respondent, he is asked to indicate the adjective of each pair that is most appropriate to that place. This church is smooth and clean and high; that barroom is rough and dirty and low. The combined answers of a group of people can then be analyzed to see which adjectives are most consistently combined over the whole set of places. These consistent adjective sets (which may or may not have some easily expressible summary meaning, such as power or danger) are presumably the principal dimensions of meaning by which these people discriminate their world. The places represented can then be arranged along those dimensions.

The method has its limitations. It deals solely with verbal stereotypes, and the verbal classes are imposed on the respondent. He must call a bar rough or smooth, however he feels about it, even if his personal word is "wetness,' or if he has a visual image of a dim, quiet room, delightful for adults and risky for children.

Forced choice
Since imagined preferences are costless, they may have little relevance for real choices. The forced choice is a device for getting closer to reality. For example, the respondent is given an imaginary sum of money and is asked to choose how she would spend it on an array of types of housing, locations, transportation, and services. Each type has its price, and the sum of their prices is larger than the money available. Most people will play this familiar game with conviction. From the choices, one learns how people might trade off the size of the house lot against the time distance to work or against the quality of the school. The method is unreal to the extent that the stated prices or the available sum are unreal. Costs are stated in the one commensurate dimension of money. But the cost that drives any real decision may be a loss of social prestige or fears for one's children.

Play
Scale models are intriguing representations of reality. Respondents can be requested to rearrange them as they would prefer to see them or to deal with some given problem. They can be asked to represent a real place by making a model out of standard parts, instead of drawing a map of

it, since map drawing is a task that many will resist. They can be requested to construct an ideal settlement as the basis for a discussion. Young children, given reasonable replicas of people, cars, and other active objects, will act out a typical day within the model. The game absorbs them; they reveal feelings and interactions. Acting out can be recorded on videotape and studied as if it were actual place behavior, heightened by the vocal and facial expressions of the players.

Personal memories of the environment, about which most respondents are pleased to speak, are a rich store of information. Childhood memories, in particular, will evoke a flood of feeling. Distorted as they may be by the passage of time, they explore strong associations. Early experiences shape present values, and there is evidence that many people seek to replicate the settings of their childhood. Such memories should be used with due caution, since they are simplified idealizations, but they can sensitize designers and managers to the needs of children. Comparing remembered delight in some wild backlot to the careful exclusion of waste space in a plan can be a salutary shock. Environmental memories are evocative but difficult to quantify. Memoirs and autobiographies are further sources of them.

Memories

The respondent's sense of what he is likely to do in the future, or would like to do, is material of special interest. Unfortunately, it is unreliable. Predictions are notoriously unlike actual choices. The inability to foresee the course of events, plus a poor knowledge of possible environments, plus an equally imperfect knowledge of self, all render answers dubious. "What kind of place would you like to live in?" will usually produce a banal answer, and in the real event the respondent might not choose it anyway. What type of open spaces would you like? Who would you like to live beside? How dense is too dense? are questions not reasonably given to a quick response. Not hearing any, planners may conclude that user involvement is unproductive.

Predictions

The error is with the planners. More likely, the question is not meaningful to the respondent, or he may never have considered it in the abstract. If it takes a planner weeks to understand a site and its use well enough to be creative about solutions, surely no less should be expected of someone not trained to such hypothetical issues. Projections of detailed future behavior are probably more reliable than general choices. "How would you like to eat your breakfast?" will get a more interesting answer than "how would you like to live?" An actual trial is a better guide but not easy to arrange.

97

Role playing—the projection of oneself "inside" another person or situation— is a powerful, risky, very human road to understanding. However difficult to standardize, it is the basis for any nonroutine communication: for intimate relations, for ethics, for literature. It is the necessary beginning of any investigation of the experience of place. By imagining what it might be like, the researcher frames his hypotheses for testing. The designer imagines himself inside his creations as he evolves them, but he must be careful not to take that empathic experience as revealed truth. Actors are trained to achieve insights into how other people feel and behave. Designers are not trained to forget themselves.

Role playing, carefully pursued with an open mind, can be a useful source of insight, a good first step. The designer, even a member of the school board, can imagine that she is a child walking to school. Adults must be pushed before they will let go of their identity in this way. It is easier for the child to imagine that he is on the school board. Temporarily, the designer should become one of the persons for whom an environment is being designed. When planning housing for the blind, spend a week living blindfold. A school architect may go to school, and the designer of a mental hospital may become a certified patient. The experience is not really the same, since one knows that one is not really blind or ill. But play is a way of learning, which is what children use it for.

Return from fantasy, come out of the laboratory, and take the users out into the real place that they know. On the spot, many of the same questions can be asked that have been touched on already: activity logs, problem identification, free descriptions, preferences, memories, predictions. All these procedures are more pungent in the presence of the real thing. Noise, bystanders, and other intrusions will disturb the flow of talk, and the investigation demands more time and energy. A more natural variant occurs when the designer, in the course of watching behavior in his chosen location, falls into conversation with those whom he meets, a conversation that is informal and casual in tone, but directed by his knowledge of what he wants to know, and of the methods of evoking it. The interview sample, of course, will be unbalanced, leaning toward housewives, children, firemen, the aged, and the unemployed.

Furnishing respondents with a camera is a productive prelude to an office interview. Ask them to photograph the things that they think are interesting, important, pleasant, or unpleasant. The photographs can be used in all the discussions described. The respondent sets the stage with the material meaningful to him. Interviewer and respondent explore the place together.

Site visits are especially useful when discussing preferences about places not yet created. Users are taken to places which represent alternative ways of shaping the new environment. Reactions and preferences can be discussed in front of the real thing, and photographs taken at the time will form a basis for group discussions later.

All of these methods were originally devised—and are still usually conducted—on a one-to-one basis: the respondent and his "neutral" questioner. Discussion within a small group can yield a more diverse response, through the sidelights and mutual support of good dialogue. But the group must be small —no more than five or six, perhaps—and the interviewer must exercise some skill to keep the discussion on track, with everyone participating. The group should be relatively homogeneous in its values and experiences, and there should be no power distinctions among its members, so that all feel free to speak. Given this, group interviews can be stimulating affairs and use any of the techniques discussed. They can be a prelude to larger community meetings, in which conflicting viewpoints are expressed and negotiated.

Some of these methods can be used with much larger populations. The interview can be converted into a written questionnaire, filled out in private, and returned by mail. The answers are now restricted to multiple-choice boxes. The meaning of questions must be patent, since there is no opportunity for on-the-spot clarification. The questionnaire must be brief, since there is no strong motive for working on it. Respondents will be self-selected to those who have some interest in the subject. The rate of return will be low and further discards will be necessary to ensure a composition of respondents which is similar to the composition of the whole using population. For all its extended reach, the mailed questionnaire is less useful to us, except as a check on some precise and widely debated issue that has arisen out of exploratory studies. But it is also possible to interview large numbers of respondents on written forms, when they are assembled in a hall. If an assembly can be achieved, then returns are largely guaranteed, questions can be explained, and visual simulations can be used.

Group
interviews

Reference 14

Careful as the outside observer may be, he yet intrudes his own feelings and images and finds it difficult to enter into the other person's inner world. His questioning presence inevitably disturbs the thing he is observing, and his information, once collected, may be used against the interests of the person observed. This can be dismissed when we study easily visible behavior relevant to some widely shared purpose—as when we analyze traffic with the aim of reducing accidents. When we study preferences as a basis for relocation, we are in greater trouble. *Participant observation* is a way of circumventing this. It is the approach peculiar to anthropology, whose literature is perhaps our richest mine of knowledge about ways of life. The investigator lives with the group he is studying, joins in their pursuits, and makes himself as much a part of their world as he can. By gaining their confidence and a share in their intimate communications, as well as by his partial transformation into a member of the group, he achieves a more profound insight into their perceptions. He begins to see the underlying, inarticulate systems of belief, the latent functions, the hidden agendas. Thus the tales of anthropology are often more useful to the designer than the more precise, remote data of sociology.

Unfortunately, the participant observer is on a fence. He is an insider and yet a stranger, one who shares intimacies and tells tales. Since he collects information that will be used by outsiders, he may be violating an unspoken trust. To maintain the objectivity necessary for accurate reporting while also participating means walking another tightrope. The method was first used by "advanced" scientists studying "primitive" societies, where the scientist had no fear of becoming a primitive and little doubt but that he knew what was right. As we apply the method to people more and more like ourselves, these ambiguities become more obvious. It is a patient business, which demands careful training and years of quiet observation. Where its results are available, it provides some of the best background material that can be found. The site designer is less than likely to engage in it herself. She may dip temporarily into this mode, pretending to be blind or ill, living briefly in a slum tenement.

Self-observation is a more radical response to these difficulties. The users of an environment can be trained to employ the observation techniques themselves, analyzing their own use and conception of their surroundings. All the methods described can be used: indirect and direct observation and direct communication. But the roles have changed.

100

Observing the response to environment becomes a self-experiment in which the potentialities of the setting and of one's own nature are explored in parallel. The ambiguity of the observer's role disappears, and new ambiguities are created. The outside expert becomes a teacher of technique, and it is possible to explore inward feelings as well as outward signs. The resulting information remains in the hands of those who produce it and to whom it is relevant. The very act of survey helps to establish the control of the setting by those who will use it.

The process of observation continues to disturb the thing observed, however. The disturbance is now radical, since feedback is rapid, internal, and self-conscious. Participant analysts will change their perception of the place, and even some of their values about it. The process may go in unexpected directions. Environmental assessment becomes a path along which people come to understand themselves, a path toward organizing to be effective. Survey becomes self-transformation.

This is mostly speculation. Self-analysis is a new way of studying the interplay of man and place—one which avoids many political and ethical ambiguities and lays the basis for participatory design. It would develop clients aware of their proper interests and able to speak for them. It has its own limitations, surely. It assumes a stable and well-organized set of users, who will continue to control a place. It takes time to accomplish, careful planning, and more self-abnegation than many designers can summon up. It can threaten the power of the paying client, or at least upset his time-table, and so it is likely to be resisted. If carelessly done, it may only raise hopes later frustrated. It is a "hot," risky technique, demanding, likely to go off in unexpected directions, and therefore full of promise.

There are many other methods for involving users in generating ideas. The planner's tools can be put in their hands: they can be instructed in doing site analysis, be given manipulable models to test site arrangement, or a large number of photos or slides of site qualities from which to compose a scheme. They can hire their own design advocate, who takes their ideas and converts them into a form comprehensible to the planners. The problem can be broken down into small units so that proposals are presented in forms—such as simulations or mock-ups—that match the user's everyday experience, rather than employing hard-to-read drawings that emphasize large-scale issues. These methods are effective only if the planning team is prepared to empathize with users and their concerns. They should be central to the planning process, not a fringe activity aimed at minimizing opposition.

It is clear that we do not conduct value-free analyses. The designer should observe *herself*, to understand the biases she brings to the task, and so that she is prepared to speak for her own values. So she probes her own images and feelings of place, her own memories. Any observation beyond the most trivial must be done with the knowledge and consent of the observed, and the information it generates should be available to them. This principle has technical consequences: it favors simple surveys, suited to decentralized execution, giving rapid returns, whose results are immediately understood. Designers are not accustomed to think of their inquiries as political, but information is power.

Other
techniques

Extended as this list of methods has been, there are still others used in research, and to some extent in professional practice: the repertory grid, gaming, thematic apperception. In others, the exact locus of attention is traced; the facial expression is photographed, as well as gesture and body movement; the tone of voice and fragmentary vocalizations are recorded; and pupil dilation, galvanic skin reactions, brain rhythms, and internal chemistry are measured. These measurements require elaborate equipment and can bury us beneath information that we are not ready to use. Respondents can be subjected to distorted stimuli: be blinded, deafened, blinkered, isolated from sensation or overloaded, subjected to very brief visual exposures or to reversals in time or space. Analysts can employ methods associated with psychiatry: depth analysis, hypnosis, dream interpretation, and the like. These studies are of great research interest, but the techniques are difficult, and occasionally dangerous in unskilled hands.

Choice of
method

How might we summarize these techniques for the purposes of practical design? The choice of method depends largely on the nature of the users. Where they are a relatively small group—available, reasonably homogeneous, and having some control over their place—then one goes directly to them for information. Individual and small-group interviews about how they actually use the place, how they describe it, what problems they find with it, what they hope for the future, and how they remember their past, will be

Reference 14

the centerpieces of investigation. Users can be encouraged to observe their own behavior in some systematic way and to visit other sites that present alternatives. The designer, or her investigator, acts as convoker, teacher, and organizer. She raises questions, presents possibilities, integrates suggestions into workable solutions. All the techniques for stimulating group debate and for bringing it to a conclusion are employed. Users take photographs, draw maps, play with models, engage in group walks and charrettes. In addition, the designer will try to identify users normally not considered, such as teens or caretakers. She will help residents bring their findings to some conclusive form and show them how participatory analysis may be carried over into design and management.

As the user group becomes larger and more complex, but where it is still present and familiar with the site (as in a renewal area), then the same direct techniques are used, but they must become more general in their form. Sample surveys and narrower, more quantifiable interviews are employed. The likelihood of conflicts between user groups, and between clients and users, rises. Designers are put on their mettle to find solutions that satisfy diverse requirements simultaneously or mediate between them. Who will be heard is an open issue. If present users are to be removed, the issue can be agonizing. Formal political means must be used to air and mediate those conflicts, and greater reliance is placed on explicit, quantified data. The designer begins to observe local behavior and movement patterns in some systematic fashion. Self-observation is still a valuable technique but is more difficult to organize, more likely to meet client resistance, and less likely to carry through subsequent stages. The designer will search the available literature for its findings in analogous situations and may conduct small experiments on the site. More of his time will be occupied with the management of user and client conflict, and with the identification of those groups who have power, or who might have power, over the environment. Where users are present but are transient and anonymous (as in a city plaza), self-observation is no longer viable, and one turns even more to the observation of action and to brief sample surveys on the street.

In many site planning tasks, however, the user is not present: the housing project is still to be built; the transit line is only planned. Users may be organized and vocal, but more often they are represented only by their predicted, indirect influence on the client: the house builder, the college administration, or the industrial firm. If assembled but voiceless (students of a college or employees of a firm about to relocate) the designer attempts to communicate with them. If not assembled, and if she cannot find a way to assemble them (as by helping to organize a housing cooperative), the planner is driven to the more indirect sources: studies of market choices or of behavior in analogous places, or consultation of the research literature. Samples of surrogate users may be interviewed to elicit their reactions to situations similar to the proposed new forms. The development may be important enough to justify a controlled experiment. In any case, the program will be framed as a learning device, and provisions will be made for changing the form as learning occurs, when the actual users appear on the scene.

Some site plans are concerned with prototypes rather than with particular places. They are illustrative designs or systems of things to be repeated in various localities. The design may be for a prototypical trailer park, a standard road cross-section, or a bus stop and its context. While site planners are less accustomed to such work, it is an efficient way of using scarce design talent, and it fits the way in which many components of our landscape are actually produced and installed. Now the user cannot be reached directly; he may even be unknown. On the other hand, the user will be engaged in some specific role within that prototype, which simplifies the analysis. The large number of settings that will be controlled by the design makes a sophisticated analysis or a carefully monitored experiment economical. It is also possible to leave room for modifying the system as experience accumulates.

Most difficult of all is the situation in which the designer faces a culture strange to him, where he cannot easily communicate with a user, sympathize with his values, or understand his behavior or its traces. In such a situation, the designer must move with caution, leaning on local informants, previous studies, and cultural precedent. He focuses on basic needs such as vital support, makes flexible plans open to user intervention, and emphasizes the training of local professionals.

Through all of these situations, the site designer continues her own private investigation of how people inhabit place: watching behavior, looking for traces, talking with people about their dreams, their difficulties and their memories, attending to the changes brought about by natural experiments. She remains open to the environment, fascinated by it, not afraid of using her own intuitions as a first step of understanding, but not relying on them.

We have attempted a synopsis of the methods of studying environmental behavior but not a synopsis of findings. The bibliography refers to some of the more useful compendiums of research. Its findings are bunched in particular areas: elderly and family housing, hospitals and other total institutions, children's play, urban pedestrian spaces, traffic behavior, shopping, large offices, man-machine interactions, hostile and isolated environments, landscape preferences, proxemics and small-group interactions. When working in a similar place, the designer may hope for useful information. He will often discover that the reported results, while suggestive, do not quite fit the puzzle he is up against. Therefore he must make inquiries on his own or engage someone else to do so. In other situations, he will find very little that he can rely on.

Findings

Reference 95

Chapter **4**

The Program

The program represents a set of agreements on the purposes and specifications for site improvement. It asks: what uses should be included? with what environmental qualities? how much of each use? to be used by whom? patterned how? built and maintained by whom? at what cost? according to what timetable? Some of the answers will be suggested by the potentials of the site; others will evolve from the motives of designers, owners, users, financiers, public officials, and others involved in the project.

Traditionally, the site program has been considered the responsibility of the immediate client, the "brief" he provides designers to explain his objectives and limit the task. This dusty document states the maximum total cost, lists the number of spaces or units or structures to be accommodated, and indicates the desired access among the components. The design will be its three-dimensional elaboration, to be "fitted into" the site. Most issues are addressed later and implicitly through the choices made during design. Such an approach can require backtracking when new considerations are discovered; it mixes decisions on details with fundamental choices; it can lead to misunderstandings between client and designer; and it usually leaves few traces of intentions against which the performance of the built environment can eventually be assessed.

An explicit programming process provides a more dependable basis for design. Programming and design are never completely separable activitites, nor should they be. Sketch

Value of
programming

designs are needed to clarify the consequences of programmatic decisions, and early designs expose programmatic choices not previously anticipated. The program may dominate attention in the initial stages of a project, but it is important to begin design explorations before its decisions are firm. Later, after the design has developed, it may be necessary to make further adjustments to the program. Emphasis will vary over the course of a project, but programming and design are continuous, interlocking activities, complementary aspects of the task of deciding site form.

For some projects, a major investment in programming may be critical. Where sites are developed over long periods of time, such as in creating a new town, the program will be the thread of continuity, allowing successive generations of designers to acquire a framework for their work quickly. Reprogramming will occur every year or two, taking account of the physical and financial results of completed work. A detailed program allows newly arrived users to challenge current policies and to inject their own views about the future of a place.

Where there are multiple clients, the program may be the principal instrument of communication from one actor to another. Public land development agencies, for example, frequently relay their intentions through a "proposal call package" to the private developers who will be responsible for design and construction. When developers must compete for a site, it is essential that the important physical, social, and financial criteria be spelled out. In this case, since the program is fixed before the developers prepare specific designs, it must be tested by design studies that explore what is possible within the rules.

Even in small sites, preparing a program can provide the impetus to think in fresh ways about environmental character. Siting a new school in a built-up area is an example. School boards have adopted rigid minimum space requirements and rule out many inner city locations because they are too small. But if the need for open space is considered in terms of activities, ways can be found to overlap uses, invent more intensive activities, and identify new locales such as rooftops and nearby lots. A difficult siting problem can give rise to a unique design response.

The expression of a program can take many forms: lists of objectives and design criteria, charts of responsibility, schedules of elements to be included and their desired characteristics or performance, diagrams of desired linkages, timetables for construction, financial statements, scenarios of how the place should seem to be when in use, examples of other projects that can serve as departure points for design, and so on. With varying emphasis, most programs will embody decisions in four domains: about the *population* to be accommodated on the site; about the *package* of activities or elements to be included, their timing, and the managerial and financial responsibility for each; about the type and level of *performance* expected from the designed environment; and about the essential *patterns* or physical arrangements the site design should seek to incorporate.

Assumptions about the *population* of a site are often thought to be the aspect least open to choice. This is true in many cases: where an existing organization is to be transplanted into new facilities; where a site's location or character seriously limits who may be attracted there; or where the site owner has decided in advance to develop facilities for specific persons. Accepting those initial assumptions, the designer learns what he can about that particular population.

But in many instances the question is open. A site may seem appropriate for housing, for example, but the market may be undefined. Even if the development will aim at low income households, their detailed character (families with young children? singles? elderly?) will have important consequences. Where many uses are possible, such as downtown, it may be essential to pin down the main groups of possible users, even if actual occupants will not be known until the components of the development have been decided on.

Constructing a profile of the probable population is an essential first step. But a simple statistical profile seldom tells the whole story. Nor is it imageable in the way that helps designers to invent an accommodating place. More detailed accounts—the ways in which these people spend their time, their likes and dislikes, their backgrounds, their social networks—complement the aggregate data. Accounts are not limited to documenting the past. Scenarios of how they might use a site with new opportunities will also make a contribution. Accounts should convey a level of social intelligence which ensures that users are actually being provided for.

Users depend on the *package* of improvements chosen for the site. In its simplest form, packaging involves deciding on the type and quantities of elements to be provided: the number of housing units and the size of each type; the square

Population

Package

109

footage of commercial floor and number of parking spaces; the recreation activities for which indoor and outdoor facilities are to be built; and so on. To this may be added a budget broken down by elements and types of expenditures and inclusive, perhaps, of maintenance costs and a staging schedule. Where there is a single client with considerable experience, these initial figures may be dependable enough to begin the design. Little is gained by refining the program before sketches determine whether it is possible to accommodate the package on the site. Later, after several preliminary designs have been attempted, a more detailed analysis of financial scheduling may be needed. Before proceeding with construction documents, these analyses will be formulated into a firm development program.

In most instances, however, the package emerges only after a more open exploration of possible mixes of uses, along with their consequences, sequencing, marketing, management, and potential difficulties. For example, in deciding on the development package for a large site in a location suitable for housing, several combinations of housing types will be considered, and for each type the densities will be varied. Financial pro formas will be sketched in enough detail to reveal the financing required, the time required to complete in view of assumed market absorption, and the expected return on investment. Within each option, basic alternatives will be tried out: what if the land were purchased in stages rather than all at one time? what if more of the units were aimed at the lower end of the market? what if portions of the land were sold to others to develop? what if a small commercial complex were included? what if parts of the site were reserved for other nonresidential development at some future date? Each combination of assumptions will have different consequences, which can be compared to facilitate decision.

Analyses may be done in the abstract, based on site size and constraints such as zoning. Better, they are done with a quick sketch of site arrangement. Designs may change what is possible: a valuable wood may be ringed by high density units; site access may limit its capacity; topography may require heavy infrastructure costs to be counterbalanced by an increase of units.

See Figure 37
Where profit is the driving motive, the comparative economics of alternative packages will be the dominant criterion. Timing, logistics, and organizational issues are frequently important to these decisions. The uncertain prospect of

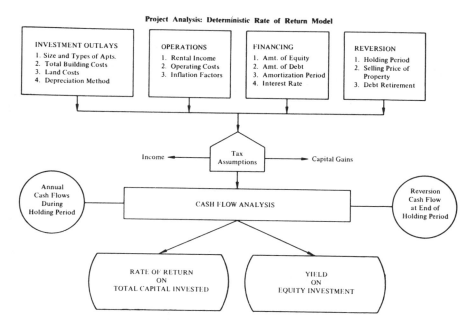

FIGURE 37 *The standard model for analyzing the financial viability of a development package, judged in terms of rate of return on equity and on total capital invested.*

changing a public regulation may outweigh the benefits of more intense development or a mixture of uses. Establishing a distinctive character may argue for an initial increment that is larger, and initially less profitable, than market studies suggest. The ability to attract one or two key tenants to begin a development may prevail, even if it means reshaping the package to accommodate their desires. Packaging is an art, not a science. It is shaped by hunches, a sense of the future economy and its possibilities. Precise estimates of cash flow, debt accumulation, and returns on investment aid in assessing possibilities, but they are seldom the only basis of decision.

Where profit is not the driver, such as in public and institutional projects, the source of funds will often have a strong influence on the package. Public agencies will have regulations on allowable costs (dollars per student housed in a dormitory or maximum rentals), while private donors will have purposes to be served by their gifts. But it is also important for institutions and governments to analyze the costs and benefits of new environments over time, and not let their decisions be distorted by the source of funds. Maintenance costs always should play an important role in this examination.

Behavior
settings

Reference 7

Reference 23

To enable financial analysis, the package will necessarily be stated in terms that can be costed directly ("so many hectares of land devoted to offices with an expected value of $X per hectare," "three play areas with an estimated budget of $Y for each," "sites for 60 townhouse units with a servicing budget of $Z per unit"). But a richer program transcribes these quantities into a schedule of behavior settings, described in terms of their type, timing, equipment, qualities, and linkages. Instead of simply specifying a children's playground (which is all too readily translated into a labeled plot of ground), the program should describe a series of play settings for children of different age groups and how they are expected to be used. This leaves open an option of one or several locations, and even of play settings integrated with other activities. The program would go on to describe the equipment desirable for play, assigning an approximate budget to each or to the entire set of facilties, and would identify the management arrangements preferred. In a program for government offices, the requirements might be described by purpose ("working groups of 50 people on the average, each group needing a place to meet outside visitors, half of each group requiring private and secure workplaces, the remainder needing spaces where considerable collaboration is possible") rather than by arbitrarily grouping activities into structures (e.g., "two buildings of 10,000 sq.m with 1,000 sq.m floors"). Activity-based descriptions not only promote more inventive design but offer a basis for collaboration between social scientists and designers because they expose the behavioral assumptions that underlie the program.

The technique of specifying behavior settings can be applied to a metropolitan region or the layout of a backyard, and the units of activity will vary accordingly. Such classification is treacherously simple. What is once assembled in a single category is rarely separated later. Having chosen "industry" as a class, one will rarely realize that different kinds of production may have different locational requirements, nor will one be aware of the rich diversity of behavior that actually goes on in most factory areas. Moreover, there will be a natural tendency to separate "industry" from other activities, excluding the possibility that residing and working might desirably happen in the same structure. Types of behavior should not be classed together because they are conventional groups, or are legally wedded in the zoning ordinance, or have similar names.

On the other hand, classification of some kind must be used if the problem is to be manageable. One looks for groups of activities that are interrelated through the purposes of their actors, or that should be located together in time and space, or that place complementary demands on their settings. Groupings are divided as finely as can be handled in the time available for observation and design. Superficial groupings are avoided, such as putting "laundry drying" and the "delivery and removal of bulk goods" into a single category labeled "utility functions." Past classifications can serve as a guide, but each new problem requires one to think out once more the strategic clusters of activities that are appropriate.

The source for specifying behavior settings may be past personal experience, but it is better grounded in detailed observation, made on the spot or in parallel situations. Where a project rebuilds an existing environment, much can be learned by systematically observing how its members now use space, as described in Chapter 3, remembering that current routines are always adapted to existing surroundings. Where the new development, or the combination of uses planned for a site, is largely unprecedented, the schedule of behavior settings will need to be composed from bits and pieces of examples and through conversations with users or their surrogates.

In some instances it may be possible, or necessary, to make a trial use of a site, with temporary fittings, before committing the major resources needed for permanent installations. Cities with little tradition of using their waterfronts, other than for industry, have organized waterfront festivals to gauge the response to new uses before building permanent settings. A richer array of water-edge activities is the result. Such a strategy provides a second meaning for "programming": it now means an initial organization of activities, which then founds a tradition of occasions that cry for appropriate settings.

Specifying desired behavior settings immediately raises questions about the levels of *performance* expected from arrangements on the site: the degree of convenience, comfort, stimulation, safety, access, fit, sense, control, maintainability, adaptability, or any other quality desired. Notions about environmental performance are often embedded in project objectives ("encourage public transit use"), or implied in

Performance requirements

standards (a design table for storm sewers based on 10 year flood conditions), or carried forward by convention (housing setbacks which, among other things, ensure a transition zone between the public and private domains). Identifying the critical performance objectives guides the site plan and later is the basis for evaluating the inhabited environment. When sites are developed in stages over an extended period, it may be especially important to monitor the performance of each new increment. To do so, intentions need to be spelled out as precisely as possible.

Requirements can be stated as thresholds ("at least 3 lux of light on pedestrian paths, with an evenness ratio of no more than 2:1"), or as absolute determinants ("no streets are to be crossed at grade by footpaths between any dwelling unit and its associated elementary school"). They also can be expressed as desired increments or qualities ("to reduce the average journey to work by 20 percent" or "to communicate a sense of privacy for each housing cluster of 20 to 30 units"). They may be phrased in comparative terms ("walking routes from houses to neighborhood shops should be more direct than driving routes"), implying how design trade-offs can be made. Specifications that anticipate conflicts and suggest how they are to be handled ("residents in the immediate vicinity of their dwellings should be unaware of passing motor vehicles, as long as police are able to overlook all public areas from their patrol cars") often are the most useful form of design guidance.

Every statement about environmental performance makes a host of assumptions about human behavior, how it is connected to settings, and how much human and environmental adapation will be tolerated. Consider, as an example, the following common performance objective: "all houses should be within a 10-minute walk of a bus stop." It assumes, among other things, that walking time is an important determinant of people's willingness to use transit (while waiting time, or the quality of service, or the pattern of destinations might be more critical); that time and distance requirements are uniform (for the elderly 10 minutes may be too far, while for youth it could be farther); that transit journeys will be home based and not linked with other activities (teenagers may use transit mainly to go to jobs after school, or working parents may drop children off at school before their journey to work); and that people desire to minimize their walking time (the exercise might be considered pleasurable or healthy). Each assumption is capable of being

Reference 76

114

tested, and it is through such studies that programmatic knowledge evolves. But since few performance standards have been scrutinized in detail, there is good reason to be skeptical about their basis.

The example also highlights the critical importance of selecting the right measure of environmental performance. Distance might have been substituted for time ("all houses to be within 600 m of a bus stop"), a translation that designers will need to make in any case. Though simpler, a single distance criterion might obscure critical human differences: elderly housing should be closer. A more complex measure might be aggregate walking time ("maximize the proportion of residents within an 8-minute walking radius of bus stops") which adds an incentive for locating higher densities in the vicinity of the stops.

Measures and values

Objectives should be significant and also discriminate between alternatives. "All houses must orient to the cardinal directions" may discriminate between plans but be a goal of little importance, while "all houses must be accessible on foot" may be important but not discriminating. Given that, the set of criteria should be complete: when a solution meets the stated criteria, all the major purposes should be fulfilled.

Direct quantitative goals and limits are easy to state: "to house 100 families," "to allow a flow of 2000 cars per hour," "not to cost more than $500,000." Objectives that deal with the quality of place are harder to establish. The level of generality is one difficulty. Shall it be "a comfortable environment," or "all south and west facades to be shaded by trees"? The first is too general to test; the second dictates the solution before the design process has begun. "To maintain summer indoor temperatures within the comfort range" might be a better statement since it is both testable and can be achieved by various means. It is generally preferable to express objectives in as concrete a form as possible, short of fixing a single solution. The best form is one that specifies the desired human behavior together with the neccessary supporting qualities: "a street that allows a pedestrian to cross with safety and without anxiety, with no more than an average delay of ten seconds." In doing so, qualities that are difficult to measure should not be neglected; sensuous form is an example. The program should describe the desired character of paths, the views to maintain, the mix of visible activity, or the legibility of the completed environment, even if judgments about success along those dimensions must be subjective. A robust program can set the terms for thinking about site experience and ensure that they are congruent with what is known about human values.

Management decisions may confound the performance of environmental features. Snow-covered footpaths lie unused in winter because public bodies do not have the budget to maintain them, even though the program required a direct connection between houses and schools. Setting the performance requirements can be a time to debate the linked assumptions about environment, behavior, and management, as well as an occasion for commissioning small scale studies that observe places in use.

Patterns

Covering all the important functions normally occurring in any place suggests an exhausting list of performance statements. The street and frontyard space in a residential area, for instance, is an access way for autos, trucks, emergency vehicles, and pedestrians; below grade it is a utility corridor; it provides for parking, serves as a play space, and occasionally is the scene of a block party; it lets neighbors watch for potential criminals, is a locale for socializing, and allows residents to symbolize who they are to passers-by. Sometimes, then, there is little gained by describing in detail how such a place should function: it is better to point to an environmental *pattern*, which resolves those many demands in a satisfying way.

Reference 1

Patterns serve as a direct bridge to design. Few site problems are totally without precedent, and so a useful program can identify workable examples. Patterns can range from solutions to single requirements ("locate parking areas 0.5 m below pedestrian walks," which is designed to reduce the obtrusiveness of autos) to complex prototypes that respond to many desires ("the Radburn housing cluster"). They may highlight aspects of the context of the site that deserve attention ("continue the six story street facade" or "cascade housing units down the steep hillsides") or focus on issues of grouping ("locate the new college buildings around a central open quadrangle"). Environmental patterns can be identified at scales from the immediate ("entrances to houses at least 0.5 m above the street") to the extended ("an orthogonal grid transportation network"). Every site design problem will demand a particular combination of patterns, some unique, others applicable elsewhere.

Patterns can be tested if they are accompanied by a note on the performance they are designed to address, the context in which they should be used, a diagram of the critical aspects of their form, and where they have been tried before. Where programming is done for a type of project likely to be repeated, or where several cycles of programming and then evaluation after occupation are possible, patterns may be compiled looseleaf. A number of existing pattern books serve as examples of form and content. Because they are concrete and imageable, patterns are an effective focus for discussion between users and specialists.

Reference 1

The four domains where program decisions must be made—population, package, performance, and patterns—are, of course, closely related. It does no good to assemble a catalogue of patterns that are inappropriate because they assume the wrong population or do not fit the constraints of resources and management. Choices made in one domain inevitably affect the others. There is no foolproof beginning point for programming, and often no easily recognized end. Several iterations will usually be needed to ensure internal consistency, and the program must be put to the test of trial before proved reliable.

How then to begin? The original assignment by the client will offer the first clues. He may be interested in repeating an earlier development that he thinks has been successful, perhaps a housing project he has built or visited. The first step might analyze that development, isolating its successful patterns, constructing a profile of its population and how they use the site, making an estimate of its development package, if not a search through its financial records. Transposed to the current site, this first cut may make poor fit. It may seem impossible to attract the same residents, so a modified poulation profile will be drawn up. The price paid for the current site may be higher, or its intrinsic character may be different, suggesting a different package. Each contingency calls into question the environmental patterns and performance of the original example. Since it is difficult to juggle all aspects simultaneously, one makes reasonable assumptions about as many aspects as possible and explores the remaining areas. Once there is a first draft for each aspect of the program, assumptions can be reconsidered and internal consistency established.

Preparing the program

For projects with no obvious precedents, programming might begin by listing objectives and then translating these into performance statements. If the project is complicated, special experts can help frame the problem from their several different perspectives. In planning a new town, bring together a diverse group of professionals with experience in community development to debate the possible aims and the ways in which performance might be judged. Emerging performance statements might lead directly to thoughts about patterns and could underpin the first crude sketches of the financial package. Programs can as easily begin from site impressions, the dreams and experience of users, or unbuilt utopian schemes. Each project will have its own process logic, its point of departure, its set of issues demanding attention.

Beyond the client

The type of project will also influence the set of actors to be involved. So far, we have portrayed programming as if it were the province of specialists and their immediate clients. But it may well be desirable to expand the circle to include those affected by development. Each group consulted has a legitimate, but partial, claim on program decisions. Site neighbors may have a direct interest in the effects on their business, their property values or rents, the extra traffic on their streets, the additional people who will use public facilities, the disruption of views, and so on. By identifying the matters neighbors will be most vigilant about early in the process, program decisions can help to mitigate oppo-

Reference 42

sition and prevent unnecessary damage. One technique is "front-end impact analysis" in which a draft of the environmental and social impact statement is begun simultaneously with the early program and elaborated as programming and design progress.

If possible, involve the eventual users of the site in the programming, or, if they are not present or identifiable, compose a group of surrogates for consultation. Direct involvement offers people the opportunity to explore and project their wishes about better places. It can result in fresh ideas about performance. Consultation is more fruitful if it begins early and continues throughout the design process. Discussions should focus on decisions that will in fact be open to influence by users. Since any site will have many types of users, who should be involved? Differences in motivation (routine users vs. visitors, owners vs. renters, employees vs. managers, etc.), in social class, stage of the life cycle, and race or ethnicity are often good predictors of variation in environmental preferences. They are logical categories for making up a consulting group which will reflect those diverse interests (see Chapter 3). Each person will hold idiosyncratic as well as representative views, and so it is important to involve enough people to allow some generalizations to be drawn. The designer can help lay participants to translate programs into terms they can comprehend, explain the consequences of alternatives, and give flesh to their proposals so that they will be considered seriously.

Before investing in acquiring an in-depth knowledge of the preferences of particular users, potential markets may be examined in other ways. When a site must compete in a metropolitan space economy, it is important to gauge whether the anticipated *market share* is realistic. For example, the anticipated housing demand at a site may be the result of metropolitan growth, or a desire among current residents to change their housing location, or a general shift in preferences among at least part of the population toward a form of housing that the site could provide, or some combination. A market analysis will identify the magnitude of trends, the competing opportunities, and the factors likely to be critical in making the site competitive. It will describe the market segments to be served and recommend the number of units which can be absorbed each year. Market analyses are commonly done at the beginning of programming and provide a barebones outline of population, package and performance objectives. They are not always necessary, of course. For many projects, the only test is to build and observe consumer acceptance. In other cases, the decision will hinge on the population the builder or institution wishes to serve rather than on financial gain.

If needed, the preparation of a financial *pro forma*—a forecast of the eventual financial balance sheet of the project—flows directly from the market study or program. For each year of the project, the forecast identifies the costs and revenues that may be expected, described by type and source. The net position of the client at the end of each year is summarized, along with the amount of temporary or permanent financing required and its cost. A variety of computations will then be made to determine financial viability: the period within which the initial investments will be repaid; the percentage return on invested capital; the possible effects of a market downturn, increased inflation or changing costs of financing; and ways in which the financial performance could be changed by altering assumptions. For projects not subject to market forces (public or institutional sponsors, typically) the pro forma will take other forms, typically focusing on the projected flow of expenditures and the funds to which these will be charged.

Many computer programs exist which simplify this financial analysis. Other aspects of the program may also be efficiently handled with computer assistance, including proj-

Market analysis

The pro forma

See Figure 38

CP and PERT

See Figure 39

($000)

YEAR OF DEVELOPMENT	1	2	3	4	5	6	7	8	9	10	11	12	13	TOTAL
Expenditures for Land and Improvements														
Land	2,199	3,596	5,140	1,338	1,338	2,214	2,355	2,348	-					20,528
Administration, Planning, Mgm't.	150	200	250	300	100	100	100	-						1,200
Streets and Storm Sewers (18,500 D.U. @ $700)	-	-	-	1,500	1,500	1,500	1,500	1,500	1,500	1,500	1,500	900		12,900
Water and Sanitary Sewer Systems (expandable)	-	-	-	2,000	2,000	2,000	2,000	-						8,000
Less: Misc. Rental Income -- Temporary Farm Rentals, etc.	(19)	(59)	(98)	(119)	(119)	(81)	(40)	(40)	(40)					(615)
TOTAL	2,330	3,737	5,292	5,019	4,819	5,733	5,915	3,808	1,460	1,500	1,500	900		42,013
Proceeds from Sale of Land and Utility Company														
Residential Lots	-	-	-	2,400	3,300	5,600	7,350	8,750	8,750	8,750	9,720	10,130		64,750
Industrial Acreage (325 acres)	-	-	-	-	500	1,000	1,000	1,000	1,000	500	500	500		6,000
Apartment Acreage (250 acres)	-	-	-	-	-	150	150	150	300	600	600	900	900	3,750
Commercial Acreage (50 acres)	-	-	-	-	-	-	327	436	436	436	545	-	-	2,180
Greenbelt Acreage (3,400 acres)	-	-	-	300	300	450	600	600	800	800	1,200	1,400		6,450
Utility Company (@cost)	-	-	-	-	-	-	-	8,000	-	-	-	-		8,000
TOTAL	-	-	-	2,700	4,250	7,527	9,536	19,086	11,586	11,195	12,320	12,930		91,130
Cash Flow from Income Properties														
Apartments ($300 per unit)					75	150	300	450	600	725	1,050	1,275	1,500	
Commercial ($.45 per sq.ft.)					30	60	94	128	138	248	289	330	371	
Industrial ($.10 per sq.ft.)					11	33	55	77	99	132	165	198	220	
TOTAL					116	243	449	655	887	1,105	1,504	1,803	2,091	
Annual Net Cash Position	(2,330)	(3,737)	(5,292)	(2,319)	(453)	2,037	4,070	15,933	11,013	10,800	12,324	13,833	2,091	
Interest on Net Capital Invested (6%)	(70)	(252)	(523)	(754)	(840)	(798)	(620)	(29)						
Cumulative Net Cash Position Unadjusted for Eq. Build-up	(2,400)	(6,389)	(12,204)	(15,277)	(16,570)	(15,331)	(11,881)	4,023	15,036	25,836	38,160	51,993	54,084	
Equity Build-up from Income Prop.					64	280	705	1,390	2,365	3,718	5,505	7,738	10,435	13,458
Cumulative Net Cash Position Adjusted for Equity Build-up	(2,400)	(6,389)	(12,204)	(15,213)	(16,290)	(14,626)	(10,491)	6,388	18,754	31,341	45,898	62,428	67,542	

FIGURE 38   *A financial pro forma for a large scale new community development. Note that revenues are not expected to repay initial investments until year 8.*

ect scheduling and the grouping of elements according to functional ties. *Critical path analysis* (CP) and the *project evaluation and review technique* (PERT) are two developed methods for modeling the tasks, costs, and time associated with complex construction projects. They identify possible bottlenecks—points where the failure to complete an element in time will delay the entire course of the project—and can help to make a timetable that prevents the project from being stalled by such an eventuality. Detailed scheduling models are constructed only toward the end of programming, but a sketch of the schedule may be useful during the early stages, since time can constrain the options to be considered. A district heating system may appear financially feasible when considered separately, but scheduling reveals that the long lead time required for its construction would delay the entire project and throw the economics out of balance.

Cluster analysis

Where many functions are to be related in complex ways on a site, there may be some advantage in performing a *cluster analysis* as part of the programming. The actual or desired strength of the links between different units is set

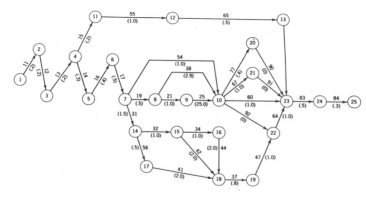

FIGURE 39 *The critical path diagram charts all the tasks (arrows) and milestones (circles) for the project. While many tasks can occur simultaneously, the length of the project is dependent on the time necessary to complete the critical sequence (from 1 to 10 to 23 to 25).*

down, then a scaleless diagram of those units is rearranged until the weighted length of the linkages is minimized, and finally the units of the diagram are redrawn as scaled areas. Such analyses can done by hand, but a variety of computer models will accomplish this efficiently, provided that the critical links between elements are known and can be expressed in comparable terms. Cluster modeling has been applied to the programming of hospitals, new university campuses, and industrial facilities. It can help decide which elements should be grouped together, and identify the constraints to this. The danger in using such analyses in a deterministic way is that they emphasize easily measurable linkages (such as walking distance or vehicular access) over others which are difficult to dimension (the symbolism of having two things located together or the possibility of future expansion) and so they bias performance.

On highly constrained sites, *envelope studies* will discover how the package will be affected by a variety of limiting circumstances. The amount of building that could occur within the zoning envelope is one obvious subject, but similar studies can be done of other performance requirements: how large a package could be created if all the housing units were assured a south exposure? if specific views across the site are maintained? if all offices have day lighting? if the perimeter is kept the same height as adjacent structures? if emergency vehicles are allowed to reach each structure? The

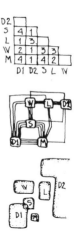

Envelope
studies

See Figure 40

121

FIGURE 40
Hugh Ferris' classic studies of the possible envelope of a skyscraper, if it is to fit within the legal rules for setbacks and bulk.

answers require a series of design studies, but they are not an attempt at final placement. Their object is to understand the consistency between package and performance and to ensure that the program can be realized on the site.

Design potential studies can be used to validate desirable patterns. If all the units for families with children are located at grade, with private entrances and outdoor space, what is the impact on site density? What social groupings may result? The analysis may demonstrate that the pattern is impossible to achieve or has unanticipated consequences. The line between design and programming becomes blurred, a reflection of how program and form are interlocked.

When a public agency or a developer conveys a site to others and cares about its patterns and performance, a *design prototype* incorporating them may be a more efficient and imageable communication device than a lengthy list of guidelines. When resources permit, it may be better to include both: clear and explicit specifications coupled with prototypes illustrating how they might be achieved.

Prototypes

Programming, as it has been described here, costs time and money. Its cost must be balanced against the risk of mistakes if it is not used. Elaborate programs are warranted where client control is indirect, where there are many actors in the design and construction process whose efforts need to be orchestrated, where the development is large and will occur over many years, where the developing agency can generalize over several projects, or must learn to improve its future performance. But even the simplest problems require a clear, if modest, program as a prelude to design. The program is not discarded when design begins. Moreover, it will be an important reference in the assessment of future results.

By federal, state or local law, the environmental impacts of most large projects must be formally reviewed. The material assembled during programming will be invaluable at this point. The threshold criteria for requiring such a review vary considerably, and there is even greater variance in the required subjects. The aim of these reviews is to enlarge the body of fact and opinion that decision makers have at their disposal when they approve plans. They expose predictions to scrutiny and invite competing opinion. They seldom require that the plan with the most desirable (or the least undesirable) impacts be chosen, but they assume that will happen if decision makers are confronted with the evidence.

Environmental impact analysis

References 12, 15

The effects of a project are summarized in an environmental impact statement (EIS). Frequently, such statements deal only with impacts beyond the site boundaries, but in large projects such as a new community, the most consequential impacts may be within the site. EISs are circulated to interested parties, and comments are invited. The responses of reviewers are then appended to the statement, which may be modified as a result of the comments received. Federal legislation allows litigation over the adequacy of coverage in an EIS, a step which can cause great delays. The understandable defense has been to paper over all conceivable subjects with as many words as possible. Each agency charged with reviewing an EIS has its own guidelines about form, contents, and the process of preparation, circulation and filing, which must be scrupulously observed since the resulting document will be held to tests of completeness and compliance. A typical table of contents will include the following:

Content of an
EIS

Description of the project—its aims, overall scope and size, and the aspects of the program critical to its success.

Description of the site—its location, present uses, legal boundaries and status, and its surroundings, along with a summary of the predesign site analysis.

Description of the alternatives considered—generally these will fall into several standard categories: the "no-action" alternative, the locational alternatives (construct the facilities elsewhere), the programmatic alternatives (different mixes of uses), the design alternatives (different layouts), the engineering alternatives (different standards and techniques), and the institutional alternatives (different arrangements of management, logistics, timing, ownership and tenure). A limited set of these myriads of alternatives is selected for detailed scrutiny (and in this "neutral" selection lies a substantial power to determine final decisions).

The impacts of alternatives—the impacts on the existing natural and cultural environment; the impacts on site and neighboring inhabitants and users. These are arranged in a comparative way, distinguishing between impacts that are adverse versus those beneficial; those that only occur in the short term, during construction and initial occupancy, as opposed to those that appear in the long run; and those that are reversible or irreversible.

The proposed plan—a detailed description of the proposal and the reasons for its choice.

Detailed impacts of the proposed plan—generally broken down by type of impact, explaining the basis for prediction as well as the results, summarizing the unavoidable negative impacts that remain.

Mitigating actions—steps that will be taken to minimize, contain, or counteract the negative impacts identified.

Official and private reaction—the comments resulting from circulating the draft EIS to agencies and groups with an interest in the project.

Environmental impact statements which deal exhaustively with these subjects can run to hundreds of pages, burying important findings in a tangle of detail. Sometimes this is deliberate but more often just a case of compliance without commitment. Whichever the reason, they discourage informed discussion. A number of checklists exist which remind analysts of the variety of environmental dimensions which may be described and analyzed in an EIS. Appendix G contains one such list. The best analysis will select only the small number of factors likely to have critical consequences for residents and neighbors, and will devote the bulk of their attention to them. Other less critical issues are dealt with in a cursory way. Sometimes it is useful to organize the analysis by the stage of decision (choice of site, grant or loan for acquisition, density, form, standards of infrastructure, layout, construction techniques, etc.). Serious attention or opposition can be focused on the stages most in need of change rather than seeming to cast a shadow on the entire project.

Programs, budgets, and impact analyses are all predictions. Programs talk of desired outcomes, and budgets set out the resources to be expended, while impact analyses consider the costs and benefits that will fall on others. Simple projects will not need an elaborate program, a pro forma, or an EIS. Simple or complex, however, all projects involve predictions. Those predictions should be stated early, be sharpened as the design develops, and be tested by occupation.

Reference 30

125

Chapter 5

Design

Design is the search for forms that satisfy a program. It deals with particular solutions, while the program is concerned with general characteristics and desired outcomes. Design begins in the programming, and programs are modified as design progresses.

By common account, design is a mystery, a flash of revelation. The genius who receives this flash learns to receive it by following the example of other people of genius. After the revelation, there are details to be developed and the labor of carrying out the revealed solution. This afterwork is separate from design, however, whether one thinks of it as a grubby nuisance or as facing up to realistic issues.

This common account is correct on one point: there *is* a mystery in design, as there is in all human thought. Otherwise, the account is mistaken. Design is not restricted to genius, or separate from practicality, or a sudden revelation. Fine places develop out of an intimate understanding of form possibility, which has been gained by constantly reframing the problem, by repeatedly searching for solutions. Revelations go by the inch and the foot, rarely by the mile. Particular methods, learned by experience, help the designer to make this journey of discovery.

A site design deals with three elements: the pattern of activity, the pattern of circulation, and the pattern of sensible form that supports them. The first, symbolized in the activity diagram, is the arrangement of the behavior settings, their character, linkage, density and grain, following the requirements of the program. The second is the layout of the movement channels and their relations to the activity locations. The third, to be considered in the next chapter, centers on the human experience of place: what we see, hear, smell, and feel, and what that means to us. The designer is concerned with what it is like to act in a place, to move through it, and to experience it. These are the subject matter of her first sketches, and remain dominant themes throughout the work. Each element implies the other, and so she faces a multitude of interlocking possibilities. She must make a set of simultaneous decisions which seem at first too numerous to grasp, which all depend on each other, like linked dancers in a ring.

Metaphors

Design is a process of envisioning and weighing possibilities, mindful of past experience. "What if I thought of the site this way?" the designer asks, bringing to mind one of a number of possible solutions. A wooded slope is seen as a "cascade," with houses "spilling" down it. Solutions frequently begin with metaphors, and the logic of the metaphor guides its elaboration. The practicalities of servicing, cost, or foundation stability then come to mind as tests of the idea. Each initial solution will fail to achieve the outcome sought. Failure points to another way of thinking about the

Reference 78

problem. The problem is reframed, and a new cycle of invention and testing follows. Thus design is a dialectic of framing and making. Leaping from metaphor to metaphor, attending to this aspect and then to that, neither dismayed by dissonance nor seduced too early by some momentary consonance, the mind begins to understand the significance of decisions in all their important dimensions. The designer imagines total systems—precise at the critical points, loose and unresolved where decisions have less significance.

To do this, designers need to construct a "virtual world," a model of what they know about site and program, which allows possibilities to be tested quickly. Diagrams and physical models are of service, but these virtual worlds are mental pictures. A site seems "fragmented," which shapes what one sees and calls to mind the virtues of unifying devices. Through past experience, designers accumulate a repertoire of analogous situations. Before each new situation, one asks what others it is like and most unlike. Likeness and unlikeness are understandings that help to imagine and test possible solutions. This virtual world will almost always extend beyond the original site boundaries, since a site de-

128

pends on its context. The designer is suspicious of limits and yet cannot deal with the universe. Therefore he decides: where shall my focus be? what shall be its context? how shall they connect? This is often a larger universe than the one first given, and thus some tension arises. The design need not harmonize with its context, should that be undesirable or ephemeral, but it must take it into account.

Designers develop a preference for a particular way of structuring their process of design and hold strong attitudes about appropriate procedure. Some prefer to make decisions along the way, moving deliberately from one step to the next, while others engage in a free-flowing inquiry in which nothing is frozen until all aspects seem right. These personal styles help shield them from the anxieties of the open search. But since the design process should fit the problem as well as the designer, a personal style is also a limitation of possibilities, a latent distortion of the problem. Ideally, designers should be eclectics. Where this is not psychologically possible, they should at least be aware of other ways of doing business and have a sense of the type of problem to which their own manner of working is best fitted. All design methods are laden with values; none are objective. Each emphasizes some environmental qualities over others and favors particular ways of judging. Bear this in mind as we outline the commonly used design methods.

Design methods

The great majority of environmental designs are adaptations of solutions previously used. Forms that are a model to be emulated become prototypes. Those that are used very often are stereotypes: the cul-de-sac, the backyard, the tree-lined avenue, the axial vista, the playground, the sidewalk cafe, to name a random few. Our heads are full of such customary forms, and we know something about the situations for which they are appropriate. People who do not call themselves designers use them repeatedly, making minor adaptations to fit to any current situation. Avowed designers review the literature for previous solutions, follow the fashions of the day, and use common stereotypes without being conscious of them.

Adaptation

Creating a new form, complete with detail, purpose, method of production, and its fit with behavior, is an exhaustive undertaking. Repeated trials are necessary to test its usefulness and fine tune its details. Since it is impossible to innovate most of the features of a place, we must fall back on previous achievements. The finest site planning of the past was a culmination of a long process of this kind.

Each designer copied a past solution while making a few adjustments to improve the functioning. Late products are miracles of well-fitted form. Where appropriate stereotypes are widely diffused, magnificent regional landscapes can develop, created by many minds, yet harmonious and visibly meshed into a way of life.

As a complete design process, incremental adaptation is useful where external changes are slow relative to the pace of environmental decision—when objectives, behaviors, technology, institutions, and settings are all relatively stable. But even in a more dynamic situation, we adapt previous forms. In ordinary work, they appear everywhere, and fateful decisions are made thereby. Bitter arguments will arise over the alignment of an expressway, but no one stops to wonder about the circumferential prototype on which any exact alignment is based. The plan for a new town in Ghana looks strangely like one in Texas. Stereotypes cannot be avoided; the danger lies in using them unthinkingly. The available stereotype must have some reasonable relation to the problem, and it must be possible to reach a good solution by a chain of small modifications. Recent fashions or forms developed in different circumstances may be radically inappropriate.

A few years ago, designers would have been embarrassed to admit to their reliance on stereotypes. Now it is fashionable to design places that "recall" or "remember" or "speak in the manner of" some past example. Where such past forms are widely known and experienced, these associations have symbolic functions (but keep in mind that *people*, and not things, recall or remember). Judging the appropriateness of some previous solution requires knowledge of its performance and proper context and an accurate estimate of the current problem. Information about performance and context is not to be had in most published examples of design. The designer is forced to guess at how the form suited its users.

A better series of prototypes appears in a *A Pattern Language*, by Christopher Alexander and his colleagues, which may be taken as a model sourcebook of forms for site design. From many cases, they extract environmental configurations (or "patterns") that seem well matched to particular human needs. Each pattern is described in terms of its appropriate context and the problem it will solve. While marred by the assumption that most of these patterns have some eternal or universal validity, the book demonstrates that the creation and evaluation of prototypes is a task of influence and value, worthy of substantial public investment.

Adaptation is the preferred method of designers who believe in the virtues of familiarity, and that truly great environments are the product of accumulated understanding. It can be an especially powerful method when carried out in the field, that is, when modifications can be made to an environment in use, the results observed, and another round of adjustments then be carried out. A close fit between form and purpose is achieved. But except where there is a decentralized management of small settings, the cost and scale of normal site operations makes this difficult to do. Working directly with the real product rather than with its simulation is the privilege of painters and potters and small builders. Site planners usually wrestle with more unwieldy institutions.

When faced with complexity, one reasonable response is to break the problem into parts. By solving each part separately and then combining the results, we reach a solution to the whole which responds to all its aspects. A traditional method of subdivision is to divide the site into distinct areas, each small enough to be fashioned without unreasonable effort. Preferably, these will be elements that can be repeated elsewhere in the plan, and if so we call them *modules*. While being small enough for easy study, the module must be large enough to coincide with some important issues of the plan: spatial form, for example, or social grouping. In a large housing development, a module of one or two houses might miss the most important issues of interrelation, while a module of 500 houses would be inconvenient and too large to be repeated. In low density housing, twenty to thirty dwelling units often proves to be a convenient module, since a plausible spatial unit can be created at that scale, and those social relations that are founded on proximity seem, in our culture, to clump at that approximate size. In other words, a module must have enough self-sufficiency so that a substantial number of internal relations can be determined, independently of the effect of outside patterns.

Modular design is convenient if such a division of the program is possible. But it should not be elevated from a design convenience to a design principle. Some sites are best planned by modules because they have semi-independent, repetitive functions. Others do not. Moreover, even if spatial divisions are used as building blocks of the design, those

Modular division

divisions need not be modular. Units may differ in size or function, or occupy unique terrain compartments, or contain distinct populations. One can focus design on the treatment of the banks of a stream, then on the cross-section of an arcaded street, and then on the form of the central meeting place.

Division by aspect

A second method of disaggregation is to consider the design by separate aspects, each of which involves the entire site. One likely division is to consider the three basic elements of site design as if they were separable.Thus one can think first of the activity settings, taking into account their various characters, densities, grain of mix, and desirable linkages. One designs them "from the inside," to become familiar with the general form and requirements of each, then places them according to their detailed requirements and the accidents of the site. The designer meditates over each piece of ground and tests the result to see that all functions are adequately housed and that each advantage of site has been utilized. Or she can make a "cluster analysis," which groups them by their most important linkages, and then apply this diagram to the ground. The designer can also begin with some formal pattern. Indeed, a general form is too often unconsciously assumed. Pattern habits are difficult to break, and the planner must willfully develop his ability to imagine formal alternatives. A set of archetypes, and a sense of their nature, is part of his stock-in-trade: the ring, the peak, the star, the hierarchy, the axis, the line, the constellation, the network, the checkerboard, the hollow square, the layering. Each has its own implications—some intrinsic, some appearing only at particular scales or in particular situations.

Putting activity layout aside, the designer next tries various road arrangements, testing general patterns—grid, linear, or concentric schemes—and playing with her repertoire of circulation devices—culs-de-sac, superblocks, loops, serpentines. She looks for circulation determinants in the site: passes, ridge and valley systems, broken or gentle ground. These trials produce a sketch circulation system that is a coherent structure and seems to fit the site and the general density and type of use proposed. Last (but there is no last or first), she works with the sensible form of the place: accentuating topography, trying out spatial prototypes (of which we have such great store), playing with images of massing or character or view. Once again, this results in some general concepts of site organization.

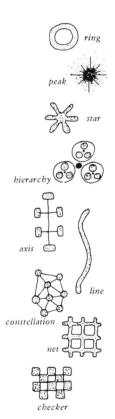

ring

peak

star

hierarchy

axis

line

constellation

net

checker

At first, these three patterns will be in conflict. By trial, they are reshaped until a coherent organization has the virtues of each: that provides well-fitted behavior settings, good access, and a compelling visual form, and in which all three aspects map onto each other. This may be a protracted process, since no law of nature states that general forms are inherent in particular situations (although some situations have their hints, due to an organized drainage system, a clear social structure, or whatever). Human ingenuity creates coherent form, or the form is borrowed from some previous exercise of human ingenuity. All too often, to avoid this painful reshaping, a designer will force a form onto the site, producing a plan that is powerful on paper and makes us grit our teeth when we experience it in reality.

Activity, access, and sensed form are not the only seams along which a problem can be disjointed. It is also common to separate it by professional tasks: the architecture, the landscaping, the engineering. This is the riskiest division since integration is then likely to be late and superficial. The misfit of building and site is a persistent example of the failed interplay of part and whole. Corridors are extensions of the sidewalk; the view from the window is significant; building shapes are landscape forms. The relation of floor levels to ground level is of special importance. Architectural and site design should be done together, whether by a single individual or by a cooperating team. The separation of site and building design raises special problems, which are treated in Chapter 11.

Thinking about separate criteria is still another way of dividing the problem along nonspatial lines. The designer begins by making plans that optimize some particular purpose—access, control, fit, sense, cost, maintenance, or narrower subdivisions of those—while satisfying other criteria only in some customary or minimum way. She works out the plan that would be safest for children (making endless difficulties for access) or the cheapest plan, without thought for its dreariness. These caricatures, like a crossfire of sidelights, cast the whole into clearer relief. Correspondences are sought out and reinforced, conflicts avoided or compromised, to reach a solution that responds to the entire set of criteria. Since these single-criteria solutions are not independent of each other, the designer must face up early to the conflicts inherent in the conflicting purposes of the plan.

Attempts have been made to carry this method further. Criteria are finely divided into concrete, operational state-

Optimizing

133

ments and solutions for each pair of criteria worked out, starting with those pairs that imply the most important conflicts, and reaching in the end a comprehensive solution that reflects the whole chain of compromises. Multiplicity is explicitly dealt with. Unfortunately, not only is this exhaustive, stepwise resolution impractical in practice, but there are criteria for the whole, as well as for its parts. Moreover, one can only judge the probable misfits between two criteria by having in mind their possible solutions. How else does one judge that "no views into private yards from the adjacent houses" will collide with "private yards to have a southern exposure"? Problems do not have an intrinsic structure; they have a structure by reference to solutions that human beings can imagine, which is all the more reason to break problems up in ways congenial to our human understandings.

Essential function

Other designers optimize in a more general way. First, they abstract the "essential" function of an environment, then develop a form that will best satisfy this general function, and finally adapt this ideal form to satisfy the other functions and constraints. One criterion leads the way to solution. For example, if an area is to be an outdoor market, it is decided that buying is the essential behavior and thus that, above all, the environment must make that act inviting. The designer considers the character of settings that invite a buyer, imagines an ideal form with that character, and then tinkers with it in order to manage the delivery and protection of goods, the arrival of customers, the cost, the maintenance, and the topography of the site. He succeeds when he does so without compromising his ideal too seriously.

This is analogous to linear programming: the optimization of a single function, subject to constraints. It is a powerful way of dealing with complexity but has limitations. It must be possible to discover a truly dominant function, whose satisfaction is far more important than any other factor. If the function to be optimized is chosen because it is more easily measured or is more dramatic, then a many-sided problem is falsified. The dominant function of a university is pronounced to be "learning," and that named function is conceived as a standard process in a standard setting. All the rich complexity of a real university is lost. Even if the dominance is real, the ideal solution may be so compromised in the subsequent process of adaptation as to lose most of its force. The correct balance between dominant and secondary functions is hard to maintain.

The search for the essential function is the working method of designers who believe that places should have an all-encompassing, immediately grasped image, and are prepared to acquire that image at the expense of other ends. It can lead to dramatic confrontations between designers, clients, and other actors. High drama is sometimes wanted, a flexible attitude more often. However, in contrast to the stepwise pairing of detailed requirements, this "seizure of the essential" is very congenial to our human way of thinking, and so it is very impressive to the client. If the designer is cautious of its seductive power, and willing to drop it when the problem screams, it can be a way to begin.

Rather than proceeding from an ideal that is then adapted to circumstance, the designer may go the other way and look for clues in circumstance itself. In site planning, it is common to begin by analyzing the possibilities and difficulties of the terrain, as analyzed in Chapter 2. One looks for a structure latent in the land: a valley system, a major division, a key pass, a focal point. One considers the ground piece by piece: place tall buildings where there is a fine distant view, and the hangout in its traditional location. Dramatize the decorative form of this old building; put row houses on this sunny slope and a park on this picturesque terrain. In this mode, it is easiest to work on a demanding site, dense with old scars and special difficulties. But the technique is not limited to the consideration of site, although it is more familiar there. The planner can also engage the form consequences of other aspects of the problem: the difficulties that led to the demand for a new setting, the structure of political power surrounding decision process, the presence of bored and resentful adolescents, or the need to rely on hand labor and local materials.

Suggestions for a solution seem to rise directly out of the situation—its difficulties, conflicts, and potentialities. Most people are better at recognizing problems than they are at imagining ideal solutions. The mental readiness to convert a bewildering difficulty into a peculiar asset is a useful set of mind. But designs do not actually rise out of problems. Something is seen as a problem because we have in mind a way of dealing with it. The designer constructs the "real" situation; it is not sitting out there, fully formed. The designer recognizes conditions for which she remembers a solution. She sees the problem she knows how to solve.

A problem focus is less risky than utopian dreaming, easier to justify, and more likely to produce a feasible so-

Problem
solving

135

lution. But it will neglect the unrecognized issue and what might be achieved by radical innovation. Since it sets its sights at solving immediate difficulties, it may undershoot. Perhaps the terrain might be exploited in unheard-of ways, or a *new* terrain might be manufactured. Analyzing the problem is always an essential step, and sometimes one begins a design by working with its structure, if one can be found. Only rarely should one confine one's work to that mode. In any case, since the recognition of a problem is a recognition of a solution, the problem first recognized is not always the right one.

Exploring means

There is still another path to take. The designer starts to play with available means—formal, technical, or institutional—to see what might come of them. Thus he may manipulate lines, circles, or checkerboards on the site, watching for something interesting. Natural forms are a rich storehouse of possibility, and so are chance happenings in the artificial environment. The designer will imagine what a new piece of machinery could do, or a special structural technique, or a new law or administrative program. These are means in search of ends. Surely this is immoral, one may say, the epitome of the worst in our society, the triumph of senseless technique! But since design is a linking of ends and means, it is just as useful to begin from one end as from another, as long as a connection is finally made.

The open-minded investigation of the possible use of things is a well-beaten path to innovation. Artists do surprising things in this mode, and so do technicians, although the latter sometimes forget to reconnect, that is, to consider what their new devices are for. Along this path, one may stray far from the original problem. Perhaps the mode is best suited to a long-term, free search, or to such open problems as the best use of a given piece of land. But even in the normal case, it can be valuable as a preliminary warm-up.

Drawing out consequences

An interesting variant of focusing on means is to simulate the future consequences of immediate actions, since they are the actions most likely to be carried out. "If I should put a road here, to begin with, what is likely to happen in ten years, and what do I think of it?" If I think well of it, the resulting plan has its means of implementation built in. This focus on first moves suggests still another way of framing a site design problem, which so frequently deals with a long sequence of development, full of uncertainties. We may ask: "What is the least that I can do to achieve my immediate aims?" This leaves subsequent decisions to those who will be on the scene at the time. Initial actions are minimal but are shaped to begin well and to leave the future open. In addition, these initial actions may be designed as experiments which explore possibilities: a novel house type, a new bicycle path, a gathering place to see what happens there, a seafood festival to learn who might be attracted to an undeveloped waterfront. Success and failure will be combed for clues about what to do next. Since these are trials affecting real users, they will be more conservative than paper simulations. Both users and developer must be protected against the risk: by prior explanation, by free choice, by making the experiment relatively independent of other actions. But as the new means embodied in such experiments work themselves out, they help us to clarify the problem and even to decide on our ends.

Designers use a particular strategy of attack. Consciously or unconsciously, they choose the mode in which to begin their design, what aspect will be key to the solution, and how it will be brought together in the end. It is a schizoid business. At times, the designer is relaxed and uncritical, allowing her subconscious mind to suggest forms and connections, most of them fantastic and unworkable. At other times, she turns sharply on those suggestions, probing and testing them. So she swings from doodling to stern and critical review, and part of her skill lies in managing those two states of mind. Her critical powers must not inhibit her creativity, while her irrational processes must not keep her from criticism. Design fails when one of those mental states overbears the other.

Reason and unreason

In almost every design process there comes a time when the designer feels blocked. All the solutions that he has tried fall short of what he is seeking; he is unable to reframe the problem in any useful way; new ideas are subconsciously shut out. As children, we are taught to suppress "irrational" ideas. In design we unlearn that lesson in order to break out of a block. Shifting the context may be used to confuse the built-in censor. Imagine the worst possible setting (which is devilishly easy) and let this suggest the reverse. Make a jump in time or scale, designing the site in the palm of the hand or as if its actions were to take centuries. How might the site be designed under socialism, or at the equator, or upside down? Or the designer projects himself into the physical thing itself, imagining that he is a playground, and wondering how he might help the children to play on him.

Overcoming blocks

At times, surprising ideas emerge from the juxtaposition of phenomena that suddenly appear to have some mysterious connection. A team may be confronted with a large number of randomly chosen, vivid visual images and asked to point out "unthinkingly" those pictures which feel as if they had some connection to the problem. In the attempt to describe that hidden connection, the team members bring to light new associations. These are children's games, and designers must be childish. Most suggestions are unworkable, but they provide new raw material. Experienced designers have just that ability for childlike observation and suggestion, free from obvious or proper association.

Design process

Great numbers of possibilities are produced. The designer carries on a dialogue with the form—almost personifying it as if it were some growing thing that responds to her suggestions and yet has a will of its own. Discoveries are made; the mind is full of images and analogies. "We could circle this bright, active place with a deep, cool arcade, damp like a wine cellar. But then it wants to trench into the ground. So perhaps it could dig right through this hill and pop out high on the other side?" The dialogue is internal, supported by silent words, quick sketches, and felt images.

See Figure 41

When a suggestion appears promising, it is developed in a diagrammatic sketch—loose, free, but complete, engaging all the major aspects.

These alternatives are not worked over by successive modification and erasure. They are set aside or redrawn as whole systems. Otherwise, valuable possibilities might be buried under layers of subsequent change. The trained designer knows where her sketch can be vague and where precise, that is, where she can reserve judgment and where she must be explicit. Some alternatives will be rejected, others retained. New ones are suggested in the process. As they flower, criteria will be rethought, the site reanalyzed, the program modified. The designer redraws the feasible alternatives, modifying them to meet the various objections that have occurred. He knows when to abandon a scheme that has been so overlaid with compromise as to lose its original force. He is alert for a hint of some new arrangement appearing momentarily in this troubled shifting of forms. In time, a basic scheme emerges as the choices narrow down and as the designer begins to grasp the whole simultaneously, in all its major dimensions.

The process is kept open and fluid until a broad range of possibilities has been created and judged. If design were a logical process that went from initial assumptions, by explicit steps, to a correct solution, it would take far less time and effort. But design is an irrational search, conducted over a ground prepared by experience, the study of principles, and the analysis of site and purpose. Systematic, rational criticism is brought to bear on the product of this search, although partial judgments have been made throughout the process, as one sniffs down false trails and then moves on. Each plan is preceded by drifts of discarded ideas; every designer is haunted by the fear that she has left some form unturned. And when a final scheme has been identified, it is wise to allow some time to elapse before confirming the choice. The designer cannot avoid an emotional attachment to these ideas that arose in the heat of creation. To a cooler eye, they may appear surprisingly flawed. In time, one learns to admit to such mistakes without taking it as a reflection on one's person.

The design has been carried forward in plan and section, with diagrams of behavior settings, sensuous quality, and circulation. Perspective or isometric sketches help to convey the sensible form. Rough models show the context and the relation to ground, since the design deals with three dimensions. Models are crudely made, for reasons of speed and easy modification. But models are insufficient because they are imprecise, they falsify detail, and they show static form rather than activity. Elaborate presentation models, moreover, are not only expensive and time-consuming but dangerously seductive.

The design process results in the developed schematic site plan. The succeeding chapters will discuss in more detail the elements which comprise that schematic plan. In the case of a large-scale, complicated problem about which fundamental decisions remain to be made, designing may produce two or three schematic plans. They show proposed building locations and form, the surface circulation, the expected outdoor activities, the shape and treatment of the ground, the principal landscaping, and any other features that will convey the use and quality of the outdoor space. The schematic plan may show an "ultimate" development, or it may indicate development stages, each stage being viable in itself and capable of enduring for some time. Schematics are accompanied by a revised program and budget. Plan, program, and budget are now formally reviewed with the client. Once accepted, the schematic plan will be elab-

Alternatives

See Figure 42

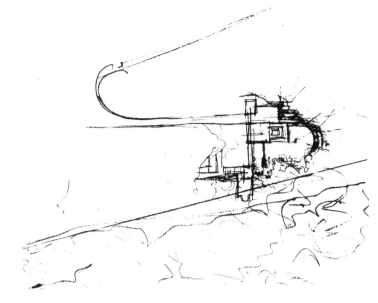

FIGURE 41
Frank Lloyd Wright's first diagrams of the organization of the Coonley House. Inside and outside, building and site are dealt with as one.

FIGURE 42
An early study by John R. Myer for Government Center, Boston. Building mass, open spaces, grades, circulation, paving and landscape charcter are being developed together in the context of the existing city.

orated into that set of technical drawings and documents which control the construction process, as described in Chapter 8.

In more complex problems, where there are several clients with diverse interests, and where conflicting choices must be weighed, then those clients will frequently require the generation and full development of a number of reasonable and desirable solutions, "well spaced" along the dimensions of the major variables. Because of our limited ability to generate and choose, only three or four alternatives will usually be made up. The clients then select the preferred alternative. But planners may try to manipulate their clients, giving them an illusory choice between one favored design and two or three unworkable dummy solutions. Even if honestly used, it is difficult to choose a solution without seeing all its implications, yet it is time-consuming to develop all the alternatives in such detail. Thus choices may be based on hunches about detailed workability.

By a different strategy, the designer develops one reasonable possibility at a time, beginning with the most likely one. Each possibility is developed far enough that it can safely be accepted or rejected. If rejected, the process recycles to seek a new solution, carrying with it the lessons previously learned. Each choice is informed by its detailed consequences. This process is economical if a good first try has been made and wasteful if not. Effective practice makes a compromise between these two approaches. First, a broad search is made to expose some well-spaced basic alternatives. One is tentatively chosen for full development and evaluation, with the option of falling back on another solution in case of failure. The more important choices may not lie among the general alternatives but be made continuously in the course of design, as modifications occur. The client may play a role in this string of choices, but if complex will tend to be limited to a veto power at the end of the process. Then the first system that produces an array of developed possibilities for client consideration at some formal stage can be preferable. But the alternatives must be honest and sufficiently developed to allow a real choice. Full alternatives are expensive in time and effort, and not responsive to the actual fluidity of decision and events. Fateful choices may be made on superficial grounds. It may be a formal necessity, or be used to give the client a stake in the outcome. It can be worth the cost when it is necessary to make decisions about large systems whose features are not expected to change rapidly.

But, where possible, the client is introduced regularly into the ongoing stream of design.

Competitions

Planning competitions are another way of surfacing possibilities. They can take many forms. The most familiar focuses exclusively on design: site documents and a detailed program are distributed to all entrants, along with firm requirements for how ideas are to be presented. The submissions are judged by a jury of distinguished professionals, the winners are announced, and the client is then free to engage the winner or anyone else. Because of the cost of preparing a proposal detailed enough to be workable, and because of the hazard of selecting a plan that may later prove unworkable, two-stage competitions have become more common. From the initial, less detailed entries, a small number of promising approaches are singled out, and their authors are paid to develop them into detailed plans. Or an invited competition may be held, in which only a handful of organizations are invited to prepare proposals, for which they will be paid a limited fee. Still another way to minimize the risk of sponsors is to hold "design-development" competitions. In this case, plans are accompanied by a firm proposal to build the project according to specific financial arrangements. But all of these schemes suffer from the necessary arms-length relationship between planners and clients. These barriers can be broken by a "charette" competition, in which competing groups work side by side at the site for a brief intense period, each having an equal chance to talk with clients and others who will be affected by their decisions.

Design teams

So far, we have spoken of design as if it were done by lone individuals. In reality, most projects involve several professionals working collaboratively who bring quite different preoccupations and skills to the task. Such teams are not simply a practical necessity; they add dimensions to the act. Where an individual may find himself in a blind alley, unable to reframe the problem, a group of designers working in parallel will ensure that there are other live options. Alternatives keyed to different value orientations are more easily done by separate individuals.

Usually, however, it is not possible for a single organization to include all the professional disciplines necessary for any project. Sometimes it is not even desirable since the opportunities for professional growth may not be present within a limited range of projects. Collaboration then involves coordinating the work of staff and consultants so that the right cast is available at each stage of a site planning

142

process. It is best, nevertheless, if all the critical elements of the site—land form, activities, and structures together—are designed by one closely knit team.

If people with diverse skills are to collaborate in producing a plan, it is essential that they begin with a common understanding of the problem. A group reconnaissance of the site, and common attendance at initial client meetings, will be a good investment. A communication system, which records the decisions reached, circulates minutes of key meetings, and ensures that maps and data are available to all, will keep everyone abreast of the project. At key points, it may be useful to assemble the entire team for an intensive working session when the main alternatives are devised and are narrowed to those that will be given detailed attention, or when the wrinkles must be ironed out of the final plan. The discussion will need to be structured to encourage the flow of ideas. Brainstorming and synectics are group dynamics methods in which members agree to suspend criticism and self-censorship in the interest of triggering new possibilities. Specialists are encouraged to invade each other's territories. Analogies and examples build a shared understanding. It is important that a strong consensus be formed around the preferred plan; later it can easily be undermined by team members who have accepted it grudgingly. Expert status alone is not permitted to decide a question: professional judgments must be opened up to scrutiny.

If the project is large, such as in planning a new town, and the organization is engaged in many projects, each with its own time scale, there may be virtue in a "matrix" organization, where the vertical lines represent disciplinary groups (engineering, planning, construction, financing, marketing, etc.), and the horizontal bands are project teams that draw together an ad hoc staff. Project managers tap the members of any disciplinary team, as required. Each professional is accountable both to a project manager and to the manager of his disciplinary group. If a project has several stages, it may be desirable to separate the short, and long-term responsibilities so that some members of the team are thinking ahead three, five, or ten years, while others are caught up in next year's issues. Matrix organizations are redundant, but they are superior—in flexibility, continuity and accountability—to organizations that separate design from engineering and production or have a more hierarchical divisional grouping.

A Diversity of Landscapes

Remarkable landscapes have been created in many diverse circumstances:

FIGURE 43
The grounds of Sanzen-in, a Buddhist temple near Kyoto: the mature Japanese garden, springing from its Chinese sources, is a miracle of refinement and meaning.

FIGURE 44
A court in the Generalife, Granada: the Moorish water gardens of Spain stand at the end of a long tradition of Islamic and Near Eastern pleasure grounds, which represented paradise in the midst of an arid climate.

146

FIGURE 45
*A cascade in the
garden of the
Villa Lante, Bag-
naia: the gardens
of the Italian
Renaissance
renewed the
landscape art in
Europe.*

FIGURE 46
Versailles: the
formal European
garden, expressing
man's domination
of space, reached
its apogee in
France.

FIGURE 47
The romantic, apparently "natural" park landscape is the work of English genius, under Eastern influences. This is Ashburnham, by Capability Brown.

FIGURE 48
Jens Jensen, a Danish immigrant, adapted the English landscape style to the plants and the climate of our prairie states. His parks and suburban gardens are calm, informal, apparently quite simple, and integral to their physical and social context. This is the yard of the Dell Plain Place in Hammond, Indiana.

FIGURE 49
Gunnar Asplund's
Woodland Crema-
torium in Stock-
holm: a spacious
modern use of
land and religious
symbolism.

FIGURE 50
As Jensen worked
with the American
prairie, so Burle
Marx creates spec-
tacular landscapes
with the tropical
plants of Brazil.

FIGURE 51
Luis Barragan's El Pedregal sub-division in Mexico City, laid in a great expanse of ancient lava. Steps, paths, roads, pools, and showpiece gardens settle among the fantastic rocks and strange plants, creating a harsh and beautiful landscape. House forms and walls were controlled to respect these unusual formations, but the controls were later lost under the financial pressures of success.

Chapter **6**

The Sensed Landscape and Its Materials

The sensed quality of a place is an interaction between its form and its perceiver. It is irrelevant in a sewer layout or in an automated warehouse. But wherever people are, it is a crucial quality. Sensuous requirements may coincide or conflict with other demands but cannot be separated from them in judging a place. They are not "impractical," or merely decorative, or even nobler than other concerns. Sensing is being alive. Perception includes the esthetic experience, where the dialogue between perceiver and object is immediate, intense, and profound, seemingly detached from other consequences. But it is also an indispensable component of every-day life.

Reference 56

The designer shapes his form so that it will be a willing partner in that sensed interaction, helping the perceiver to create a coherent, meaningful, and moving image. What we look for is a *landscape*, technically organized so that its parts work together, but perceptually coherent as well, one whose visual image is congruent with its life and action. In nature, an integrated landscape is shaped by the consistent impact of well-balanced forces. In art, it is the result of comprehensive purpose skillfully applied.

References 32, 44, 81

The designer works to enhance the expression of place: to communicate its nature as a system of living things residing in a particular habitat. To this end, he will open up a wood-

153

land, put a meeting house on the dominant point, accentuate the topography, or create an oasis in an arid climate. Using his knowledge of perception, he sharpens the rooted, indigenous character by means of simplification and contrast. Some of this knowledge is newborn, but much of it is old craft knowledge.

Historic styles

There have been many historic styles of site design, meaning by style a characteristic way of arranging space, activity, and material that is linked to an idea of how a place is to be used and what it should express. Historic styles provide an enormous storehouse of form possibilities, through which it is legitimate and useful to rummage in search of hints for solving a design problem. It is less legitimate to copy past solutions wholesale, unless they are part of a living tradition and still fitted to the present problem, or unless we mean to make a historic peepshow, divorced from any association with use. We have, or should be developing, our own apropriate style, out of our own time and place. It will grow out of the past but cannot replay it. The great axes of the formal French garden depended on the power to control the form of an extensive area and the will to display that power. The sophisticated Japanese garden depends on meticulous maintenance and an intricate set of cultural associations. The lively Italian piazza depends on a way of community life. The traveled designer has enjoyed these places, and their qualities are part of his memory. But he is creating new prototypes, fitted to existing or emerging landscapes: the rehabilitated and "densified" suburb, the "new town in town," housing for new forms of family living, the city freeway, the cluster of low-rise, high-density houses, the mixed agricultural-recreational rural zone, the crowded coast line, the office and factory workplace, the educative

Reference 31

adventure landscape, or soon even new settlements on polar ice or in outer space. So he is interested in new vernacular forms (mobile home tracts, squatter settlements, hand-made houses and their settings, allotment gardens), and, since artists are so often the barometer of coming storms, in the current projects of "environmental art," which put man-made traces on the ground, often at enormous scales, in order to sharpen our sense of our habitat.

Space perception

The sensuous experience of place is first a spatial one, a perception of the volume of air that surrounds the observer, read through the eyes, the ears, and the skin. Outdoor space, like architectural space, is made palpable by light and sound and defined by enclosure. But it has characteristics of its

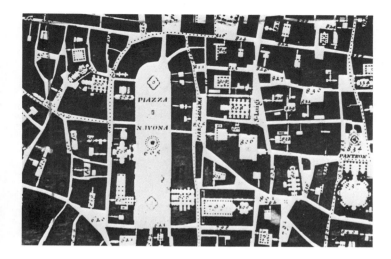

FIGURE 52
*A portion of
Nolli's map of
Rome in 1748,
showing interior
and exterior
spaces as an inter-
connected system.*

own, and those characteristics have implications for site planning. Site space is more extended than architectural space and looser in its form. Horizontal dimensions are normally much greater than vertical ones. Structures are less geometric, connections less precise, shapes more irregular. A deviance in plan that would be intolerable in a room may even be desirable in a city square. The site plan uses different materials—notably earth, rock, water, and plants—and is subject to constant change: the rhythm of human activity, the natural cycles, the cumulative effects of growth, decay, and alteration. The light that gives it form shifts with hour, day, and season. The place is seen in sequence, and over an extended period of time.

These differences call for corresponding variations of technique. The looseness of outdoor space, combined with the difficulty that any but a trained eye has in estimating distance, plan form, or gradient, allows a certain freedom of layout. Flaws can be masked and illusions created: two water bodies coalesce because their outlines seem to match; a large object disappears because it is blocked out by a small thing nearby; an axis appears straight, although in reality it is bent. Level areas tilt by contrast with adjacent counter-slopes. The apparent relative elevations of two objects may be reversed by the treatment of the grades adjacent to them.

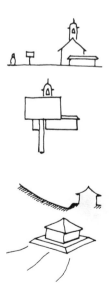

This freedom to deceive imposes a corresponding responsibility to make a clearly connected whole. A simple, readable, well-proportioned outdoor space is a powerful event. Structure is explained in a way that purely natural

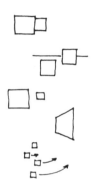

Enclosure

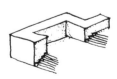

forces rarely accomplish, connections established that defy time and distance. Dimensions difficult to grasp are made legible by visual measuring devices. Part is connected with whole by echoes of shape or material. The designer uses every resource to confirm the form she intends to establish. Unless she seeks an air of mystery and doubt, she makes sure that spaces are well defined and clearly joined. Changes in plan are coordinated with changes in section.

Spatial dimensions are reinforced by light, color, texture and detail. The eye judges distance by many features, and some of them can be manipulated to exaggerate or to diminish apparent depth, such as the overlapping of distant objects by closer ones; the parallactic movement of objects disposed in depth when seen by the moving eye; the way in which distant things "rise" toward the far horizon; the smaller size and finer texture of things far away, and their bluish color; or the apparent convergence of parallel lines. Used with restraint, the manipulation of such features heightens the spatial effect, whether by making real depth legible, as by planting a line of trees whose interspacing, overlap, and convergence in perspective mark off an otherwise "empty" distance, or by creating an illusion of depth, as by using smaller, blue-green, fine-textured trees in a background. In any illusion, there is always the danger that from some other viewpoint the trick will be exposed. An illusion of some characteristic that is indirectly perceived (such as level, or geometric plan) is easier to maintain. An illusion of direct perception, such as an imitation of the color and texture of some other material in a substitute, is far more difficult to carry off.

Outdoor spaces are defined by trees, hedges, buildings, hills, but are rarely completely enclosed. They are partially bounded, their form completed by the shape of the floor and by small elements that mark off imaginary aerial definitions. Since horizontal things dominate the out of doors, vertical features take on an exaggerated importance. We are surprised to find that our photographs of an awesome mountain landscape record a minor disturbance of the horizon. Level changes can define spaces and create effects of dynamic movement. A regularly organized space will tilt uneasily if it contains a steep slope. Thus it is safer to make up vertical differences in the approach or in the transitions between important openings. The general shape of a site plan may have less bearing on its success than its levels, or the small projections or focal objects that make up the real visual space on the ground. But once a readable space is established, it has a strong emotional impact. The intimacy of a small enclosure and the exhilaration of a great opening are universal sensations. The transition between the two is even stronger: the powerful sense of contraction or release.

Spaces are enclosed by opaque barriers, but also by walls that are semitransparent or broken. Space definers may be visual suggestions rather than visual stops: colonnades, bollards, even changes in ground pattern or the imaginary extensions of things. Buildings have been the traditional enclosers of urban space, but the demand for open areas around the buildings has grown. Such breaks may be masked by overlaps and staggered openings, by bridging the street, by screen walls and colonnades, or even by a continuous line of low fencing. More often now, enclosure is achieved with trees and hedges, supported by the shaping of the ground. Trees may form great walls, or columnar lines, or canopies overhead. Shrubs, on the other hand, are human height, and so are more decisive obstacles to our vision and our movement.

Spatial character varies with proportion and scale. Proportion is the internal relation of parts and may be studied in a model. Scale is the relation of size to the size of other objects: the vast sky, the surrounding landscape, the observer himself. A few tentative quantities can be assigned to the latter scale, that is, to those dimensions of external spaces which seem comfortable, due to the characteristics of the human eye and to the size of our bodies. We can detect a human being at about 1200 m (4000 ft), recognize him at 25 m (80 ft), see his facial expression at 14 m (45 ft), and feel him in direct relation to us—pleasant or intrusive—at 1 to 3 m (3 to 10 ft). Outdoor spaces of that last dimension seem intolerably small. Dimensions of the order of 12 m (40 ft) are intimate. Up to 25 m (80 ft) is still an easy human scale. Most of the successful enclosed squares of the past have not exceeded 140 m (450 ft) in the smaller dimension. Beyond that, there are few good urban vistas over 1.5 km (about a mile) in length, unless they are distant panoramas seen over a featureless or hidden middle ground, such as views over water or from high places. All this refers to the stationary observer or to the man moving slowly. Space perception at high speed is another animal.

Proportion and scale

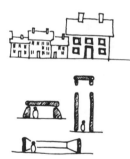

Other effects are due to our angle of vision and to the way in which we scan a scene. An object whose major dimension equals its distance from the eye is difficult to see

as a whole but can be scanned in detail. When it is twice as far away, it appears as a unit; when it is three times as far, it is still dominant in the visual field but tends to be seen in relation to other objects. As the distance increases beyond four times the major dimension, the object becomes one element of the general scene, unless it has other qualities that focus our attention. Thus, an external enclosure is most comfortable when its walls are one-half to one-third as high as the width of the space enclosed, while, if the ratio falls below one-fourth, the space begins to lack a sense of enclosure. If the height of the walls is greater than the width, then one ceases to notice the sky. The space becomes a pit or trench or outdoor room—secure or stifling depending on its scale with respect to the body and how the light falls into it. Another example of a visual rule based on the human anatomy is our sensitivity to an ambiguity at eye level as might be caused by a narrow barrier at that level or by a vertical surface terminating there. Vision should be kept clear at that touchy elevation or decisively blocked. Walls should either be low or over six feet high; railings at eye level are to be avoided.

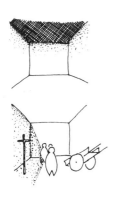

The appearance of a space is modified by the activity that goes on within it, by the way one passes through it, by the color and texture of walls and floor, by the way it is lighted, and by the objects with which it is furnished. Wall Street on a Sunday is very different from Wall Street at a weekday noon. A familiar square can be mysterious under artificial light. An empty room is notoriously smaller than the same room when furnished; distances are shortened over open water. A few man-sized objects can establish a scale relation between a person and a big space, and a tall object can relate a small space to a larger world. Blue and gray surfaces seem farther away, while hot, strong colors advance toward us. Downhill views are long, and uphill views foreshortened.

Light

The light that bathes a space is a determinant of its character. Light will sharpen or blur definitions, emphasize silhouette or texture, conceal or reveal, contract or expand dimensions. An object frontally lit is flattened, while side lights bring out its surfaces. This is the effect produced by the grazing rays of morning and evening or the vertical illumination of a tropical sun. Light reflected from below brings out unsuspected qualities, which may be dramatic or disturbing. Backlight makes silhouettes and polarizes tones to black and white. Silhouetted objects are prominent visual

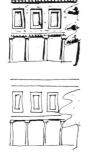

158

FIGURE 53   *Siena's central square has an entirely different character*
when the Palio fills it with crowds and wild riders.

features, and the designer is always careful about things that appear against the sky. She knows of the apparent outward radiation of bright surfaces, which causes light sources to seem fat and silhouetted objects thin. Shadow patterns can be attractive features—large masses or delicate traceries, dark and opaque or scintillating with light. Shadows may explain the modeling of a surface. A lighted opening, seen beyond a shadowed wood, is a dramatic vision. So the designer arranges her light effects, orienting and modeling surfaces, disposing of openings, casting shadows, reflecting or filtering light. But, since natural light shifts with hour, season, and weather, she is less concerned with some special dramatic effect than with a form that receives that changing light gracefully. To do this, she must be aware of the geometry of sun and moon position and of light effects in varying weather. She must be sensitive to that quality of light particular to the locality: the low, crisp light of a continental interior, which clarifies distant things, and lights them from one side and then from another, or the soft grey light of a northern littoral, which softens form and makes us attend to things nearby.

Reference 50

She has another resource in artificial light, more subject to her control and full of dramatic possibilities, but also costly, normally unchanging, and subject to limitations of technology and the requirements of safety and of functional illumination. Most sites are now used at night as well as in the daytime, and some even more intensively after dark. Artificial light can modify a space, even create it after the sun has set, transform textures, pick out entrances, indicate the structure of paths or the presence of activity, confer a special character. Fine trees or monuments can be dramatized. Moving water can be made to glow and sparkle. Changing light can be an intriguing display in itself. This resource is rarely used effectively. The fear of crime, our obsession with the moving vehicle, the false standards of the lighting industry, and the costs of energy and of maintenance have all conspired to impose a harsh, even, yellow glare on us. The varied requirements of pedestrian and driver, the need to differentiate and structure the night time scene, the pleasures of modulation and visual drama, the qualities of moonlight and of starlight, indeed the wonder of darkness itself, are all banished. Utilitarian standards, mechanically applied, flatten out the visual landscape, except in an occasional extravaganza of signs or shop windows.

The sense of hearing also conveys the shape of space. Nocturnal animals and blind human beings use echo location to move through the world. We interpret an absence of echo, for example, as extended openness. Similarly, if to a lesser extent, we are affected by the feel of a surface (or how it looks as if it should feel) and by its radiation of heat to our skin, or vice-versa. The visual presence of a wall is reinforced if it reflects sound, or looks rough to touch, or radiates heat. Places have particular smells that are part of their identity, even if it is undignified in our culture to say so. The microclimate is a marked feature of a place: it will be remembered as cool and moist, hot, bright, and windy, or warm and sheltered. All these sensations of light, sound, smell, and touch can be exploited by the designer, although he is not accustomed to do so.

Touch and hearing

Space forms have common symbolic connotations: the awesomeness of great size and the pleased interest of diminutive scale; the aspiration of tall, slender verticals, and the passivity and permanence of the horizontal line; the closed, static appearance of circular forms, and the dynamism of projecting jagged shapes; the protection of the cave versus the freedom of the prairie. Strong feelings are evoked by fundamental elements of human shelter, such as the roof and the door, and by basic natural materials, such as earth, rock, water, and trees.

Connotations

A landscape is normally seen from a limited set of viewpoints: the paths along which the observer moves and certain key stations, such as windows, seats, or principal entrances. The lines of sight from these critical points should be analyzed, whether by quick sketches or by traces of the cone of vision on plan and section. A site model is studied by placing the eye close to ground at these points, and not by a synoptic view from above. Simple devices permit this displacement of the eye: pinhole viewers, small mirrors, or periscopes that project the viewer down to ground and allow us to see the model as if we were walking through it.

Viewpoints

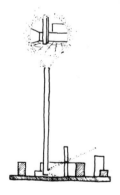

Sight lines are manipulated in the design by slight shifts in ground level or path direction or by the position of opaque barriers. The eye may be directed by framing or subdividing the view or be drawn along a path or rank of repeated forms. The visual attraction of some focal object can blot out the surrounding detail. A distant view is enhanced by a foreground with which it is contrasted. Indeed, it is often the middle ground that is most difficult to manage, and a design

161

References 4, 25

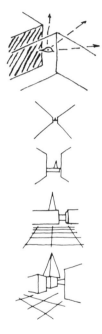

Reference 81

may mask out that middle ground—by planting or by a drop in level—so that some carefuly chosen foreground detail can stand against the distant landscape. The distant view itself can be organized by what is permitted to be seen. In the Japanese garden, distant hills are "borrowed" into the small enclosure. Seats and shelters are located at key points for some special contemplation: to watch the dawn, see the moon on the water, enjoy the autumn foliage or the wind in the bamboo. The garden is a set of carefully prepared sensations, linked but distinct.

Since the landscape is usually experienced by a moving observer, especially in our day, the single view is not as important as the cumulative effect of a sequence of views. Any lack of formal balance at one moment is of less consequence than the balance over time. Coming out of a narrow slot into a broad expanse is a strong effect. The dancing of the landscape as one moves by it can be a pleasure. Potential motion takes on importance: a road suggests direction and the eye follows it as a connecting thread. Broad, flat steps invite one; a narrow, curving street leads to some hidden promise. Orientation is significant: the direction to some goal, the marking of the distance traversed, the clarity of entrance and exit, the location of the observer in the structure of the whole. A major view may be hinted at, that hint be succeeded by an intimate scene, the view then reappear behind a dominant foreground, to be replaced by a tightly confined space, and at last open fully before one. A succession of arrivals, like the runs and landings of a stair, will be more interesting than a protracted approach. Each new event prepares for the next: an ever new but coherent development. A number of graphic languages have been invented to make the design of sequence possible.

The form of motion itself has meaning: direct or indirect, fluid or formal, smooth or erratic, purposeful or whimsical. Objects can be disposed to heighten this sense of motion. The observer's speed is significant since vision is restricted to a narrow forward quadrant as speed increases, and spatial effects that are pleasant at a walking pace may be imperceptible at 60 miles per hour. The spatial form, seen as a sequence, is a fundamental component of the site plan. So it is often useful to outline the spaces lying between the opaque objects in order to study this primary visual sensation. These spaces must not be thought of flatwise, however, but as a progression through which one moves. Sequence is the radical difference between landscape and pictorial compo-

FIGURE 54 *Coming from confinement into spaciousness is a strong experience: a principal entrance into the Dvortsovaya Square in Leningrad, with the Winter Palace in the background.*

sition, and, along with our perception of space by scanning and peripheral vision, explains why it is often impossible to take good photographs of fine environments.

Spaces are primarily defined by vertical surfaces, but the only continuous surface is underfoot. The configuration of this floor is determined by the existing topography, although modern machinery now allows rapid, cheap (and risky) reshaping of the land. Careful inspection reveals key points in the shape of the land, such as the point at which the gradient changes abruptly or from which a commanding view may be enjoyed. The land may be divisible into small regions, each of homogeneous character, linked to one another along certain strategic lines. Most sites have their own special character or some pivotal features to which the plan can respond. Sites of strong character will dictate the basic organization of the plan and call for a simple arrangement that clarifies the terrain. Flat ground and sites of more neutral character allow a freer, more intricate patterning.

There is an easy visual relation between a man-made structure and rolling topography when the long dimension of the structure, whether a road or a building, lies along the

Reference 44
Ground form

FIGURE 55
In old Cordoba,
this narrow, twist-
ing lane leads one
on from one event
to another.

164

FIGURE 56
On a road near Naples, the pines planted along one edge explain its forward direction.

FIGURE 57
The great English garden of Stourhead is a rich succession of space and incidents along a path that encircles an irregular lake. Here we look from the Temple of Flora to the Temple of the Sun.

contour lines. The base level of the structure meets the ground happily, its alignment accentuates the land form, and the natural contours are left relatively undisturbed. This is often the cheapest solution. On the other hand, if contour following is used on steep ground, then the land falls sharply toward or away from the structure on either side, and this may cause difficulties of drainage, use, or harmonious appearance. Here the best solution may be to let the road or axis of the building plunge directly across the contours. Road gradients will then be steep, and the cross fall across the face of the building may have to be handled by step-like forms, but the topographic structure is dramatized, just as the streets of San Francisco, which seem to ignore the contours, are in fact very expressive of them. When the structural axes are diagonal to the contours, however, a more awkward relation occurs.

The designer places her structures, and arranges her views and approaches so that the basic form of the land can be grasped. She may plant the hills and clear the valley bottoms to emphasize the drainage and exaggerate the heights. But if trees are planted on a hill, they should continue over the crest from all viewpoints and not stop halfway up. The "natural" pattern, with its tall trees on the rich bottom land, and dwarf plants on the hills, actually tends to blur our sense of the underlying ground. Nature is not always right, to our eyes. Straight lines of planting across rolling ground make vivid the swelling forms, and a deep cut through a crest exposes the earth. Buildings of uniform height, with their differentiated planes of roof and facade, may be arranged in step fashion on a hill to give the sense of "piling up." Tall buildings can take the heights, and low structures nestle in the valleys. Long slabs can be set back in echelon as they climb. Yet if structures are not intended to dominate the land or to be visible from great distances, it is best to place them not on the very crests of the hills but on the military crest (the "brow" of the hill), where the ground commences to fall more rapidly to the foot, a location which commands a more continuous view, and where rooflines will be backed by the hilltop rather than be silhouetted against the sky.

Inevitably, any new development changes the old contours. The new ground shapes should fit harmoniously into the old or else be intentional intrusions. If the former, the new ground forms must be of the same family. In humid, temperate climates, for example, slopes are usually contin-

168

uous and flowing, curve running into curve, hillside meeting hilltop with a convex, and hillfoot with a concave, profile. Every region will have its own family of landforms, a product of the base material, its stratification and its angle of repose, its history of vulcanism or glaciation, the work of water and wind, the climate, and the vegetative cover. But rather than simply smoothing over his traces, the designer may choose to shape the ground willfully, to reveal and conceal, to make the movement of a path seem reasonable and interesting. An obtrusive road may be made to disappear by dropping it into a shallow, steep-sided cut.

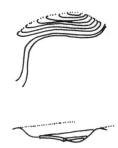

Where the existing topography is monotonous or shapeless, or where it must be radically disturbed, then modern earth-moving capabilities allow the designer to create artificial terrain. The problem shifts from the expression, or harmonious modification, of a preexisting structure to that of abstract sculpture on a vast scale. This is frequently done for engineering purposes, and often enough with dismaying results. It has rarely been done for conscious visual motives. The vast terraces in the hills of Los Angeles, meant as platforms for small houses, are awesome forms, before they are occupied by their little boxes, more "mountainous" than the original hills. It is difficult to make a convincing imitation of a large natural topography, but obviously man-made shapes have a potential, which we glimpse in recent works of "earth art." We also get some intimation of their possibilities when we look at a great dam or pass through a complex highway interchange.

These qualities of topographic form are best studied on a model, even though eventual decisions are more accurately conveyed by a contour map. The work is sculptural; there is no substitute for pursuing it in a sculptural medium. Simple cardboard contour layer models are built up, and cut and patched to show the new dispositions. In more complex ground, it may be best to use a plastic material. If the plastic model is reshaped without any addition or subtraction of material, then the solution is one in which cut and fill will roughly balance. Decisions are transposed to accurate contour drawings, for earthwork calculations, and to specify construction in the field. Some preparatory analyses can be done on a contour map, however, as by shading the ground not visible from some key point (and therefore indicating those locations from which it cannot be seen). This is similar to a military reconnaissance for fields of fire, which are just like fields of view. Concepts like *defile* and *military crest* are

Models and maps

169

common to both. On larger, complex landscapes, perspectives of the ground as it would be seen from a given point can be displayed by a computer.

Textures and materials

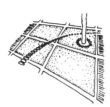

The textural finish of this ground helps set its visual character and can be source of delight in itself. It may be no more than a harmonious background that unifies the scene, or it can be a dominant surface that sets the pattern of the plan. It can express the disposition of surface activity, and play a role in guiding that activity. It imparts sensations of touch as well as sight. Raised beds protect planting from surrounding traffic, and ribbons of smooth paving guide walkers through a cobbled square. Changes of level act as space definers. A valley guides our vision along its course, while a centrally dished floor gives us a static feeling. Fine ground textures—moss, monolithic pavement, or close-cropped grass—emphasize the shape and mass of the underlying ground and increase its apparent size. They act as a background for the objects that rise from them. Coarse textures—rough grass, cobbles, bricks, or blocks—work in the opposite way, calling attention to the surface itself rather than to the underlying mass or the objects above it.

Since the ground has such visual importance, we should consider its enrichment and not leave it to casual attention.We use too scanty a palette: little more than mown grass, bituminous macadam, and monolithic concrete. We skin the ground clean, or put it under trees or buildings. The result is monotonous, sometimes ugly, often unsuitable. Concrete is poor for running, deprives the land of water, and makes an uncomfortable summer climate. Asphalt is black. Grass cannot bear intensive traffic and requires constant management and plentiful water. A wide range of other ground surfacings are available. They include cutivated or stabilized earth, rough-mown grass, low ground covers, shrubbery, tanbark and other soft granular materials, water-bound macadam, sand and gravel, asphalt or concrete with fillers, jointings, or surface aggregates, wood block or decking, terrazzos or mosaic, and pavements of bricks, tiles, asphalt and cement pavers, cobbles, and stone blocks or slabs. True enough, many of the alternative hard surfacings are expensive relative to plain asphalt or concrete, or require frequent weeding, cleaning, or replacement. And grass is still king of the soft surfaces, since most other ground covers are sensitive to wear, and, in the sunlight, cannot meet the competition of grass or weeds. See Appendix I for a more complete listing of these possibilities.

170

FIGURE 60   *In the gardens of the Saiho-ji temple in Kyoto, moss and low bushes make vivid the skin of the earth.*

Self-maintaining surfaces, such as rough grass, a natural woodland floor, or mixed stands of native shrubs and herbs ("weeds," that is) could be employed more often. Hampstead Heath in London is a model of a seemingly untended rural recreation area, which is in fact carefully managed for urban use. The grass is mown late in the summer to allow spring flowers to mature and ground-nesting birds and animals to rear their young. Paths and areas for more intensive activity can be mown or surfaced within the larger, "unkempt" areas. Small curbs and mowing strips at the edge of the finished areas make care easier. The edge between two habitats is always the interesting location and demands greater design attention, whether it be the edge of a walk, the edge of a wood or pond, or a doorway between inside and outside. Here we prefer to linger, here the diversity of species is at the maximum.

If visible space is the element over which the designer   Visible activity
traditionally exerts his control, it is nevertheless not the salient impression of place for most observers. We equate design with things, as the lifeless photographs of the architectural magazines will testify, but places that conceal

the human trace, as so many new buildings do, are depressing and cold. To see and hear people in action is endlessly entertaining. We want to know who is there, what they are like, what they intend toward us, what they are doing. Seeing and being seen, promenading on a busy street, watching a cobbler or a construction crew, are recurrent pleasures. The site planner does not control this aspect of place, which is fortunate enough. But the site plan can support or suppress visible activity; it can help people to become aware of each other. Activity locations can be concentrated and mixed so that they are intervisible. Spaces and seats can encourage the passerby to linger; places for meeting and celebration can be provided. Productive activity and the flow of traffic can be exposed to sight. The setting can have a form and substance such that human action can easily leave its trace. The presence of other living things can be encouraged by the way in which habitats are arranged and food and water are provided. An untended acre of woodland, brush, and small glades will support many different kinds of birds and animals. The margins between these types of cover are particularly attractive to wildlife. The small clearings, to be effective, should be at least 20 m across. If these small wildernesses are connected by strips of rough vegetation, such as along neglected hedges or unmown drainage ditches, they will allow for wildlife movement from haven to haven. Small water bodies add to the attraction, and certain plants provide favored food. Planned neglect has its value for wild things, for children, even for ourselves.

Reference 33

Congruence and transparency

One quality of a warm, life-saturated place is its *congruence*—the degree to which its visible form matches the form and scale of its activity. Visual climax corresponds to activity climax; space is sized to the intensity of activity. A lively central square would appear vast and lonely at the periphery. A footpath can be a long journey along the empty lots, or relatively brief if bordered by activities. Spaces should not only be fit for the activities that occur within them, in the direct behavioral sense, they should *visibly* be fit for them. Action can be clarified and expressed, its emotional mood visibly reinforced. Distance and light will determine whether we can read faces; the sound level makes conversation easy or difficult. There may be a comfortable niche in which one can sit to watch the action. The shape of the space and the location of its detail will help or hinder the effort to delimit behavioral territories. Part of the pleasure of an outdoor concert is the sense of being one with the audience. Some outdoor activities, like the *paseo* or the hot-rod parade, are essentially concerned with this mutual visibility. Openness, transparency, and overlook bring what is happening into view. Here we skirt the reefs of privacy, the danger that we may reveal activities that the looked-upon prefer to keep hidden. So we expose only those actions which by consensus are deemed public, or which both viewer and viewed wish to communciate, or which consist in the impersonal trace of human action: the movement of cars and ships, the work of great machines, the hollowed step, the handworn rail. By these means a place becomes warm and alive.

Where a public place is to be managed by some single agency—a merchants' association, a university, a park administration—it is possible to go further. The program and the design may include the direct promotion of certain activities on the site. One can arrrange for festivals, encourage street vendors, provide a street clown to interact with passersby, or create a ritual of founding or remembrance. The act of construction can be celebrated and explained, or the closing of a street excavation can be commemorated by allowing the public to throw small objects into the pit for future archaeologists to find. Piles of cleared snow might be shaped for visual effect, just as the raking of sand in the Japanese garden has evolved into an artistic patterning. If these devices appear overstrained and peculiar, there is indeed some danger of overmanagement. The road to Williamsburg and Disneyland is alluring. But it remains true that site design should deal with activity as well as physical form and should consider, and at times even prescribe, the form of those activities that will occur in any case, such as the acts of construction, maintenance and renewal. *(margin: Activity management)*

Beyond the direct perception of space and activity, a landscape is also a medium of symbolic communication, whether by means of explicit, conventional signs or by the implicit meanings of shapes and motions. Symbols are a social creation and may be unintelligible to the stranger. They tell us about ownership, status, the presence of people, group affiliations, hidden functions, goods and services, values, proper behavior, history, politics, time, and events to come. Meaning arises automatically in a settled landscape, long occupied by the same group of people who have been engaged in the same activities and hold the same values. In more mobile, pluralistic situations, the consciously designed symbol is more important. The designer may manipulate *(margin: Symbols)* these symbolic forms in order to increase the resonance of his setting. Many contemporary architects, inspired by recent work in semiotics, now use symbols in a free, eclectic way. But deep symbols grow slowly, and this game may soon exhaust itself. The site designer will be well advised to restrict himself to sharpening the direct perception of his basic materials—space and time, earth, living things, and human activity—and allow the underlying symbolism to grow of itself.

Sense of time

Reference 58

The communication of a sense of time, however, is as important as the conveyance of spatial form, since time and space are the great dimensions within which we have our being. A good design saves evidence of the previous occupation of a place, especially such evidence as conveys intimate human use (a seat, a threshold) or evokes profound feelings (a cross, a grave, an ancient tree). Contrasting new with old, we feel the depth of time. Former buildings, or parts of buildings, can be remodeled for new use and existing planting patterns salvaged. The plan also leaves room for the coming inhabitants to make their mark. Materials are chosen that will weather handsomely. How plantings will mature, grow, and decay, how structures will be destroyed and replaced, is part of the scheme. The place should be evocative of season and of time of day: the shift of light, the cycle of growth, the rhythm of activity. The planner provides for the celebration of the present time, the great anniversaries and events, so that there may be a "sense of occasion" as well as a "sense of place." He also provides permanent features against which that flux may be measured. Even some features of the possible future might be marked out on the ground. We scarcely think of such things but like to imagine that a site design is isolated in time, something that appears suddenly, itself changeless and enduring. We may save a few historic scraps but never express the *stream* of time that a place has endured. Yet it is this very rootedness in time that attaches us emotionally to any place.

Rock and earth

Rock and earth are the primary site materials: our environmental base. Cuts and fills, pits and outcrops, cliffs, caves and hills communicate a sense of mass, a sense of endurance, an intuition of the planet whose surface we inhabit. Rock is a handsome material. We hide it with topsoil or prettify it in rock gardens. But it expresses strength and permanence, the working of powerful forces over long spans of time. It displays a great range of color, grain and surface

FIGURE 61
*Giant ammonites
in a limestone
wall in England
are eloquent of
geologic time.*

FIGURE 62
*If one looks to the
left in this quiet
courtyard of the
Parroquia del Sal-
vador in Sevilla,
one sees with a
shock that time
has almost buried
an old arcade.*

FIGURE 63
*Expressive
strength and rich
texture: stone
walls, lichen, and
natural rock at
Machu Picchu in
Peru.*

Water

Reference 96

texture, especially when it is long weathered. It appears as pebbles, cobbles, boulders, thin beds and massive outcrops; men fashion it into setts, blocks, slates, slabs, and crushed fragments. The Chinese and Japanese are connoisseurs of stone and use them to great effect in their gardens. Stone is expensive but can be the ideal material for walls, steps and pavings. Weathered stones are stunning objects in the landscape. If they are intended to be part of some natural landscape, then the manner in which the local rock is exposed must be carefully observed, whether as ledge, or talus, or scattered boulders. On the other hand, the bold artificial cuts through rock strata seen along our highways are often their most striking feature.

Water is equally elemental but extremely varied in its effect. The number of its names in the common language marks its richness: ocean, pool, sheet, jet, torrent, rill, drop, spray, cascade, film, stream, rivulet, mist, wave, pond, lake— to which add the words for liquid motion: trickle, splash, foam, flood, pour, spout, spurt, ripple, surge, run, seep. The range of form, the changeableness and yet the unity, the intricate repetitive fluid movement, the suggestion of coolness and delight, the play of light and sound, as well as its intimate connection with life and its attraction for birds and animals, all make water a superb material for outdoor use. It affects sound, smell, and touch, as well as sight.

Moving water give the sense of life, still water conveys unity and rest. But water must appear to lie naturally within the land: it appears tilted and unstable unless the ground slopes down to it. Water plays with light, and if still can act as a mirror. Unruffled, brimful, and with open borders, it reflects the changing sky. If dark and low, it catches the images of sunlit things nearby. If shallow, a dark bottom improves reflectivity. Water running in the shade is a grateful thing in a hot and arid climate. In a grey, humid one, it will seem damp and gloomy and so is better disposed where it will be open to the sky.

The sound and movement of running water is enhanced by the form of its container. A well-crafted channel will throw water into the air, strike it against obstacles, make it swirl and gurgle. If the lip of a fall is undercut, then all its volume will be visible, its force heard and seen, as it drops into a pool below. A small amount of water can perform repeatedly, to make a surprisingly large effect. The Moorish gardeners were masters of this. Even a tiny drip will strike a musical note. Baroque gardeners led their small streams

FIGURE 64
A courtyard in the Alhambra, Granada: a few plants, sun, shade, and a small flow of water have their maximum effect.

FIGURE 65
*The famous water
displays of the
Villa d'Este, near
Rome.*

down stepped cascades, concealed them, and caused them to spurt up, only to disappear once more. The Japanese may use only a slow-dripping source in the shade, or even a symbolic stream of rock and sand.

So magnetic is the attraction of water that observers look inward toward it, and so it can be the centerpiece of a design. Its edge is the important feature and requires careful thought. That edge can be abrupt and definite, or low, shelving and obscure. A simple form conveys clarity and stability. If complex and partly hidden, it evokes expectancy and extended space. Stones just below the water surface make its depth legible. Objects at the water's edge are sharply seen; the Japanese place their waterside stones with great care. To make a natural shore, one must attend to the ways of water in that region. But if there will be many people about, it will be wiser to pave the water's edge, since it is sure to attract hard wear.

For all its quality, water can be expensive to introduce and to maintain, especially in an urban setting. It may raise safety problems. It catches trash and dust, and exhibits them proudly. It breeds insects and weeds; it floods, erodes its banks, and fills with silt. It is a dynamic, transitory element of the ecosystem. The designer must decide whether to provide clean water, free of plants and other living things, or to make a balanced ecological system. If the former, he uses filtered and recycled water in artificial basins and provides for frequent cleaning. In the winter and during shutdowns for repairs or scrubbing, these containers will be dry and must be handsome in that guise. If the latter, he introduces the bottom soil, plants and fish which will compose a complete nutrient cycle. Along with them, of course, come the algae, mud, and insect life which are part of that cycle, just as down timber and brush are part of a natural woodland. A "clean" pond can be extremely shallow and can be located anywhere. A balanced pond needs sunlight, and of at least a foot and a half of depth, if small fish are to survive the winter. Either pond requires a watertight lining of masonry, puddled clay, or plastic sheeting.

Next in importance is the living plant material, the trees, shrubs, and herbs, the material popularly associated with landscape work, which is usually thought to be concerned with the spotting of trees on a plan after buildings and roads have been located. More correctly, the plant cover is one element in the organization of outdoor space. Some great landscapes are treeless, and there are handsome squares that

Plants

FIGURE 66
The Riverwalk through the heart of downtown San Antonio: a small, neglected stream, which was about to be thrust into a sewer, has been transformed into a delightful, active promenade.

FIGURE 67
A sparing use of vegetation may enhance its visual power: a street in the Cyclades, Greece.

do not include a plant of any description. Nevertheless, plants are one of the fundamental materials. If in public we worship the tree, in practice we destroy it. Planting is the "extra" in site development, the first item to be cut when the budget pinches.

Site planning is concerned with groups of plants and the general character of planted areas rather than with individual specimens. Trees, shrubs, and ground covers are the basic materials. Trees are the backbone; they form the structure of the plan, while the occasional specimen tree may be used for particular effect. Simple in essence, intricate in form, fluttering and swaying in the wind, leafless or deep with foliage, they are enduring and yet alive. The shrubs, man height, are the effective space formers. They are privacy screens and barriers to movement.

References 10, 37, 77

Plants take on a bewildering variety of forms under the influence of their environment, and those forms change as the plant grows and ages. But each species has its own habit of growth, its own way in which leaves, stems and buds are connected and succeed each other. This pattern, distorted in any one individual by the accidents of age and exposure, produces the characteristic mass, structure, and texture of that species. When working at the site planning scale, dispose plants according to their habit of growth, their texture, and mass as a group, rather than by their individual form, since the former are the features that can be predicted and are less likely to vary from different points of view. The surface of a plant may have a texture that is fine or coarse, shiny or dull, closed or open, stiff or trembling, clustered or even, smooth or modeled in depth. The habit may be prostrate, upright, vasiform, fastigiate, main-stemmed, crookedly branching, or high canopied.

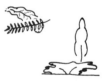

Other characteristics, such as growth rate, eventual size, color, life span, scent, and seasonal effect, are the next considerations. Species must be chosen which are hardy for the given microclimate and soil condition. They must stand up to the expected traffic, be resistant to disease and insect attack, and demand no more care than can be furnished at the expected level of maintenance. Dense urban areas are particularly difficult for plants because of the lack of water, light, and humus, as well as the air pollution, the reflected heat, and the presence of poisonous chemicals. Trees must be specially chosen for this harsh habitat. Impervious paved surfaces must be kept at least three feet from their trunk. Appendix I lists a selected number of trees, shrubs, and

The landscapes attractive to human beings are generally not the stable ecological climax states—salt marsh, dry desert, rain forest, high grass prairie, or mature dense woodland with its underbrush and decaying trees. We prefer some intermediate stage, in transition to the climax, which is more productive or more pleasant to us—meadow, grain field, park, orchard, or suburban garden. In consequence, we labor to maintain these unstable, intermediate landscapes. We dominate the land, and sometimes it is as if we looked on vegetation as a medium for exercising machines. The typical suburban garden lasts for less than a generation. Farmlands demand heavy labor, paid for by their economic return. When this return ceases, the land lapses back to brush. City landscapes, with their extensive paving, hold out longer, but after ten years of neglect the lots have grown up and the pavements are cracked. The ecosystem reasserts itself.

Any system of plants is growing and dying. The designer preserves sound existing trees, but in dense development this is usually possible only with old avenues, substantial clumps, or occasional fine specimens, and these must be carefully protected. It is difficult to save extensive cover within the construction zone, since the ground surface is too *Reference 84* disturbed. The existing cover will not endure in its present form. It will change as human use puts new pressures on it. Feet and wheels will compact the earth above the feeding roots of trees, if nothing else. The water table will fall, pollution will appear, the climate will change. Mature trees will not survive a violent change of habitat. They can lose some of their roots (even up to one half, if carefully managed and pruned), but the ground must not be lowered within their root spread. It can only be slightly raised, and that only if a large well is built around the trunk and filled to the new level with coarse stone. Any change in the groundwater or the microclimate will be fatal. It is also a mistake to preserve only the large trees, while cutting out the young plants that would have replaced them, and unwise to save large, ancient trees long past their prime, whose removal after development will be costly.

New sites are barren and old ones overgrown. The designer imagines her effects in youth and in maturity: the scattering of small whips, the half-grown stand within the lifetime of the client, the fifty-year maturity, the trees decaying and replaced. Permanent trees must be set far enough apart from structures, and from each other, to prevent interference, unless a distorted shape or a solid mass of vegetation is what is wanted. Large forest trees, for example, must be set 15 to 20 m (50 to 60 ft) apart, and 6 m (20 ft) from a building, if they are meant to come to full size. The initial emptiness can be filled with quick-growing plants, which will be removed or crowded out. Mature specimens may be transplanted, but this is expensive and should be reserved for key locations. When it is done, however, the tree can be turned and shifted in its place, taking account of its particular shape just as if it were a piece of sculpture. Occasionally, it is possible to pre-plant trees for future development. The initial investment is small, and subsequent development is given a mature setting from its beginning. Where this happens by chance, as in a resumption of development in an abandoned subdivision, the effect is quite handsome.

The management of a place is as important as its initial form. To reduce maintenance cost, base the design on some minimum simplification of the climax ecosystem proper to that place, consistent with the given human purposes. Where the climax state is woodland, the design may take out the understory and simplify the ground cover to emphasize the form of the wood and to open it up to human access. It preserves the dominant plants and their replacements and maintains a diversity of species to allow for natural evolution and to reduce the risk of failure. The wood may be opened up in places and new species introduced for visual effect, species that are either indigenous or are established exotics. Rough grass and wild herbs instead of lawn will occupy the open ground. Paving and dense turf is used only where heavy wear is expected, while traffic is deflected from more sensitive growth by elevated ground or barriers. Less expensive maintenance practices are prescribed: grazing, burning, or annual mowing. Where close-cut grass is necessary, then the mown areas are made large and simple, accessible to machines. Trees and other permanent plants are emphasized and invasive plants avoided. If possible, costs of upkeep are balanced by some productive return, as from harvested timber in a parkland, from fruit trees along a city street, or from open spaces devoted to cropland, pasture, or allotment gardens. Nonaggressive weeds are tolerated; shrubs and roadside trees are rough cut, not pruned; ragged mulch is thrown on the ground. Insect control is limited to crucial moments in the life cycle or to epidemic outbursts. In any

Maintenance

Reference 38

FIGURE 68 *Hampstead Heath in London: what appears to be a rough rural landscape is in reality carefully managed to endure heavy city use.*

case, any landscape plan must include a plan for maintenance: a budget, a set of priorities, a calendar of routine upkeep, and an allowance for that intensive care and partial replacement which must always follow the establishment of a new planting.

Exotics

None of this excludes the use of a highly "unnatural" setting—a water garden in the desert, a greenhouse in the arctic, a paved plaza in the jungle—whenever the resources can be concentrated to maintain it. By its very contrast, such a setting heightens our perception of surrounding reality. But we fall in between and support large, rather characterless landscapes which stretch our ability to maintain them and neither echo the natural situation nor make some vivid contrast to it.

Many landscape designers feel that plants exotic to an area should never be used, except in gardens that are obviously artificial. This guarantees that plants will be hardy to the area, will evolve naturally within it, and will appear harmonious, since they are customarily associated together. But many self-maintaining, apparently natural species are in truth fairly recent exotics, and the visual harmonies that depend on familiar association may be enlarged by new experience. The objective requirements for hardiness and maintenance, and the subjective requirements of visual fit, are the underlying principles. New methods of control may create stable plant systems that were previously thought to be completely unnatural. Therefore, use conscious, even artificial, means to heighten our sense of the natural system, within the limits of continuous maintenance and of the human use to which the ground is put. Tall trees and low shrubs will clarify the vertical layering of a natural woodland; lower ornamentals will mark the border between wood and meadow. Certain species make a sudden show in spring or fall or have a striking skeleton to be seen stark against the winter sky. A delicate fern brings out the character of a massive rock.

While a natural area may contain a large number of species, and an unmolested ground may in time achieve the same diversity, it is usual to limit the plant list in a design, for reasons of economy, and for power of effect. Restricting the planting to a single species along a street, or in a flower bed, will make a vivid impression. But it is risky, when dealing with long-lived plants and extensive areas, since a new disease may obliterate the species and since succession is difficult to provide. It is wiser to use a mix of species, but their number need not be large. In a stand of trees, for example, it is rarely necessary to use more than three, or at the most five, species, since beyond that number the visual impression remains unchanged, and the security from species failure is not markedly improved. But the various species are not evenly mixed within the stand, since then the character of each is lost. Locate each kind in small clusters, which thin out into clusters of another type.

Planting is not a frill or a green stuffing to be packed between buildings. The main framework should be completed before occupancy and should be conceived as a total pattern in which public planting is integrated with the private lots. Lines of tall trees, visible from a distance, mark the major axes of the plan, plant masses define the major spaces, particular textures indicate the important areas.

Walls and fences, thin lines on the plan, mark out space just as do the trees and hedges. Along with the surface paving, then, they are the most important of the artificial outdoor elements. Their position and height, their texture and condition, are significant. Fences are often added at the last, and with little thought. The common choice is chain link, which has the emotional meaning of barbed wire and

185

filters the view through its countless holes. Along with asphalt paving, it is one of our less than happy contributions to the beauty of the world. Unfortunately, like asphalt, it is cheap, durable, and effective. To reduce its visibility, it should be dark in color and it can be planted out.

There is a large vocabulary of alternative fencings, from low, polite reminders to high, solid barriers. Wooden fences—rails, pickets, stakes, lattice, close boarding, sheets, or woven saplings—are in our tradition but require frequent painting and must be protected where in contact with the ground. Cast and wrought iron openwork is splendid and durable but quite expensive or even unobtainable today. It is sometimes imitated in painted plastic or cast aluminum, or more often in mild steel, which must be frequently painted to prevent rust. The modest stretched wire fence, with its wood or metal posts, is cheap, appropriate, and does not interrupt the view, but is easily damaged by fence climbers. Brick and stone make the finest solid walls, but stone is very costly, and brick not cheap. If their material is well chosen, they weather beautifully, and can support fine climbing plants, mosses, and lichens. In a brick wall, the choice of brick, the bonding, the coping, and the treatment of the joints determine the visual texture. Concrete block is a less expensive material and makes a good masonry wall if carefully laid and given a well-designed coping. It can be patterned or perforated. Fieldstone can be laid up in a dry wall. Even earth makes a good fence, whether as a planted berm or as a rammed earth wall with a weatherproof coping. A fence is subject to severe exposure on both sides, and must be well made. But the trace of time and weather on an old, substantial fence is its greatest charm. The height of a wall in relation to the eye defines its meaning for us. It can be perforated to permit vision, but even a perforated fence will seem opaque if seen obliquely or if light in color. To make a fence transparent, its members should be thin and black. An obtrusive fence can be lost in a hedge or under a vine, or set at the bottom of a swale. Many of these variations will be part of a regional tradition, and their symbolic connotations strong. Throughout the world, gardens are a rich source of fence patterns, and new forms are always being invented.

A site includes many other man-made details. Think of the normal furniture of any urban area: seats, traffic signals, signs, utility poles, light poles, meters, trash cans, fireplugs, manholes, wires, lights, plant containers, alarms, newsstands,

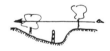

Site details

References 9, 16, 18

186

telephones, bollards, bus shelters, notice boards—the list goes on. It is curious that that mere list conveys a sense of disharmony, a feeling quite opposed to that evoked by saying: houses, trees, water, walls, paths. This near world of detail affects the appearance of the whole, and if it accumulates without design, as it usually does, it can create a sense of clutter. And yet designers may put too much stress on these details or stress the wrong details. The user is affected by the texture of the floor, the shape of the steps, or the design of a bench because he uses them and is in direct contact with them. Other details, not directly used, may escape his conscious attention. He sees the light but not the light pole, uses the telephone but does not notice the wires overhead. The designer invents a special form for the light pole, and at some expense puts the wires underground, while neglecting to put a back on his bench. Details require an investment of design and supervision if they are to be finely shaped, and the effect for the user should justify that investment.

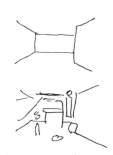

Most details are normally left to the customary operations of many separate agencies. This may be successful where there is a strong tradition or when the particular detail is not crucial. The designer focuses on the details critical for the perception and use of the site, which brings her to putting telephones, alarms, and mailboxes where they can be found; makes her think about how the trash cans are moved; reminds her to provide comfortable seats and public toilets. Instead of hiding the power lines, she might think how they could be made handsome. When possible, she installs examples of the features crucial for the user—such as benches, walks, or pedestrian lights—for trial and comment before the entire landscape is furnished. If lamps and benches are donated by individuals, the setting will acquire a further, more personal meaning.

One site detail merits additional discussion: the signs that have become so dominant in what we see. Design theory thinks of them as ugly necessities to be suppressed or minimized. But a landscape must communicate to its users. In a complex and mobile world, many messages must be carried by contrived symbols. If signs are ugly, it is not by their nature but because they are thoughtlessly used, ambiguous, redundant, and fiercely competitive. They are intended to deceive or manipulate, or at least to dominate someone else's sign. On the other hand, signs could make us aware not only of goods and services, names and prohibitions but also

Signs

187

of history, ecology, the process of production, weather, time, politics, events to come, and many other interesting things. A spectacular sign can be a dazzling piece of scenery. It should be our objective to enhance these beneficial powers—not to suppress, but to clarify and regulate, even amplify, this flow of information. Therefore the designer is concerned that signs be accurate, rooted (that is, located in the same space and time as the thing to which they refer), and intelligible—in other words, that they communicate well.

Environmental
art

The purpose of other details is solely visual and symbolic: those traditional sculptural memorials to distinguished persons and events, for example, or those more recent embellishments of civic space funded by the "1% for art" provisions of public budgeting. Occasionally these works catch at the public mind, and become well-loved landmarks: the lions before the Art Institute in Chicago, Daniel French's Lincoln in the Washington Memorial or his Minute Man in Concord, the memorial to Lewis Carroll's Alice in Central Park, or, more recently, the monument to Einstein in Washington. Far more often, public sculpture is ignored by the passerby, and at times even resented. It commemorates someone he never heard of and has no love for; it is a thing put there by some remote official for reasons of state or status or because the expense was mandatory. Savage civic battles erupt over these expensive objects, particularly if they are "modern," and therefore puzzling, in their form. Art and architecture, or art and landscape design, are still in a very uneasy alliance, although the recent murals painted on urban facades have been more happily received.

One answer is the collaboration of artist and site designer from the beginning of a project, but such team efforts have at times been stormy. Another piece of the answer, and perhaps a more fundamental one, is to bring the user into the process of programming and judging the artistic project. It may be wiser, for example, to allow a site to accumulate some experience of use, and a basis for an organization of users, before its special works of art are created and placed. People who have participated in this process will be far more interested in its results. Recent efforts at "place-making," which develop objects or murals that commemorate, and are particular to, the local community, seem to generate attachment to their products.

Perceiving an environment is creating a hypothesis, building an organized mental image of space and time that is based on the experience and purposes of the observer as well as on the stimuli reaching his senses. In building this organization, he will seize on congenial physical characteristics: symmetry, order, repetition; continuity and closure; dominance, rhythm, common scale or similarity of form or material. Sharp variations are also a way of relating parts, if there is some underlying continuity between them. A dark, narrow street is related to the broad avenue on which it emerges, a quiet park to the intensive shopping that fronts on it. Related contrasts bring out the essence of things. The Chinese garden masters made much use of complementaries, pairing rough with smooth, upright with recumbent, rock with water, mountain with plain. Near and far may be set together, fluid and fixed, familiar and strange, light and dark, solid and empty, ancient and new. Continuity depends on the important transitions: the joint between house and ground, gateways, decision points on a path, skylines, sunsets, shorelines, the edges of a wood. These transitions must be articulate if the times and spaces are to be readable and well joined. The classic architectural emphasis on cornices, base courses, and door moldings can be echoed in the edges, entrances, and pivotal events of the site.

As a consequence of the great numbers of objects and events in the outdoor scene, grouping and contrast must be used to bring it under perceptual control. The sought-for effect is usually broad and simple. Richness is inherent in the material; an intricate plan may end in confusion. The material is complex, in motion, and seen on different occasions, and the scene must accept this variation without losing its form. This does not demand formal geometry but simplicity. A good site plan, while highly refined at some critical point, may be almost coarse overall.

The principal structure of the plan is often some type of hierarchy or centrality. There may be a central space to which other spaces are subordinated or a main path linking many minor paths. There can be a principal approach, entered by a gateway and reaching a climactic point where one is at the heart of things. Such hierarchies are not the only possible structural plan, especially in large, complex, changing landscapes. The designer may use many-centered

189

FIGURE 69   *The Majolica Cloister of Santa Chiara in Naples: a memorable refuge of quietness in a dense and hyperactive city.*

forms, interlinking path networks, continuously varying activities and spaces, multiple sequences that have no determinate beginning or end. Such structural plans are more difficult to employ without a lapse into disorder, but they fit our situation more closely. They still rely on variations sequentially organized, on contrast, continuity, emphasis, and grouping.

The designer uses a strategy of concentration since he is always confronted by a shortage of resources. He conserves his views and displays them at their best, brings things together at focal points and along main lines, economizes here for luxury there, and avoids spaces beyond his ability to equip, maintain, or fill with activity. How much area or activity or visual experience can he effectively organize? Can he control a large landscape by means of numerous axes and focal points, or should he be content to structure one strategic location?

Frameworks
and programs

In some cases, the designer will not be in complete control of the site form, since he is making a long-range plan to be developed by others. In such cases, common

Reference 56

practice would entrust sensuous quality to those latecomers,

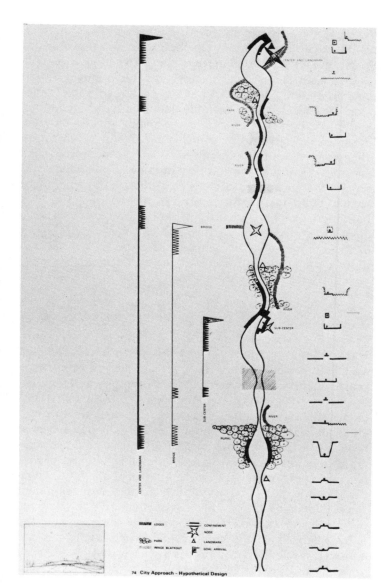

FIGURE 70
An imaginary highway as it enters a city, illustrating one graphic language for the explicit design of visual sequence. The diagram deals with turns, up and down movements, the opening and closing of space, the forward views, and the things that pass alongside.

191

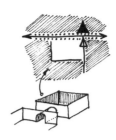

laying down only certain technical aspects of the plan, such as the street layout, the land subdivision, or regulations as to use, density, and building envelopes. But it is quite possible to deal with the sensed form even at this remove, as will be discussed in Chapter 11. Not only can the design framework be specified—for example the cross-section, planting, and succession of views from the major streets—but the designer may also specify a sensuous program for the future elements, without attempting to fix their exact form. Thus she might indicate the location of some major landmark, require that its public activities be visible, that the nature of former buildings on the site be expressed, that the new building be visible and identifiable from a certain distance along three major approaches, and that it distinguish each of those approaches from the others. Many particular solutions could satisfy these visual performance requirements, which can be as explicitly specified as requirements for fireproofing, access, or structural stability.

Languages

The accepted languages of site planning—site and planting plans, sections and profiles, details, specifications, perspectives—are designed to control the physical forms, and so they communicate many of the sensuous aspects of a site, but not all of them. They are not designed to convey sensuous program requirements, for example, and they fail to convey such immediate qualities as visible activity, ambience (the light, sound, climate, smell), sequential experience, the stages of development, or the daily and seasonal rhythms. Additional notations must be used to do so: diagrams of program requirements, of visible activity, of ambience and of sequential form, or a series of drawings which illustrate the moving view, cyclical change, or development stages. Notations for some of these qualities exist. Simulations of change and motion can be produced by computer graphics or by making videotapes through a periscope moving through a model. While these techniques are promising, they are as yet slow and expensive, better suited to the public presentation of a complex project than to the rapid and uncertain flow of the design process. For the latter, the quick freehand sketch—plan, view, or diagram—is still most useful.

Chapter 7

Access

Access is the prerequisite to using any space. Without the ability to enter or to move within it, to receive and transmit information or goods, space is of no value, however vast or rich in resources. A city is a communication net, made of roads, paths, rails, pipes, and wires. The economic and cultural level of a city is in some proportion to the capacity of its circulation. The cost of that circulation system is the most significant element in site cost.

In this system, one element influences and substitutes for another. Telephone calls replace personal trips, and the flow of gas in a pipe makes hauling solid fuel unnecessary. Bus trips reduce car trips. The layout of streets affects the pattern of underground utilities, and the location of telephone cables depends on the method used to transmit power. Since one kind of communication can substitute for another, a circulation plan seeks an optimum balance of modes, not blind reliance on a single one. We are not wise to depend so heavily on the car, given the diversity of present need and the unpredictability of the future.

There are various types of channels: the graded and surfaced rights-of-way for pedestrians or wheeled vehicles, the rail systems, the wires conveying power and information, the gravity flow pipes carrying off surface drainage and waterborne wastes, the pressure pipes suppying such fluids as water, gas, and steam, or even bulk materials in water suspension. Of all these, the vehicular ways are the most critical.

Access systems

193

Reference 76

They convey persons as well as objects; they are demanding of space and sensitive to alignment; and they are fundamental to the usefulness and quality of the locations they border on. The other channels tend to be patterned in conformity with this dominant system. Too often, indeed, even the walkways are thought of as insignificant adjuncts to the street. It is possible to consider the layout of roads and walks first and then to refine this layout by a study of the other components of circulation.

In general, circulation systems may be integrated or dispersed. That is, water may come through great aqueducts from a single metropolitan reservoir, or each house may have its own well; sewage may go to a central disposal plant or be disposed of in individual septic tanks; roads may lead from the village to its fields or be connected in a nationwide system. Today, road systems are usually integrated; storm drainage systems are usually dispersed.

There are systems in which materials, energy, or information are conveyed under some external force that is confined to the channel: the water, gas, electricity, and telephone lines. The channels are small in cross-section, continuous, flexible, flowing full, fitted with valves and subject to frequent breaks. Their pattern will usually appear as a fully interconnected network. There are systems in which materials flow by gravity, the storm and sanitary sewers in particular. These must be laid to consistent slopes; they are rigid, jointed, relatively large, flowing only partially full, and have a tree-like pattern in plan. Finally, there are the channels along which objects move by self-propulsion: the walks, roads, rails, and air lanes.

Along some lines, materials move out from a central source; along others, they go to a single terminus. In others, origin and destination are multiple. There are systems in which the moving elements are not interchangeable but must go from a particular origin to a particular destination: streets and telephone lines. Switching is then required: there is interference at the joints and capacities fall. Person movements are the most complex of all. Here we must consider the moving experience itself, as well as the fact of arrival. If only drivers were unconscious and could arrive at any address, how simple highway design would be! Finally, circulation systems must be considered not only for the way in which they handle their assigned flows but for their influence on the surrounding activity.

Despite this variety, physical circulation has certain consistent general characteristics. When the quantity of flow is more than insignificant, it must be placed in defined channels, with terminals and interchanges. These channels are organized into networks, which distribute the flows over large areas. This is true not only of roads or pipes but of footways, wires, and air lanes as well. The greater the flow, the greater the necessary definition, control, and specialization of the channel, with more elaborate terminals and interchanges. The route from origin to destination becomes more indirect. The network is more clearly separated from the region it serves, and is more difficult to live with. Superhighways are an example.

Channel networks may take one of several general forms, most frequently a uniform grid. Grids are useful where flows are shifting and broadly distributed. They are clear and easy to follow, and well suited to complex areas at large scales. The seldom encountered triangular grid produces difficult intersections but allows straight travel in three instead of two directions, and so comes closer to providing uniform access. A hexagonal or triangular grid can be used for a street system, but at a small scale it tends to produce awkward sites for development.

Grid patterns

The rectangular grid, the most commonly used street pattern, has been criticized for visual monotony, for disregard of topography, for vulnerability to through traffic, and for a lack of differentiation between the heavily traveled and lightly traveled ways, which prevents specialized design and an economical use of space and paving. These faults are not inherent in the pattern. Heavy or through traffic can be directed onto particular lines of the grid, and monotony can be avoided by varying the building and landscape pattern. The grid can be curved to fit topography. The essence of a grid system is its regularity of interconnection. It need not be composed of geometrically straight lines, nor must it enclose blocks of equal size and shape.

The grid may be further modified by controlling the flow through it. All flows may be made one-way, alternating between one line and the next parallel one. Capacities will increase, and intersections will be simplified, with most of the conflicting maneuvers eliminated. But travel requires more forethought and a lengthier journey. An extreme example of this type is the "steady-flow" system, in which movement is directed clockwise and counterclockwise around adjacent blocks so that flow in any one channel is one way but reverses its direction between each intersection. There are no direct crossings, only weaving movements, as in a rotary. The system will work for small-scale networks where flows are heavy, but it makes any continuous trip exceedingly indirect. Blocked grids are a further refinement. In order to concentrate through traffic and to allow for a differentiation of paths, occasional interruptions are made in the grid while leaving the whole pattern intact. This system will often take a swastika form.

Radial patterns

Another general form is radial, in which channels spread out from a center. This is appropriate where flows have a common origin, interchange, or destination, such as a common workplace or even a symbolic center. The radial system affords the most direct line of travel for such centrally directed flows, although at high levels of traffic the central terminus becomes difficult to handle. It does not respond easily to shifts in the central activity, nor does it work well if some flows have neither origin nor destination in the center. Rings may be added to make a radioconcentric net, which still favors central flow but allows bypassing movements as well. In its outer reaches and at a large scale this net acts like a rectangular grid. A radial system of local streets creates difficult building sites.

A modification of the radial system branches at other points than the center. This is the classic pattern—in nature as well as in design—of central distribution or collection. It allows the most direct line of travel, favors the specialization of major versus minor arteries, and makes the intersection problem manageable by distributing them. But it is especially frustrating to noncentral flow. The use of dead-end streets in residential layouts, which is a form of the branching layout, permits lightly built, safe, minor streets, but creates difficulties for emergency or delivery vehicles. Any branching system is sensitive to interruptions at single points on the main lines, whether it is a broken water main or an arterial occlusion in the human body.

Linear patterns

The linear system is the third general pattern. It may consist of a single line or a parallel series, to which all origins and destinations are directly attached. It is useful where major flows run between two points, rather than to or from a single point. In addition, since all activities are grouped along the line, subsidiary flows also have direct lines of travel. It is an economical form when the first cost of the channel is high but terminal cost is low and when there is little saving to be gained by building branches for lower

196

capacities. Since there are no intersections, frontage along the channel is used to its maximum. The linear system is used along freight railroads, canals, and trolley car lines, in pioneer agricultural areas where road cost is relatively high, and in strip development along highways. Its disadvantages are its lack of focus and the overloading of the channel because of the innumerable on-and-off movements along its length.

At the site-planning scale, this system may appear as a linear settlement or "roadtown," or may be used perforce, because of the limitations of a site lying along a topographic edge. The linear pattern may be modified by specializing the channels, some to take the through movements and others the local flows. Thus a spinal street is bordered or intersected by minor ways. Another variant connects minor loops on alternate sides of a major way, providing two continuous paths, one major and direct, the other local and sinuous.

Closing the line upon itself to form a loop improves the characteristics of flow by giving two choices of direction to each destination. A loop distribution system is generally preferable to a branching system for the distribution of electricity or water. Similarly, a minor residential street that comes off the main artery as a loop rather than a dead end is more efficient, unless the cul-de-sac is very short. The loop allows alternate exits, as well as continuous progressive movement for service circulation.

A deliberate disorder of local streets may be created to discourage through movement, to adjust to intricate topography, or to create interest. This disorder need not waste land or cause excessive street frontage. It can be justified where the ground form, rather than the streets, will convey a sense of pattern. It can be used in small areas, enclosed within a more regular layout, to give a sense of intimacy, mystery, or special character. Continued over areas of any size, the scheme becomes exasperating.

Defined channels usually have a consistent cross-section, located along a continuous center line. This center line must have a definite location in three-dimensional space, an *alignment*, which is separated for design convenience into a horizontal and a vertical component. The rigidity of normal alignment standards conflicts with the fluidity of the landscape. It takes skill to make a major road "flow" with the land, to create a harmonious joint between a tree and a telephone wire, or to grade the land smoothly between a

Alignments

Reference 49

197

driveway and a sloping garden. Alignments are detailed toward the end of the planning process, but the designer is thinking of their requirements even as he first sketches the circulation system.

Specialization of channels

A recurring issue is that of *grain*: the degree of specialization of the flow and the fineness with which these specialized types are mixed. Greater flows can be accommodated with greater safety if pedestrians and vehicles travel on their own ways. Efficiency will also increase if one sorts out trucks, bicycles, children, strollers, long-distance and local traffic, the fast and the slow. Homogeneous flow is more efficient, and the light pavements of the minor streets will save money.

But each gain in specialization is a loss in flexibility. It becomes more difficult to change from one mode of transportation to another, and paths are more indirect. The system is more complex and more difficult to change as need arises. If trucks, cars, and pedestrians are all completely separated, the system will require grade separations, and each building will have three entrances. Our superhighways have increased capacities and speeds for a particular type of flow. Should this type of circulation lose its importance, this specialized system may become a serious obstacle to a readaptation of the environment.

There are always pressures both to increase and to decrease the grain of circulation. The appropriate solution provides highly specialized traffic where the flow is intense and low specialization where the flow is small: freeways and pedestrian malls at one end and walking-driving-parking-play areas at the other. In the latter, the street maintains its ancient role as outdoor living room.

Hierarchies

One general distinction between street types is often expressed. This distinguishes the *distributors*, which have no access along their frontages and carry vehicles bound to or from distant origins and destinations, from the *access roads* along which activities front and whose traffic is restricted to vehicles associated with those particular activities. Distributors are continuous over long distances, allow high speeds, and may exclude all but vehicular traffic. Cyclists and pedestrians travel in networks orthogonal to these roads and cross them at grade separations. Access roads are short, have low speed limits, and carry cars, pedestrians and cycles along parallel alignments or even, in very intimate localities, within the same channel. This distinction is difficult to apply as a pure solution, due to diversities of mode and activity,

198

the space and expensive engineering it may require, and a certain bleak emptiness in the road landscape that this separation produces. But some hierarchy of streets is usually advisable. The conventional one begins with the *minor streets* (loops or culs-de-sac) fronted by low-intensity uses. These lead to the *collector streets* on which occur local centers, special small-scale activities, and uses of moderate density. Collectors empty into major *arterials*, built for heavy flows, with intersections at longer intervals, intensive fronting uses, and access controlled but not excluded. If any moderate-intensity use occurs on this arterial, it will front onto an intervening service road. Foot and cycle ways parallel the arterial, on their own separate tracks, and cross by means of bridges or tunnels or at controlled intersections. From the arterial one enters the *freeway*, solely devoted to cars, with no parallel walks, crossed only by totally grade-separated intersections at wide intervals, and having no fronting access.

Reference 90

Large superblocks, enclosing as much as 20 hectares (50 acres), and penetrated but not divided by minor loops and finger streets, increase the grain between the circulatory and noncirculatory zones. They improve the amenity of the living areas, at the price of frustrating through traffic. By eliminating many street intersections, they minimize the expensive street frontage per unit. They concentrate the through traffic, keeping loads light on the minor streets. Large and relatively inexpensive interior parks can be provided. If interior footways are included, pedestrians can cover substantial distances without crossing a street. At first, pedestrian and motor access was completely separated within these blocks, but experience has shown that the point of motor access is also used as the principal foot entrance to the units. It attracts most of the pedestrian flow, much of the close-to-home play of the children, and becomes the social focus. Therefore it should be linked with the main walkway system inside the superblock, while branch walks, giving access to the rear of individual units, can be dispensed with.

Superblocks

At the normal residential scale, a complete dissociation of foot and vehicular travel now seems neither necessary nor desirable, except for the traditional separation of street and its bordering sidewalks. And even this segregation may be erased where cars are strictly controlled, as in the Dutch *woonerf*. Complete separation is difficult to achieve, and sporadic separation may actually increase accidents. But major walks or cycleways that cut across long blocks, or pass through their landscaped interiors at some distance from the streets, will carry a substantial number of pedestrians and are desirable additions to the normal channels. These separate walkways must be adequately maintained, policed, and lighted. The sidewalks along the streets need not follow the road alignment slavishly but can merge and diverge in response to minor accidents of terrain, in consonance with the nature of pedestrian movement. Sidewalks, as well as being footpaths, are places for meeting and play and are an essential element of the plan.

Superblocks and dead-end streets impose a more and more circuitous path on local traffic as their size increases. If no internal cross-walks are provided, movement on foot becomes difficult. For this reason, there are commonly accepted maximums for the lengths of blocks, culs-de-sac, and loop streets. But some of the disadvantages of long dead-ends may be mitigated by interconnecting their ends by footpaths, waterline easements, or emergency service roads—in other words, by converting them into loops for special purposes. To facilitate circulation and social intercourse, there are distinct advantages in keeping block lengths short, particularly where flows are not disruptive.

Interchange and arrival

Interchanges and terminals are problems when the elements of flow are individually oriented: when a given vehicle or message must reach a particular destination. The problem becomes acute where flows are intense, channels are specialized, and single trips use a combination of modes. The delays and conflicts at the interchange become the chief losses in the system, as in the notorious terminal time of an airline trip. These difficulties may block further specialization or force the distribution and reduction of termini. Intersections and intakes are the bottlenecks of channel capacity. This is most marked where the automobile predominates, since the carrier is large in comparison with the object carried, is individually operated, and is idle much of the time. Parking can become insoluble by site planning means alone.

How best to enter a building when arriving by car is a typical puzzle. There are functional problems of deceleration, of entry and vehicle storage. There are esthetic problems of a change of scale and a danger of isolating the entrance behind a forecourt of parked cars. There must be a visual transition between velocity and repose and a clear orientation throughout. The car may have to pass the entrance before parking, after which its passengers approach the same entrance a second time on foot. Parking may be dispersed, disposed in separate levels, or threaded with activities or landscaping that invites pedestrian access.

The circulation system is the most expensive feature of site development. Operating costs should be considered together with first cost, but this is rarely done. A few general rules may be stated for reducing initial cost at least. The first rule is simply to minimize the length of channel per dwelling or other unit of activity. This requires a small number of intersections and continuous, narrow-fronted development on both sides of the line. A heavily developed, endless line is the cheapest layout, and increasing the size of blocks approximates it. The second rule of economy is to specialize, short of the point where elaborate interchanges are needed. A plan with arteries and minor streets will be less expensive than an undifferentiated grid. Third, it is usually cheaper to lay out channels so that they have gentle gradients and no more than gentle curves. Sharp curves and steep grades, but also very flat grades, all increase costs because of earthwork and drainage.

Minimizing cost

The road layout also has a decisive effect on the development potential of the land because of the shape and character of the plots that remain: the holes in the net. Other things being equal, the larger and more regular these plots and the more nearly they approximate squares with right-angled corners, the easier they are to develop. A road that runs parallel to the contours of a slope permits level foundations for the buildings fronting on it. If the cross slope is sharp, however, then access to these buildings may be labored, sewers difficult to reach, and the visual space lopsided. In this case it may be advisable to widen the right-of-way, in order to take up the cross slope within it, and to disassociate the facing buildings visually. Or it may be necessary to use separate utilities for the lower structures, or one-sided frontage or special building types on the lower side of the street, so that they can be entered at an upper story. For these reasons, contour-following roads should normally be kept back from the brow of a hill if double frontage is intended. Roads perpendicular to the contours avoid these problems, although foundations must now be stepped (a somewhat more expensive process), and street and utility gradients may become too steep. Rear lots may have awkward cross slopes, requiring substantial terracing, but it will be possible to use special step-down buildings in a dramatic way. Roads diagonal to the contours produce plots that are the most difficult to use and should be avoided

Effect on
development

except where slopes are gentle or where they are so steep that neither parallel nor perpendicular roads will serve. The negative effects of circulation must be taken into account: the noise, the pollution, the danger of accident, the actual or apparent difficulty in crossing, the ecological damage, the taking of valued space or structures. Buchanan suggests one standard for residential streets, which sets a maximum time delay that would be experienced in crossing a street by a prudent adult.

Social effects

Wherever people are moving, there are social and esthetic effects to be considered. These effects occur wherever people go, and not only when they happen to be on foot. In reaction to the horrors of American traffic, we think of persons as being unrelated to cars, which are mechanical monsters to be kept in tunnels and garages. But cars have drivers.

The path system affects communication between people. One way to encourage contacts between neighbors is to open their dwellings on a common pathway. Friendships are made along the street, and not across the park. Conversely, the plan can foster privacy, division, and isolation by providing separate or masked routes, such as apartment hallways or doors not mutually visible. As the scale of flow increases, the path becomes more difficult to cross. Entrances no longer open directly on it. It will then reverse its role and become a barrier. A crowded but slow-moving downtown street can be a central place, but an expressway is a wall. A cul-de-sac will focus a neighborhood group, and a broad planted parkway will delimit it. These effects can be inferred by going through routine movements in the imagination and noting what casual contacts would thereby arise.

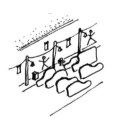

The traditional street served many functions beyond that of passage. It was market, workroom, and meeting hall. We have shouldered these functions out of the right-of-way, to the advantage of traffic and to society's loss. We improve streets by widening the auto lanes, at the expense of pedestrians, trees, and other marginal nuisances. Sidewalks are still playgrounds, however, and street corners are hangouts. Pathways should support all their functions. In very local or very specialized streets, the pedestrian can take over the pavement again, or share it with the car, wherever the latter is sufficiently tamed. Shoulders and medians are unexploited wastelands. Seeing the road and its associated uses as an opportunity for integrated development is a fairly new approach in site planning.

The public street can be a significant focus for site design. The street is a true community space, the visual foreground of any urban landscape. It is already under public control and can be changed with less disturbance to private activity. A site design for streets may be system-wide: a tree planting scheme, a lighting system, new signing, a traffic plan that imposes one-way flow or prevents through movements on local streets, the replacement of utilities underground, changes of the rules for curb-side parking, or a widening of the walkway or the planting strip. Most often, such moves are considered separate functional questions, questions of lighting standards or utility installation, or ways of moving traffic. The right-of-way becomes a flood channel, with room at the edges on which it is convenient to collect public fixtures. But the ordinary street is a basic element of the city landscape, and policies for its form and maintenance are a legitimate field of site planning. Trees, signs, lights, conditions at the curb, and the rules for traffic and parking should be considered as a whole.

The street as design focus

See Chapter 6

Minor residential streets are now receiving long overdue attention. The basic problem is one of safety from the automobile and the desire to recapture the street space for walking, talking, play, gardening, and neighborly sitting out. This must be done without denying access to the individual dwelling and without completely disrupting the general traffic circulation. Refusing entrance to the car stirs up rebellion, and so does preventing through movements over any substantial area. Such precinct plans have been successful in many places, but they impose costs on those who must bear with the added traffic which has been pushed out to the perimeter. The Dutch *woonerf* (or "living yard"), now being imitated here, is one solution to this dilemma. A small piece of local street—a block or two—is marked off. Cars may enter within that stretch, but only at very reduced speeds—8 to 15 kilometers per hour (5–10mph)—and the responsibility for any accident involving a pedestrian is automatically assigned to the driver. He must therefore move with great care, although the pedestrian is not allowed to block his passage in any deliberate or permanent way. Within the woonerf, some modest physical changes may also be made: a speed bump and sign at the entrance to remind the driver, the marking out of parking spaces allotted to residents, a few new trees, or the placement of an occasional planter or other obstacle in the pavement to force the car to take an indirect course. But the physical changes are modest. The

Reference 3

FIGURE 71
A woonerf in Delft, Holland, showing the shared street space, the planting, the unified pavement, the indirect vehicular path, and the breaks in visual continuity.

FIGURE 72
Plan of a typical Dutch woonerf. Note the strategy of locating the parking, the warning signs at the entrance, and the indirect path for vehicles.

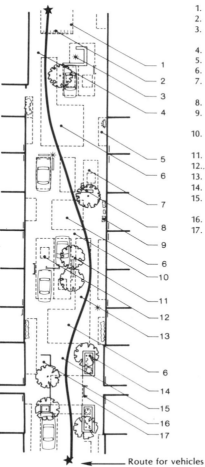

1. no continuous kerb
2. private access
3. bench around low lighting column
4. use of varied paving materials
5. private footway
6. bend in the roadway
7. empty parking lot place to sit or play in
8. bench/play object
9. on request plot with plants in front of facade
10. no continuous roadway marking on the pavement
11. tree
12. clearly marked parking lots
13. bottleneck
14. plant tub
15. space for playing from facade to facade
16. parking prevented by obstacles
17. fence for parking bicycles etc.

1
2
3
4

5
6

7

8
9

6
10

11
12

13

6

14
15
16
17

Route for vehicles

key change is in law and expectations and in the changed use of the street that ensues.

In new development, the pattern of streets or paths will provide or destroy the sense of coherence in the plan. People in motion are oriented to the forward direction, and a focusing of paths gives us the feeling of a strategic common point. A sense of association or disassociation with neighboring areas can be produced by connecting or disconnecting one local street system with another. Real estate developers are well aware of this effect and attach their roads to those of the "best" districts in their vicinity.

Pathways are the points from which the development will be seen. Therefore they have a profound effect on visual character. They should have a clear order of their own and build an image expressive of the function and nature of the site. Along them the traveler should experience a pleasant sequence of space and form (see Chapter 6). The path system is a powerful way of expressing the underlying topography, whether it runs along the contours or aggressively opposes them. Roads and paths are seen as foreshortened objects in perspective, and not as patterns from the air. Minor deviations are significant, pronounced curves will seem startlingly abrupt, and complex patterns will be incomprehensible. Pathways should seem to go to their destination, and changes in direction should appear reasonable. To do this, it may be necessary for the planner to introduce artificial obstacles or to mask a possible shortcut.

There is some conflict between the functional desirability of a continuous network and the visual pleasures of bounded space. The long straight street seems to go nowhere, and even the curving layout, though blocking the "infinite" view, becomes wearying as the endless curves pass by. Designers may resort to T-junctions on minor streets, with an important structure on the axis. This is useful where minor roads intersect an arterial, since it reduces traffic conflicts as well. Other techniques include the opening and closing of building or planting lines to make visual compartments along a continuous road and the use of abrupt direction changes, with important objects at the break to act as visual termini.

The character of the line should depend on the speed with which it will be traversed. A footpath responds nervously to minor changes in terrain; a highway takes a sweeping line. Pedestrian motion, like the flow of water, has an apparent fluid momentum. It follows the lines of least resistance, shortening distances by cutoffs. The flow may be

The moving view

Reference 4

Path character

See Figures 55, 56, 58

Reference 81

smooth or turbulent, purposeful or meandering. It can be deflected or encouraged by visual attractions, by levels, openings, and the character of the floor. A walk may be arcaded, heated, cooled, or its floors warmed to melt the snow. It can be provided with benches, plants, kiosks, cafes, display cases, or information devices. As a fine highway expresses the nature of vehicular movement, so a good walk system reflects the pleasures and characteristics of motion on foot.We incline to think that roads and utilities are regretful but necessary—things that should be hidden. Yet the flow system is one of the two basic attributes of a developed site and has much to do with its interest and meaning. Power lines and highways are components of the landscape; exposed pipes can be handsome.

Evaluation

The circulation system should be tested in every dimension. The plan is checked by mentally making routine trips and noting their nature. How does one get from the car to the house? How do children walk to school or adults to the bus? How does one reach a building for repair? Can one ride a bicycle safely? Can an efficient set of bus routes be laid out? Can the channels carry the flow desired, given the predicted distribution by mode? Are the interchanges and terminals workable? What damages are imposed on the surroundings? The social consequences of the path system are analyzed, as well as its visual impact—the views of and from the road.

Finally, judge the circulation system as a whole. Will it seem orderly and well oriented to someone on the ground? Does it provide for a balance of the diverse modes of movement? Is its structure coherent with the structure of use and in balance with the intensity of activity? Will it help to express site and function? Does it connect with the surrounding systems?

The circulation system is exposed to technological change and therefore must be adaptable. If a self-contained water and sewage purification cycle becomes economically feasible for the individual unit, then it may become unnecessary to tie a building to an underground water and sewage system. If future land vehicles will hover over the ground on compressed air rather than rolling on wheels, then road characteristics will be revised. If urban areas are roofed with vast spans, then surface drainage loses its significance. If we develop a good dispersed transit system, we can shake off our dependence on the automobile. When we learn how to move large numbers of people in three-dimensional conveyor

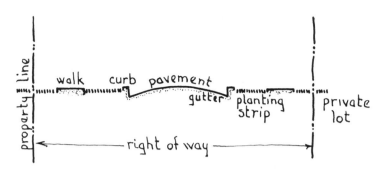

FIGURE 73
*The elements of
the normal street
cross-section.*

systems, then central districts will be transformed. Video-phones and dispersed computer terminals may change commuting habits. Certainly there will be less radical innovations that will modify the design of circulation. Thus general considerations such as pattern, balance, diversity, and social and visual impact should have more weight than precise technical standards.

Vehicular ways are usually laid out with a cross-section that remains fixed for substantial distances, and is located by the center line of the pavement. The principal features of that common cross-section, not drawn to scale, are shown in Figure 73. Many other cross-sections are possible, each with its own implications. The dimensions of the cross-section are controlled by the regulations of local governments, often with unnecessary rigidity.

The pavement itself is usually crowned at the center for drainage, the cross-sectional slope being 1:50 from crown to edge for concrete and bituminous pavements, and 1:25 for earth and gravel roads. Pavements sloping all to one side are used when a height differential between opposing curbs is allowable, as when there is a median strip. Where heavy rain or freezing is not likely, the pavement may be sloped to its center line, using the street itself as the drainage channel. Both schemes save on the length of storm drains. A 150 mm (6 in) vertical curb and gutter is used on major streets, while a 100 mm roll (4 in) curb, which allows driveways at any point, may be used in rural areas or on low density residential streets. A vertical curb should never exceed 200 mm (8 in), or it will cause difficulties for the elderly. The curb must be ramped down to the street pavement at each crossing to allow the handicapped to negotiate it. A simple turf or gravel shoulder, without a curb, flanked by a shallow

Street cross-sections

Reference 49

207

ditch about 1 m (3 ft) wide and probably sodded, can be used at very low densities. The ditch allows surface water to seep back into the ground but requires a culvert under every driveway and at each intersection. This may be more expensive than a curb, which converts the street into the drainage channel. The curb also prevents breakdown of the pavement edge.

Depending on traffic, the pavement may be concrete, bituminous macadam, gravel, stabilized soil, or simply a graded and drained earth surface. We seem to have forgotten the technique of building an earth or gravel road, which, if dusty, is quite suitable for light traffic if crown and ditches are maintained. In the simplest case, the topsoil is stripped off, the soil underneath is compacted and graded to drain, and gravel is added, or the soil is stabilized by adding small amounts of portland cement or hydrated lime. A workable sand-clay road can be made by adjusting the soil to the approximate proportion of 10% clay, 15% silt, and 75% sand. Temporary, expedient roads may also be built of corduroy (logs and brush), of planks, or even of wire mesh and burlap.

Road width is computed by summing up the traffic and parking lanes required. Curbside parking, if provided, should be 2.5 m (8 ft) wide. Each traffic lane should be 3 m (10 ft) wide on minor roads, and up to 3.5 m (12 ft) wide on highways. Minimum vertical clearance is now 4.25 m, (14 ft) to allow for the passage of trucks with high loads. A practical minimum pavement width for minor residential streets with light parking is one parking lane plus two traffic lanes, or 8 m (26 ft). If parking will never occur or will only be sporadic because of very low densities, this minimum pavement may drop to 6 m (20 ft) for a two-way minor road. On a one-way street with parking only on one side, the pavement may be 5.5 m (18 ft). Such a street might be used as a short loop or as a marginal access road alongside a major thoroughfare.

The purpose of the planting strip is to separate the walk from the street, to allow room for utilities and street fixtures above and below ground, to provide for piling snow, and to permit the planting of street trees (although this usually places them too close to the moving traffic). The strip should be at least 2 m (6 ft) wide if it contains trees, or 1 m (3 ft) wide for grass alone. If paved and used only for utilities, it may be reduced to 0.6 m (2 ft). In commercial areas it is sometimes eliminated, and poles and hydrants are placed in the widened sidewalk. In any case, street poles should be set 0.6 m (2 ft) back from the curb for safety. On important roads, the opposing traffic lanes may be separated by another planting strip or median, for reasons of safety, the channelizing of intersection maneuvers, the management of steep cross slopes, or visual amenity.

The private property line is set only a nominal distance beyond the edge of the walk, unless this is the location for public planting. Indeed, street trees are perhaps best planted here, or in private front lots, rather than in the street-side planting strip. This prevents branches from interfering with overhead poles, lights, and wires, keeps roots from disrupting the pipes and cables underground, and protects the tree from all the chemical poisons used in road maintenance.

Sidewalks should have a minimum width of 1 m (3 ft), which allows three persons to pass or walk abreast, although where they lead directly to the entrance of a single dwelling they may be only 0.8 m (2.5 ft) wide. Collector walks handling numbers of pedestrians must at least be 2 m (6 ft) wide. In central areas, where large pedestrian flows are expected, sidewalks must be sized to demand, just as roads are. Walks, like street pavements, should be crowned, or have a 1:50 cross slope. They are normally, and rather monotonously, made of concrete or asphalt, but gravel, brick, or stone may also be used, or the concrete may be textured, colored, or laid in patterns. In low-density residential areas, walks may occur on only one side of the street. The major walk system may be designed to be independent of the road system, passing under principal streets in subways approached by easy grades. But there must be a walk on at least one side of all streets, except very short local streets, service drives, or roads in rural or semirural areas with no substantial fronting development. People persist in walking along the road. Walks are useful for children's play and quite necessary where snow is frequent. In high-density areas they cannot be skimped but must be wide enough to accommodate all the movement and social activity that will take place on them.

Walks and pedestrian spaces should be analyzed for capacity. When there is more than 1.2 sq m (12 sq ft) per person, space for standing is unimpeded, and it is easy to move about. This is a desirable standard for spaces that will accommodate crowds. Below this point, circulation is somewhat impeded, and people must resort to polite warnings or touches to move about. Below 0.65 sq m (7 sq ft) per person, standing becomes constrained: only limited internal

Sidewalks and pedestrian flow

Reference 72

209

circulation is possible, and people move as a group rather than as individuals. This is the tolerable minimum for crowd spaces. At 0.3 sq m (3 sq ft) per person, there is no internal circulation, and people are forced into physical contact with each other, an unpleasant situation in this culture and dangerous if a panic occurs. It is, however, physically possible to pack people into spaces of even less than 0.15 sq m (1.5 sq ft) per person.

The capacity of walkways is summarized in Table 2. Since average speeds vary from over 90 m (300 ft) per minute (a brisk walk) in open flow to less than 45 m (150 ft) per minute (a shuffle) at maximum rates of flow, the total walkway space occupied by a single pedestrian in the examples given can vary from over 55 sq m (600 sq ft) in open flow to less than 0.5 sq m (5 sq ft) in a jam (that is, in the condition of "constrained standing"). Twenty persons per minute per m of walk width (6 per min per ft) may be taken as the desirable maximum rate of flow.

Pedestrian flow usually comes in pulses, or "platoons," as crowds are intermittently released or interrupted and as slower walkers impede more rapid ones. This effect is more noticeable where flows are moderate rather than where they are heavy or very light. Rates of flow will also vary throughout the day, when employees pour in and out of an area at the rush hours, or when shoppers and lunchers frequent the

TABLE 2. CAPACITY OF WALKWAYS

Quality of Flow	Rate of flow (persons per minute per meter of walkway width)
Completely open	under 1.5
Unimpeded: free movement; walking groups are maintained easily	1.5–7
Impeded: groups must shift and reform; much maneuvering but few conflicts	7–20
Constrained: groups cannot be maintained; cross flows cause conflicts	20–35
Moderately congested: touching necessary; frequent conflicts throughout the stream	35–45
Heavily congested: even slowest walkers are obstructed	45–60
Jammed: enforced mass movement or a standstill	0–85

stores and restaurants at midday. Flows can be calculated from direct observation or from assumed relations between the quantity of residents, employees, or shoppers and the quantity of floor space provided. In midtown Manhattan, for example, 300 sq m (3000 sq ft) of residential floor space attracts 6 in-and-out trips per day, the same amount of office space 14 trips, and of department store space, 300 trips.

Two-directional flow on a sidewalk is not much less efficient than one-way flow, since pedestrians adjust themselves into nonconflicting streams. This is not true, however, when there is a small reverse flow opposing a major stream. When the reverse flow is only 10 percent of total flow, for example, total walkway capacity may be reduced by 15 percent.

Public stairways, under normal and easy conditions, do not average more than 7 persons per minute per m (7 per min per ft) of width. This rate may rise to a maximum of 16 persons per minute per m (5 per min per ft) when a crowded stair is fed by a permanent queue and there is no passing or any reverse flow. Escalators do not increase the rate of flow moving up stairs; they simply reduce the effort of mounting. To maintain access for the handicapped, public stairs and escalators must be supplemented by ramps or elevators. Wherever the flow exceeds 7 persons per minute per m, bunching at the head or foot of stairs and escalators will occur, and reservoir space must be provided for this.

Similarly, reservoir space should be provided where pedestrians wait at street crossings, especially when the flow of the feeding sidewalks is more than the same 7 persons per minute per m. Crosswalks should be *wider* than the incoming sidewalks, since two pedestrian streams will meet head on. And when adjacent walk flows rise to 20 or 35 persons per minute per m (6 or 10 per min per ft), grade intersections will be chaotic, with people waiting in the street or crossing against the lights.

Travel by bicycle has the advantages of quietness, economy, no pollution, good exercise, and easy parking. At the same time, it is easy to steal a parked bicycle, and the accident rate is very high when cyclists are mixed with automobile traffic. Ideally, cycles are never mixed with cars or with pedestrians except at very low volumes. As a minimum, separate cycleways are necessary wherever the flow of cyclists is likely to exceed 1500 per day, or where heavy peaks are expected, as at industrial plants or schools. In tight circumstances, but only where curbside auto parking is prohibited, cycle lanes may be reserved at the edge of the street.

Cycleways

Cycleways are normally built of light pavements 3.5 m (12 ft) wide, with curving alignments and easy grades. They should be grade separated from heavy motor traffic or their crossings controlled with signals, since to merge cycleways back into major traffic may actually cause a heavier accident rate than to have no cycleways at all.

Mopeds, electric carts, and other low-powered, low-speed vehicles can run in lanes at the edge of the road where traffic is light. They may be allowed in the cycleways, but separation is better. Very slow public service carts can at times be operated on major footways. In general, however, mopeds should have their own lanes or be classed as powered vehicles, while cycles are classed with pedestrians.

Although standard cross-sections are commonly used for roads of similar type, and simply applied to the changing ground surface as if a rigid template had been trundled along the center line, it makes much more sense to adapt the cross-section to the context. Walks may move to and away from the curb; road lanes may separate to save some landscape feature or change elevation with a dividing strip between them; cut-and-fill slopes may match the flow of the terrain; trees may be planted in groves. Such adaptations mean added design and supervision but contribute to appearance and usefulness and often decrease construction costs as well.

The right-of-way is the total public strip of land within which there is public control and common right of passage and within which all pavements and utility lines are located if possible. Its width depends on the features included within it. The minimum is commonly given as 15 m (50 ft), but this width can actually be reduced on minor streets to as little as 9 m (30 ft). This makes for a more economical and flexible plan, particularly in rough ground, and improves the visual scale. Where the future traffic load is uncertain, it may be necessary to use a wider right-of-way, while beginning with a relatively narrow pavement. At the other extreme, a major freeway may use a right-of-way that is 180 m (600 ft) wide.

Horizontal alignment

Reference 49

The horizontal alignment of the road is based on the pavement center line, which is marked off in 30 m (100 ft) "stations" for reference, beginning at some arbitrary end of the system. A separate numbering system is used for each single continuous line. All significant points, such as the intersections of one center line with another, or the beginning and ending of horizontal and vertical curves, are located by reference to this numbering system. The horizontal alignment

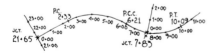

of the center line is made up of two elements, normally used one after the other: straight lines, called "tangents," and portions of circular curves, to which those straight lines are tangent. If two curves are directly joined without an intervening straight line, both curves are made tangent to the same imaginary line at their junction. On minor streets, two tangents may be joined without an intervening horizontal curve, where the angle of intersection is less than 15 degrees. This may also be done at much sharper turns, where it is obvious to the driver that he must slow or stop before negotiating the turn, as at a street corner.

Tangents and circular curves are used for ease of layout and so that curves, once entered, can be negotiated with one setting of the steering wheel. On major roads, the joint between tangent and circular curve may be softened by a "spiral" curve, whose radius begins by being infinitely long (and so is a straight line) and then progressively decreases until it reaches the radius of the circular curve that it is introducing. These spiral curves of transition are rarely used on minor roads and will not be treated here.

The circular curve has the elements shown in Figure 74. The sharper the curve, the shorter is its radius. The minimum allowable radius of a curve depends on "design speed," that is, on the maximum safe speed that can be continuously maintained on that piece of road. See Table 3. It is preferable to avoid two curves in the same direction, separated by a tangent less than 60 m (200 ft) long (a "broken back" curve). It looks awkward and is hard to drive through. Similarly, it is best to avoid two sharp curves in opposite directions, separated by a tangent of less than 30 m (100

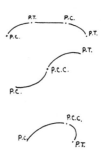

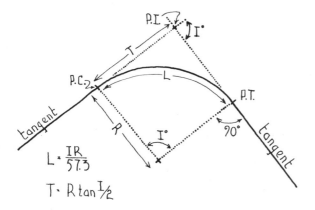

$$L = \frac{IR}{57.3}$$

$$T = R \tan \tfrac{I}{2}$$

FIGURE 74
The elements of the circular curve used in constructing a horizontal alignment.

213

ft). Gentle reverse curves may be directly joined without a tangent, however. Two curves of the same direction but of different radius that are directly joined together ("compound" curves) should be avoided where possible but are occasionally necessary.

Intersections

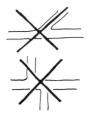

Street intersections should be within 20 degrees of the perpendicular for 30 m (100 ft) each way from the intersection. Intersections of acute angle are difficult to negotiate and make it difficult to see an approaching car. Where a minor road crosses a major one, an offset of about 50 m decreases the chance of accidents, since conflicting maneuvers are separated. But a slight offset increases the danger, while a long one frustrates crossing traffic. Direct crossings are clear but should be designed with channels or with signal lights. Similarly, between two minor roads, where the in-direction imposed on either flow is not important, the T intersection may be preferable to the straight cross, not only for reasons of safety but also for closure of the visual space. Successive intersections with an arterial road should be no closer than 250 m apart to prevent disruption to the major flow. On freeways, intersections will be limited to 1500 or 1000 m (5000 or 3000 ft) intervals. The curb at corners should have a radius of 3.5 m (12 ft) for minor streets, or 15 m (50 ft) at intersections of major streets to allow easy turns.

When traffic flow is heavy, the critical limit to capacity is the intersection. Even where total volume through an intersection is as low as 500 cars per hour in all directions, up to 50 percent of the approaching cars may have to stop before going through or turning. Such an intersection, or any one handling higher loads, will require some treatment. The simplest is a stop sign on the secondary street. From there, the designer may go on to traffic signals, channelization, or grade separation. The design and analysis of high-capacity roads and intersections is a matter for traffic engineers, but the site planner must have some sense of the problems involved. Intersection design is briefly treated in Appendix J.

See Table 3

Minimum forward sight distance must be maintained at all points on the line to give drivers ample time to react to dangers appearing in the road. It can be scaled from the plans and should take account of buildings, hills, landscaping, and other blocks to vision. The minimum value depends on the design speed. A driver 20 m (65 ft) from an intersection should see the entire intersection plus 20 m of the intersecting street on each side. Houses should be located so that car

214

headlights will not shine into ground floor windows and so that there will be no danger of any house being struck by cars out of control. This argues against axial positions at sharp curves, especially at the foot of slopes.

Lengths and endings

The maximum total length of a loop drive is usually given as about 500 m (1600 ft) and that of a cul-de-sac as perhaps 150 m (500 ft). The maximum allowable block length might be put at 500 m (1600 ft). All of these standards are based on the same reasoning: as block, loop, and cul-de-sac length increase, general circulation becomes more indirect, service deliveries longer, and emergency access more liable to misdirection. These rules are commonly held to be reasonable. Not all site planners agree to them. The rules would not apply where through circulation is already blocked for other reasons, as on a narrow peninsula, ridge, or pocket of land.

A minimum turnaround at the end of a cul-de-sac should have a 12 m (40 ft) outside radius free of parking so that vehicles such as fire engines can negotiate it. This requires a large circular right-of-way and may defeat the economic and visual purposes of small culs-de-sac. A T-shaped terminus or shunt is an alternative way of providing for backing turns on very short dead ends, but the backing of a vehicle always includes the possibility of overrunning a small child who is out of sight. The wings of the shunt should be at least a car's length deep on each side, exclusive of the width of the street, and at least 3 m wide exclusive of parking. The inside curb should have a 6 m radius. As long as these turning requirements are provided for, free of obstacles, a small short residential cul-de-sac need not adhere rigidly to these shapes. A freely formed parking and arrival court may be quite desirable.

Individual driveways should be 2.5 m (8 ft) wide, the curb at the entrance being rounded off with a radius of 1 m (3 ft). Driveway entrances should be at least 15 m (50 ft) from any street intersection, to prevent confusion with the turning movements there. Separate driveways and entrance walks should be provided for each dwelling unit unless they are made common to large numbers of units. Walks and drives that jointly serve only two or three units are potential sources of friction over who should maintain them.

For carrying convenience, the distance from the street to the door of a dwelling unit should not be too long or include a steep grade. This maximum distance is in dispute: some would restrict it to 15 m (50 ft); others would relax it to 100 m (300 ft). The number has an important effect on cost and on layout. It depends on the way of life: in North America, this maximum distance is shrinking. In countries where walking is customary, the distance could be substantially longer.

Parking

Reference 17

Parking may be provided in various ways: on the street (which is convenient but expensive and disturbing to moving traffic), in small parking bays, in large parking lots (which is the cheapest method but may be inconvenient or unsightly), underground, or in ramp structures or garages (the most expensive ways of all). Parking lots can be laid out if the following dimensions are kept in mind: each stall for the full-grown juggernaut should be 6 m (20 ft) long and 2.5 m (8 ft) wide, or even 2.75 m (9 ft) wide to give a sense of ample room. Stalls reserved for the handicapped should be 4 m (13 ft) wide to allow the use of a wheel chair. But those set aside for the increasingly common small car can be reduced to 2.5 x 5 m (8 x 16 ft).

Stalls may be parallel, perpendicular, or at 30-, 45-, or 60-degree angles to the moving lane. Angled parking requires one-way traffic flow, which may be confusing. Aisle widths range from 3.5 (12 ft) m for one-way lanes serving 30-degree and 45-degree parking, to 6 m (20 ft) for two-way lanes serving perpendicular parking. For efficiency, there should be stalls on each side of each moving lane. Herringbone dividers placed between the inner ends of angle stalls will save further space. Dividers and curbs hamper snow removal and future rearrangements of the lot, however. The perpendicular layout is the most efficient and 30-degree angle parking the least. As a rough guide, overall space requirements of large and efficient lots run from 23 sq.m (250 sq ft) per car for attendant-parked lots in which cars are stored three or four deep, to 37 sq m (400 sq ft) per car for generous self-parking. The maximum allowable slope in any direction across the lot is 5 percent and the minimum 1 percent.

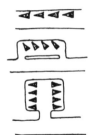

The circulation within large lots should be continuous, with dispersed exits and a minimum of turns. Lot entrances should be at least 4 m wide if one way. Thought should be given to the movement of pedestrians to and from the cars. If they are to walk down the aisles, then the aisles should run in the desired direction. A raised and planted strip between the ranks of vehicles makes a more pleasant path, but it requires space and fixes the lot pattern. Tree planting will improve the climate and look of a parking lot, but trees require substantial room for root feeding. Lots may be screened with walls or planting or sunken a few feet to allow vision over them. For convenience, visual scale, and individual control over the car, it is preferable in residential areas not to allow parking in groups of over six to ten cars. Even in large lots serving commercial areas, it is desirable to keep the cars within 200 m of their destinations unless special transportation is provided.

Large tractor-trailer trucks are about 15 by 2.5 m (50 by 8 ft). They require a minimum outside turning radius of 18 m (60 ft) and a vertical clearance of 4.25 m (14 ft). Curb radii at street corners must be 9 to 12 m (30 to 40 ft) where such trucks are common. Loading docks for trucks should be 3 m (10 ft) wide per truck, set at truck-bed height—about 1.2 m (4 ft) off the pavement—and arranged so that, when backing, the trailer swings clear of the driver's line of vision. A 15 m (50 ft) parking and maneuvering apron is needed in front of the dock. A general rule is that the floor of a loading dock should be about twice the floor area of the beds of all the trucks that could be brought up to the dock at one time: this allows room for unloading and temporary stacking.

Trucks

The capacity of a road depends on the characteristics of the road—its width, surface, alignment, and conditions at the edge— and the characteristics of the traffic—vehicle type, speed, control, and driver skill. The theoretical capacity of one lane of traffic is 2000 cars per hour where this flow is completely steady, uninterrupted, and at optimum speed and spacing. It might be approximated by an organized convoy moving on an ideal pavement. In practice, a multi-lane freeway may carry up to 1500 or even 1800 cars per hour per lane, while a congested street with frequent side friction due to cars parking and entering may carry only 200 to 300 cars per hour, on the outside lane. A local residential street will carry about 400 to 500 cars per hour per lane. Four lanes in each direction seems to be the widest road that one can drive on without loss of sanity. Expected local street volumes in suburban areas may be roughly estimated by assuming that each dwelling will generate about seven one-way vehicular trips per day or one or two per peak hour. Larger, denser, or more complex areas require more careful traffic assignment studies.

Capacities

Reference 41

The vertical alignment of a road is also made up of straight tangents—constant upgrades or downgrades— joined by vertical curves. These vertical curves are parabolic rather than circular. Parabolic curves are used because they

Vertical alignment

are easy to set out in the field, and they make a smooth transition between intersecting grades. The grade of a tangent is expressed in percentage, or the meters of rise and fall per 100 meters of horizontal run. By convention, grades are given as positive percentages when they go uphill in the direction of increasing numbers in the stationing, and negative when downhill. This vertical alignment is conventionally shown on a series of *profiles*, or continuous sections of the center line of a stretch of road, drawn to an exaggerated vertical scale, and flattened out on the plane of the drawing, as if the center line were straight in plan.

The minimum grade of a tangent that allows water to drain off the road is 0.5 percent. In special cases, the pavement may be laid dead flat, but if possible the street profile should have positive drainage throughout. That is, there should be no sag curves or any downhill loop or dead-end streets that occur at points from which the adjacent land does not slope away.

Maximum grades

The maximum grade of a street depends on its design speed. See Table 3. Maximum grades should not be long sustained. A passenger car cannot stay in high gear if the grade is continuously above 7 percent, while a large truck must shift down on sustained grades of over 3 percent. A 17 percent sustained grade is the most that a large truck can climb in lowest gear. Maximum grades are somewhat flexible, depending on winter conditions and local custom. Where icing is severe, anything over 10 percent may be too steep, while in San Francisco regulations allow grades up to 15 percent on minor streets.

The grade of a sidewalk should not be over 10 percent, or less if icing is frequent. Short ramps at breaks in grade may go up to 15 percent, however. If steps are used, there must be at least three risers, so that they will be noticed and not cause accidental falls. The steps should be designed to prevent bypassing. In a stepped ramp, there is a single riser to each long, gently sloping tread (5 to 8 percent). The ramping tread is made long enough to require an odd number of paces to traverse it (so that steps are not always taken on the same foot). Since a normal pace is about 0.75 m (2.5 ft), preferable tread depths are therefore one, three or five times that distance. The size of the normal pace should also be remembered in placing stepping-stones. A useful general rule for proportioning conventional exterior steps is that the height of two risers added to the depth of one tread should equal 700 mm. Riser height may vary between 165 mm as a maximum and 75 mm as a minimum. Stairs in heavy public use should never rise above a gradient of 50 percent. Ramps for the handicapped should not exceed 8 percent.

The parabolic vertical curve has the elements shown in Figure 75. This curve drops below the original tangent line in proportion to the square of its distance from the point of curvature, but it can easily be laid out graphically with sufficient accuracy for residential work. Choose the length L, locate the PC and PT so that they are equidistant horizontally from the PI, and draw the chord. The intermediate point of the parabolic curve is then halfway, vertically, between the chord and the PI. The PC, the intermediate point, and the PT are three points on the required parabola, which can be drawn freehand, or with a French curve.

The required length of the vertical curve is controlled by the need to maintain adequate sight distance, and by "roadability," or the avoidance of an unpleasant jolt caused by an excessive acceleration or deceleration of vertical velocity. For roadability, a vertical curve is required wherever the algebraic difference in grade is 2 percent or more. (In Figure 75, the algebraic difference between the intersecting tangents would be x% − (− y%), or x plus y%.) The minimum length of the curve depends on design speed and that difference. See Table 3 for how this required length varies. If, for example, the intersecting gradients were plus 5 percent and minus 8 percent, and the design speed was 60 km per hour (at which speed Table 3 requires 9 m of curve for each 1% change in grade), then the required curve length would

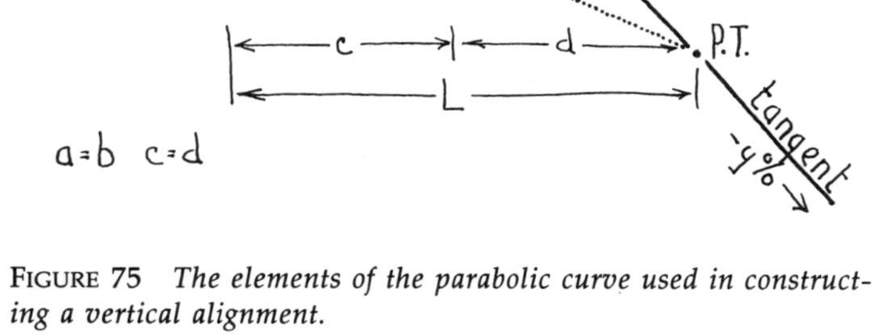

FIGURE 75   *The elements of the parabolic curve used in constructing a vertical alignment.*

be: 9(5 + 8) = 117 m. Vertical curves may be dispensed with in individual driveways, except that the long modern car will strike the road in passing a break in grade greater than a difference of 9 percent. Therefore, vertical curves must be inserted in any driveway where such break occurs, using a curve at least 0.3 m (1 ft) long for each 1 percent of algebraic difference in grade.

Minimum forward sight distance must be maintained throughout the vertical as well as the horizontal alignment. This is computed as being vision from a point 1.2 m (4 ft) above the road to a point 10 mm (4 in) above the road, and may be scaled from the profiles. It depends on design speed and is given in Table 3. Sight distance may sometimes require longer vertical curves at summits than are needed for road-ability alone. In sag curves, the resulting length of headlight beam must also be checked to see that it is equal to the minimum sight distance.

Profiles should be flattened at street intersections so that halted vehicles need not hang on their brakes and can start easily. There should be a "platform" of not over 4 percent grade extending at least 12 m (40 ft) each way from the intersection. This often causes difficulty where many cross streets intersect a street on a steep gradient. This rule must sometimes be sacrificed.

Alignment
standards

Table 3 indicates the variations in alignment standards according to design speed. An appropriate design speed for minor residential streets is 30 or 40 km (20 or 25 miles) per hour. Major streets would be designed for 60 km (40 miles) per hour and highways for 90 km (55 miles). Maximum grades at the slowest speeds may be increased somewhat where ice and snow are infrequent, but these grades should not be continuous for long stretches.

Horizontal and vertical alignment must be considered together, since what is being planned is actually the locus of a center line in three-dimensional space. The perspective view of that center line is an important visual feature of the landscape: it is markedly different from the road alignment as it appears in plan. Small dips and bumps look awkward, especially when they are clearly visible, as when a long flat curve or a long grade is seen from the side. Some shapes give the sense of discontinuity or twisting: a dip just before a curve, a dip in the tangent within a broken-back curve, a horizontal curve that begins in a dip, or a bridge that is skewed to the road or whose deck does not fit smoothly into the vertical alignment. There are also handsome com-

TABLE 3. ALIGNMENT STANDARDS IN RELATION TO DESIGN SPEED

Design Speed (km/h)	Minimum radius of horizontal curves (m)	Minimum length of vertical curve for each 1% change of grade (m)	Minimum forward sight distance (m)	Maximum percent of grade
20	25	2.75	40	12
30	30	3	45	12
40	50	5	55	11
50	80	6.5	65	10
60	120	9	75	9
70	170	15	95	8
80	230	22	115	7
90	290	30	135	6
100	370	45	160	5
110	460	60	180	4

binations, as for example when vertical and horizontal curves coincide, or when the approach alignment is arranged to display a fine bridge from the side. It is a good general rule to avoid the partial overlapping of horizontal and vertical curves, or at least to make sure that no visual distortion results from that overlap. It is often useful to construct a simple string or cardboard model of the road center line, to analyze its appearance directly.

For reasons of safety, sharp horizontal curves should be avoided on high summits, in deep cuts, or at the foot of steep grades. The change in direction in a reverse curve should not occur when going over a summit. Where a horizontal curve occurs on a grade of over 5 percent, the maximum allowable percent of grade on the curve should be reduced by 0.5 percent for each 15 m that the curve radius is less than 150 m (500 ft).

Chapter **8**

Earthwork and Utilities

Site construction involves many physical features that later sink beneath our notice—pavements, curbs, foundations, grading, sewer pipes, power lines—all those technical underpinnings economists dignify with the name of "infrastructure." We are astonished at their cost and at the chaos that accompanies their installation on the site. But their absence, or their faulty design, will remind us of them. They are the central concerns of site construction, and their specification is the meat of the working drawings.

Construction begins with the accurate location of the property boundary and of the area within which construction is to occur. The topsoil is stripped off this working area and stored in heaps—from which it will in the end be respread over the new-shaped ground. The principal structures (roads, buildings, underground utilities) are then precisely located on the ground. Foundations are laid and pipes trenched in. When the major structures are complete, or nearly so, the exposed subsoil is graded by machines to its new shape, following the indications of frequent grade stakes marked with the required new levels. The road base and surfacing are installed, and then the above-ground features such as light poles and hydrants. Last, the topsoil is replaced and new plant materials put in. This normal sequence will often be modified, however. For example, when new grades are very different from the old, grading must precede the erection of buildings.

To control this construction process, the builder is given a sheaf of technical documents. These include a precisely dimensioned layout of the roads and buildings in plan, sufficient to locate them exactly on the ground; a profile of each road or other critical linear feature, such as a large sewer main, to set its vertical elevation throughout its course; a grading plan which shows the new shape of the ground by means of contours and exact spot elevations at critical points; a plan layout of all utilities, with an indication of their sizes and their elevations at controlling points; a landscaping plan showing the quantity, species, and location of all planted material; a series of detailed drawings of such items as manholes, inlets, curbs, seats, lights, and walls; and finally a set of written specifications which controls the quality and installation of all elements.

These documents are normally developed out of the schematic site plan in something like the following order: first, a precise plan layout of structures and roadways is made, which reduces street alignments to exact curves and tangents and specifies the geometry and location of buildings and property lines. Then the road profiles are constructed— a succession of straight grades and vertical curves lying over a plot of the existing ground. The spot elevations of critical points, such as the floor levels of buildings or the ground levels necessary to save existing trees, are then determined. From this, and following the form envisioned in the schematics, the grading plan is constructed, which, as a minimum, makes a smooth transition between the road profiles and the critical spot elevations. Then the utilities are laid out, beginning with the storm drainage, which is the one most likely to have a significant influence on the plan. The landscaping plan is prepared, again following the ideas of the schematic design. Plant lists and quantities are drawn up. Finally, detailed drawings of special objects are made, and the construction specifications are written. Much of this design development in the future will be accomplished by computer.

Put so simply, this sequence is of course misleading. Working details are not just the mechanical consequence of a design idea. Grading, profiles, road layouts, landscaping, and details are being considered and developed even as the schematic plan develops, and they influence and are influenced by that basic design. Even within the process of final technical development, the consequences of a later step cause the designer to reconsider preceding steps. A problem of sewer flow requires the readjustment of a road profile, which in turn affects the grading plan, a house location, and the landscaping. As always, it is easier to explain the details of a design process as though its elements were orderly, linear, and separable. Once in command of those elements, however, one carries them forward in a looping, iterative game.

This chapter explains the considerations that govern the grading plan, the precise street layout and profiles, and the location of utilities. Along with the landscaping plan, discussed in Chapter 6, these are the technical bedrock of site design.

All site development requires a remodeling of the earth's surface, and sometimes it calls for a very large disturbance. The remodeling is specified by the grading plan, which comes to be the key technical document in site planning. Grading has a strong influence on cost, utility, and appearance of the completed project. Changes in earth-moving technology have been more striking than in any other aspect of site construction.

To control the grading operation, grade stakes showing the required new levels are set at intervals in the subsoil. They are set out at the critical points, such as peaks, changes in grade, outlets, culverts, roads, and buildings, as well as at regular intevals in any featureless ground. Stakes also indicate the lines along which the areas of cut and fill merge back into the existing grade or into each other. Machines then cut or fill the ground to the staked levels and shape it into a smooth curve between the stakes. Allowance is made for the depth of topsoil that will be replaced and for the expected settlement of the fill.

Material cut out of the ground fluffs up as it is being handled in a loose state and then recompacts as it is replaced in fill. The final ratio between the volume of earth before it is cut out and after it is filled in varies according to the material and the method of handling. This ratio must be known when earthwork volumes are calculated. If the soil is not compacted after the fill is in place, the volume of fill may exceed the cut from which it came by 15 or even 25%. If it is compacted well, there may be 10% less fill than cut, or even less if many roots, stones, and other debris must be taken out of it. In normal work, it is customary to make the preliminary assumption that the filled material will be 5% less in volume than it was before being cut. This is only a first guess.

Earthwork

References 49, 77, 94

225

The degree of compaction is partly controllable and ideally produces a soil dense enough so that it will not settle after the occupation of the site, yet loose enough so that internal drainage is not destroyed. In areas in which settlement of the ground will not be critical, the fill can be dumped as it comes, from various sources. When settlement must be controlled, the composition of the fill will be selected, its moisture content will be set so there is just enough to allow the soil grains to slide into stable positions at the right density, and the fill will be pressed down by rollers or loaded vehicles that run over it a specified number of times. Where greater stability is required, the fill will be placed in thin layers, each of which is independently moistened and compacted. On the contrary, particularly in areas to be replanted, the subsoil may have inadvertently been compacted too much by the movement of heavy machinery over it so that it will form an impervious layer under a waterlogged topsoil. In that case, it is necessary to break up the top layers of the regraded subsoil by plowing and harrowing before the topsoil is respread. The stable balance of the original soil system is difficult to regain.

Other disturbances appear during the grading process. Topsoil and subsoil may be mixed together, and thus valuable organic material is lost. Even when the topsoil is saved, as it should be, the natural soil profile is a continuous gradation down to the bedrock, and the overturning and mixing of the subsoil usually means that the biological performance of the new surface will be impaired. In addition, surface erosion will affect newly graded ground stripped of vegetation, even on 2% slopes after a light rain. This results in a loss of soil and the pollution of downstream rivers and ponds. Heavy silting in the lower watershed is a common accompaniment to large-scale development. All newly graded areas should be dammed at their lower edges by temporary berms (low banks) of earth, sufficiently high to impound the local runoff for the time required for the soil particles to settle out. The impounded water seeps through the berm or runs out through small pipes, which act as weep holes. Berms are removed when site construction is complete and the ground cover reestablished. Another remedy is to schedule grading so that it does not remain unfinished but is quickly followed by replanting. Spraying new ground with water, seed, and liquid fertilizer is one technique. Nevertheless, construction sites are notorious for their mud, dust, and polluted outwash.

Despite these difficulties, earth-moving technology offers many compensations. The power that can be applied to moving ground is now so large that hills can be regraded, solid rock cut out, large lenses of soil removed or imported, hard infertile soil pulverized and made productive. It becomes economical to terrace the Santa Monica mountains for small houses, to make smooth new land in Michigan for cherry orchards, or to throw up artificial hills for recreation in Detroit from the spoil of highway cuttings. The results may be good or bad; at least they are startling.

Earth-moving machines

Earth is moved by a large variety of machines, and the designer should know something of their capabilities. The tracked bulldozer can push the earth ahead of it with a heavy blade that can be raised, lowered, or tilted. It is the most versatile of the earth machines. It is particularly good for making banks, plateaus, and extensive irregular surfaces but is used wherever a pushing or pulling force is needed— including the felling of trees, the removal of boulders, and the traction of other earth machinery. It can turn on circles of 3.5 to 6 m (12 to 20 ft) radius and work on slopes up to 85 percent.

Reference 94

The huge wheeled scrapers, self-powered or drawn by tractors, take up earth from their undersides and carry it along to be released at will. They are particularly useful for shallow cuts and long hauls over rough ground. They can operate on slopes up to 60% longitudinal and 25% transverse. The high-wheeled graders, with the long, delicately adjustable blade suspended beneath them, are used for the final shaping of a surface, especially a road bed. The power shovels, which cut into material from below with their toothed scoops, load dump trucks for long hauls, handle weak or broken rock, and excavate hills, rock faces, and other volumes at their elevation or higher.

The buckets of the draglines hang from cables at the end of long booms, which in some monster mechanisms may be 100 m (330 ft) long but are more normally 7.5 to 25 m (25 to 80 ft). The buckets are dragged toward the operator, through the material to be excavated. Draglines are useful for large cuts and channels below the level of the machine and for making valleys, mounds, slopes and banks. Occasionally, soil may be moved hydraulically, being transported as a slurry of water and soil, through pipes whose outlets are moved from point to point. After the water runs off, the soil is left at the outlet location as an alluvial fan. Finally, there are various kinds of rollers and scarifiers to compact or break up the ground.

An economical grading plan will respect the limitations and capabilities of these machines, in order to avoid expensive hand shoveling. The curves of new contours should not be sharper than the minimum radii of the expected equipment. Equipment cannot work on slopes that are too steep for it or work economically in confined spaces or on small scattered sites. The machines want broad simple forms. Fussy shapes and shallow cuts and fills are to be avoided. Undulating hill and valley forms are cheaper than terracings. So are repetitive landforms. All these cost rules refer especially to larger areas, those perhaps over 5 acres in size.

Grading criteria

Normally, new grades are kept as close to preexisting grades as possible, since these usually represent an established equilibrium. Departures upset the drainage pattern, expose or bury the roots of plants, disturb old foundations, and may make visually awkward shapes. Moreover, even in urban development, the agricultural value of the land should be conserved, since it is a fundamental resource that only slowly renews itself. Topsoil is stripped, stockpiled, and replaced. Even then, the disturbance to the total soil profile can be serious, especially when the soil will be cut away. One therefore avoids unnecessary, shallow cuts in particular. But the site must be disturbed to some degree, and sometimes a dramatic disturbance is best—a hill sheared off, a river drained. One does not do this lightly, but never excludes the possibility.

The basic criteria for any new surface are its fitness for the purposes of its occupants and its ability to be maintained as part of a stable system. Imagine acting and moving over it; check it for its plant cover, for erosion, and for drainage. Grassy slopes should be kept below 25%, although special ground covers like ivy may hold stable cut slopes of up to 100%. Beyond that, it is necessary to crib or terrace the ground. The angle of repose (the limiting steepness beyond which soil grains will slip downhill) is a further constraint, if one is making slopes of new fill. These limiting slopes range from 30% for very wet clay and silt, to 80% for wet sand. A stepped slope, a terrace at the foot of the slope, or drainage at its top will help prevent slippage.

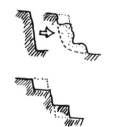

The ground should have positive drainage throughout, without any isolated depressions, to prevent local flooding. Drainage from sites upstream should not be blocked, nor should the discharge upon downstream sites be increased. Water should flow away from buildings and roads, and not be directed into valleys and swales in which no provision has been made for the additional flow.

The new ground must have a pleasing visual form, harmonious with its landscape context. In most instances, this will be a simple, smoothly curving, visually stable surface. The ground shape must be imagined from many viewpoints and approaches. Most likely, it will be studied in a model.

For economy, the amounts of cut and fill (less the allowances for compaction) should balance out over the site as a whole or, if the area is large, within subareas of the site. But this is not true in some situations, as when bedrock is close to the surface or large volumes of peat are present. Then net volumes must be imported or removed.

The most common difficulties that appear in a grading plan are excessive or unbalanced cut and fill; drainage pockets in the land, on the roads, or against the sides of buildings; steep grades that allow erosion, or are dangerous, or which make use, access, or maintenance difficult; a poor visual or functional relation between a building or a road and its immediate surroundings; a visually awkward transition between one section and another; the destruction of existing trees by changes in the ground level; the loss or degradation of good agricultural soil; or the frequent use of expensive and undesirable steps and retaining walls.

The new surface is usually represented by a drawing that shows the new contour lines in relation to the old ones, supplemented by spot elevations at key points. Occasionally, in small areas where there is little to be done, only the spot elevations may be shown. Or if a small area is to be graded to a very exact surface, the new elevations may be given at each corner of a close-meshed imaginary grid. In any case, it is best to sketch the contours first, or to use a model, in order to visualize and control the topographic form.

Representing elevations

More often than not, the new form is simply the best transition that can be found between the set of fixed points— the roads, buildings, sewers, and special landscape features— and the existing land at the site boundaries or at the edge of construction. This sought-for transition respects all the criteria mentioned: function, economy, drainage, appearance, and minimum ecological damage. Sometimes, however, the designer is not merely arranging a trouble-free transition but is handling the ground as a sculptural medium. In either case, contour sketches are his language, and he must be fluent in that language.

Balancing cut and fill and estimating site costs requires a calculation of the earth volume to be moved. Among the several methods of calculation are the contour-area method,

Cut and fill calculations

the end-area method, and the use of elevations at grid corners. The first is best for general site planning purposes, since it is accurate enough for first estimates, fits directly into the process of developing a contoured grading plan, and gives an immediate graphic picture of the quantity and location of earthwork over an extended area. The use of end areas is common in highway work or any linear earth moving, where it is appropriate for determining the best strategy for hauling cut to fill. The last method, like the first, can be used in more extensive earth moving but also for deep excavations. It allows greater precision and correspondingly less graphic control. All these can be supplemented by studies from the model. These various methods are discussed in Appendix K.

Soon it will undoubtedly be customary practice to enter the existing topography in a computer file in digitized form, where it will be manipulated during development of the schematic plan, and whence it will emerge as a final grading plan, a computation of earthwork, and exact street and utility layouts and profiles. In present practice, technical development of the site plan begins with a precise layout of the structures and paths shown on the schematic plan, to the degree of accuracy required for their location on the site. This drawing specifies the geometry of streets, buildings and property lines in relation to bench marks and compass directions. The freehand sketch of the road center line is approximated as closely as possible by a succession of exact circular curves and tangents that conform to standards. Station points are marked on this precise center line.

Profiles

The vertical dimension of the plan is then detailed. This task begins with the design of the road profile, which is a succession of straight grades and parabolic vertical curves. On a sheet of cross-sectional paper, a continuous section through the existing ground at the center line is drawn along each road or consecutive run of station points. The horizontal scale is that of the road layout; the vertical scale is exaggerated ten times. The designer plots the existing surface along this line, as if this sinuous vertical section had been flattened out onto the plane of the drawing. In several trials, a new road profile is approximated by drawing a series of straight tangents over the profile of the existing ground, usually adhering rather closely to it.

The designer searches for a new line whose grades are neither too steep nor too flat, which has positive drainage (no sag curves at points difficult to drain in the plan), and

230

which minimizes and balances cut and fill. Once he has found such an arrangement, he draws the necessary vertical curves at the intersections of the tangents and readjusts the line where difficulties develop. He also checks the profile in relation to the horizontal layout to judge the shape of the road in three dimensions. The designer makes sure that the profile is self-closing—in other words, that elevations are the same on different profiles where they intersect with each other.

The relation of the profile to the grading plan is more difficult. The balance of cut and fill along the profile itself is sometimes a misleading indication of total earthwork. Since the profile tends to generate the detailed grading plan, this profile must permit a good shape for the ground surface as a whole. In drawing the profile, a skilled planner will usually be aware of how he is influencing the grading plan, but the subsequent development of the grading plan will often force him to reconsider.

Spot elevations at other critical points in the plan, such as the elevations of finished floors in the principal buildings or those at the base of existing trees to be saved, are now set to conform with the sketch. These spot elevations are then transferred to a precise layout on which existing contours have also been drawn. Since the profile of the road center line has been established, tick marks showing where the new contours will cross this line in plan can also be put on this layout. And since the road cross-section is known, these new contours can be drawn as far as the tops of curbs or the edge of the road shoulder.

Knowing the fall from crown to gutter, the draftsman can see that the new contour will cross the gutter at a point proportionately as far uphill toward the next contour above as the fall from crown to gutter is in proportion to the contour interval. Thus, if the gutter is 200 mm (8 in) below the crown and the contour interval is 1 m (3 ft), then in plan any new contour will cross the gutter one-fifth of the way uphill between the point at which that new contour crosses the center line and the point at which the next higher contour crosses the center line. This can easily be approximated by eye. In the same way, the new contour crosses the top of the curb, in plan, as far downhill from the gutter crossing as the height of the curb is in proportion to the contour interval.

Once the draftsman has located where the contour crosses the center line, gutter, and top of curb with tick

Grading plans

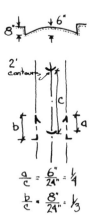

marks, he can draw freehand a smooth curve between them, a curve that has the exaggerated form of the road cross-section itself. The degree of exaggeration is less on steep slopes and greater on flat ones. Like all local contour forms, it points downhill. Thus, a road that is first rather flat, then rises, then falls steeply into a sag, and finally rises again more gently would if contoured have the appearance that is shown below in Figure 76:

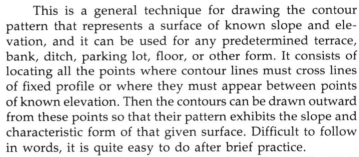

FIGURE 76 *The contours which might appear on the surface of a hilly road.*

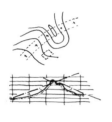

This is a general technique for drawing the contour pattern that represents a surface of known slope and elevation, and it can be used for any predetermined terrace, bank, ditch, parking lot, floor, or other form. It consists of locating all the points where contour lines must cross lines of fixed profile or where they must appear between points of known elevation. Then the contours can be drawn outward from these points so that their pattern exhibits the slope and characteristic form of that given surface. Difficult to follow in words, it is quite easy to do after brief practice.

The next step is to make the grading plan itself, which will specify the new shape that the entire ground is to have when development is complete and which is shown by drawing the contours of the new ground surface wherever they will differ from those of the existing surface. This new surface, at a minimum, will make an easy transition between any predetermined new surfaces (roads, the spaces close by new buildings) and the existing land which is to be left undisturbed. It respects any features to be retained, such as trees, outcrops, or existing roads and buildings. While the grading plan, if it is simple, may be indicated in final contract documents only by spot elevations at key points, it is essential to develop it as a contour drawing in order to control the landform as a whole.

The grading plan is the most delicate and significant element of the technical documents. As it unfolds, it may cause the basic plan to be modified. The skill with which it is made will have much to do with the technical adequacy of the plan and its visual and functional success. It therefore requires care and time for proper development. It is most likely that the road profiles and the spot elevations of buildings will have to be revised to make good transitions possible. Eliminating problems will be slow work until the designer has become skillful in reading contours on paper as if they were actual forms in space. Their interspacing, linear quality, degree of parallelism, and general pattern all have meaning. But the modeling of the ground surface should have been an integral part of the general plan from the beginning.

The storm drainage system takes off the flow of surface water. It is a substitute for the natural surface drainage, and it may be unnecessary in low-density development, at fewer than 5 families per hectare (2 per acre). It need not be a continuous system but can discharge into local streams, lakes, and gullies wherever this will not cause flooding or increase pollution. Storm waters are not free of pollutants once they have run over disturbed land, or through the debris and chemicals of the streets, or have taken up the fertilizers and pesticides of the fields. Large storm discharges must be controlled or treated, and every effort must be made to decrease pollution at the source, both by restraining the use of chemicals and by stabilizing the new surfaces. If natural water bodies or main drainage lines are not available for discharge, it is possible to empty storm flows into recharge pits or retention basins. These are made in pervious soil and must be big enough to hold water from the worst storm. They economize on the length of main that would otherwise be needed to reach a stream or a public sewer. Retention basins require a substantial piece of ground and, since their level must fluctuate, they are not very handsome. Yet a heavy runoff from development not only overloads downstream channels and imposes costs for artificial drainage works, but also denies water to the earth, and thus lowers the water table. Therefore it is becoming good practice to install recharging pits and basins where possible, so that the runoff is restored to the soil. Large flat roofs with parapets, even occasionally-used parking lots, may also be used for temporary ponding as a way of reducing peak rates of flow in the sewers.

Since the required pipe sizes are often large, the underground storm drainage system is expensive, and every effort is made to minimize or eliminate it. Where economic resources are scanty, underground drainage may be avoided

Storm drainage

Reference 87

by keeping development at low densities, decreasing paved surfaces and increasing planted ones, grading carefully to ensure gentle slopes and positive flow, and relying on ditches, check dams, short culverts, and good maintenance. The large diameter pipes at the lower ends of underground sewer systems may cause difficulties in the grading plan by tending to ride up out of the ground as they maintain sufficient elevation to reach their destination or as they flatten out to prevent scour inside the pipe. Nevertheless, since roofs and paved surfaces usually interfere with existing surface flow and sharply increase the runoff, some kind of artificial drainage structure, however simple, is usually required to prevent flooding. This storm system is kept separate from the sanitary drainage to reduce the volumes that must be treated in sewage disposal and to prevent the backing up of sanitary wastes.

Elements of the system

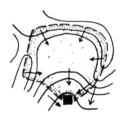

The storm system is made up of a drainage surface, a set of open gutters and ditches, and probably a series of underground pipes, usually made of vitrified clay and laid straight to line and grade, connected by manholes and fed by inlets. Large sewers, over 1 m (3 ft) in diameter, are made of concrete instead of clay. When the pipes are large enough for a person to enter them for inspection or cleaning, they can be gently curved in horizontal alignment. It is now becoming accepted practice in some localities for all sizes of sewer lines to be laid in regular horizontal curves, as long as the radius is not less than 30 m (100 ft) and the vertical grade is constant. Particularly where streets are curving, this technique minimizes sewer length and the number of manholes and allows the sewer to remain in a standard relation to the street and other utilities. The lines cannot then be inspected visually, and the flow is somewhat slower, but modern cleaning machinery can easily be sent through such curves. Small curved sewers may not be permitted by local ordinance, however.

Manholes—man-sized circular pits—are used to enter the lines or to look down their length. They are placed at the upper end of lines and at every change in horizontal or vertical direction or curvature. They should also be placed no more than 100 to 150 m apart, to permit the use of cleaning apparatus. An economical design will minimize their number. Recharge manholes, designed to deliver storm water back to the ground rather than simply to conduct it from pipe to pipe, are made with porous sides and set in pits filled with gravel in order to enlarge the soil surface which will absorb the water.

Surface water first flows in a film across the ground,
and it is kept spread out as long as possible. The aim is to
keep this surface water moving, but not so fast as to cause
erosion. Allowable slopes therefore depend on the volume
of water expected, the surface finish, and the amount of
damage that can be done by local flooding. Planted areas
and broad paved areas should have a minimum grade of
1%, although open land far from structures, where occasional
ponding can be permitted, may slope as little as 0.5%. Streets
and other paved surfaces that are laid to exact elevations
may also have a minimum grade of 0.5%. Land should slope
away from all buildings for 3 m with a minimum grade of
2%. Planted drainage swales and open ditches require a
similar minimum of 2% and cannot go over 10%, or 5% if
the area drained is over 0.2 hectares (half an acre). Lawns
and grass banks can have a maximum slope of 25%, while
unmown planted banks can be as steep as 50%, or perhaps
60% in firm, undisturbed soil. Expensive cribbing or retaining
walls are needed to hold steeper ground.

The ground is sloped so that undrained depressions are
avoided unless a settlement basin is intended. The designer
must be aware of the quantity of flow entering his site from
the outside and of how it may change in the future. On the
other hand, if he wants to avoid claims for damages, he
contrives to direct any water leaving his own property along
previously existing drainage courses, and not in greater
amounts than before. Preventing any increase will be difficult, however, and will require a combination of devices.

Even over a uniform, moderate slope, surface flow will
begin to cut small rivulets within 150 m (500 ft). Before it
concentrates naturally to form these gullies, it is concentrated
artificially in man-made channels. It is picked up by the
walks, or in grass ditches or in open concrete channels, like
walks with inverted crowns. These deliver the flow into the
street gutters or ditches. Where swales or ditches drain more
than one lot of land, they must be open to common maintenance, and easements are required. For economy in open
development, a small pilot sewer, sized to carry ordinary
storms, is often run underneath a wide, planted swale, which
will carry off any extraordinary downpour. Natural creeks
and gullies may receive increased flows because of hard-
surface development. They will erode and become laden
with silt. Bankside trees will be undermined. To prevent this
erosion, check dams must be installed to reduce velocity, or
the channel may be paved, or piped drains may be installed.

But if drainpipes are laid along a wooded stream, the trees will be lost in any case because a broad swathe must be cleared for construction. The best solution is then a bypass drain, leading water away from the draw.

Storm water can be allowed to flow for some distance in the street gutter before being taken up by underground drains or being discharged into streams or off the property. Gutter flow cannot be allowed to run across a street or walk, and thus it must be picked up at least once on each block, at the lowest corner, or be carried under the crossroad in a culvert. Usually the gutter will have sufficient capacity to carry the flow from one block, although it is desirable not to allow water to run more than 250 to 300 m (800 to 1000 ft) before reaching the sewers, and then only in fairly level ground with an efficient inlet system. No substantial gutter flow should have to turn a sharp corner or meet a sudden obstacle, such as protruding driveway apron. Otherwise, any heavy flow will jump out of the gutter.

The flow from gutters and ditches, if not previously turned into a natural drainage course, is finally caught by inlets placed in the gutter or the face of the curb, usually at street intersections or at low points in streets or grounds. Inlets have a grating to hold back large debris and are connected by short branch lines to the main drain, preferably at a manhole. Catch basins (or "trapped inlets") are sometimes inserted here to collect the grit and trash. But since these basins will require frequent cleaning, they are used only where much grit is likely because of sandy soil or earth roads and where slopes are flat and velocities are low.

Gradients

Sewer lines must be covered deeply enough to prevent breakage and freezing (over 1 m (4 ft) deep in the latitude of New England, for example), but if they are buried more than 6 m (20 ft) deep, the excavation will be costly. Lines must have a minimum slope so that the flow is fast enough to keep the pipe clean. The slope required to achieve this velocity depends on pipe size and quantity of flow, but it may be taken as a minimum of 0.3% in preliminary trials, before size and quantity have been determined. In later calculations, this minimum velocity is taken as 60 cm per second (2 fps) when flowing full, which will provide for sufficient speed when the sewer flows only partially full. On the other hand, the slope must not give velocities over 3 m per second (10 fps), which begins to cause a scouring of the pipe lining. This may require flat slopes and large pipes in the lower ends of lines, as quantities build up.

236

Changes in slope can be made only at manholes. Manholes can be of the drop type, where the upper line enters above the lower receiving one. Otherwise, the ends of two connecting lines are laid so that the tops or center lines (not the bottoms!) of the pipes are at the same level. However, the vertical position of a pipe is traditionally specified by giving the elevation of its *invert*, which is the lowest point on its internal surface. A pipe is never allowed to discharge into one smaller than itself, since floating matter might jam at the smaller entrance.

The storm sewer system is initially laid out in plan, with the first inlets located as far down the slopes as possible, within the limit for flow in the open gutter. The pattern of converging sewers is then arranged so that there is a minimum length of line and a minimum number of manholes, which are nevertheless placed to be close to all necessary inlets and to allow straight runs (or perhaps regular curves) between themselves. Since repair and cleaning are usually done at the manhole rather than in between, the manholes must be in the right-of-way, but the sewer lines themselves may occasionally run through easements separate from the right-of-way. Preliminary profiles of the top of the sewer pipe are then plotted on the street profiles, with the pipe as close to ground surface as possible within the limits stated for cover and minimum slope. Since the system must meet the outfall sewer, settling basin, or stream at the right elevation, it is easier to draw this preliminary profile upward from the discharge point.

System layout

Finally, pipe size must be computed by the site planner or his engineer in order to estimate cost, check velocities in the pipe, and avoid excessive depth of cut. Required pipe size depends on the slope of the pipe and the volume to be carried, and the latter on the area being drained, the coefficient of runoff, and the intensity of the storm at the time that the peak flow arrives at that point in the line. The coefficient of runoff—that fraction of total rainfall that runs off on the surface rather than penetrating the ground—may vary from 0.9 for roofs and pavements, to 0.5 for impervious soil, 0.2 for planted areas, and 0.1 for wooded land. The momentary intensity of rainfall depends on two factors: the chosen "year of the storm" (that is, the decision to provide for anything up to a storm likely to occur once every ten, or twenty-five, or one hundred years), and the time since the storm began (since it is assumed that most storms gradually slacken in intensity as time progresses). The combined

Computation of pipe size

effect of all these factors means that pipe size (which means cost and downstream damage) can be reduced by any one of the following: 1) increase the slope of the pipe; 2) reduce the area drained; 3) decrease the coefficient of runoff by reducing paving, by increasing the planted land, or by installing recharge pits; 4) decide to risk a lower "year of storm"; and 5) delay the storm flow by using retention basins or by causing the water to make long runs over unpaved land.

In any case, the minimum diameter of a sewer that drains a street is 300 mm (12 in), or 250 mm (10 in) for one that drains a yard, to prevent any stoppage by trash. Drains at the lower ends of large projects can be very large. The velocity of flow within any pipe is kept between 3 and 0.6 m (10 and 2 ft) per second, to prevent internal scour on the one hand and to encourage self-cleaning on the other. On that account, the slope of very large pipes may have to be flattened and that of very small pipes steepened.

Technical problems in the storm drainage system sometimes require modification of the general site plan. In laying out the system and computing pipe size, the designer must take account of other areas draining into the area under study and of the possibility that more intensive development may increase future drainage.

Occasionally, a development is laid out on a completely flat or swampy site, which causes problems for all the utilities. Storm drainage can sometimes be handled by keeping the crown of the road dead level, while letting the gutters alternately rise and fall so that they will discharge into a series of inlets along their length. Here the water falls into the underground system, or runs off through ditches to overflow basins, where the water is ponded until it seeps into the ground. The land surface is graded so that building sites and paths are above the pond levels and so the critical elements of the site are protected from flooding.

Culverts   A short length of pipe inserted under a road or other barrier to carry storm water or a small brook is called a culvert. In effect, it is a fragmentary storm drainage system. Normally, culverts are circular in cross-section and are made of concrete or corrugated metal. They should be straight, should cross the road approximately at right angles, and should use the line of the old channel if possible. But in any case they should cross the road at the first opportunity and should not allow water to course along the uphill side of the road, which causes erosion.

Where possible, culverts are laid at the slope of the old channel, but with a maximum grade of 8 to 10 percent and a minimum grade of 0.5 percent. The gradient just below the outlet must be at least as steep as the slope just above the inlet to prevent silting. Inlets and outlets require wing walls and aprons to prevent erosion around the pipe. To protect it from being crushed, the culvert should be covered with a depth of fill that is equal to one-half the pipe diameter but at least 300 mm (1 ft). The size of culverts is calculated in the same way as the size of sewer pipes: by computing the quantity of flow from the acreage of the watershed and its average coefficient of runoff. The flow should be calculated for a 25-year storm, or even for a greater one, since the culvert cost is small and the consequences of an underestimate serious.

Sometimes subsurface drains are installed to carry the water away from wet ground, to prevent seepage through foundations or at embankments, or to correct frost heaving or a high water table. Most often these are 10 to 15 cm pipes, perforated or with open joints, laid in a gravel fill. They lead into the storm system or into natural drainage courses. They are put 0.75 to 1.5 m below ground: deeper and more widely spaced in permeable soil, and shallower and closer together in more impervious soil.

"Sanitary" (a euphemism for insanitary) wastes, such as those from sinks and toilets, are kept out of the storm drains but carried down in a system of quite similar form. Waste is carried to a disposal plant, which converts the sewage into an effluent that can be safely discharged into some natural body of water. It is no longer tolerable to allow raw sewage to flow into lakes or rivers. Moreover, we are learning that we have as much to fear from chemical and thermal pollution as from biological pollution and that elaborate treatment, or recycling, of wastes is now imperative. Indeed, if we cannot modify our habits of polluting the water, air, and land, we may soon be able to dispense with site planning and other problems of civilization.

Sanitary drainage is typically a converging system of manholes and straight pipes, or pipes of gentle horizontal curvature, leading to a disposal plant. Unlike the storm system, it is likely to be continuous over large areas, and it sometimes must be pumped up over divides in order to reach the common point of discharge. Pumping is avoided if possible at the site planning scale. Sanitary drains may

Sanitary
drainage

be critical for the large region, but their layout is rarely controlling in site planning.

Unlike storm sewers, sanitary sewers form a closed drainage system. They are not connected to open inlets but directly to sink and toilet drains via traps that seal off the sewer odors. The branch lines (or *laterals*) leading to houses connect into the main all along its course rather than just at manholes. If permitted by local regulations, manholes may be replaced by simple and relatively inexpensive cleanouts at the upper ends of lines, and also at the branchings or breaks in alignment of laterals from single houses or small groups of houses (not more than 10 to 12). Where a cleanout is used at a change in direction, the change must be less than 90 degrees. Where two branches join at a cleanout, only one branch should change direction. Lines, particularly short laterals, need not always be entirely within the right-of-way as long as manholes and cleanouts are accessible: a properly designed system rarely needs repair or even cleaning. The street mains must be set low enough to receive the house laterals, which are dropping at minimum gradients from the cellars of buildings. The mains are therefore likely to be set at least 2 m (6 ft) down, and more where the land slopes down from the street, or where there are deep basements. Otherwise, the layout technique is similar to the storm drainage system. The minimum size of sanitary sewer pipe is set rather large in relation to flow in order to prevent stoppage: 200 mm (8 in) pipe for mains or laterals and 150 mm (6 in) pipe for house branches. Only the main outfalls of extensive areas require a larger-size pipe.

Sewage disposal

If a public disposal plant is not within reach, it is possible to construct an economical private disposal plant, although this will require operation and maintenance. A small private plant would consist of a septic or Imhoff tank, followed by one or more sand and trickling filters. This plant should be set 100 m (330 ft) from any house and could be economically designed to serve from 50 to 500 dwelling units.

Where the soil is sufficiently pervious and the groundwater low, it is possible to dispense with a common drainage system in low-density development by giving each unit a septic tank discharging into an underground drain field. Drain fields must be kept 30 m (100 ft) from any surface water or well, and they should not be heavily shaded, or crossed by any vehicles, or installed in land with a slope over 15%. Their required size will depend on the absorption capacity of the soil. If properly installed, septic tanks should give no

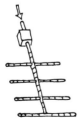

future trouble and are more economical than a sewage system complete with disposal plant. The small community disposal plant, on the other hand, has the advantages that it can later be hooked into a future public system, with no loss of the investment in the sewers themselves. Either system, however, tends to make a future extension of public sewers more difficult to justify.

The absorption rate for a septic tank may be checked by digging a test pit at the drain field site in the wet season to the depth that the field will lie. The pit is filled with 600 mm (2 ft) of water, which is allowed to fall to a 150 mm (6 in) depth, and then the drop is timed, as it falls further, from 150 to 125 mm (6 to 5 in). This procedure is repeated until it takes the same time to make this 25 mm (1 in) drop for two tests running. The allowable absorption rate of the soil, in liters per square meter of drain field area per day, is shown in Table 4 below. If the time of fall is much longer, it is doubtful if the drain field is usable. Given the rate, the necessary total field area can be calculated in a housing development by assuming that total sewage flow will equal 400 liters (90 gallons) per person per day.

These two water-borne systems are almost universal in the developed world. They are expensive, wasteful of a precious resource, and can pollute astonishing volumes of ground and surface water. There are alternative systems that use no water, or very little of it. The pit privy is the simplest of these. Despite our distaste for it, it is quite acceptable if reasonably maintained and if it will not pollute the underlying groundwater. The water table should be at least 7.5 m (5 ft) below the bottom of the pit, which is usually 1 to 2 m (3.5 to 7 ft) deep, and the pit must be at least 30 m (100 ft) away and downhill from any well. The soil must not be impermeable, nor yet so extremely permeable (gravel or fissured rock for example) that any effluent will travel a

Dry disposal

TABLE 4. ALLOWABLE ABSORPTION RATES OF SOIL

Time for 2.5 cm (1 in) fall in min.	Absorption rate in liters per sq m [gal. per sq ft] per day
5 or less	120 (2.5)
8	100 (2.0)
10	85 (1.7)
12	75 (1.5)
15	65 (1.3)
22	50 (1.0)

long distance underground. The pit is made tight for half a meter below ground and is unlined below. The privy is moved when it fills this unlined portion, and the waste material is left underground for at least a year before it is removed or used as fertilizer. The pit cover must be tight and the privy ventilated and screened to prevent flies and odors.

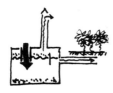

The somewhat more expensive aqua privy may be preferable, especially where there is danger of contaminating the groundwater. It is a simplified version of the septic tank and is equally acceptable. A water-tight tank, filled with water, is located directly under the toilet or squatting plate and is connected to an overflow drain. Sludge falls to the bottom, and scum floats on top. The sludge is pumped or dipped out once every several years (and can be used as fertilizer after having been allowed to decompose for yet another year), while the scum is restrained by a baffle from entering the overflow drain. Drain and toilet inlet are both submerged, providing a water seal, and the tank itself is vented to allow the escape of any gas. The meager daily outflow of contaminated effluent falls into a soakpit, or, if the natural soil is impermeable, into a small trench filled with loose earth or gravel and planted to increase transpiration. If, even then, there is a danger of groundwater pollution, then the effluent must go into a sewer system, although, since the volumes are very low, the flow from a cluster of houses may easily be directed to some nearby location that will absorb them safely. About 7 liters (1.5 gallons) of water per person should be added at the inlet each day (as against 400 liters (90 gallons) in our sewer systems) to maintain the level in the tank and a sufficient degree of dilution of the wastes. This small amount need not be potable and can be used to wash the toilet. Thus the aqua privy is safe, free of nuisance, modest in cost, and very saving of water. The tank itself must have a capacity of about 120 to 150 liters (25 to 30 gallons) for each person who will use it.

The anaerobic digester is a rather bulky sealed tank in which water, vegetable waste, and excreta are held for 30 to 80 days, producing methane gas, which is useful fuel, and a safe, fertilizing sludge. It will work only in a warm climate unless the tank is artificially heated, and there must be a safe way of storing and using the methane fuel. It is reasonably expensive—a technology best suited to a tropical agricultural settlement, with some modest capital.

The aerobic digester, the so-called composting toilet, decomposes the same mix of vegetable matter and excreta in a large ventilated bin, from which odors and water vapors are drawn off by a flue. A safe fertilizer can be removed from the bottom of the bin in about 30 to 50 days. The digestive process heats the mass to over 65° C (150°F). The bin is bulky and moderately costly; it must be screened, well ventilated, and adequately insulated in cool climates. Care is needed to maintain the proper mix in the bin and to avoid a fire. But no water is used; odors and flies are controlled; there is no risk of disease; and the by-product is useful. With further development to reduce cost and the care needed in operation, the aerobic digester may become the preferable technology in many circumstances.

The quality and quantity of our water supplies are vital to our health. Clean water is the most critical utility, a necessity even in the most primitive settlement. Yet while it may make the development of a given site either feasible, costly, or impossible, it rarely imposes controls on the pattern of the site plan itself. The pipes of a pressure system can be laid with bends and gentle curves and so adapt easily to most layouts.

Water lines leak or break rather frequently and must be located in a public right-of-way that can carry repair vehicles. Care must be taken to prevent contamination. The mains for potable water are directly connected to the using fixtures, without cross connections to other lines. Sewer lines are laid below the water mains, and where possible on the opposite side of the street or 3 m (10 ft) distant horizontally. Water is usually brought into the buildings, but in low-cost development it may be conveyed only to a public tap or fountainhead, from which it is carried by hand into the dwellings.

As with any pressure system, there are two basic distribution layouts that may be used. One is a treelike pattern, with lines branching out from the point of entry. A second is a loop or interconnected network, which may have more than one point of entering supply. The treelike pattern is likely to minimize length of line and thus be cheapest, but the loop or network is preferable since it avoids the drop in pressure that occurs at the ends of long branches, and the difficulty of keeping the dead-end pipes clear, and few units

Water supply

will be cut off from service when a main breaks. Where dead ends do occur, as at the ends of culs-de-sac, hydrants or blowoffs must be installed to allow occasional cleaning.

Since this utility is the one most seriously affected by frost, in New England it is normally laid under 1.5 m (5 ft) of cover. The line may rise and fall with the slope of the surface, as long as positive pressures are maintained at the high points. Since water supply is paid for according to the quantity delivered, meters are installed at individual dwellings, at groups of dwellings, or at the boundary of an entire development. Valves are placed in house branches where they leave the mains and in the mains at points necessary to cut off sections in the event of breaks. These valves must be no more than 300 m apart. Fire hydrants are put along vehicular ways at intersections and other points, so that all parts of buildings may be reached by hose lines not over 100 m long from one, and preferably two, hydrants. Yet to keep them usable in case of fire, no hydrant should be closer than 7.5 m (25 ft), and preferably 15 m (50 ft), from any structure. In high-value commercial districts, a special high-pressure system for fire fighting is sometimes installed separately from the potable supply.

Capacity   In site-planning work, sizing and detailing the system is left to specialists, whose calculations of pipe size must assure adequate delivered pressure during periods of maximum instantaneous demand, while accounting for frictional losses, network patterns, and variations in elevation. For the site designer, the layout of the water system is usually confined to the location of the lines, valves, meters, and hydrants in the public right-of-way. This rarely calls for changes in the design itself. The minimum diameter for water mains is 150 mm (6 in), or 200 mm (8 in) in high-value areas, which is usually adequate for developments of up to moderate size.

Calculations for the capacity of the water supply, rather than of the distribution system, use average rather than instantaneous demand rates. These requirements depend on population, climate, industrialization, and the prevailing standard of living. In U.S. cities, for example, average demand varies from 450 to 900 liters (100 to 200 gallons) per capita per day. In rural or low-density developments, individual wells can replace a common water supply, but they are not recommended except where unavoidable. They are unreliable, often expensive, and not easily supervised to maintain purity. A private group water supply is quite feasible, and its maintenance can be supported by water charges on the users. Such a system, consisting of a well, or group of wells, a pump, and pressure or gravity tanks, can serve developments of 50 to 500 houses. The wells must be at least 30 m (100 ft) from the nearest sewer or drain field. There is a threshold in cost at about 200 dwelling units, where more than one well must usually be driven. But the principal cost is in the distribution system rather than in the pump or well. A large, professionally operated public water system is still the preferable solution.

Power is brought in on primary high-voltage lines and then is stepped down at transformers to enter secondary low-voltage lines going to the points of use. Since low-voltage transmission is wasteful, secondary runs should be shorter than 120 m (400 ft). As with any pressure system, the electric lines may follow a branching pattern, fanning out from the point of entry to the points of use, or a loop distribution. The first pattern is cheaper, the second preferable. However, the difference is not as important here as it is in the case of the water system.

Electric power

The conductors may be placed overhead on poles or underground in raceways. Underground distribution may be two to four times as expensive in first cost, but it reduces breaks, does not interfere with trees, and eliminates the clutter of poles. Once breaks occur, however, they take longer to repair when underground and cause more disruption.

If the overhead system is used, it is possible to string the secondary lines on the buildings. But this entails a risk to building repairmen and adventurous children. Normally, all lines but those directly entering a structure are strung on poles, which are guyed at changes in direction and at the ends of lines. The poles are spaced 40 m (130 ft) apart or less. Transformers are hung on the poles or installed partially or wholly underground, with exterior venting. Where poles or raceways do not follow streets, a 2.5 m (8 ft) easement is required. The choice of putting pole lines on the street or at rear lot lines is usually dictated by minimizing the length of secondary runs. Placing poles at the rear to "beautify" the street is questionable when buildings are low, since the poles are even more prominent on the skyline than when directly overhead. Poles at the rear lot lines are also more difficult to service. Furthermore, power poles located on the street are useful for mounting street lights, telephone lines, signs, and callboxes.

Residents may be willing to pay the premium for underground electric lines for visual reasons. Costs of underground installation are most favorable in light soil, and new techniques of laying cable are making them more favorable. Where there is rock or a high water table, however, the cost difference is likely to be prohibitive, and poles become mandatory. Elsewhere, the principal difficulty may be the transformers, which must be designed to disperse internal heat if put underground or which bulk large in a residential area if left above.

Lighting

Reference 50

Exterior lighting is required on all streets other than rural or local ones in low-density development, and also on pedestrian ways along which people may be expected to move at night. On local roads without street lamps, individual dwellings can be required to maintain door or post lamps to illuminate their entrances and the adjacent walk. Light is especially needed at entrances, intersections, steps, dead ends, and remote walkways. Powerful lights high in the air give a strong, even illumination and are therefore specified for roads, but they produce a general pallor that lights up houses unpleasantly. Walkways are safe with much lower and variable illumination, as long as entrances and potential lurking places are well lit. Unfortunately, sodium, halide, and mercury vapor lamps are the most economical of energy and last five to ten times as long as an incandescent bulb. Hence the eerie yellowish or greenish glow of our highways, which is not only unpleasant but may possibly have effects on our health given protracted exposure. The old incandescent lamp has the warmest color and emits the widest spectrum of wavelengths but dissipates much of its energy in heat. Incandescents may be used on walkways, however, or highway lamps may be color corrected at some cost. In any case, the visual requirements of drivers and pedestrians are quite different, and their lighting environment should be different.

Standard mounting heights for lights are 9 m (30 ft) over roadways at spacings of 45 to 60 m (150 to 200 ft). Lamps are designed to give average illuminations of 10 lux (1 footcandle) on arterial roads or large parking lots, or 5 lux (0.5 footcandles) on local roads. Areas of lowest illumination are not allowed to fall below 40% of average levels on arterials or below 10% on local streets. Tall lamps must be shrouded to prevent glare into windows, private sitting areas, or drivers' eyes. Their location must be correlated with adjacent buildings and plantings.

Lamps on walkways are normally 3.5 m (10 ft) high. One can see physical obstacles at very low illuminations; the critical factors are the quality of the light and the psychological sense of safety. Thus shrubs and recesses should be well lit, as well as doorways, steps, and intersections. Such spots may receive as much as 50 lux (5 footcandles), while the path itself is irregularly lit at average levels of a fraction of a footcandle.

Power and light poles are intrusions in the daytime visual scene and must be sited carefully. But sketching how an area will look at night should also be a normal part of its design. Night lighting can structure a darkened landscape so that people find their way and recognize the familiar daytime features. Light conveys a sense of warmth and activity. But the floodlighting of unused grounds, or lighting empty buildings, may only underscore the absence of people. Unless they are symbolic landmarks, buildings should be lit from inside, in accordance with their nighttime use. Outdoor light should be concentrated where people are and where they want light to see by. Darkness is as necessary a foil for light as silence is for sound. Outdoor lighting has generally been guided by one simple rule: as even and as high a level of illumination as possible over every inch. The result is ghastly.

Gas is piped underground by a system similar to the water distribution network, in a branching or a loop pattern, with its own valves and meters. The pipes are of small diameter. The principal problem here is the danger of leakage or explosion, and so these lines are not laid under or close to buildings except where they enter them, nor are they put in the same trench with electric cable.

Other utilities

Telephone lines are strung overhead on the electric power poles if the voltage characteristics of the power lines are suitable. Otherwise, telephone lines are rather easily laid in underground conduits or more simply as buried cable. They can be placed in the same ditch with the electric lines. In urban areas, connections to central computers and additional lines for cable television are now common.

Where central heating is provided, the heating medium, usually high-temperature steam, is distributed in insulated underground pressure mains, set in raceways or running through the basements of structures. Space is required for a central plant in one of the buildings or in a structure of its own. This heating plant must have a tall stack and provision for large fuel deliveries. Its location is preferably in the middle of the development but on low ground to facilitate the return of condensate. In unusual situations, group cooling systems may be installed.

The choice between central or group heating plants, operated by management, and individual plants, operated by the tenant or owner, as well as the choice of fuel to be used, is an economic issue. It depends on the type and number of dwelling units, the attitude of residents, maintenance costs, the relative efficiency of plants, and the relative cost of coal, gas, oil, and electricity. A central plant is worth investigating when one is dealing with from 100 to 200 families or more. The choice has an important effect on the site plan. When individual plants are used, provision must be made for the delivery and storage of fuel. If coal is burned, it should be possible to chute it directly from truck to bin over no more than 6 m (20 ft). Hoses on oil delivery trucks have a maximum reach of from 30 to 60 m (100 to 200 ft). Gas and electricity can be brought directly into the unit.

Solid waste

Large quantities of solid waste, including organic material and combustible and noncombustible rubbish, must be removed from inhabited areas. These may be picked up in varying combinations and at various times. Some of this material may be destroyed on the site in incinerators, but this method puts the burden of waste disposal on the atmosphere—a dangerous practice. If householders are willing to make the effort, a good portion of the organic waste can be converted to useful compost at the site, or the various types of wastes may be separated for more efficient recycling. But the noncombustible material must in any case be hauled away unless, in a rural or low-resource situation, it is locally buried. Group collection stations may be used if they are screened and drained, but separate collection from each dwelling unit is preferable. For separate collection, a drained and protected area must be provided for the waste cans, convenient to the dwelling unit and as close to the curb as possible. The route from the waste cans to curb should not be too steep and preferably should be paved. If structures are close to the road, it is possible to put waste containers within the unit, placed so that they can be filled from the inside and picked up and emptied from the outside. Compactors, which reduce the volume of the wastes to be transported, are recent innovations, as are duct systems which convey the solid wastes underground, directly from the unit to a central collection point.

Once the grading plan has been completed, the layout of utilities is made, usually beginning with the storm drainage, which is the system most likely to be significant. As a minimum, this layout will include the plan of the utility lines. The designer will now check to see that no critical problems of elevations or sizing will occur. It is not likely that any major revisions of the plan will be required, although they may sometimes be necessary. But it is quite possible that utility considerations will require changes in the precise layout, or in the grading plan, or will suggest economic or functional modifications.

The location of all utilities must be considered together to avoid cross connections, minimize trenching, and maintain the required separations between incompatible systems. In particular, the layout must be checked in three dimensions to see that crossings in plan will not result in actual intersections below ground. The technology of underground circulation is rather backward in comparison to surface systems. Subsurface structures are expensive and inelegant, their design traditional, their layout chaotic, as opening up a street will make apparent.

Where curves or grades permit, it is desirable to keep utilities in a uniform location relative to the street. It is further desirable to put them underneath the planting strip in order to prevent periodic digging in the road. In intensive development, where utility systems are numerous and of large capacity, it may save installation and maintenance cost if groups of them are placed in a common conduit, big enough to allow people to enter and inspect the lines. Where the site plan consists of fairly continuous structures under single control, it is sometimes better to run all the utilities except gas in basements or crawl spaces, saving excavation and simplifying repairs.

The layout of all utilities may be shown on one sheet, or it may be more convenient for the storm drainage to be shown on the grading plan because it is so intimately related to topography. Depending on the extent to which engineering consultants will prepare construction drawings of their own, the utility plans will go beyond general layouts to show subsurface elevations, structural details, and the sizing of conductors.

When technical development is complete, it must be checked for internal consistency and for compliance with the basic plan, the program, and the budget. The plan may be evaluated once more in the light of these findings and readjusted. The developed design has now been expressed in a series of final technical drawings, consisting most often of a precise surveying layout, a set of road profiles, a grading plan with spot elevations at key points, a utility layout, a landscape plan, and a sheet of details. These are the working drawings of a site plan. Together with the specifications for pavements, utilities, grading, landscaping, site maintenance, bidding procedures, the timing and interrelations of the trades, and the general and special conditions of the work, they form the contract documents on which estimates and work are based. However, they may not cover all legal and administrative needs. Requirements vary over the United States and include such items as plats for legal record or sketches for approval by public agencies. Many of these technical drawings and documents will soon be developed, stored, and exhibited by computer graphics rather than by draftsmen and typists.

Important as these technical drawings may be, they are not the essence of the site plan. The essence lies in the sketch, which may be a drawing or a model, and which sets forth the three-dimensional pattern of activity, circulation, and physical form. The correctness of this essential pattern will be tested in use, as it conforms to purposes, resources, and the spirit of the site.

Chapter 9

Housing

Housing is the most common and possibly the most difficult form of site development. Over two-thirds of the area of a typical American city is devoted to residences. To remain desirable over many years, housing areas must have qualities that transcend the values of any particular wave of residents. We consider those qualities, but as the discussion becomes more concrete, it will apply less and less generally. Much of this chapter is rooted in North American practice.

The elementary component of any housing site is the dwelling unit, traditionally thought of (even if not always occupied) as a nuclear family's living quarters, and often legally defined by its possession of a separate entrance and separate cooking facilities. Today, a housing unit is just as likely to be inhabited by a single-headed household, an unrelated group of singles, members of an extended family, or some other unconventional household. Thus it is difficult to predict the type or number of residents from the size and number of units on a site. Nonetheless, self-contained units that have cooking and bathing facilities continue to serve as the basis for computing densities and for constructing typologies of housing.

In a general way, there are four broad categories of housing form:

1. *Detached housing*: each dwelling unit is in its own isolated structure, movable or fixed in place, on its own site.

2. *Attached housing*: each unit has a separate outdoor

entrance and often a private outdoor space, but units are joined side by side or one above another. Duplexes, semi-detached houses, town or row houses, maisonettes and stacked townhouses are the common forms.

3. *Apartments*: several dwelling units share a common (usually an indoor) access and are enclosed by a common structural envelope. Apartments can be walk-up buildings, where upper floors are served by stairs, or elevator buildings. A unit may be on one floor (flats) or have internal stairways to serve two or more levels. Apartments take a variety of shapes, including slabs, towers, and units arranged around courtyards.

4. *Hybrid housing*: two or more forms are mixed. A detached house may have an accessory apartment; a large apartment structure may devote the bottom two floors to self-contained units with private yards and entrances; access along outdoor galleries causes an apartment structure to resemble attached housing.

Density

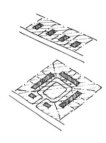

Each housing type has its own appropriate density, although a considerable range is possible. There are also a variety of ways of measuring density, which leads to some confusion. The most common measure relates land and dwelling units. *Net density* is the most precise relationship of land to units. It divides all the lands that may unequivocally be assigned to particular structures by the total number of units. For subdivided, single-family detached housing the measure is simple to compute: divide the total area of the building lots by the number of lots. In other housing forms, where there are privately owned but common streets, parking areas or open spaces, these must first be excluded from the calculation. Thus, the measure more often used for housing projects is *project density*, which uses as its base all the land to be developed as a single project, and thus may contain certain local streets and other areas of common use immediately adjacent that cannot be separated from the total development pattern. The term *neighborhood density* includes the area occupied by housing plus all its local support facilities, such as streets, parks, pedestrian ways and public facilities. This is the more stable measure, if local and nonlocal facilities can be distinguished, but it necessarily lumps private and public activities together. In larger planning studies, a coarser measure of *overall density* is sometimes used, which lumps commercial and employment areas, and even undeveloped lands, into the numerator, along with residential uses. The overall densities of two cities are occasionally compared by such measures, which may be useful for some regional planning purposes but for site planning are largely meaningless.

Along with unit density, the floor area ratio (FAR)—sometimes called the "plot ratio" or "floor space index"—is a common measure of development intensity in North America. This is the ratio of the total usable floor space of all buildings, divided by the total area of the site. Still other indices are used in other countries, such as population, or habitable rooms, or children per hectare, and these measures may be more sensitive to wide variations in household size.

FAR 0.75

The densities associated with particular housing types are not rigid: a skilled designer can move them up a little, or site constraints may decrease the density below what is otherwise possible. Much depends on three decisions: how to store the automobile (and how many to store); the amount of private and common open space to be provided; and the privacy distances to be maintained between facing windows. Nonetheless, as a general guide to the site planner, Table 5 indicates some typical densities for common housing types.

See Figure 77

TABLE 5. DENSITIES BY RESIDENTIAL TYPE

| | | families per hectare (per acre) | |
	FAR	net density	neighborhood density
single-family	up to 0.2	up to 20 (8)	up to 12 (5)
zero lot line detached	0.3	20–25 (8–10)	15(6)
two family detached	0.3	25–30 (10–12)	18 (7)
row houses	0.5	40–60 (16–24)	30 (12)
stacked townhouses	0.8	60–100 (25–40)	45 (18)
3 story walkup apts	1.0	100–115 (40–45)	50 (20)
6 story elevator apts	1.4	160–190 (65–75)	75 (30)
13 story elevator apts	1.8	215–240 (85–95)	100 (40)

Any housing type can be built at lower densities than those shown, although it may be difficult to justify much lower figures economically. It may prove impossible to maintain community facilities and services if densities are too low. Single detached houses are commonly built at very low densities, ranging down to one or two houses per acre in some suburbs or one house on four acres in others. Such development is costly to service and wasteful of land and infrastructure.

Each housing type also has a range of tenure possibilities on which the site plan is necessarily based. In the most basic

Fee simple tenure

253

FIGURE 77 *Housing types can be built at a range of density. The dense town houses of Beacon Hill, Boston contrast with those in the open landscape of Reston, Virginia.*

sense, there are only two tenures—freehold and leasehold—but there are a myriad of variations. Rights to housing usually derive from the land on which it sits; hence site arrangements are important, and tenure decisions bear on how a site can be organized.

Fee simple freehold is what people normally refer to as "ownership." It means that all claims by others have been discharged or have been agreed to in the form of "covenants," and the owner has a deed to the land which spells these out. Except through taxation, he has no further obligations to pay for the land, although he may grant others a mortgage on the land as security for repayment of a promissory note. He can exclude others from his property within the rules and mores of the society. All adjacent property is divided into two categories, privately owned and publicly owned, and the latter is assigned to some public body. Easements registered in the deeds may insure access or views across the private land, however. Generally, all privately owned land fronts on a public street, and its subdivision follows the rules established by the local government. Under such tenure, common facilities are best dedicated to a public body with taxing powers.

Detached housing, and much street-fronting row or semi-detached housing, is usually developed under fee simple ownership. If the houses are attached, property is subdivided along the party walls. But where apartments and certain other attached housing forms are to be owned by their occupants, they require a way to hold and maintain shared property, ranging from common areas (a private street, parking area or playground) to shared structure (stairways, corridors, foundations or roof). At least four variations on fee-simple ownership provide for this collective responsibility.

The simplest method is that each fee-simple owner holds an *undivided interest* in a common facility through a provision in their deeds which passes that interest along to successive owners. The system relies on a sense of obligation among owners for maintaining the property, and so this arrangement is only workable if the ownership group is small and close-knit, the costs of ownership are minimal, and the interests in maintaining the common facility are equal and apparent. Five homeowners may share an undivided interest in a wooded ravine at the rear of their lots, viewing it as an extension of their outdoor living areas and having no ambitions for changing its character. But where the facility de-

Interest in common

255

FIGURE 78
Sunnyside was built in Queens, New York, in 1924–28 on land already divided into narrow blocks. Modest row houses were put around quiet courts which became a commons for the block, protected by 50-year easements.

FIGURE 79
Now the easements have expired at Sunnyside and housing owners have moved to reclaim the commons as private grounds. The meaning of the open space has shifted.

mands more upkeep and attention, we must look to other arrangements.

Most jurisdictions permit the creation of *mandatory homes associations,* a second way to manage shared facilities. Membership in the association is automatic upon purchasing a home in the development area. By vote of the membership, annual maintenance charges are levied against all property owners. If these charges are not paid, the association can place a lien on the owner's property. Large developments give their homes association permanent responsibility for many facilities—open spaces, lakes, clubhouses, golf courses, swimming pools, parking compounds, day care centers, and the like. They can, if so chartered, offer services beyond maintenance (social events, a newspaper, etc.). They frequently become a miniature government. One example is the Columbia Association, which takes responsibility for most of the shared facilities in that Maryland new town.

Homes associations

Reference 62

On a much smaller scale, a homes association could be created to ensure that pavement is maintained and snow is cleared along a private cul-de-sac serving, say, three houses. A common motivation for assigning facilities to a homes association rather than to a public body is to escape some straitjacket of public policy: the desire to cluster housing on small lots to preserve an open area, a preference for narrower streets than public bodies will accept, the wish to create a level of amenities or facilities well above what public bodies are prepared to provide, and so on. But in cases where these facilities duplicate what local governments would otherwise provide, the owner faces a system of dual taxation, which can be a serious financial liability. In most cases, however, homes associations are a workable way of providing for facilities that are neither public nor exclusively private.

Creation of a *condominium corporation* is an alternative to the homes association when there is greater interdependency among the shared facilities. The corporation not only owns and maintains the common elements—in the case of an apartment structure this may include everything except the internal finish and space of the units—but typically it also holds the land on which the housing sits. The condominium was originally devised as a form of fee-simple ownership for apartment dwellers. Recently, however, condominium tenure has spread to moderate density townhouses, semi-detached, and even detached housing, where consistently high maintenance is desired for building exteriors and grounds, such as in exclusive resort and retirement developments.

Condominiums

FIGURE 80
The common park and clustered housing of Baldwin Hills, Los Angeles is possible because of cooperative ownership. By contrast, the surrounding areas are developed for fee-simple ownership, and all facilities beyond the lot are publicly maintained.

Owners of condominium units must meet at least annually to agree on the budget, type of maintenance, and regulations for the coming year—issues which can be quite divisive if members regard their units differently. While the practical size of a condominium depends on what is to be shared (how many units are needed to afford a swimming pool or to warrant a full-time maintenance person?), experience has shown that beyond about 150 housing units it is extremely difficult to maintain a cohesive management group. Many professional managers favor projects of no more than 50–75 units, or even smaller if possible. Mixing units with quite different maintenance responsibilities should be avoided. Coupling high-rise apartments (whose elevators are prone to breakdown) and low-rise townhouses (which front on open spaces that need to be manicured) is a sure formula for conflict. Minding these constraints, condominium tenure provides considerable flexibility for site design and allows continued control over the appearance and use of a housing area.

The final step in the continuum from individual to collective ownership is represented by the *cooperative corporation*. Here the owner becomes a tenant in a building owned by a cooperative, of which he is a shareholding member. The entire ensemble—exteriors and interiors, grounds, parking facilities, and common spaces—is owned by one entity, although maintenance responsibilities may be divided. Cooperatives are preferable to condominiums when members wish to control the future occupants of units if they are sold. Because all shareholders are equally liable for any expenses (including sometimes a "blanket" mortgage on all or part of the property) the cooperative corporation normally reserves the right to approve any transfers of shares. In stratospheric New York City coops (we refer both to height and price), this is a license to discriminate; in low-income cooperatives it is a way to ensure that newcomers are prepared to shoulder their share of maintenance. Arguments over new occupants will be added to conflicts over levels of maintenance, but tenants have substantial control over the future of their neighborhood. One critical issue typically surfaces: should departing tenants receive the market price for their units, or only their original cost? That is, who gets any unearned increment or inflated value: the individual or the group? Cooperative tenure means that the entire complex can be thought about without property subdivision. Occupants regard themselves as owners, not as renters, and are likely to adopt a long-term view of their housing.

Cooperatives

259

Leasehold

Leasehold tenure is the opposite of all of these forms, and can take many forms beyond the standard one- or two-year term. A very long-term leasehold (say 99 years) is almost indistinguishable from ownership. Even a 10- or 20-year lease may encourage an occupant to make improvements and do maintenance. Buildings may be owned on land that is leased. Under such a scheme, the regular lease payments can provide funds for the maintenance of common spaces and facilities, much as in a home association or condominium. Leases may be prepaid, so that the situation is virtually equivalent to freehold purchase, except as the end of lease term nears. As a practical matter, land lease periods must be long enough to provide the security needed for mortgaging the owned property, and so that there is an incentive for continued maintenance. Even so, the arrangements for renewal or termination are difficult issues.

Many public bodies are beginning to lease their land instead of selling it to allow for the recapture of the unearned increment, that is, any increase of land value that is not due to improvements on the site but to more general changes. This value is captured by periodically raising rents to reflect general rises in land values. Leasing land at favorable rates can also be a way of lowering the down payment, and so making it easier for lower-income households to buy a house. But there are many political difficulties with the latter form of land leasing: rates seldom keep pace with inflation because of the impact on those least able to pay; it is virtually impossible to evict homeowners at the end of the lease term even if the land is needed for other public purposes, and a long period of uncertainty, even disinvestment, can precede the expiration of the lease.

Finally, there is the option of strict leasehold, or rental development, where the occupants do not own their units. Many apartment buildings have been rented for decades; they are not necessarily prone to deterioration, but must be designed with different expectations of tenant responsibility. Much depends on who the tenants are, how transient they regard themselves, how much they expect of management, and what sense of social obligation they feel toward other residents. Increasingly, housing is first built as rental units and later converted to condominiums once desirability is proved. But there will be design conflicts to be resolved, if housing is to work equally well for both types of tenure.

Tenure choices, density, housing form and the management system are intimately linked. So are a number of other choices in virtually every housing development project. These include:

the scale and form of the residential module,
providing access to the unit,
storing the car,
orienting the units,
supporting everyday life,
assuring privacy and views, and
increasing security.

If by *module* we mean that group of housing units that appears, and is thought of, as a distinct unit, then its proper size is set by many considerations. Where a consensual management coincides with that module, the grouping must not be so large that members lose their common interest. The desired common facilities will suggest a natural size.

There are social imperatives. An area designed for families with small children must be large enough to make it probable that there are at least two or three children in each two-year age bracket below, say, 12 years of age. If only half of the houses will have children of that age, this might imply a module of at least 24 housing units. Among adults, there should also be a reasonable chance of finding a friend or two nearby with shared interests, but, since adults are more mobile and their interests more diverse, this is more elusive to translate into group size. Much depends on the stablity of the population, the breadth of its social spectrum, and its customs of neighboring. There is some evidence that, after living in an area for several years, people are able to greet by name other people from about 15 households and that they will recognize other people from up to 30. Casual observation suggests that groups of 15 households are a typical social-spatial unit in suburban areas, and that when a street has 30 or more units along it, it is seldom considered one social entity. But the context matters. In a dense urban setting two hundred families may feel they "belong" to a tight-knit block, especially if they have organized to defend and improve their turf.

Social ties are more easily formed among households of similar socioeconomic class. We can increase the chances of such grouping by creating modules of perhaps 15 units of similar type, size, tenure and cost. Avoid abrupt changes in these factors on adjacent sites. Within a wider radius, there is a virtue in mixing, to avoid social isolation and to break down common stereotypes. We can hope for more: that diverse groups will choose to live together to share each other's worlds, but this is not achieved by coercion.

Size and social composition are not the only issues of the residential module. There are physical choices in how these small groups of houses are to be related, internally and to the outside world. Module and access are linked. The common scheme is the street front pattern, in which the building units—houses, rows, or apartment towers—line both sides of a street. Access and orientation are easy and there is little ambiguity in the plan. If visually monotonous, the corridor space can be varied by path alignment, building setback and landscaping.

In a second type, rows of units are disposed end-on to the street. The street frontage per unit, which is one index of site development cost, is sharply reduced. Units are removed from the noise and danger of the street but also from its convenience. Successive rows of units may face toward each other on common entrance pathways, or they may turn their backs on each other to enjoy some favorable orientation. Rows may run through from one street to the next, to form a continuous path system at right angles to the streets.

A third module is the court arrangement, in which groups of units face inward on a common open space. This is done for social and visual reasons: to promote neighborly relations, to exclude outsiders, to provide a pleasant space. Vehicular circulation may be allowed to enter the court, perhaps in a narrow one-way loop, or may pass through it in some indirect fashion (as in the English square), or may be excluded, as in the "close." The court with its circulation may shrink to the width of a cul-de-sac. The internal space of the court or cul-de-sac may be open to the street, forming an inlet of the major street space, or the entrance may be narrowed—even formalized with a gateway—to produce an independent place, secure and well identified. The land behind the buildings may be committed to public open space, to private yards, or to service access. Any resulting land in the block interiors is relatively inexpensive to provide since it adds little to the street frontage. If raw land is cheap, then large parks, gardens, or allotments may be provided at little additional cost.

Court systems are economical except when loops are brought into the court, and are favorable (sometimes too favorable) to neighborly intercourse. They may complicate the street system, lengthen the journey for service vehicles, and make units difficult for a stranger to locate. Courts look best on fairly flat ground or when sloping uphill from the observer. A marked cross-slope destroys the visual unity of the space, and a downhill cul-de-sac gives its terminal buildings a peculiar sense of inferiority and instability, and raises problems of surface drainage and utilities.

A fourth general module is the cluster, in which units are concentrated and surrounded by open space. The street may pass alongside the cluster or penetrate it. This module produces a strong visual effect of mass, the opposite of the spatial focus of the court type. Access may be complicated, but a visual sense of unity can be achieved without forcing social intercourse. There are significant savings on roads and utilities, and overall density can be maintained even while preserving substantial open space. A number of recent developments have used this principle to conserve a handsome piece of landscape. The most difficult problem is likely to be the interrelations between individual buildings, in terms of privacy and the use of adjacent land. These modular layouts apply to all types of residential units: single-family houses, mobile homes, rows, even slab and tower apartments. Differences in scale of course will change the effect.

The relation of parking and housing is another set of decisions. Most people prefer to park within arm's reach of their kitchen door. Parking is inevitably troublesome, especially where densities are high. The parking space is the second most costly item of real estate, after the housing unit itself.

Parking

How much parking should be provided? The type of occupancy, the size of units, and the traditions of transit usage will dictate this. It is now customary in North America to provide one to one-and-one-half parking or garage spaces for every dwelling unit. Many suburban localities require two spaces per unit, particularly where singles are expected. When parking is pooled and unassigned, the ratio may be slightly lower. In central city housing, the parking ratio may drop as low as half a space per unit, although some rationing of parking privileges may then be necessary. In elderly housing areas, still fewer spaces will be needed, perhaps only one space for each three units. Because many residential parking spaces are vacant during daytime hours, they can serve double duty if shared with a complementary use such as offices. In the inner city, approximately 65% of the overnight parking requirement may be available for sharing during the day. These figures are only rough guides. A brief study of local experience in a comparable project is the most reliable way to peg the parking ratio.

The parking supplied and demanded has a circular relationship. If parking is inexpensive and easy to obtain, more people are encouraged to own autos and drive them, even in areas where transit is a good choice. Mortgage lenders may mandate high parking ratios to enhance marketability, and some local governments do so to avoid overloading on-street parking areas. On the other hand, since parking is expensive in land and construction, it is worth the attempt to roll standards back to the absolute minimum. One solution is to construct spaces according to a low estimate of need at the outset, reserving land and money to add more spaces later if required. If not necessary for parking in a year or two, that land and money can then be devoted to other purposes.

Garages

At low densities, surface parking is relatively simple, being provided at the curb, or in small one- or two-car parking stalls beside the unit. In wintry climates most people prefer to have a garage to protect their car. In more temperate climates, garages are equally prevalent but find many other uses, ranging from active storage to home enterprises to inexpensive expansion space. A carport is a partial substitute for a garage, and open parking, while workable, is third best. Placement of the garage has never been satisfactorily solved, except in low-density, single-family areas. The old location at the rear of the lot entails a long driveway, reducing the size of the private yard, or an alley, which is costly. A position directly at the edge of the street right-of-way masks front entrances and destroys the street space, while endangering passing pedestrians, particularly children. Raising the dwelling unit above its parking is expensive, produces internal stairs, and reduces street surveillance from the active indoor areas. Location alongside the dwelling, on the same building line, is often the best technique if there is sufficient space between units, although it may block access to the rear yard. Garages can be paired. If attached, the garage can be entered directly from the house, but a fire separation must then be maintained. In any case, direct association of parking with the unit to which it is assigned is generally preferred if net densities are 10 units per acre or less.

At middle densities—25-75 units per hectare (10-30 per acre)—there is a choice between consolidated or distributed parking. Most occupants will prefer to have parking near the door. But pavement for parking and access roads will consume a large proportion of the ground surface—approximately one-third of it at a density of 75 units per hectare (30 per acre). Street spaces are dominated by the automobile. Where there is a change of elevation across the site, it may be possible to tuck the automobile under the unit on one side while maintaining a connection between living space and the ground on the other side, one level above. This may also be accomplished on flat sites by lowering the roadways half a story and raising outdoor spaces an equal distance.

Sometimes it is possible to group two to six garages together, between or behind the units, or in small courts so that they are convenient and not visually disruptive. If budget permits, an even better solution is to create a parking "street," partly below grade, in which the parking area is covered by a deck that becomes a vehicle-free outdoor space. Such arrangements simplify snow management when they cover access and parking together but are costly if the parking area must be fire contained. By covering the area only partially and separating it from the dwellings, more conventional construction may be possible.

In many cases, it will be impossible to avoid open storage of the car, along the curb or in parking lots. Curb parking can be ameliorated by occasional projections of the planting strip, to break the line of cars and to provide a safe launching pad for crossing the street. Curb parking must be kept away from intersections. But parking on the street is expensive, since it devotes highly accessible and heavily paved space to a low value use. Where cars are grouped into off-street parking lots, it is preferable to keep these lots no larger than six to ten spaces, since larger lots will be remote from most of the units and visually depressing. The site should be organized so that the parking area can be seen from most of the units. But it is possible to improve the look of small or medium-sized parking lots or stubs by dropping them a few feet below pedestrian grade, so that the line of sight passes over the car. This also makes it easier to screen the lots with planting or low walls. Parking lots also serve a social function—as meeting place, auto maintenance center, or hard surface play area for children—and this must be considered in design.

At net densities above 75 units per hectare (30 per acre), automobiles will overwhelm the site unless at least some are placed in garages. In many suburban apartment areas

Curb and lot parking

(often advertised, with some irony, as "garden apartments") virtually all the ground space is occupied by the buildings and the parking lots. Because parking in structures costs five times as much as on-grade arrangements, it will be avoided unless high land costs justify an added intensity of development. Above-ground garages are generally less expensive than underground ones, since they do not need ventilation equipment, or waterproofing where there is a high water table. Garages are frequently an eyesore. The simplest form of structure parks one level of cars on a pavement a half-story below grade, and a second level on a light open deck above them. Their access ramps are short and inexpensive, and two levels are obtained for the price of constructing one. Where multi-story structures are necessary, it is worth investigating whether all cars must be housed that way. Some cars may only be used occasionally and can be parked in remote lots at a distance from the site.

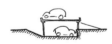

So intimate to our way of life and so necessary in suburban areas, the automobile bedevils the site planner. Wherever other modes of transport are in use—walking, bicycling, bus travel—residential areas are more pleasant, economical and commodious, as well as freer from pollution and danger. But most North Americans are not easily divorced from their car. It provides too many satisfactions and meshes with too many aspects of their lives. Divorce might be wise but will require fundamental changes in the pattern of living and in the technology and ownership of the means of transport. It might require a return to compact densities, plus a renewed and efficient public transit system, clustered services, and a loss of freedom in vacation travel. Or city travel might have to be restricted to some new, small, low-powered vehicle, while large cars were stored on the periphery—perhaps rented or communally owned. Or living at moderately low densities might be coupled with a diffuse microbus system, routed on call, plus special paths for bicycles, horses and electric carts, while larger private vehicles would be restricted to infrequent use by means of permits or user charges. To be successful, the solution must satisfy all the functions for which the automobile is used today.

Orientation

Many have hoped that the rise in energy costs during the seventies would trigger a reappraisal of the private automobile. So far it has not. However, it *has* led to a reawakening of concern for thermal performance. Good solar orientation and attention to wind direction and microclimate can measurably decrease the energy requirements of a

References 48, 60

266

dwelling. An ideal orientation is sometimes proposed, but, under ordinary circumstances in the temperate zone, properly spaced single- and two-family structures can be designed to fit many orientations. The problem of standard orientation only arises when stock designs are used. There are several simple rules for good thermal performance: in temperate climates, principal daytime living spaces should face south; outdoor decks or patios should not be on the north; openings on north faces should be reduced, especially where winter winds are from that direction; westerly openings should be protected from the late summer sun by deciduous vegetation or other form of screen; winds should be broken near entrances and openings; cross-ventilation should be provided to all living and sleeping spaces. By varying interior plans, these criteria can usually be met regardless of street orientation.

Orientation is more of a problem as densities increase and units have fewer open sides. With two exposed sides, row houses, maisonettes, or gallery access apartments are usually oriented to face east and west so that all rooms have some sun. But the west face may then suffer from heat and glare, and buildings can as well be designed to face north and south if principal living areas are placed on the south. In very hot climates, of course, much of this is reversed: large glass areas must be avoided on the south and especially on the west; outdoor living spaces must have shade; and orientation to capture prevailing breezes is essential.

Two-sided units have the benefit of cross-ventilation. In apartments, this virtue often persuades designers to advocate multi-level through-units with internal stairways instead of flats entered from a double-loaded corridor. Small walkups can at least place their units at corners. It is the orientation of the typical tall, central corridor, slab apartment building that is the most difficult problem. Not only does it have a serious external influence on wind and sun shadow, but each of its dwelling units has only one orientation. In the higher latitudes, facades facing north and south must be avoided to prevent sunless dwellings and sunless ground. A north-south axis, while preferable, is not ideal, since it exposes some dwellings to the hot western sun. In the tropics this can be intolerable. The local climate must be consulted for the preferable alignment of this awkward type. In the Boston region, this might be a slab facing somewhat north of east and south of west, which is a compromise between the demands for winter sunlight and summer breeze.

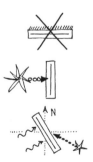

Orientation is more difficult if the building skin is considered as an impermeable membrane. As an alternative, the entire zone immediately around the dwelling can be regarded as a place where indoor and outdoor climates meet. On tall apartments, balconies may belong to the outdoors in summer, but then "button up" with glazing to become sunrooms in winter. The landscaping nearest the dwelling can be designed to temper the climate in each of the seasons, providing pools of shade in summer and warm sun traps in winter.

Spaces for
children

Reference 23

The grounds of a housing site are, for many of its residents, the most important setting for social life. Children are not only the most committed group of users but also the brokers for many adult friendships (or enmities). Acquaintances are formed across back fences, on front walks, at formal playgrounds where the youngest children play, at garbage disposal areas, coming and going from a common laundry, waiting at an adjacent transit stop, at a host of other points of contact. They may blossom into something more if there is desire and reason. For young children, for their mothers and for the elderly who are confined to a site, the nearby settings and possibilities for contact are a large component of their everyday world.

A common solution bundles all the stereotyped activities of children below adolescence into a single facility, tucked away in an unusable corner of the ground. Teenagers are usually forgotten altogether. The remainder of the ground is then designed for its appearance to the adult eye. A few hours on the site will uncover the unreality of this approach. Toddlers may spend time in a playground, supervised by their parents, but older children will roam from place to place. They seek out a hard-surfaced area for games and cycling, another place to dig the earth, an isolated area where they can construct a primitive shelter, some casual water where they can risk getting wet, trees to climb, and any other possibilities for adventure and stimulation. It is better to distribute a varied set of play opportunities in many locations rather than to concentrate them in one area.

This places heavy demands on landscape construction and maintenance. Parking areas will be hockey arenas, baseball diamonds and basketball courts. Retaining walls will be climbed and walked along, benches will be stages, and flowerbeds will be ideal for earthworks, especially in spring when they turn to mud. All this can be restrained by strenuous adult supervision, but it is preferable to design the site to

268

withstand the assault. Regular maintenance will always be necessary when children are present. In low-income housing, if regular maintenance cannot be assured, the child density may have to be limited. It has proved difficult to maintain the grounds of North American public housing areas when there are more than 50 children per acre. This is not an absolute limit but one that reflects our usual maintenance commitment.

In regard to teenagers, the best strategy may be to ensure that the "hanging out," the socializing centered on the automobile, and the noisy events will occur at arm's length from adults. The alienation of the adolescent, associated with their drive to carve out a separate identity, mirrors our confusion about their place in the larger society. At best, site facilities provide an outlet, but the underlying confusion remains. If numbers warrant, a separate teen center, an auto workyard, a place for a small business enterprise, or an active recreation area (basketball, tennis) can be useful additions.

There are many communal uses which cut across the age groups and can encourage social contact. Allotment gardens, group drying yards, areas for picnics or barbecues, putting or bowling greens, swimming or wading pools, tennis courts, sidewalk cafes, an animal courtyard, are only a few. Until recently, communal provisions have been relatively neglected in this country. We favor the individual lot, plus services for larger areas installed by local government. But the growth of homes associations, condominiums and cooperatives demonstrates that community management is an attractive and affordable alternative.

The private yard is still an important use of the ground in a family housing site. In an approximate order of frequency, it is used for sitting, playing, cooking and eating, clothes drying, gardening, entertaining and storage. Children under the age of 3 will spend the vast majority of their outdoor time in the yard, particularly if it is fenced and can be overseen by parents from indoors. To serve these functions, a space of 12 by 12 m (40 by 40 ft) is likely to be a minimum. But if that quantity of ground is not available, then a simple "outdoor room" of 6 by 6 m (20 by 20 ft) may be provided, simply for sitting. When outdoor spaces shrink to 3.5 by 4.5 m (12 by 15 ft), they are hardy used at all, and if fenced seem claustrophobic. Private outdoor space should be intimately related to the unit, with a suitable slope and a good orientation. On steep ground, it may be necessary

Private spaces

Reference 20

Reference 23

269

to build open decks or to do massive grading. At all but the lowest densities, at least some part of the yard should be given visual privacy by a fence or hedges. Visual privacy from above is equally essential, and it must be considered from the start since it is affected by building location and orientation. As one example of a general standard for adjacent open space, housing developments in Sweden are required to provide at least 100 sq m (1080 sq ft) of usable open space within 50 m (165 ft) of any dwelling entrance, reachable without crossing any vehicular way. To be counted, this space must not be occupied by any nonresidential use, or be within 3 m (10 ft) of any road, or be located on over a 50% grade, or have less than one hour of sun at the equinox, or be subject to noise of more that 55 dBA. Thus a multitude of qualities are condensed into one performance requirement.

Privacy and view

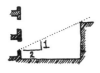

The spacing between buildings not only affects the ground left over for outdoor use but also the livability of the interior rooms. If structures are too close to each other, especially if they surround a space, noises will resonate within them. Every room should have adequate light and air. A substantial piece of sky should be visible through the windows from normal standing positions in the room to ensure good daylight and prevent claustrophobia. A minimum standard may be that from each window of any principal room, the view should not be obstructed by any artificial element that rises more than 30 degrees above the horizon. This suggests spacing buildings at more than twice their height, but denser arrangements will also pass the test if windows are carefully placed.

Even where this rule is observed, it is unpleasant to look directly into windows close enough to destroy visual or acoustic privacy, and it is advisable to avoid any layout in which one eye-level window faces another more closely than 18 m (60 ft) away. Blank walls or high windows may be needed where units face on to the private areas or facades of other units. Similarly, no principal window should be closer than 4.5 m (15 ft) from any public way, unless that way is well below the sill.

Taken together, these standards make it impossible to duplicate many older dense residential areas considered charming and urbane (usually by visitors). However, there are innovative arrangements which fulfill the spirit of these standards and yet permit high densities. Opposing windows can be angled to prevent direct vision. Ground floors can be raised three to four feet above the street to allow windows on the property line above the eyes of passers-by. "Blinders" can be installed alongside a window to prevent vision into adjacent yards. Deep balcony railings discourage views down into private space below. Some rooms in particular types of units may not need windows—the sleeping areas of studio apartments, for example. But for visual and psychological relief, at least some windows of a dwelling should command a long, free view.

The desire for privacy often runs afoul of another objective—the security of residents and their possessions. Vandalism, larceny and assault are common dangers. Trained police and changes in the organization of society are the most effective ways of dealing with human aggression. But where such dangers exist, the layout and organization of exterior space can make a place more or less secure. The key techniques are surveillance and giving local residents a sense of territorial responsibility.

To provide for surveillance, one arranges doors, external pathways, parking areas and building corridors so that they are visible from a number of windows and from the street. A delicate balance must be struck here: residential units and spaces must be sufficiently on view to detect any criminal activity but not so open as to destroy privacy or give potential offenders a clear signal about vacant units or low probablities of detection. Electronic and optical devices can be used to supplement the eye. Paths are laid out so that the pedestrian sees his route well ahead, without encountering nearby hiding places. Routes and their bordering spaces are lighted with moderate illumination levels. Grounds are organized so that they can be easily patrolled in some rapid, systematic way, and so that multiple escape routes are not provided for the criminal.

Surveillance increases when residents have a clear sense of the territory that is their responsibility. Territorial concern means defining spaces so that they are either clearly part of the public street, or as clearly attached to a dwelling or a specific group of dwellings, and thus subject to resident control if they choose to exercise it. When the governance of a housing area puts the responsibility for security in the hands of local residents, control improves. Walls, locked doors, fences and other barriers are useful only if they can be monitored. Their greatest value is to define territory, to delay the trespasser, and to make him visible. Many of these security techniques interfere with privacy, on the one hand, or the sense of openness and warmth in the landscape, on the other. But where social peace is lacking, a defensive stance is necessary.

Detached houses

Every site design must reconcile these multiple require-ments for access, parking, management, social interaction, orientation, behavioral fit, privacy, view and security within the context of density and tenure. While there are many possible housing forms, a number of stereotypes have proved their worth. We include them here by way of example and as a challenge for further invention.

The *single-family detached* house remains the mainstay in North America, accounting for half or more of annual housing starts. Its advantages are well known: it receives adequate light and air from its four exposures and provides room for gardening, play, parking and other outdoor uses. It enjoys direct access to the street and its own private grounds, which can be shielded from noise and view. It can be built, maintained, remodelled, bought, and sold inde-pendently. It can be constructed at reasonable cost, using light frame materials, although it is not the least expensive type of housing. In many parts of the world, it is popularly considered to be the ideal house. It symbolizes the individual family.

The archetypal single family detached house is built at a net density of 12 or 15 per hectare (5 or 6 per acre), on lots with a frontage of 18 to 22 m (60 to 75 ft). Houses are set back uniformly, often 7.5 m (25 ft), from the front property line and a minimum of 1.5 or 3 m (5 or 10 ft) from side property lines, depending on local regulations. The units may be one or two floors, adorned in a variety of popularly understood styles. Cars will be parked in an attached garage or in the open beside the house.

There have been many criticisms of the detached house: that it is the main cause of city sprawl, which eats up rural land; that it makes public transit service uneconomical, that it is only suitable for two-parent families where one is pre-pared to (wo)man the home front. These presumed liabilities have not deterred home buyers, but the steady rise in land and servicing costs has spurred a search for detached housing forms that can be built at higher densities and use less street frontage per unit. One direct response is simply to reduce lot widths to 12 or 14 m (40 or 45 ft), which is adequate if houses are modest in size and two floors in height and if any garages are set in front or at the rear of units rather than at their sides.

Reference 51

272

Another way of reducing lot size is to do away with one of the side yards, setting the house directly alongside one property line. Such "zero-lot line" housing can be built *Reference 46* at a net density of 25 to 30 units per hectare (10 to 12 per acre). Maintenance easements on adjacent properties are required for painting and repairing walls located on the lot line. Because of the close proximity of units, it is essential to distinguish the walls that may have windows, from those that must be kept blank to preserve the privacy of neighboring yards. Fence and driveway locations must also be controlled. These site-specific rules are frequently recorded as covenants to prevent subsequent owners from upsetting a delicately balanced scheme.

Rather than reduce lot size, the average frontage can be reduced by changing lot shape. "Flag lots" are permitted in some localities. They make two tiers of development, the one served in the normal manner along the street, the second located behind it and reached by a driveway. This rear lot may have only 3 or 4 m (10 or 12 ft) of actual street frontage. If house services are also combined, significant cost reductions are possible. There are many other variations on this system.

Mobile homes are a further response to the problem of delivering detached housing at affordable prices. They require Mobile homes less land and are considerably less expensive to build than *Reference 65* site-framed housing because of the materials used, the lower cost of factory labor, the economies of scale, and the more lenient codes that apply to them. "Mobile" is a misnomer, since most of these houses will move only once—to the site where they are first located. Indeed, the trailer industry, whose products originally served summer campers and migratory workmen, has evolved into a prefabricated house production system, manufacturing 3.75 and 4.25 m (12- and 14-ft) wide modules that now constitute 20 percent of the new housing units delivered in the United States. These units range from narrow, self-contained trailers to "expandables" and "double-wides," which are indistinguishable from a normal bungalow. There have been many experiments with stacking modules or inserting them into structural frames, but none has proved as successful as the single-floor manufactured house.

These manufactured houses have substantial advantages, especially to the new family or the retiree. They are inexpensive; they are easy to buy (though not as easy to sell); the buyer knows exactly what he is getting; they are

See Figure 81

Reference 91

compact and easy to maintain; often they may be purchased fully equipped and furnished. They have the glamour of newness, and some of the social camaraderie of camping lingers on in the trailer parks. But that image has also meant that manufactured houses are frequently banished to the outskirts of cities and towns, onto land that is not suitable for normal housing or is being held speculatively, awaiting a more permanent use. Mobile units are placed on leased sites, and usually little is invested in landscaping or common facilities. Over time, these developments become a clutter of parked vehicles and impermanent self-improvements— storage sheds, lean-tos, children's wading pools, clothes drying lines, and the like—filling the spaces between regimented rows of trailers. Normally set on the diagonal, units have no privacy, and there is little sense of responsibility for order and maintenance. Small wonder that they are resisted by so many communities.

Manufactured houses which look like site-built ones can easily be integrated into regular subdivisions if their construction standards meet local codes. There are also examples of well-planned mobile developments. Landscaping is important, softening the hard, shiny appearance, creating street spaces, providing privacy to the individual yards. Setting units at right angles to each other or clustering them around a common space can break the deadly regimentation. Sometimes permanent false fronts are erected, and units are inserted within them, hardly noticeable from the street. In a few places, automobiles have been parked at the edge of the site, and electric carts are provided to reach the units, allowing roadways to be given a more intimate scale.

Mobile houses highlight the visual problem in all detached housing areas: how to avoid the appearance of endless repetition, on the one hand, while guarding against total disorder, on the other. The problem arises from the size of the separate units, relative to the development area, and the car, and the associated right-of-way. Where houses can be clustered or related across a footway or pedestrian space, the proportions become much more pleasant, and the ground surface can be designed to unify the whole. Any reduction of street width or of the depth of the front yard always helps.

There are other devices for giving unity to small structures. Individual houses may be linked with screen walls, planting, garages or porches. Garages may be paired or grouped in compounds to improve their proportions, although this may mean new ownership arrangements. House

FIGURE 81
*Homes developed
from manufac-
tured models
which bear little
resemblance to
their mobile home
predecessors.*

spacing and setback may be varied to create visual groups
or to modulate the street space. Tall forest trees may take
over the role of space enclosure, contrasting with the low
roofs of the houses and providing a larger-scale structure.
Individual houses may use similar roof slopes, wall materials
or proportions of window openings. Low-density houses
suffer from a particular discontinuity at intersections, just
where a strong enclosure is most desired. Screen walls can
counteract this, or special house groups, or corner units designed to be set closer to the street. Diminuitive scale is not
by itself unpleasant: the tiny wooden houses in Oak Bluffs,
on the island of Martha's Vineyard, Massachusetts, are
packed together along the pedestrian ways of the former
tenting ground, and the effect is charming. But everything
is in scale with these highly decorated houses: the pathways,
the gardens, the vistas, and the spaces devoted to car and
service vehicles.

Older cities provide a rich array of attached housing: **Semis and**
the Boston Triple-Decker, The Philadelphia-Style Duplex, **duplexes**
the Queens Quad, the Toronto Semi, and so on, each a
response to local populations and norms. One unit of these
two- or three-family houses is often occupied by the owner,
while the others are rented out, so that houses serve different
types of households. Internal apartments and rear-yard units

275

are now being added to single-family houses in our middle-age suburbs to regain such diversity.

There are at least three distinct varieties of two-family housing: the *semi-detached house*, of British origin, where the units are joined side-by-side, the *duplex*, where one unit is over the other, and *rear-lot housing*, where one unit occupies the front half and the other the rear half of a lot. The "semi" has almost all the virtues of a detached house. With three exposed sides instead of four, it can provide private entrances and outdoor areas, and has relatively few sound separation problems if properly designed. By eliminating one sideyard, land and service frontage is reduced. Traditional examples also share driveways with the next unit. While in divided ownership, semis may look like one large house, especially if the entrance of one unit is tucked around to the side.

The duplex, on the other hand, usually joins an owner-occupied unit with one which is rented out, providing an opportunity for small-scale investment and management. Creating private outdoor spaces for each unit is now more difficult. One solution is to give one unit the front and the other the rear ground space; another is to provide a balcony for the upper unit (traditionally facing the street) while allocating the rear yard to the lower one. Another variant follows a pattern that has developed by individual initiative in many older areas: a small apartment without an outdoor area is set over a large family housing unit. The apartment may be rented out for extra income or may house older parents or other members of an extended family.

The duplex and the semi are being rediscovered as housing costs increase and ways are sought to bring ownership within reach. Rear lot housing is also being reconsidered. Granny flats attached to the rear of houses are one example; another is the conversion of garages in rear yards into living units. Identification and access can prove difficult when existing housing is converted, but in the case of new construction, a front-to-rear division may be the most desirable way to double densities without eroding low-density character.

Another unit type is the *quad* or four unit building, of which there are many varieties. Frank Lloyd Wright's "Suntop Homes" in Ardmore, Pennsylania, organized units in a pinwheel pattern; each had a private yard without being overlooked by another. Pinwheels have at least two difficulties: they require street frontages on two sides, which is costly in terms of services, and their private yards must abut

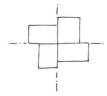

public street space, making screening essential and converting streets into inactive corridors. Other quad designs are, in effect, attached duplexes. Their problem is how to accommodate so many automobiles in so little frontage. The Queens Quad resolves this in a totally unsatisfying way by making the entire front yard an auto court. Except as an infill unit, it may be better to build a row of four ground-access units than to attempt this complex pattern.

Among ground-access types, the *row house* provides the most space at the lowest cost and is the cheapest to maintain and heat. It will provide as much outdoor privacy as the semi, and more than the duplex, while making more efficient use of the land that would be otherwise lost in narrow side yards. Row houses can vary in width from as little as 3.5 m (12 ft) to as much as 10.5 m (35 ft); they can be one or more stories high but usually are two. It is much easier to achieve coherent visual spaces with continuous rows of units, particularly if they curve to follow the terrain or are shaped to enclose an area. Since the term "row house" has working-class connotations, developers frequently refer to it as a "townhouse" or "terrace house." Row houses

A fundamental choice in planning row houses is whether to aim for fee-simple ownership with no residual spaces or accept some form of collective ownership. In fee simple, every property must front on a public street, automobiles must be accommodated on each unit site, and private yards away from the street will generally only be accessible through the unit. The main barriers to such traditional row houses today are the burdens imposed by public regulation—excessive rights-of-way, costly services, and other restrictions such as limits on the frequency of curb cuts. Private streets, and the institutions necessary to maintain them, are a circumvention of these restrictions. But once some form of collective tenure is accepted, there are many options for grouping the units.

When row houses have one street frontage, the internal arrangement will depend on cultural attitudes. Some prefer the living and dining rooms to be on the street side, which become the limit of how far guests will penetrate into the home. The kitchen and private yard are backstage. Others prefer the kitchen and its eating area to be in front, reserving the living room for special access and allowing a direct link to an associated outdoor space. With either arrangement, storage and service functions must be provided for at the front or rear entrance. The most frequent complaints about living in row houses stem from a poorly conceived entry, storage, disposal, cycle parking or other service arrangement.

Another concern, equally bound up in cultural attitudes, is the fear that personal identity may be lost in a row house complex. But it is quite possible to design row houses so that each unit has a different physiognomy or so that each can be personalized by the occupant. That units can be visibly individualized is important to some people, especially those with modest incomes (and also designers, regardless of income), for whom the house is a critical symbol of self. Others choose different ways to assert their identity, and may wish their unit to be outwardly similar to their neighbors, personalizing only the most discreet details (address number, door plate) and the interior spaces.

Laying claim to a place through decoration is only one aspect of adaptation; such changes are superficial. If structural or volumetric changes are to be made possible, they require much more forethought. The paths of circulation must be placed so that they will not be upset by changes. Equally as important is a set of public regulations that does not frustrate an owner who seeks to add rooms or a deck, relocate windows, enclose a parking area as a garage, or extend his living space in other ways. One solution is to have the limits of extensions approved in advance, leaving the owner the freedom to decide when to modify and what form these modifications will take.

A wealth of experiences can be tapped for the design of row houses. Many of the finest North American urban neighborhoods are composed of this housing form, yet each is distinctive in style and detail. The bow-front houses of Boston's South End, the brownstones of Park Slope in Brooklyn, the plain-faced Federalist houses of Georgetown, Montreal's gray Victorians, Chicago's ornamented limestone southside townhouses, and the houses of San Francisco's Russian Hill are only a few examples. These areas have often changed occupancy, and their density has shifted up and down over the years. A generous single-family row house may have become several floors of flats or a rooming house or a set of tiny apartments, two to a floor. With gentrification it may have been reconverted to a duplex or single-family house. These possibilities were created by a dimension between the party walls which was wide enough for two bedrooms or a living room, by a depth of the units sufficient to accommodate interior rooms (especially kitchens and bathrooms), when they became flats, and by a strategic placement of the vertical circulation, which works equally well for single or multiple units. It was also helped by the divided ownership pattern, which allowed the area to change unit by unit. Few housing units are built today as large as nineteenth-century row houses, but it is possible to design units of any size with future conversion in mind.

Row houses are the most accepted moderate-density attached housing form. They are typically built at net densities between 35 and 50 units per hectare (15 and 20 per acre), but there may be as many as 75 units per hectare (30 per acre) if the houses are three-story, narrow-fronted 3.5 or 4.5 m (12 or 14 ft) units. Above those densities, it is more difficult to provide private entrances and outdoor spaces for each unit, to accommodate parking and to respect unit privacy. The designer is forced to construct decks for private or group outdoor spaces, or expensive garages for storing the automobiles. Hence land values must be considerably higher, and the market must strongly favor self-contained units before the construction of attached units is warranted at densities of 75 to 110 units per hectare (30 to 45 per acre).

The *stacked townhouse* is one higher-density form that allows private entries and outdoor spaces. The effect is of a row of attached duplexes, and many of the choices are the same. The upper unit, which begins on the second or third floor, is reached by a private stairway. Fire exit regulations usually make it advantageous to locate the smaller of the two units below, minimizing the climb to the upper unit. Private yards may be separated, with each unit having all the ground space on one side, or the ground space may be dedicated to the lower unit, with roof space and decks serving the upper unit. It is nearly impossible to make outdoor spaces completely private, but each unit can be provided with an area for its exclusive use and the site can be designed so that there is little outdoor space needing shared management. Because of the density, parking must occur in some form of a structure, either below the housing units or covered by a deck between them.

A variation on this housing form is the European *maisonette*, whose upper units are reached by a common outdoor gallery at the second or third floor level. These corridors can pose security problems. The most extravagant (and also most costly) prototype for gallery-access attached housing is undoubtedly the Habitat '67 complex constructed at the Montreal Exposition. Units are stacked within a frame in an irregular piled-up form. While the densities are no higher

Other attached houses

than for stacked townhouses, a great deal more outdoor space is available on the roofs, so that virtually every room has access to the outdoors, albeit in the sky.

The difficulty of all of these housing forms is their cost: because there is not enough ground surface to accommodate automobiles, humans at leisure, and building footprints, expensive new "ground" must be constructed in the form of garages and decks. As a result, rather little attached housing is built at densities between 60 and 100 units per hectare (25 and 40 per acre). Within this range, most housing is in apartments, and above this range, it inevitably is so.

Walkup apartments

The walkup apartment was at one time the cheapest kind of housing available. It would still be so today if the fire laws had not banned nonfireproof construction in structures three or more floors in height, and if people had not lost interest in walking up greater distances. Two- or two-and-a-half story walkups (which stretch the permitted nonfireproof height to its limit) have become the mainstay of suburban "garden apartment" developments, providing low-cost apartments at an intimate visual scale and allowing parking to be handled on grade. Buildings are designed with minimal corridors, and most units are reached directly off the stair landings. As densities are squeezed to their limits, the entire outdoor ground space can be consumed by the automobile. Transient adults may not object, but families with small chidren may find suburban walkup areas too limiting.

An important virtue of the walkup apartment is that it can easily be broken down in scale, even in a very large project. Only a few units need share a common stairway, and a common courtyard can become an outdoor living room. Ground floor units can have private outdoor space so that perhaps a third of the apartments are like attached dwellings. Parking can be grouped in small lots near each building, allowing surveillance for security. These possibilities are worth exploiting, especially in varied topography where entrances can be made at several levels.

Elevator apartments

Greater building heights require the introduction of passenger elevators, the use of fireproof construction, and often the installation of mechanical ventilation systems. Since these are costly items, they usually entail a significant jump of density above the walkup apartments, to compensate by reducing per-unit land costs. *Elevator apartments* can have many plan shapes, but the basic forms are the tower, where the units on each floor are grouped tightly around a core of elevators and stairs, and the slab, in which units are arranged along an extended corridor on each level. A variation on the latter is the *skip-floor system*, where access hallways are located on every second or third level and living areas above and below are reached by stairways within the private spaces of the units. The tower block provides better light, offers more chance for cross-ventilation, and when tall is visually handsomer. The slab often has unpleasant proportions and may block the view, cast broad shadows, or adjust clumsily to terrain, but it is the less expensive type. The skip-floor system can provide through units in a slab building, thereby offering advantages of cross-ventilation, but this is done at the expense of access for the handicapped.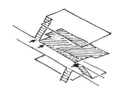

The tall apartment has advantages in addition to its usefulness at high densities. Tenants acquire some anonymity and social freedom, if that is what they seek, and they may be lifted up high enough to enjoy fine views and cleaner, cooler air. Apartments are more secure, particularly if there is a 24-hour control at the entrance, although their elevators can be dangerous places. The buildings themselves provide dramatic accents at the urban scale: they compose well within large spaces and can relate to powerful natural landscapes. Moreover, at the densities at which they are generally built, it is possible to supply special services: catering, nurseries, convenience stores, social rooms, swimming pools, squash courts and other special recreation, all within the same structure.

Thus, for some households the tall apartment may be a preferred setting, and it need not be confined to central areas. But where there are small children, the stresses on them and their parents can be considerable. It may deter their early sense of independence, since they will need to be accompanied by an older person whenever they leave the apartment. The parent will not be able to supervise outdoor play while working indoors. There will be constant anxiety over the danger of high balconies, elevators, and contact with strangers. Children may have a lessened sense of their family's separate identity. For all these reasons, many will advise against housing children in high-rise buidings. But there are exceptions where it is perfectly acceptable: where nannies, or members of an extended family, provide a network of care and supervision; where there are other substitutes that encourage human development; where home is considered less important as a mark of identity than summer place, or school and family ties.

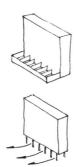

Elevator apartments have other problems that must be addressed in site planning. They can create winds at ground level that make outdoor spaces unpleasant to use. At the same time, because of winds, balconies above the twentieth floor may be largely unusable, placing more demands on ground-level outdoor space. These problems are multiplied in climates with heavy snowfall. Ground-level units can suffer from the nuisance of the intense activity at the foot of the building, and it will be necessary to protect them with a screen or even eliminate them entirely. Common facilities can be located there instead. The once fashionable device of leaving the ground-level open, raising the structure on *pilotis*, creates more problems than it solves: wind, expense, and a lack of ground level surveillance among them. Orientation must take account of ground level use, the solar exposure of units, and overlooking views from above.

The cost of elevators in relation to other equipment, and the imagined preference for high-speed service and short waiting time, often leads to several conclusions: that elevators should be grouped in a single location; that buildings should be high; and that many units should be served at each stop—a sure prescription for giantism. But if each of the assumptions is looked at more closely, the conclusion may not be as obvious. People may be willing to trade a few seconds of added waiting time for the less impersonal situation where fewer residents use any elevator and there are shorter corridors. A shift to pneumatic elevators, which are slower but cost only a fraction of the typical high-speed installation, may be hardly noticeable and allow much lower structures to be built economically. If skip-stop corridors are used, time may actually be saved over a high-speed installation that stops at each floor. Thus it is possible to consider six- to twelve-story apartment structures, grouped along streets or around squares. Perhaps this may develop into a new form of urban apartment dwelling.

Hybrid types

Different housing types may be mixed within projects or structures. Units with separate access and outdoor space can be placed in the lower floors of apartments. By interlocking, this direct-access base can be as many as three floors high. To save on the cost of elevators, apartments above the third floor in a five- or six-floor structure can be served by bridges from an adjacent high-rise structure, as in Peabody Terrace at Harvard University. Row houses and walkup apartments for rent can easily be mixed on the same site since they are of similar scale. They appeal to different groups and thereby broaden the occupant mix. The addition of granny flats, student apartments, or small rental units can multiply the lifestyle opportunities in single-family areas. When there is greater choice of accommodation, residents can stay in a single neighborhood as they move through their life cycle. We have neglected here many special housing types, some traditional, others now emerging: apartments for the aged, congregate housing for the elderly and the disabled, hospices, hostels, apartment hotels, single room occupancy (SRO) housing, dormitories, communes, second homes, time-share resorts, flop houses, halfway houses, nursing homes, crisis centers, religious homes, and so on and on. Each has its special requirements for site planning.

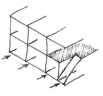

Infill housing

Reference 74

While residential development continues to spread outward at the urban fringe, a substantial quantity of vacant land still exists within. A recent study in three major U.S. cities showed that there was sufficient usable vacant land within the built-up city and its suburbs to provide for all, or almost all, of the expected residential growth in those metropolitan areas for the coming decade. These were mostly small parcels: 90% under 2 hectares (five acres). While a good deal of this land is clustered in low-income central areas, the great bulk of it is in the suburbs. A small part of this vacant land is unusable due to its extremely small size, lack of access, steep slope, or bad soil, or due to the presence of some threatening structure, such as a transmission line. But most of it is quite usable, especially for small groups of houses.

This is land that can be built on without displacing anyone and without impairing the function of any present structure. Most land will not require any further infrastructure. Building here would substitute for growth at the fringe and in so doing would conserve energy, service costs, transportation, and agricultural land. Internal growth stabilizes the old neighborhoods and adds to the tax rolls. Officials are therefore in favor of infill development. Neighbors may also look favorably on it if it means stability, the removal of unkempt vacant land, and the provision of housing that is within their means. But they may well oppose it if it will bring in people of a different class, or cause the loss of a pleasant open space which they have enjoyed, or pose threats of heavy traffic or an unwanted density or style of building.

Builders have their doubts as well. Few large developers work with scattered sites. They look for at least 8 to 16 hectares (20 or 40 acres) for their residential projects. They are convinced that working on dispersed sites would be uneconomic. (There is little evidence that this is true.) Even small builders generally do custom work or put up units on finished lots bought from larger developers. The small builder tends to work within a restricted sector of a city—for familiar clients and within familiar restrictions. Infill housing is erected by only a minority of the small builders, quite often by contractors and tradesmen in their spare time.

Costs and conflicts

Site development is only marginally cheaper at infill locations, and construction costs are basically the same. For the builder, the sure advantage of fringe land, whatever its disadvantage for society, is that he need deal with only one local government and one client group and that the surrounding neighbors will not be nearby and watchful. Moreover, production can easily be coordinated in a single location. Lots passed over by previous development, on the other hand, may no longer be fitted to modern building and zoning codes and may need variances.

The builder wlil attempt to increase the allowable density on his infill site, relative to that prevailing in the neighborhood, in order to compensate for his land costs, to meet his market, and to enlarge his scale of operation. The local neighborhood will resist, fearing the consequent traffic and parking, the loss of open space, and the introduction of inharmonious buildings and unknown neighbors. The result of this struggle is usually a modest upward shift of density, accompanied by a design that attempts to downplay its actual scale. The likely outcome is a small group of row or two-family houses, inserted within an older area of single-family or mixed housing.

On the fringe of the inner city, small walkup buildings have become the standard infill housing form, built on lots 15 m (50 ft) wide and up. They are often the vanguard of an area transition from a family to a largely adult neighborhood. Units are typically built from standardized designs and sold to small investors. They are cursed by city officials, adjacent residents, architects and almost everyone else other than their builders, investors, and occupants. They are, indeed, often banal and insensitive in appearance and siting. But there is a need for low-cost units with minimal maintenance, which can be inserted into the fabric of relatively dense neighborhoods. We lack good prototypes for this.

A fit with context is best accomplished by recalling existing building types, materials, scale, and mode of entrance and by achieving a clear external expression of the individual dwelling unit. Each unit is visibly differentiated and given its own entrance, directly off the same public street on which existing units face. The sense of crowding is avoided. Noise problems are attended to, especially at the joint between infill and its setting. Wherever outdoor territory will be arranged in a different way than is customary in the surroundings (such as in a common, instead of in private backyards), then thought is given as to how neighbors will perceive and use that space. Neighbors are consulted in the process of design (indeed, it may be impossible to do otherwise). Symbolic details can be important: shutters, fences, doorways, flowers. If possible, the future occupants are identified and organized prior to construction—not only to participate in design but so they can discuss those issues with their future neighbors and in the process get to know them and be known as persons. The small size, irregular shape, or peculiar site condition of an infill lot, when added to its tight fit to context, raises special problems, and this means additional design time. Yet these special difficulties can usually be parlayed into special quality and interesting form.

However, we should not forget the other values of abandoned open spaces. Much passed-over land might happily be converted to public open space, or at least to space tended for private enjoyment. Some inner cities have taken to "lotsteading," whereby tax-delinquent vacant lots are sold (or leased for long term) for a nominal sum to the resident of an adjacent lot on condition that she will landscape and maintain it and pay the subsequent taxes. In other cities, delinquent lots are converted to pocket parks on condition that neighborhood organizations will assume responsibility for their upkeep.

Housing and support facilities must be considered together. There is an extensive literature on standards for nonresidential facilities in residential areas. The usual warning must be made that these standards refer to urban North America, to the present day, and to the completely average situation. In those cases they have some value as quick first checks.

For example, about 0.2 to 0.3 hectares (one-half to two-thirds acres) per 1000 inhabitants is cited as being required

Shopping

285

FIGURE 82 *Infill housing can capture the spirit of a neighborhood while using thoroughly modern forms. These townhouses are among the many new units filling gaps in the Woolloomooloo area of Sydney, Australia.*

for neighborhood convenience shopping. This is exclusive of community and central shopping, but includes such facilities as supermarkets, drug stores, laundries, beauty parlors, barber shops, shoe repair and auto service stations. This area provides for the stores, their access, and customer parking at a ratio of 2 square feet of parking for each square foot of selling space. How this space is clustered will have much to do with the type of enterprises sought and the competitive opportunities elsewhere. If national chain merchants are desired, the shopping floor may need to provide at least 4,600 sq m (50,000 sq ft) of built space, including a major supermarket of 2,300 sq m (25,000 sq ft). The market area needed to support this will average 10,000 persons, with some variation depending on incomes. But creative packaging may allow a smaller shopping area serving fewer people. And what if store keepers take on other functions than selling, or stores are cooperatively owned, or goods are not distributed by retailers selling for profit?

There is much to be said for scattered convenience stores within the housing area. The offices, restaurants, clinics, libraries, meeting rooms, motels and other facilities that the community needs are often located in the commercial strips, and they are there partly as a result of being excluded elsewhere. Strips offer many advantages—they serve a distant as well as a nearby market; they give each enterprise equal billing; they allow for considerable additions and changes— even if they are offensive to the eye and almost impossible to use on foot. Is there an equivalent form, more ordered and less automobile dependent, which would provide for small incremental commercial developments nearer the residential areas? Or could strips be more closely linked to the residential zones that flank them?

Recreation areas are a second important residential support. Here standards are much more arbitrary. A quoted norm for playgrounds serving the age group from six to twelve is 0.5 hectares (one and a quarter acres) per 1000 people. These should be within 1 km (half a mile) of their users, or preferably 0.5 km (0.25 mi), with a minimum size of 1 hectare (2.5 acres). But why one hectare? Do all children play the same space-demanding games in the same locations? Available space and actual modes of play will surely modify this standard. The elementary schools are commonly combined with the playgrounds, which simplifies supervision but restricts playground locations. These schools demand approximately 0.2 hectares (half an acre) per 1000 pupils for building site, setting, access, and expansion room. The minimum size for a combined elementary school and playground is 2 hectares (5 acres), which can make a large hole at the center of a residential area. If the school is separate from the playground, then additional play space must be added to the school site itself. Where there are no private yards, additional play lots must be included in the plan, close to the dwellings, at a scale of about 5 sq m (50 sq ft) per child between two and six years of age.

These standards do not provide for parks, whose standards are more variable, or for schools of other types. They represent only the minimum, local, formal requirements for the education and organized outdoor recreation of children up to twelve years of age. They are not based on studies of where and how children actually play and learn but are only a summary of the kinds of provisions we are accustomed to make for those purposes. They are not relevant to other age groups. Is this why our playgrounds all look alike? We have already quoted the Swedish standards for close-in open space in residential areas. To these standards they add that there

Recreation

See Figure 8:

Figure 83   Built in an ordinary schoolyard in Berkeley, California, the Washington Environmental Yard has become a laboratory for learning through play.

288

must be a nursery school and a *supervised* playground within 300 m (1000 ft) of each house, and a school, a convenience store, a public transport stop, and a park, all within a 500 m (1500 ft) safe walk. What a primitive society—still on foot!

Higher density developments nearer the city center will have great difficulty meeting these norms, and they should not be held as absolutes. By beginning with an accurate profile of housing occupancy and a careful examination of the activities to be supported, it may be possible to design playgrounds that are much smaller, but still fully adequate. Elementary schools can be put on sites as small as one and a half acres if their roof spaces are used for play. And there are many opportunities for doubling up: the parking areas for churches can be used as basketball or tennis courts during the week, shopping center parking areas can serve the same use on Sundays; streets can become playgrounds at certain hours of the day; the ground floors of apartment buildings can be used for schools.

See Figure 84

Schools and playgrounds may be nuisances for immediately adjacent dwellings because of the noise and activity they generate. For this reason and because of their conventional large size, they do not fit easily into housing areas. It is advisable to locate tall apartments near them, to turn low dwellings at right angles to their boundaries, to screen them, or to place them next to nonresidential uses. A workable but expensive solution is to bound play areas with roads on which housing faces from across the street. A location next to shopping and other community facilities is of mutual benefit if the large play areas do not dilute the necessary accessibility of the center.

Recreation is a broad function, being both organized and unorganized, indoor and outdoor, daily and intermittent, local and distant. Sidewalks, for example, are a more important recreation facility than playgrounds and should be designed with that use in mind. Normal residential streets can serve the ancient functions of play, work, and outdoor living, if they are regulated as is the "woonerf" described in Chapter 7. Particularly important for the child is the chance for adventure and for play of his own invention in woods, swamps, back alleys, junkyards, and vacant lots. For the adult, the important recreation facilities may be special sports fields, commercial entertainment, access to natural scenery, city promenades, or the private garden. Many special recreational facilities will be needed: swimming pools, boat

Reference 3

See Figures 74, 75

FIGURE 84
By using its roof
spaces, the Quincy
School in Boston
demonstrates that
inner-city schools
can fit on sites a
fraction of the size
usually prescribed.

landings, parks, allotment gardens, golf courses, skating rinks, walking and riding trails, and picnic grounds. It is becoming more and more common for small housing developments to provide some of these facilities privately and locally, on a cooperative basis. Properly organized, they are very successful. As we grow more doubtful about uniform recreational space standards, we will turn to the actual diversity of recreational place and activity and think of providing for this complexity according to the particular people we house.

Many other community facilities are needed in relation to residential areas: clinics, community centers, fire and police stations, churches. Most of these facilities do not make large demands on gross land area at the scale we are considering, except perhaps for churches and community centers, which can generate substantial traffic and parking and should be sited at accessible points where they will not disturb residential uses. With their heavy off-peak parking requirements, they can be associated successfully with commercial parking. Fire stations, on the other hand, must be near several major roads, close to the center of the area served, and yet not at any point that is likely to be jammed with traffic, such as on a major intersection or near a large parking lot. $\quad$ Other community facilities

Facilities and the institutions that will use and maintain them should be planned together. Neighborhood associations that manage a local park and swimming pool are already commonplace. In many trailer park and apartment developments, the local management provides and maintains pools, playgrounds, laundries, meeting rooms, and restaurants. If teen-age youth form their own associations for recreation and learning and have the territory and resources to support it, we shall see new kinds of facilities. A school can use local residents as teachers and could be completely dispersed in the residential living space. Conventional forms and conventional institutions are mutual brakes on each other. Planning a new environment is an opportunity to plan form and management together in a way that supports innovation in each.

The chance to innovate across a broad front increases with the scale of the residential area being developed. One concept of residential organization is the doctrine that houses should be grouped into "neighborhoods," units of from 2000 to 10,000 people, insulated from through traffic, bounded by greenbelts or other barriers, and self-contained with regard to all daily facilities except the workplace. This concept usu- $\quad$ Neighborhoods ally centers about the elementary school and includes such devices as superblocks, neighborhood centers, and the separation of motor and foot traffic. The idea is based on a presumed unit of social organization and has been applied in many different situations throughout the world.

Reference 85

Although the idea of neighborhood units developed in the urban United States, it does not often apply there. Most city dwellers are not organized socially in such units, and their life does not center about the elementary school. Nor would they desire to be confined to such self-contained areas, with all the implications that has for local isolation and lack of choice. The attempt to fit all services into the same unit size is basically inefficient, a typical product of our professional weakness for solutions in which components are sharply defined and neatly grouped. In urban America, at least, the neighborhood unit seems to be a fiction, except when it springs up as a temporary political defense against some exterior threat.

Nevertheless, it has been a convenient fiction. It contains some valuable ideas and has attached itself to other valuable ideas. The idea worth saving is that local facilities should be distributed to be easily accessible to dwellings, and that when some facilities are associated in common centers, they have a special convenience. It is not necessary for all functions to occur at the same center, however, nor need their service areas coincide. A resident should have a choice as to his school or store or playground.

Areas need not be neatly packaged, single centered, or of a magic size. Yet it is important to keep speeding vehicles out of residential streets and to see that small children do not have to cross busy streets on their way to school. The superblock is a useful device, and so is the separation of foot and motor traffic, where the flow becomes intense enough to justify it. But major arteries need not surround an inward-looking cell. Local shopping, for example, may best be placed along major streets rather than inside the area those streets delimit.

It may be desirable to group dwellings to encourage the formation of true neighborhoods, that is, into areas within which people are on friendly terms because they live close to one another. Such neighborhoods are much more likely to be of the scale of 10 to 40 families than the 1500 families of the conventional unit. Physical arrangement may aid neighborhood formation, especially if the population is socially homogeneous, but factors such as class or personality

292

are likely to be more influential. Our urban areas are far too complex to be ordered by such a simple cellular device as the traditional neighborhood unit.

Having said this, we will calmly reverse field whenever the social situation is altered. If true communities exist or are realistically intended, where residents hold vital interests of work or worship or family life in common, then their spatial expression and support makes good sense. Such units may be found in village economies, among religious or socialist communities, in special ethnic groups, and in temporary special-interest camps. In these cases, the spatial unit would logically be far more thoroughly integrated than in the conventional neighborhood unit. Political, social, and economic organization is relevant to the organization of space.

Chapter **10**

Other Uses

Housing is the principal man-made environment and constitutes most of our urban living space. Site planning deals with many other situations, and several of those recur frequently. We will outline the issues, solutions, and difficulties peculiar to those situations and refer the reader to more detailed information.

Institutional site planning—planning for such things as universities, hospitals, and cultural centers—has its own characteristics, and some consultants specialize in this field. Although a hospital is in function very different from a collection of theatres or a college, yet there are similarities that derive from their common administrative structure. The typical institutional complex is under the control of a single agency, which will be responsible for the site over a long period of time and whose professed motives—of healing, education, or artistic expression—are presumably directed toward the welfare of the using population rather than toward profit or efficiency. At the same time, the complex is also a collection of diversities (medical specialties, artists, academic departments), each with its own requirements and only partially under the control of the central administration. In Robert Hutchin's famous phrase, a university is a collection of buildings united by a steam line. Moreover, the functions of these special parts are likely to change in unexpected ways and to have conflicting, or at least diffuse, objectives.

Institutions

Thus institutional site plans are usually complex overlays of successive plans, plagued by growth and cross-purpose. The symbolic form of the environment is important, and is defended at some cost, but it is constantly threatened by the demands of parking or of building expansion. The spatial plan is dependent on the long-range policy of the institution, but the latter is difficult to specify for the whole, and so will be fudged by vague generalities or buttered to conceal the cracks between the firmer parts. Space wars are endemic, motivated by conflicts of growth, and the considerations of prestige. Much of the energy of the institution's planning arm must be devoted to allocating existing space among the competing entities, keeping accounts of space use, and attempting to predict shifts in the near future.

It is not always clear how the complex should best be organized, since while the linkages between the parts are important, they are often subtle. Moreover, *whose* linkages should be favored: those of the prestigious specialists (the doctors and professors), or those of the hard-pressed services, or those of the bewildered visitors? Should parts be grouped by administrative department, or by functional requirement, or by existing linkages, or by linkages to be encouraged? Should the parts be well separated to allow for pleasant landscaping and future growth, or should they be packed together to permit easy intercommunication? Should the institution display a distinct identity, or should its parts do so, or should it simply look familiar? Will parking be brought to the door of each unit or kept at arm's length? Are the best parking spaces to be reserved for the highest status people, and, if so, how are they to be defended from the assaults of the unwashed?

Large institutions are almost always in difficulties with their neighbors. They are likely to be growing actively, and they draw in large numbers of visitors and staff. Since they often sit in central city areas, and their margins are fully occupied by other uses, they will burden their neighbors with their traffic and their demands for housing or threaten them with plans for expansion. Intent on their own compelling purposes and drawing on a much larger region for their support, institutions and their neighbors are not usually aware of any mutual benefit.

While the external setting has a symbolic role in institutional site planning, it is primarily thought of as a mere frame for those interior settings that carry out the basic purposes. Site planning attention focuses on a dignified appearance, adequate parking, utilities and access, sufficient expansion space, and the like. The external space is something to pass through on the way to somewhere else. Institutional sites can be splendid achievements since they are based on humane purpose and long-term commitment and have a rich diversity of elements and much symbolic importance. Most often, unfortunately, these advantages are lost in the space wars or sacrificed for an expression of forbidding majesty.

The site plan of a hospital or other medical center will exaggerate these characteristics. Medical procedures today are sophisticated and evolving rapidly. Physical flexibility is paramount. Conflicts are exacerbated by the complexity of the modern hospital and by its high density, which is a product of the intense internal traffic. The typical site plan packs its structures close together or envelops the whole in a single vertical shell. At the same time, it uses every device to gain adaptability. Structural supports, utilities, and vertical communications are concentrated and regularly spaced, leaving broad spans of clear floor space open to change. "Hard" functions (those that are very demanding in their location and supporting services) are placed next to "soft" or undemanding functions, so that the former can displace the latter if necessary. The arteries of circulation and of utilities are organized into a regular, three-dimensional network. Each medical department is given a corridor of expansion into an outside space, despite the dense packing.

These devices of adaptability are thought of in terms of architecture and are only partly reflected in the site plan, most often in the form of two-dimensional zones reserved for future expansion. The linear pattern is one general strategy of this kind. In Cambridge, England, the colleges lie between the river and the commercial high street. Historically, they expanded sidewards, while maintaining this stable relation. More complex and fast-growing sites might better be conceived of as three-dimensional from the start. A network of aerial rights-of-way, horizontal and vertical, associated with standardized floor levels, could be reserved for future circulation and utilities, just as we plot future roads on a two-dimensional map. Functional zones and reserved corridors of expansion could also be specified within this three-dimensional matrix.

Traffic on the hospital site is very varied. Each type has its own requirements, often antithetical: doctors, staff, patients, visitors, services, supplies, emergencies. These flows

Hospitals

See Figure 85

297

must usually be separated, and sometimes even be hidden from each other. Doctors demand preferential parking and access. Ambulances must have a special entrance and be shielded from patients and visitors. The result is a complex, densely structured site plan.

Moreover, since many of the users will be arriving for the first time or come only infrequently, there is a severe problem of orientation. Finding the unit where one should go for treatment or where some friend lies ill can be a formidable task, compounded by the fear that accompanies a trip to the hospital. While the technical problems of adaptability, precise function, complex circulation, and close packing of activity are the preoccupations of hospital planning, the psychological problems of patients and visitors are relegated to a few homey touches in the waiting room, which have little impact on people expecting to hear the worst. The human experience of hospitalization is rarely addressed, except perhaps in certain hospitals for children or the more recent hospices for the dying. The hospital grounds, if more than a parking lot, are designed as a park-like setting which will assure the outside observer of the competence of the institution which sits in them. It has little relation with getting well.

See Figure 86

Schools

If the grounds of the large educational institutions exhibit these same problems, but less sharply, they have characteristics of their own. Activities within the individual buidings are a collection of singularities rather than a repeated series of houses or of production spaces. The diversity of campus use makes it difficult to specify important common objectives that might bear on its physical arrangement. In particular, universities rarely connect site planning to learning. They see no vital link between the site plan and their central purposes, other than the obvious requirements for shelter and access. So it falls to the site planner to raise the learning-related issues of environmental stimulus or openness, or the need for spontaneous interaction or privacy, or the possibilities of the environment as a setting for education. He must also press for an educational policy plan on which he can base his site plan. He can sometimes inflame this debate by presenting physical alternatives that would have direct consequences for educational policy.

Institutional buildings contain a shifting set of activities, with many complex and imperfectly understood linkages of people and of information. Time distances or psychological barriers between activities may be critical. A traditional

FIGURE 85
Ingenuity is essential in expanding urban institutions while they remain in use. The Massachusetts Eye and Ear Hospital in Boston could only go upward—over the existing hospital.

FIGURE 86
A consistent spatial vocabulary, despite much variation in the age and style of buildings: an aerial view of Trinity College, Cambridge.

grouping may ignore such a sensitive linkage as that between research workers in different fields or the opportunity for casual meetings of students and faculty. Movement is typically on foot or in slow public vehicles such as elevators or escalators. Face-to-face interaction is important. As walking distances increase, the institution will begin to operate in sectors rather than as a unit. Students then cannot get from class to class unless curricula are compartmented; staff do not meet those from other branches without special arrangement. The natural barriers of academic specialization are reinforced.

Grain

The problem is an interrelated one of total size, of density, of the arrangement of circulation and meeting points, and of the grain or mix of units. For example, should student housing be in one location or in several locations? be separated from or integrated with other types of housing? be close to teaching facilities or distant from them? The size and density of the school, its purposes, and the rhythm of its student life will suggest a unique solution. Should teaching and research units be grouped by administrative classification, which is the most common method? This fits management convenience and prestige, corresponds to the accepted boundaries of maintenance and control, and reinforces internal communication within the administrative units. But it will discourage cross-connections within the institution as a whole and decrease future flexibility. If they are not organized in this typical way, should the various spaces then be grouped by their physical type and requirements, as by clustering the libraries, the laboratories, the classrooms, the large meeting halls, and the service functions? This can be functionally efficient and more responsive to shifting loads. But it may thwart desirable interactions as well as administrative identity, and, in large systems, produce an inhuman scale.

Other institutions may choose to cluster the various functions in repeated modular units, which correspond to some small social community, as in those university "colleges" intended to be communities of learning and of residence that will be held together by informal as well as by formal ties. Where such units exist and are stable, this can be an excellent organization. Elsewhere, these communities may be fantasies, unrealized hopes of which the physical setting is only a reminder. Worse, they may be subversive of broader links within the institution. Last, a university may try for a more "urban" solution, in which functions are intermixed and are held together by good communications. This arrangement can favor complex interactions and continuous shifts in function. The grain or fineness of the mix will now be an issue. Spaces must be usable for changing purposes, and communications must be excellent.

Linkages

In any case, interactions and successive relocations must be monitored. The site planner wants to know about current communications: the meetings, messages, flows of students, research contacts, library use, the social roles of hallways and lobbies and dining rooms. He needs to understand the policy of the institution: what interactions does it seek to encourage? If chance meetings are an important part of its workings, then the form of its corridors and central spaces may be crucial. One looks for the connections that lie behind the formal table of organization, the communities that actually exist and how they seem to be changing.

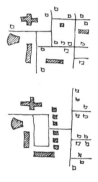

Links to the outside world must be analyzed: to housing, shopping, restaurants, private offices, support services. Should the university be open to its surrounding community or retire within a defensive perimeter? Should housing for students and staff be located on the grounds, be dispersed within the local neighborhood, or simply not be furnished by the institution? A mix of housing or a campus that is open to community use may be socially desirable but difficult to achieve because of the social distance that exists.

The large institution is often seen as an alien intrusion by its neighbors. It performs no service for them, draws its clientele from a wider sphere (and often from a different social class), and exerts a severe pressure on local housing, traffic, and protective services. That most institutions are tax-exempt only adds to the hostility, and tax exemption requires that the campus be kept pure of any revenue-producing uses. Yet wherever there is a harmonious joint between town and gown—as one may see in Cambridge, or Berkeley, or Harvard Square—a special vital character arises. Conflicts appear in the site plan as questions about the institutional boundary, the location of entrances, the provision of housing or of institutional "outposts" for local service, or even the possible dispersal of the whole campus, rather than secluding it within a territorial enclave. No university can be planned without considering the heavy demands it will make on its surroundings—demands that sometimes are tantamount to the facilities of a new town.

In addition to all these requirements of shifting linkage and function, universities are symbols for the values of

Symbolic role

301

knowledge and culture, and we are disappointed if their grounds do not express those values. The campus landscape supports the fond memories of alumni. If it has a strong character, its image conveys a sense of unity to what often enough is a very heterogeneous enterprise. (Think of Oxford or the University of Virginia.) So the visual setting plays a special role in campus planning. Natural features can be used as visual anchors. Outdoor spaces are laid out to provide a stable setting for unknown future buildings. Landscaping, lighting, and pathways can be designed to ensure a unified expression. Taking advantage of the promised continuity of management, the planner can propose a sensuous program for future growth: a palette of materials, rules about height and coverage, a characteristic way of forming outdoor space, the preservation of certain views and landmarks, or a procedure whereby any new building is forced to pay attention to its neighbors.

See Figure 87

While the symbolic importance of the campus landscape is widely understood, and as often effectively nurtured, the possible role of that setting in the actual process of education is as neglected as it is in the process of healing. Only an occasional class meets in springtime on the lawn—a special and somewhat awkward event. Might not the outdoors be shaped for teaching, just as indoor rooms are? Do not outdoor paths and focal points serve for spontaneous discussions, just as corridors do, and could they be designed with that in mind? Can the site be a biological laboratory, and the buildings and corridors display something of the immense variety of studies of which a university is comprised?

Predicting future growth is a continuous responsibility for the campus planning staff. Short-run demands are compiled from the needs of the various units, constrained by budget limits and arranged in priority order, and the staff strives to reallocate existing space in accordance with them. These allocations are naturally a field of fierce internal combat. Long-term growth, on the other hand, is gauged by estimates of the future growth of the base population, to which are applied ratios of space per person for the various kinds of facilities, as derived from experience and modified by current trends. Classroom requirements, just to take one example, will depend on the number of students, the space occupied by a single student, the normal extent to which a room is filled when in use, the hours per week that any room is usually in use, and the average number of hours per week that students are in class. Growth predictions based

Space requirements

Reference 28

FIGURE 87 *The University of Virginia, designed by Thomas Jeffer-*
son, stands as a prototype of the ordered American university
campus.

on so many linked assumptions are shaky and must be regularly revised. Many institutions underestimate future demand or even look on the next building program as their
last.

Overall floor space requirements in the typical university
may range from 10 to 30 sq m (110 to 330 sq ft) per full-
time equivalent student. Future land requirements are then
computed by fixing a desired structural density, or floor area
ratio. A college of open plan may stay below a ratio of 0.5
or even 0.3, while an urban university will commonly go
up to 2.0, or higher. If we apply the extremes of these two
quantities—of the overall floor requirement and the floor
area ratio—a college of 5000 students that might require
over 50 hectares (130 acres) in the one case could in the
other be achieved on 2.5 hectares (6 acres). Land costs, potential neighborhood displacement, political resistance due
to tax losses, and the reduction of internal time distances
will encourage dense, integrated sites in central city areas.
But these high floor area ratios incur expensive structures,

much vertical transport, high service loads, and the possibility of an oppressive environment. They ensure protracted struggles to maintain open space for amenity, recreation, or future growth. Low ratios, on the other hand, allow easy vertical or lateral growth of buildings and the landscaped settings we associate with educational institutions. Clearly, the assumed structural density is an important choice.

Parking

Parking is likely to be a problem for the university. Staff, students, and visitors will drive directly to their destination if they can. Much space is consumed by the parking lots, and the overspill of cars conflicts with neighborhood uses and with the symbolic image of the campus. Large institutions may be driven to extreme measures, such as underground garages, distant fringe parking served by a shuttle bus, heavy parking fees, the rationing of parking permits by lot location, the prohibition of student use of cars, or a joint surveillance with local police of the parking on surrounding streets. Since professors and research directors will demand convenient parking along with tenure and an attractive office, the institutional parking system is likely to differentiate between users and to require a full-fledged control system. A longer walk from parking can be imposed than might be tolerated in a shopping center or a housing project. Public transport can be encouraged, as well as the use of bicycles if climates and grades are not severe. Cycle ways and secure cycle parking must then be provided. But a massive use of bicycles introduces new problems, including bicycle theft, a rise in minor accidents, conflicts between cycles, pedestrians, and cars, and the intrusion of cycles into the buildings.

Participation

Most institutional site planning decisions are made without consulting the persons vitally concerned: students, secretaries, maintenance men, or even faculty. Yet, if one discounts for the turnover of the student body, universities are one of the more likely situations for user participation.

Reference 2

Christopher Alexander proposed a radical reduction of the scale of campus planning projects in order to allow direct participation in design by staff and students. University dormitories have been successfully designed with the collaboration of students similar to those who will eventually inhabit them. Universities have the structural base and the common purpose on which user participation might be erected. While this will cause delays and reveal dissensions, it will result in a better-fitted environment and can itself be an education. Beyond that, participation could be extended to neighborhood people on issues of joint concern: local service, parking, housing, and recreation. This will be a touchier business since there are real conflicts between the parties. Most institutions will look on community meetings as negotiations rather than participations.

Other institutional complexes, such as concentrations of cultural facilities, raise most of these same general issues: those of mix and density; the intrusive effect of parking; the relation to context; the creation and preservation of environmental character among a heterogeneous group of shifting activities; the encouragement of communications between the separate units; the use of the outdoor environment in a positive way in addition to its role as a passive symbol; the problem of flexibility and change. Clusters of museums and concert halls are not single institutions. Since their visitors rarely visit several at one time, one wonders whether they should be clustered at all. Tight groupings increase peak traffic and the separation from surroundings. However, it can be desirable to concentrate them to some degree, as within a general district of mixed use. Still other institutional complexes, such as the so-called "government centers," while they also have an important symbolic role, are in reality simply concentrations of office workers.

Unlike the institutional case, site planning of the work-place is carefully controlled, and for a clear-cut purpose. But it is also more often relegated to subordinate importance. Two-thirds of the adult population now work outside the home, and the workplace is their environment for long periods of the day. Work, we think, is an unpleasant necessity, and considerations of efficient production dominate its setting. While the well-being of the employee has begun to affect interior design, it yet hardly touches the site plan. Albert Kahn, the preeminent designer of industrial buildings, put it succinctly: "The purpose of a factory building is to facilitate production."

Much of the outdoor work environment is not subject to professional site design, consisting as it does of yards, construction sites, or the environs of those offices, shops, and factories that are completely immersed in the city setting. But the role of the deliberate site plan is enlarging, as first industries, and now offices, are concentrated in large, single-purpose districts. The advantages of controlling the site for efficient production are increasingly recognized, and so the work environment becomes increasingly isolated from other life functions.

Workplaces

Industrial
districts

See Figure 88

References 47, 55, 63

The planned industrial district first appeared in Manchester, England, in 1896 and then in Chicago in 1902. Industries of moderate size found it advantageous to cluster together in order to get protected, accessible sites, well-serviced, of adequate size, and free from conflict with neighboring uses. Specialized real estate developers now organize districts of this kind, and, in the developing countries, the districts can be an important public tool for encouraging industrialization. In this country, districts range upward in size from 15 or 20 hectares (40 or 50 acres), with an average somewhat above 120 hectares (300 acres), and moving upward.

Good access is their primary requirement, both for goods and for workers. While many industries make very little use of rail service today, and some districts are now wholly oriented to the highway, it is still advantageous to locate along a rail line in order to preserve transportation options for future tenants. More recently, districts have been located close to major airports in response to the growing importance of air freight. Some factory sites are directly connected to airport runways.

Most U.S. workers arrive by car, and so it is advisable to locate the district close to one or more superhighways. But direct access to a network of good secondary roads is more important, since that will allow a rapid dispersion of the concentrated flows that occur at shift times. Connections to public transport are not considered critical, although bus lines may later be rerouted to serve these locations. This self-imposed dependence on the small gasoline engine may in the long run prove shortsighted as fuel costs change our modal mix. In other countries, and particularly in the developing ones, most workers arrive on foot, by bicycle, or by public transport.

The peak flows of workers' cars have become the principal conflict between adjacent residential and industrial uses, surpassing the traditional nuisances of noise, smoke, and dirt. Wherever industrial traffic can be separated out and noise and pollutants properly controlled, there is now no reason why industry cannot be located together with other uses. But homeowners are averse to industrial neighbors, and industry prefers to avoid the chance of residential complaints, as well as the possibility that their future expansion may be blocked. So industrial uses are segregated at an increasingly coarser scale, and workers must travel farther from home to work. In outlying suburban districts, with no

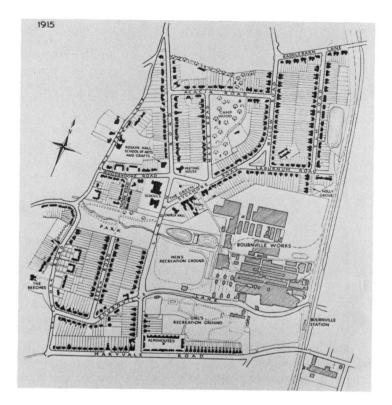

1915

FIGURE 88
Bourneville, in England, is a rare example of the intentional location of recreation and workplace side by side. The town, shown in 1915, was an early model industrial village, and the builder valued the health of his employees.

moderate-priced housing nearby, this isolation may impose daily work trips of more than ninety minutes in each direction. Access to working-class housing has become as important a criterion for district location as is access to goods, services, and markets.

Industrial districts require substantial areas of inexpensive, moderately flat land, well served with capacious utilities. Grades should not exceed 5%, or preferably 3%. The ground itself should be able to carry heavy loads. Utilities must be checked for their size as well as for their presence, since some industries are heavy users of power or water, and capacities must allow for expansion and unanticipated use. Other utilities, such as gas, telephones, steam, or compressed air, will also be required. "Wet" industries, which use water in their production process, are particularly demanding of sewer as well as water capacity. Provisions for waste disposal and recycling have become more stringent, and we are just becoming aware of the hidden burden of toxic waste. In-

Land and utilities

dustries produce larger and larger quantites of novel chemical effluents.

Buildings are generally low and extensive to allow for long, single-level production lines and heavy floor loads. But in some cases this may shift, wherever lighter machines, hand assembly, the electronic sorting of material, and the energy advantages of compact, sealed-in structures cause a reevaluation of the multi-story factory, or where production, marketing and management are so closely entwined that factories are best located in office districts. Substantial space is required for open parking, material storage, and future expansion. Thus industrial estates tend to be prodigal of land. Floor area ratios are quite low, ranging from 0.1 to 0.3. But these low initial ratios build up as growth occurs, and in central locations, or in other countries where land is more dear, the ratios may go up to 0.5 or 0.8. The U.S. norm of employee density is 25 to 75 workers per hectare (10 to 30 per acre) in a new district, while elsewhere those densities run from 125 to 200 per hectare (50 to 80 per acre).

District layout

Districts are typically laid out in a grid-iron of large blocks, 300 to 600 m (1000 to 2000 ft) long and 120 to 300 m (400 to 1000 ft) deep. If there is rail service, then the tracks run through the middle of the blocks, parallel to their long axes, so that each plot will have a street in front and a rail line behind. Rail spurs need a 12 to 15 m (40 to 50 ft) right of way, a vertical clearance of 8 m (25 ft), grades under 1 or 2%, and curves of more than 120 m (400 ft) radius. Road widths and curves at intersections must be ample to accommodate large trailer trucks. Rights-of-way are typically 15 to 20 m (50 to 60 ft) for secondary roads and 25 to 30 m (80 to 100 ft) for major roads. While plot depths are set by the layout of the blocks, frontages are not subdivided until a buyer is on hand, and so lot sizes will vary according to the requirements of each particular industry. Industrial land is often absorbed slowly by the market, while the extension of roads and heavy utilities is expensive. Thus a developer prefers to hold his land in an unimproved state and looks for a layout in which the infrastructure can be extended piecemeal.

Extensive parking is needed for workers' cars. Counting on some doubling up, in the United States it might be sufficient to allow one car space for every 1.2 workers, but some planners prefer to allow one space for each worker. Unfortunately, since one shift arrives before the next one leaves, it is necessary to allow for two shifts at a time. Since

308

FIGURE 89 *The workplace has been dignified by its parklike setting, but it is empty and totally disconnected from the workers inside.*

almost all drivers are going to a destination that is well known to them, parking can be more dispersed than in a shopping center and closer to the particular point of work. But shift-long parkers can be asked to walk as much as 300 m (1000 ft) to their door. Just the same, internal circulation should be simple and understandable, especially since the roads are not spatially well defined by bordering buildings. District entrances should be well marked. Road congestion at shift time is likely to be pronounced. Interchanges, exits, and the exterior road network immediately adjacent must be checked to see if they can handle the flow. A district agreement on the staggering of shift hours will help.

Some highly automated activities such as warehouses may have very few employees and a small parking demand, but the district developer may insist on some minimum provision of space for future parking to prevent congestion if the use should change. This insistence may be cast in the form of a required minimum area for future parking spaces, but is more likely to be expressed as a maximum allowable coverage of the plot, such as 30% or 50%. On-street parking will be prohibited.

In order to protect their investment, the organizers of an industrial district will control use within the district as closely as they can, within the limitations of the market, by

Controls

309

means of deed restrictions and leasehold covenants. In addition to a prohibition of on-street parking and rules about maximum coverage, they are likely to enforce a front setback line and the landscaping of all or part of this front yard. Outdoor storage may be limited or its screening be required. Building designs will be reviewed, or must even have formal approval, under guidelines about general appearance, adequate parking and loading, and the prohibition of certain construction materials or building types, such as temporary metal-clad structures. Maximum levels will be set for the emission of noise, light, odors, smoke, vibration, heat, and other nuisances, as measured at the property line. Residential or commercial uses will be prohibited, or the latter can be limited to particular clustered locations. The size, location, and type of signs will be regulated. In all this the industrial developer is acting just like a public regulating agency, whose constrictive rules he so deplores.

Factories

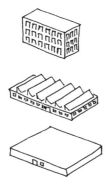

Factories have evolved from dark, chaotic structures, through the multi-story, side-lit buildings of the nineteenth century with their high ceilings and restricted depths, then to the deep, top-lit, one-story sheds of the early twentieth century, covering acres of ground, and then most recently to sealed-in, "blind," barn-like buildings, artificially lit and ventilated. Freed of the vagaries of exterior weather and the variations of natural light, they preserve a uniform internal environment throughout the twenty-four hours, illuminate work areas evenly, and conserve energy by reducing heat loss or gain from large glass surfaces. Their facades, now free of any requirements beyond that of making a seal, can be used for publicity or concealment, the expression of a few selected structural components, or a free play of forms. Architectural composition is easier, and, for the passing observer, more detached from meaning.

The worker is effectively isolated from the outside world. The site is only an approach to the real world inside and is composed of a parking lot and a showpiece lawn. Complaints about isolation may be met by cutting a few observation windows in the exterior skin, or occasionally by opening a glass-enclosed lightwell into the interior space. But this will interfere with the free layout and remodeling of the production lines. So these vast interiors are effective for production but less than ideal as a daily environment for the worker (if those two conditions can be separated).

Service facilities

It is not unusual now to provide industrial services within the district, such as banks, post offices, business advisory services, repair shops, and fire stations. Employee services are typically limited to company cafeterias, toilets, medical aid stations, and the free-lance lunch truck at the factory gate. Restaurants and health clubs are finding their way into the newer districts. Might other amenities of urban life be introduced, such as shops, bars, day nurseries, schools, libraries, and clinics? Might the factories have park-like settings designed to be looked at from within the factory, rather than solely from the road that passes by, or to be attractive places in which to walk, eat lunch, or spend a brief leisure time? Could one even imagine a work environment that would draw workers to spend their holidays on the grounds or to show their children what they do?

The contemporary industrial district is characterless, even when individual buildings are competently done and the cosmetic landscaping is heavily applied. The low structures are sprinkled across the grass and asphalt. Since the interesting industrial processes are invisible, one factory looks much like another. The grounds are for show and for storage, not for active use. The view from the nearby road is important for its advertising value, but this is fulfilled by large signs. The advertising would be more effective if the plants were visually open or were expressive of their internal activity or if the grounds were developed for active use and pleasure rather than as an empty land to be made decent with grass. *See Figure 89*

Industrial areas are not just unpleasant necessities, at their best neat and reticent. Roads, dams, bridges, pylons, cooling towers, stacks, quarries, equipment yards, production lines, even waste heaps, can be compelling objects. They are big enough, and meaningful enough, to take their place in a large landscape. They could be woven into the extensive recreational open spaces that we need. Making joint use of parking and services, visually complementary, close weaving would allow employees to enjoy their leisure, and park users to learn how things are made. But we isolate the working world. A recent publication of good modern factory design only occasionally shows the site plan. When it does, the plan is solely of the factory, never its context. Even the photographs show the factories as formal objects, devoid of people, alien in an empty land.

Office work is becoming the more common mode of employment in this country, displacing the previous preponderance of factory labor. The monumental "government center" is, in its essential function, merely another concentration of office workers, although it also has a certain sym- Office parks

FIGURE 90
*White-collar
work in a pastoral
setting: The
Wellesley Office
Park, Wellesley
Massachusetts.*

See Figure 90

Reference 67

bolic role, and may be visited more frequently by the general public. "Office parks" (how the word "park" recurs, even as its meaning is denied!) are more recent than industrial ones and soon may be as frequently encountered. Most office structures are single buildings in mixed urban surroundings, but clusters of offices are now appearing in suburban settings. Here they exhibit many of the characteristics of the planned industrial district, if in a less acute form. Goods handling and utility capacity make no unusual demands, but employee access and its attendant parking and congestion can be a greater problem since the ratio of employees to floor space is higher. Once again, the site is primarily for parking and for external show rather than for employee use. While some attention has recently been given to employee well-being, as in contemporary studies of territoriality and office behavior, or in the concept of the "office landscape," none of . this has spilled outside. A new book on office design includes 28 premium examples of low and midrise suburban offices in the United States and Canada. The large landscaped grounds contain lawns and lakes to look at, ceremonial entrances, and parking lots. Only two use the site for any other purpose: one for a rather mean sitting space under the administrative eye, the other for some interior landscaped courts with benches. While most office workers would probably prefer to spend their free time at home rather than in disporting near their offices, since we keep working and living well apart, still they have breaks and lunch hours.

Office buildings, like factory buildings, tend in suburban locations to become isolated from other uses, so that employees must drive off to shop or eat. Offices have not yet forsaken the window, however (although it is now a sealed window), so workers can at least look out. Or they can look out if they have sufficient status. Thus outside observers see an articulated skin. But office buildings, again like factories, are silent about the people inside and what they are doing. A firm simply has its sign on the wall. In this case, the lack of visual meaning is more intransigent, since offices are distinguished by few variations in their immediately visible process or product. It is the network of human relationships, and the way in which ideas are communicated, that makes one office distinct from another, and these networks are invisible at a distance. Those rare offices that are organized in any way different from the paperwork pool, or the repetitive boss-and-secretary pairing, are distinctive at close hand, but most still rely on a sign to convey the substance of the information they are processing.

But if conveying the nature of office activity to the outside observer is elusive, it would be easier for the site to be shaped to serve the needs and pleasures of the employee, since no manufacturing demands are made on it and commercial and service facilities are quite compatible with office labor. Yet normally it is only the office worker in the central city, thanks to the adjacent mix of uses and to the parks provided at public cost, who has the opportunity of a pleasant stroll or an interesting lunch hour.

Shopping centers

Site planning for shopping is quite different from planning the workplace. In both cases, a single profit-motivated developer is in control. In the case of shopping, however, the individual user (the shopper, not the employee) has a strong, albeit indirect, voice in the design, since his attraction is essential to making the profit. In a consumptive society, shopping is the one aspect of community life that unites all classes,and its exemplar is the urban downtown. But the techniques of site planning are most relevant to the deliberately planned shopping center, which by now has captured the lion's share of retail sales. Their design is quite sophisticated.

References 35, 61

Planned shopping centers are commonly divided into three types: the *neighborhood center*, selling standard con-

313

venience goods, with a supermarket at its core, and serving an immediately adjacent population; the *community center*, featuring a discount store and competing with other centers within a 5 to 8 kilometer (3 to 5 mile) radius; and the *regional center*, containing two or more full-line department stores and a complete range of shopping goods, and thus able to compete with any shopping cluster, including an established central business district, within a half hour's drive. The neighborhood center might have something like 4500 sq m (50,000 sq ft) of selling area, serve perhaps 10,000 people within less than five minutes drive, and require a 1 to 2 hectare (3 to 5 acre) site. A community center might serve 40,000 to 150,000 people with 9000 to 27,000 sq m (100,000 to 300,000 sq ft) of selling area on a 4 to 12 hectare (10 to 30 acre) site; while a regional center would serve upward of 150,000 people with 27,000 to 90,000 sq m (300,000 to 1,000,000 sq ft) on a site of at least 20 hectares (50 acres). Locations are chosen after a detailed analysis of the distribution of the resident population and its buying power, the location and composition of competing centers, and the access to the site, including its capacity, mode, and the time distances involved. The mix of stores to be provided is carefully considered and is the basis of the physical plan.

Typical layouts

Shopping centers have evolved from simple rows of stores along a street, with their parking in front and service behind; to shops fronting on an outdoor pedestrian mall, all surrounded by surface parking; to fully enclosed pedestrian malls; to two- or three-level malls around an interior atrium, linked by escalators and bridges, and flanked by, or sandwiched between, multi-level parking, a form that brings a large and complex shopping assemblage within a brief walking compass.

Within the center, whatever its form, the basic principle is to expose the internal storefronts to intense foot traffic, while keeping this traffic in concentrated channels and well distributed over the center as a whole. The primary attractions—department stores and large fashion or specialty stores—which are assumed to draw customers by their own power, are located so as to pull buyers past the smaller stores. The primaries are therefore placed at either end of a single mall or at the multiple ends of converging malls. Secondary attractions are distributed along the malls to encourage a balanced pedestrian flow. Other stores subsist on this distributed foot traffic and support the primary stores by the variety of goods and services they offer. Some of

FIGURE 91   *Woodfield Mall, Schaumburg, Illinois, one of the largest shopping centers in the world, follows the now classic plan: perimeter roads, two-level shopping with half the parking at each level, and anchor stores on each axis connected by specialty retail outlets.*

these are grouped by type of goods to facilitate comparison shopping. If certain facilities will stay open later at night, they will also be kept together. Those shops selling goods bought on impulse, such as candy, pastry, gifts, or tobacco, are sprinkled about. Small kiosks within the mall are highly profitable. Cinemas, sellers of car accessories, grocery supermarkets, and the like, whose patrons wish to park close by but who are not likely to shop in the other stores, are put in separate, free-standing buildings within the parking area or in fringe locations or dead corners where they do not preempt active mall frontage except for a narrow entrance. Service outlets—post office, beauty shop, shoe repair, cleaner—are also located at the fringe of the main block or in the basement.

The mall itself, along which all these glittering establishments are ranged, is kept less than 120 m (400 ft) in length and about 12 m (40 ft) wide for most of its course, which is a width likely to give a sense of animation without congestion, and which allows an easy view of the goods on either side. To prevent monotony, the mall may meander, bend into an L, S, U, or figure eight, open into more spacious courts, or expand into a connected network. Where it en-

315

larges, it contains some active feature, such as a skating rink. It must always be kept compact, lively throughout, easy to comprehend, without dead ends. It can rise into two or more well-connected, easily visible levels, but then there must be equal parking at each level.

Parking

Reference 98

Convenient customer parking is crucial. The location of parking, along with that of the primary stores, determines the traffic flow within the cluster. An in-town center, built at high density and drawing part of its trade from transit passengers, may be served with as few as three parking spaces per 90 sq m (1000 sq ft) of selling area. Suburban centers, on the other hand, used to provide as many as five and a half spaces, which will satisfy the needs of all but the ten highest hours of parking demand per year. But that high tide leaves empty wastes of asphalt in other seasons. Four and a half spaces is the current rule of thumb, which is calculated to serve the needs of all but the peak ten *days* of the year. Dual use of the parking space is advantageous: as between day and night if paired with cinemas; weekdays and weekends with offices and churches; or seasonally with sports arenas. The most distant parking should be no more than 200 m (600 ft) from the stores, and this will be used only in peak periods. Everyday parking should be within 100 m (300 ft). Where land is scarce or expensive, or where in large centers it is necessary to shorten the car-to-store distance or to distribute traffic evenly between shopping levels, multi-story parking decks are provided.

. It should be possible to have a general view of the parking when entering and to move through it systematically while locating a space. Drivers will strive to get near their point of first purchase or the one where they will pick up heavy packages. Many will not be well acquainted with the layout. Surface parking will be preferred to the mysterious, confined maneuvers of a parking garage, and so the entrance ramps to the latter are sometimes designed to draw in the driver unwittingly. A ring road is usually put at the outer edge of the parking area. Loops project inward to the stores, to allow for the pickup of goods and passengers, as well as for general circulation within the lot.

Parking turnover is rapid, and shoppers enter their cars with bulky packages. Car spacings have therefore been generous, allowing up to 40 sq m (400 sq ft) per car, exclusive of main circulation. But in the areas reserved for compact cars, now more widely used, this requirement may fall to as low as 25 sq m (250 sq ft). For ease in identifying one's machine, these huge lots should be divided into marked sections of no more than 800 cars. Trees humanize the lot and shade cars and people, which is much to be desired in hot climates. But trees need root room, and they are sensitive to the salt applied in winter to melt the ice and snow. Thus planting is usually confined to large clusters, or to the inner or outer perimeters, or perhaps to berms which divide the major parking sections. Customers are expected to walk down the parking aisles, rather than on separate walkways, and so these aisles must point toward the stores. Walkways and curbs between the parking bays will interfere with cleaning the lot and with changing its arrangement should loads or vehicles change.

The extensive paving and building coverage causes a dramatic rise in the rate and quantity of storm runoff, which calls for large, expensive, storm drains. Heavy runoffs may cause the flooding and pollution of nearby water courses. One solution is to create landscaped retention basins on the property, which will hold the rain water for subsequent slow release. It is also possible to pond water temporarily on the roofs of buildings. Parking may be slightly depressed below the level of the surrounding roads, to allow a view over the car tops. The lots must be evenly lighted to one footcandle, or two to three footcandles within the garages, where security is always an issue. Lots must be signed, kept clean, and monitored to prevent employees from preempting the close-in spaces. A transit connection is desirable but introduces a further conflict since shoppers' parking may be taken over by the cars of commuters. Office buildings, particularly if they are in peripheral locations, can share the parking area without conflict if their floor area is less than 20% of the shopping area. Above that level, they must be given additional parking of their own—perhaps four spaces per 1000 square feet of office floor.

Shopping centers are located along the major arteries and should be visible from them. It is desirable to have more than one line of access, but a position directly at a major intersection, or immediately alongside a fast, congested, through highway, or too close to a freeway ramp, can make access complicated. Some major centers will secure their own access ramp, directly into their parking area. In any case, the internal circulation system must be adequate to take up or discharge its traffic without backing up and long enough so that entering traffic can slow down gradually. Peak loads come at exits and may amount to as much as

Circulation

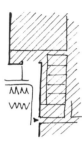

two trips per 1000 square feet of selling area, concentrated in a single half hour. Discharging the lot into more than one secondary road is advantageous, provided that the pattern of entrance and exit is clear.

The first big centers separated trucking and other service traffic from customers' cars by means of separate roads and truck tunnels under the stores. These proved to be very expensive. Servicing is now usually done in screened courts on the periphery of the shopping block, entered from the main circulation of the parking lot. Major stores have their own loading docks, while small stores are reached from these service courts by segregated internal corridors or by carts along the mall after hours. Truck deliveries are also sometimes hidden from customers by scheduling them at other times than principal shopping hours.

Access to these intensive selling concentrations is a valuable commodity, and the interrelation of cars, trucks, and pedestrians is a recurrent problem. Generous parking, a short walking distance, easy servicing, and a pleasant environment are all wanted and are all in conflict. Heavy traffic and overspill parking are the principal nuisances that shopping centers may impose on their neighbors, since other affronts such as noise and glare are relatively easy to screen, given the deep surround of parking. This vast ring is itself a barren sight, but a planted margin can blot it out. On a regional scale, however, the major shopping center is a prime generator of air pollution since it is the focus of so many vehicles, and much of the exhaust pollutants are emitted on starting, or when the engine is old. Air pollution, traffic impact, and economic consequences for existing shops are the key issues for public bodies when considering the regulation of shopping centers.

Shopping center design has ample scope for adornment, since the development is under unified control, the locational values are concentrated and high, and there is a strong economic motive for display. Special lighting, landscaping, and paving can be justified, as well as careful attention to detail and the provision of resting places, exhibit spaces, kiosks, nurseries, and play areas for children. Signs are carefully coordinated for harmony and legibility. Enclosing the mall permits maintenance of an equable climate and the introduction of special plants, birds, sounds, and odors. By removing shop windows, it allows storefronts to immerse the customer in a tantalizing display of goods. The mall provides a gay and orderly framework for all these displays.

FIGURE 92
The contrast between interior and exterior of large shopping centers is often stark. Indoors, they are scaled to the pedestrian, landscaped and invite social interchange; outside they are the opposite.

Outside, the landscape is more difficult to manage. The vast parking areas, broken by occasional clumps of planting, display either barren asphalt or ranks of dead cars. Hot in summer, windswept in winter, evenly lit at night with yellow sodium vapor, they are always exposed ground. The buildings turn inward on their delights, and once one is inside the mall, one is cut off from time, weather, or any sense of the world without. On the outside, the mall is a featureless bulk, whose blank walls must be enlivened with large identifying signs. Special form must be given to the pedestrian entrances. In comparison, the "primitive" streetfront store, with its bright shop windows, was a public asset.

Relation to community

Although the planned shopping center serves as a community focus, it is isolated and internalized. A nearby resident cannot nip out to the store or slip down to the corner to see who's there. To walk into a shopping center is to cross a hostile desert. Given our reliance on the private automobile and its voracious demand for space, these difficulties are not easy to solve. Parking decks above or beneath the shopping level will reduce the encircling band of parking. Landscaped pedestrian fingers can be extended through the parking area and into its surroundings. If they were lined with stores they would make an even more attractive approach, but then the potential neighborhood customers must be sufficient to support those stores. One might front one face of a center, complete with display windows, onto a busy public street. Revealing a view of the internal mall and its activities, making a clear connection of internal and external circulation, will help. This was easier to do in the unenclosed mall, in which people never lost a sense of outside, and where natural landscapes could be created between the shops. Good external linkages remain the advantage of the older shopping district, wherever it resists the temptation to imitate the suburban mall.

Old shopping streets

Redesigning this older shopping street has now become a common site planning task. These existing ranks of stores have advantages of mix, depth in time, central location, and street vitality that newer shopping centers cannot match, and they are refurbishing themselves in order to survive. Many of these enterprises would not exist if they had to start from the beginning today.

Some typical issues immediately arise. Shall vehicles be excluded from the street, to make a pure pedestrian mall, or shall buses be allowed in, bringing shoppers, noise and fumes? Or should the plan exclude only curb parking so that

FIGURE 93
The IDS Center, Minneapolis, Minnesota: interior crossroads of the central city, privately constructed and maintained. It is connected to adjacent blocks at ground and skywalk level.

FIGURE 94
Gigantic rocks, transported from the surrounding countryside, provided a special sense of place for the Burlington, Vermont, pedestrian mall.

the sidewalks can be widened? Curb parking will be fiercely defended by the merchants, even if few of their customers use it, but its removal to bordering lots affords room for planting, shop extensions, sidewalk sales, and ample passage. The exclusion or inclusion of buses and automobiles depends on larger traffic patterns, but also on the expected density of pedestrians. A local shopping street of customary width will go dead without some moving traffic, in contrast to a downtown street whose bed would be enlivened by the released flood of shoppers. Delivery and emergency access is a related problem. Are there rear alleys by which deliveries can be made, or must trucks be allowed on the street, and parking bays be provided for them? Can they be restricted to night and early morning delivery? How do fire trucks, ambulances and police cars get into the mall? How is garbage collection to be accomplished and snow removed? The usual answer, unless there is adequate rear access, is to provide a narrow, perhaps indirect, traffic lane through the mall, which is exclusive to these special vehicles.

Reference 18

New trees of substantial size are usually planted, although it may be difficult to find root room for them. Benches and other special street furniture are provided. The street and its walks are repaved with some higher quality material, often as a single, unbroken surface. But removal of the old curbs may raise drainage problems. Arcades may be introduced along the shop fronts, although there is always an issue of how to relate them to variations in the old facades. The old facades are restored and their window displays improved.

See Figure 94

In the most successful cases, a district development corporation is organized to carry out these improvements, as well as to provide new parking, and later to maintain the street and conduct activity and advertising programs. These renovated streets, with their planters, lanterns, benches, brick pavings, and refurbished fronts, begin to resemble one another, just as our new shopping centers seem interchangeable. Nevertheless, they work; they are enjoyed and used. The older buildings and activities give them some distinction, some local tie.

Street behavior

References 72, 97

We have some substantial information about how people—or at least North American people—act on a shopping street: where they prefer to sit and stand and talk, where they bunch up or linger, what they avoid. As a very broad generalization, they will be found at the edge of the action, talking and watching the people pass, where there is sun and easy seating, and perhaps some food to eat, or a fountain to watch and to listen to. Spaces can be analyzed to suggest those small, subtle modifications that will make them more attractive. Human activity is the key to attraction, along with micro-climate, shopping activity and the detailed placement of furniture, levels, entrances, and paths. The management of activity is as important as the design of the physical form, and successful projects of this kind fill the street with a succession of planned activities—sidewalk sales, festivals, and the like. The lengthy period during which the street is being torn up and rebuilt is a typical difficulty, however. Access to the stores must be maintained and special promotions organized to prevent any withering of custom.

Where they have successfully overrun the older centers, planned shopping centers are becoming the social foci of extensive suburban areas, at times to the developer's dismay. Teens hang out there; the elderly come to watch the world go by; political rallies are held and leaflets distributed. This is reinforced as large centers begin to add theaters, banks, post offices, hotels, medical clinics, and cultural facilities. Some developers look for very large sites so that they can build apartment houses, offices, employment, and public services adjacent to their shopping, and so assure some part of their market. They may donate a piece of it to the public, to allow the erection of a city hall or library. Various events and performances are staged in the mall, to give it life and animation. In these ways, the regional center begins to resemble the old central district.

But the relative narrowness, specialization, and "purity" of its function continues to distinguish it from the older center. Since space is totally controlled to extract maximum rent, there is no room for those marginal activities that one finds in the fringes or the historic niches of the central business district: the second-hand stores, cheap restaurants, churches, community places, teen hangouts, lofts, coffeehouses, discount outlets, social clubs, porno shops, working-class bars, bus terminals, flophouses, and cheap hotels which make downtown a place for all classes. Some experiments have been made with providing low-rent space in shopping center basements or parking decks, or with providing subsidies by manipulating rentals. Parking lots may be given to flea markets on slack days. But this is necessarily limited and must still be confined to socially acceptable activities such as churches, libraries, and community meeting rooms. Activities cannot approach the shady margin or eat into the profitability of the whole.

The regional shopping center is a highly sophisticated device for selling goods with convenience and profit. Its site planning is as advanced, and more solidly based on human behavior, than any other in this country. The interior malls are marvels of comfort and delight, if somewhat unreal or even a little oppressive in their material display. Built for selling, they have become important social foci. To fulfill that latter purpose, they are hampered by their isolation and by the restricted range and close control of their activity. It is uncertain if they can fully meet that social role within the institutional setting that has created them. Could a public developer do otherwise?

Changes

Shopping centers continue to change, becoming more complex, adorned with further comforts. The centers of intermediate size are beginning to specialize into discount centers, outlet centers, boutique centers, or "fashion" centers serving people of higher income, leaving the social mix of the old downtown still further behind. But one current innovation is the in-town center, located in, and more or less integrated with, the older central business district. Some occupy rehabilitated buildings, around which a pedestrian precinct is created, or they imitate an "historic" effect. Given the fierce competition and the pace of change, the life of a planned center is about 15 or 20 years, and now we see an occasional abandoned one, boarded up and ripe for conversion. More often, since these properties have high value, they are rehabilitated to meet the competition: new lead stores are brought in; the mall is enclosed and redecorated; parking garages are built and the old parking lots devoted to more intensive use. Thus a site plan should allow for future growth. Yet at any one time it cannot leave a gap at the heart of the selling area. The center must operate as a compact whole from the beginning and at any subsequent stage. Primary stores can grow vertically and new primary locations be provided by allowing for a cross mall. Other stores may be added at the periphery. Aerial rights-of-way can be reserved, levels and bay sizes be coordinated, and structural members be sized to permit a future three-dimensional network. Main utilities are designed for expansion, and parking is laid out to allow a future development of its air rights.

Dependence on the private car may in the long run prove to be the Achilles heel of these creations, although Americans will surely put up stubborn resistance to being deprived of their individual mobility, and the weekly shopping and entertainment trip will be a last stronghold of that resistance. Nevertheless, the wise developer will integrate his center with nearby intensive residence and employment and provide convenient access by foot, public transportation, or even bicycles. Electronic shopping and entertainment might portend the demise of spatial congregation (as Bellamy foretold in *Looking Backward* and as the telephone was first predicted to do). But even if this proves true for standardized convenience goods, yet it seems likely that most people will continue to flock together—to enjoy their shopping, their leisure, and the sight of other people.

Designing public open space is an important branch of site planning. There is an intense demand for outdoor recreation, and a growing realization of the need for conservation. Parks are heavily used, some so heavily loaded that their plant cover is breaking down, and the natural character that made them attractive is disappearing. Providing space for hiking, picnicking, camping, hunting, and fishing, especially within close range of the great metropolitan regions, has become an urgent matter.

Open space

Large recreational areas should contain a variety of landscapes: challenging, autonomous places for the teens, serene rural quiet, or crowded areas for those who want stimulus and companionship. Park design has usually been based on an appreciation for certain natural landscapes and on a settled view of what is wholesome outdoor recreation. Backpacking and nature observation are rated high, trailer camps and fun fairs low. It has produced fine landscape. Now the problem is to see how this may be reconciled with the changing ways in which open space is used by more and more of our people.

References 8, 83

The *openness* of open space is not a matter of how few buildings stand on it but rather of whether it permits the freely chosen actions of its users. Openness is a product of physical character but also of access, ownership, and management: the rules and expectations that govern activity. An open area need not be a "natural" one, a place untouched by man: there are very few of these in any case. An "open" space can be densely occupied by man-made structures, or even be an interior volume. This is a behavioral definition: an open space allows people to act freely within it. Openness is not a characteristic of most urban spaces, whether interior or exterior, nor of farms, playfields, single-purpose reservations, or even carefully tended parks. These are all places

Openness

where one is constrained to act in a prescribed way. This is not to say that playfields and tended parks should be abandoned, but rather that in designing large open spaces we must ask by whom the space will be used, what their varied desires are, and how that variety can be met and enlarged. Recent work with children has shown how indiscriminately they use their living space for play. They make occasional use of the areas organized for standard games, but more often they course through the entire environment, redefining it by their imagination. They use it for dreaming, for exploration, for self-testing, for trial runs of adult life.

Two criteria

The first criteria for open space design have to do with the quality of the human experience there: a free choice of activity, a release from exacting urban stimuli, a chance to become actively engaged, to exhibit mastery, an opportunity to learn about the nonhuman world, an ability to meet new people and experiment with new ways. These are psychological ends and cannot be attained by strict preservation of the preexisting natural state. Concern with the ecology of the site is the second set of criteria. Man and his works are part of nature. Ecological systems change; they cannot be frozen. The ecological aim is *continuity*, finding a new balance, in which human activity is an integral part of the whole and which will continue to renew itself. A good open space offers both psychological openness and ecological continuity.

Park planners often use the concept of "carrying capacity," borrowed from range management. It refers to the number of people, or the intensity of activity, that a ground can support without losing its ability to renew itself; that is, it expresses the limits within which the ground cover may be expected to hold, the trees to succeed each other, the water to cleanse itself. But a new use, newly managed, may strike a new balance. The stream is oxygenated, areas are rotated through resting periods, access regulated by entrance permits, the ecology stabilized with new weeds. Carrying capacity must refer to the experience desired. One person will feel that his two-week pack trip is spoiled if he meets a single stranger, while another is frightened as soon as he is out of sight of someone. Two thousand people on a mile of beach will seem pleasantly open to a city dweller and unhappily crowded to a person used to solitude. It is foolish to set universal density standards.

FIGURE 95   *Water and lush vegetation give special character to*
Maria Luisa Park in Sevilla, Spain.

Large open spaces serving varied populations require a
gradation of access to spread out conflicting activities. High-
capacity roads come up to some edge or focal point. Here
are the centralized facilities, the dense camping areas, the
intensive functions. From this point, activity density and
access capacity progressively diminish, finally reaching regions without man-made structures, sporadically occupied,
and penetrable only on foot at the cost of substantial time
and effort. A ring of highways, camp grounds, and picnic
groves may surround a core wilderness approachable only
over difficult pack trails. One strip of beach may be complete
with parking lots, restaurants, toilets, and life guards. A mile
away, the beach is a lonely stretch of sand. Conflicting preferences are resolved. One locale can be designed and managed to sustain a heavy load, while a fragile area is protected
from intrusion.

Large recreational areas need not be "pure," or devoid
of commerce and production. They can include motels, trailer
parks, teenage camps, orchards, self-built summer housing,
conservation work camps, education centers. Lumbering,
mining, and grazing are traditional occupants of our national
forests, and they are compatible if they do not pollute the

327

environment, disrupt its ecology, or, in the more remote areas, destroy the psychological sense of wilderness. Under the same restrictions, open spaces may also include other industries, especially when operations are open to view and have some visible relation to the natural resources of the place. Recreation and production can be integrated in ways that enhance the experience of worker and vacationer alike. Those operating farms that board vacationers in season are one successful example; the agriculturally productive public parks of China are another. Might lumber camps in the national parks give guided tours of their operations or even temporary employment to vacationers?

Territory

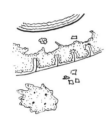

Since the experience of openness and freedom is psychological, it can be supported by the organization of space into small territories, even when large numbers of people are using the same ground. Natural or artificial masks of cover and terrain make special localities, shielded from each other's sight and sound, each with its own access—temporary kingdoms. Given the opportunity, people will usually choose their camp, picnic ground, or beach location by some possibility of delimiting a small territory, however subtly marked. They will look for partial enclosure, easy access, a position on the edge of something, a choice of sun and shelter, even while the actual distances they set between each other may be small. Thus the carrying capacity of a beach or meadow may be increased by providing a scalloped edge of wood or grassy dune or by introducing screens, trees, or boulders to be used as territorial anchors. Buildings should fit quietly into the landscape and not be set off by awkward placement, formal yards, or special planting. At the same time, it is good to locate diverse activities close to one another so that different members of the same visitor group can follow their preferences and move easily from one activity to another. Dramatic juxtaposition will intensify diversity. A leafy glen next to an active amusement area seems by contrast to be all the quieter.

Since many users of an open space will be new to it, or even unaccustomed to a rural landscape, or may be accompanied by small children with a wanderlust, it is important that the area be clearly organized in its more actively used portion. The general structure must be easy to picture in the mind: approaches direct in skeleton, if winding in detail, sequences clear. Legible maps and signs will supplement this.

The distribution of users within the park can be controlled by the location of access and facilities, even if as individuals they are following freely chosen courses. Water is the strongest attraction; people and structures gravitate to its edge, resulting in a mutilated shore and a neglected interior. The water edge is vulnerable. It is better to keep structures back, where they still enjoy the view but leave the desirable edge unencumbered and accessible to a more extensive interior. This is one instance of a more general principle: a permanent structure should never be placed directly on an attractive feature, since occupation destroys what is valued. It sits best on some less attractive margin which looks at that feature. The feature is preserved, while the new structure enhances an otherwise featureless terrain. On an island, camps are put in the interior, leaving the ocean beaches free. A house is not set in the middle of a fine meadow, but at its wooded edge, looking over the grassy expanse. Leave a screen of undisturbed trees around the shores of a pond, and let buildings look through them. Set your house on the brow of a hill, rather than on its top, and it will enjoy the view without demeaning the elevation that affords it.

Much of the delight of a place lies in how one gets to it. Open space design must think of its forest tracks, its bus routes, waterways, and horse trails as recreational experiences. In tight places, routes can be masked from one another. Each can have a memorable visual sequence suited to its own mode of travel. Waysides can expose the local geology and life. Special places can be made to seem remote, while previously inaccessible areas are opened up by beach buggies, snowmobiles, and underwater tractors. The access system regulates the intensity and the experience of use.

Roads may range from asphalt to cleared, barely passable tracks. Surfaces that might be dubious in ordinary practice—stabilized earth, loose gravel, or wheel tracks—may here be the appropriate choice. Built for the quality of the moving experience rather than for speed, they can follow far more flexibile standards: wind about to reveal terrain or to catch a good view. Design speeds may be as low as 30 kmh (20 mph), and lightly used two-way tracks can be 3 m (10 ft) wide, with turnouts for passing. Even primary roads may be no more than 6 m (20 ft) wide, with 1 m (3 ft) shoulders. Parking is made unobtrusive by screening and dispersing it, by using gravel or other porous surfaces. Camper vehicles

Cycles, horses, and pedestrians

Learning

and trailers are accommodated by planted back-in spurs or pull-through parking spaces. Where service roads must penetrate farther into the park than the public roads do, they should not extend beyond the public parking areas—which must seem to be the very limit of vehicular penetration—but branch off before these areas are reached.

Bikeways should be 1.5 to 2.5 m (4 to 8 ft) wide and have a firm, smooth surface. Foot trails, 1 to 1.5 m (3 to 5 ft) wide, need only be cleared and drained in the low spots, with logs laid cross-wise on the steep slopes to divert run-off and prevent gullying, and occasional stepping-stones in the difficult places. Adzed logs, rope suspension bridges, and flat stones carry walkers across the streams. The maximum grade, for any sustained distance and for experienced walkers, is 10% or 15%. Horses want earth to walk on and a path 1 to 2 m (3 to 6 ft) wide, while their riders hope to avoid decapitation by overhanging branches. Both enjoy an occasional long straight run.

The interpretive trail is the recent addition to the park vocabulary. Each successive station explains something about the landscape and its inhabitants, how they function, and how they came to be. But one should think of the entire park as an occasion for enhancing the meaning of place. Parks are places for learning about nature, but also for learning about oneself. They can encourage that direct action and accomplishment increasingly denied us in a highly organized society. People might learn new skills, plant gardens, build summer houses, climb, jog, hunt, or camp. The current popularity of the outdoors is undoubtedly due to what was learned in children's summer camps more than a generation ago. Ice boating, spelunking, and cross-country skiing are old games, now widely popular. Skin diving, orienteering, gliding, sky diving, and water skiing are more recent inventions. We can design new sports and new landscapes: caves, pit mazes, aerial runways, underwater jungles, do-it-yourself boat yards, bulldozer playgrounds (like giant sandboxes), complex climbing fences, video games played outdoors in three-dimensional space. Open spaces can be familiar and strange, places where one feels at ease and yet can move off onto unknown ground. They are places for developing our human capabilities.

Playgrounds and sports fields support specific games, and thus are not open spaces in our sense. Their required forms and dimensions are covered in an extensive literature. "Adventure playgrounds" are an exception. Used building

FIGURE 96 *The ornate glass canopy, carefully preserved, provides a focal point for the rehabilitation of Seattle's Pioneer Square.*

materials are stocked in a cleared space, in which children are assigned small building plots. Under supervision, they build to their own fancy and for their own use. The children are intensely engaged, and the results engaging. In the process, they learn much about the crafts of building and social cooperation. Another exception is Robin Moore's "environmental yard" in which children under his leadership transformed a barren school yard into an intricate setting for nature study, group endeavor and creative play.

See Figure 83

The creation of a modest new open space to complement existing development is an effective act of public improvement. A vacant lot is converted into a "pocket park" or a community garden. An abandoned rail line or canal, an easement for an aqueduct, sewer, or power line, becomes a linear park, a walk or bikeway, or a chain of vegetable plots. Elsewhere, some older city open space may be refurbished or a small enlargement created just where activity is intense, as by seizing a niche in the building wall at some busy intersection, or furnishing a barren traffic island.

Rehabilitated space

See Figure 96

One must be certain that the space will be valued and used. Too many attempts at inexpensive "beautification" result in scraps of littered, untended ground, which make their surroundings even more depressing. Observe what people are actually trying to do in the locality to infer how they will use a new space. An experiment with temporary features may inform the design, although there is always the risk that temporary equipment will bias the result toward failure. One inquires into the emotional landscape of the community: which are their sacred places, which are the places of fear? Persistent previous efforts to decorate a place are significant. Indeed, the fanatic efforts of some obsessive pioneer may rouse a community to support some neglected location.

The scale of these recovered spaces must be within the means of the community to use and maintain them. Many spaces built with great enthusiasm slowly lapse into disuse and disrepair. An adequate maintenance budget is more important than the initial investment. Individuals or small groups may be given the responsibility for a place: the care of a tree in front of a house, their own garden plot on leased ground, a memorial bench. In the case of a community space, it is useful to organize a group of unofficial "proprietors" or "friends of . . ." who will worry over it, press for its continued care, help to raise money for improvements, protect it against attack. Vandalism is always a problem in any city open space, especially when no definite body has a stake in it. There are devices that reduce such damage, such as planting very large trees, installing sturdy furniture, or using cleanable surfaces. But the best defense is a sense of local ownership and an effective maintenance that responds quickly to any defacement. Best of all, bring the vandals into an active partnership in its upkeep, use, and control.

Chapter 11

Weak Controls, Built Places, Few Resources

Sometimes site planning must be done without that comprehensive control of form we have described. This "imperfect" site planning is neither less important nor less productive than the conventional mode. There are two general occasions for it: first, when control or communication is impeded, so that site design is no longer a unified process; second, when resources are scarce, and many desirable features must be sacrificed for a few urgent necessities. We begin with the first, the lack of unity.

Fragmentation of the design task may be due to a passage of time, or to the intervention of multiple agencies on a single site, or to conventional divisions of what should be one process. Among the conventional divisions, the common example is the subdivision, in which vacant land is divided up into lots and rights-of-way, providing sites for future buildings. Subdivision may or may not be accompanied by the actual provision of roads, utilities, and landscaping. This is a common way of putting land into use for low-intensity residence and for industry, agriculture and commerce. It is a technique with a long history, the historical basis for urban development throughout the world, one still frequently employed.

In a subdivision, the designer controls the position of roads and utilities, the location of public open space, the shape of the private lots, perhaps the shaping of the earth

Subdivisions

and the landscaping. But she influences the siting of buildings only indirectly: she can only speculate whether site and structure will fit together. Things may go fairly well when the character and siting of buildings is prescribed by custom but much more uncertainly when design traditions are weak and technical possibilities numerous. Circulation and property boundaries are emphasized; spatial effect must be neglected; internal and external design cannot be coordinated.

There are good reasons why development by subdivision is common practice. It does not require large capital: the subdivider need only invest in the land and its survey and legal division, although he may do more. It is the device of a modest economy, frequent in this country and widespread in the Third World. It decentralizes decision, relieves the developer of the burden of architectural design, and allows subsequent owners some choice about their buildings. Land can be put to use piecemeal, as demand develops, and public agencies can control the general lines of development without being asked to make similar deliberations each time a building goes up. Thus subdivision has many social advantages, despite its unpredictable effect on site quality. It is more effective at low or moderate densities, where uses are not complex, and buildings are either detached or simply connected. It is a strategic juncture at which the site designer can have a permanent effect.

Good subdivision design can prevent the worst. It can insure good circulation, adequate locations for common facilities, sufficient open space, a basic order. The circulation system may be designed and tested by all the criteria discussed in Chapter 7, and the utilities be properly located. The road pattern should conform to the general circulation plan for the area and provide for future connections, and so must the utility system. The first test for any subdivision plan is to imagine moving through its rights-of-way and then to check the flow of surface waters and utilities. Streets and lots must so fit the ground that the former receive the runoff of each lot, or cross-lot or rear-lot swales and easements must be provided to carry it.

Buildability

The second test is to make sure that each lot has at least one good building location on it for the purpose intended. Detailed standards are often cited for the grades, widths, depths, and proportions of ideal lots, but the potential for placing a building is the crucial test. Minimum frontages, areas, and standard patterns, so commonly used in subdivision regulations, may impose an uneconomic and monotonous design. Performance requirements about access, drainage, space, privacy, and utilities will allow more flexibility without the risk of substandard arrangement. Usable house lots in low-income areas can be as small as 100 sq m (1100 sq ft); row houses can occupy frontages as narrow as 4 m (13 ft). Lots nearly rectangular in shape and tending toward the square are usually the easiest to develop, but deep, narrow lots, circles, hexagons, and interlocking Ls or Ts may be advantageous if buildings will be designed to conform with them. No reasonable rule would require all lots to be of uniform size or shape.

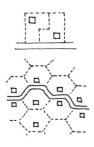

Building lines, which are the limits within the lot beyond which structures may not protrude, are often part of a subdivision plan. They may be private covenants or controls prescribed by law. Their primary purpose is to ensure access, privacy, light, and air. They may also be intended for visual effect or to allow for a future street widening. They further restrict the "buildability" of the lot. If used, they need not be uniform. A mechanical set of front, side, and rear setback lines will usually waste land and result in a uniform building location, repeated monotonously down the street.

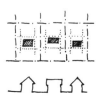

By giving thought to the street widths, to the buildability of the lots, and to the provision of sites for community use, the subdivision designer can insure basic functional adequacy. She can also do something to create a more positive character. Her best resource is the street pattern, since people will see the development while moving along its ways. The sequence of motion along the roads, their fit to the ground, the way they point to the intensive uses or more important buildings, will all have a visual impact. Intensive uses and open spaces can be disposed to create a focal point or a spatial release. Building setback lines can be varied to produce clusters or enclosures. Lotting can locate buildings at some desired point, such as at the head of a cul-de-sac for visual closure, or at the end of a block, to prevent a view down backyard fences. The public face is composed by the chosen arrangement of pavement, planting, lighting, walks, edges and fencing, and how this will respond to any changes in ground or use. Trees are planted or cleared, on the lots as well as the rights-of-way, to make a spatial structure.

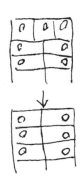

Yet the subdivision process is inevitably a disruption of the normal stream of site design. The disjunction between site and architectural design blurs and coarsens the final product. To escape this dilemma and yet reap the social advantages of subdivision, might it be possible for the sub-

Site and building design

division plan to deal only with major streets and utilities and their points of connection to the minor lines, and with use and density, principal landscaping, and necessary grading and drainage? Minor paths, lots, and details could then be planned as actual buildings were needed, subject to performance standards. This would permit incremental growth and also an intimate marriage of structure and site. In industrial subdivisions, for example, lots are rarely fixed before a buyer and his building requirements are known. But this will require a more sustained concern with the land than most residential subdividers are accustomed to, and involve public regulatory bodies in two stages of approval, as first the general, and then the detailed, plans were proposed. The first objection might be skirted by opening up subdivided land in chunks, to be divided and built on later in detail, subject to agreed standards. The review and control of detailed siting could be delegated to a permanent association of lot owners.

A like gap between the design of the building and its site will often occur for no better reason than the conventional boundaries of professional attention. Engineers or planners lay out the subdivision. Architects enter at that point to compose the building. In the end, the landscape architect is called in, to adjust the site and to decorate it with plants. When in the last hour we call in an engineer to dimension beams or the interior designer to choose colors for the rooms, we make the same error. Astonishing misfits can result from these jealous professional boundaries.

Another occasion for disarticulation appears in the use of standard, prefabricated elements—houses, trailers, or industrial sheds. The building is predetermined to the last detail and must somehow be fitted onto the site. In this case, at least, the site planner should be the dominant professional. The site is analyzed and chosen with the given prefabricated structure in mind. Mobile home courts, which provide new housing at the lowest cost, are a particular challenge to site planning skill.

Multiple developers

A distinct case of disjointed site design occurs on the large, dense, or complex site, which is to be developed in a continuous operation, by several independent agents, bound together only by a temporary contract. This is a frequent feature of urban renewal schemes, dense commercial areas, "new towns" or other large residential projects, world's fairs, or the like. The bridging field of "urban design" is most often focused on just such problems. In this case, the site planner's client, public or private, is a "super-developer" or packager—one who assembles the land, the financing, the market, and the subdevelopers, and who provides a general plan and installs the infrastructure. As in subdivision planning, a framework site plan must be made without firm knowledge of detailed use or building design. Conflicts between the parties are inevitable. Purposes, clients, and programs shift rapidly as the package is put together.

So multi-developer design is fractionated, like subdivision design, but not so hopelessly, since the development period is relatively short, the contractual relation close, and good communication is at least possible. Indeed, rapid and accurate intercommunication—of constraints, criteria, and possible solutions—is essential here. The designer must respond continually, preparing a whole sequence of possible layouts that gradually explore and define the problem and give form to the ensemble. The coordinating plan is fluid, an object of bargaining, rich in illustrative detail and alternative possibilities. As it becomes fixed, contractual controls are developed from it.

The packager attempts to anticipate the capabilities of his subdevelopers. He devises controls that will carry out his own intent while allowing for a subdeveloper's motives and for the unforeseen. In his detailed plan, the subdeveloper follows the spirit of the general plan, and yet must know when to break out of it because of some new idea or new situation. Both parties try to penetrate each other's function, the subdeveloper by remolding the general program, and the superdeveloper by making detailed plans to illustrate or test his principles. Analyses of site, market, and social need, plus the generation of performance criteria, illustrative solutions, and financial calculations, are the substance of this interplay. In the end, the site plan, the program, and the various financial and legal undertakings form the agreement between the parties. Where such communication is blocked for some reason or where there are substantial time lags, then familiar financial and human disasters occur.

Contact with the ultimate user is difficult in this situation. The shifts and conflicts among builders absorb all the administrative energy. Many ultimate users are transient or voiceless or only very indirectly represented. Standing at the top of this technical pyramid, the designer may be unaware of his remoteness. But he can get information from professional studies of the behavior and attitudes of potential users, and from the analysis of past market response. Using a subversive strategy, he may communicate information and cultivate special interest groups, to provoke a reaction upward from the bottom of the pyramid.

Long-range site planning

Site plans for the next twenty years, or even further, are at times made by large, stable organizations, occupying a permanent site and expecting to exercise long-term control over it: a university, a hospital, a large manufacturing plant. Long-range site planning is like the preceding cases in that future uses and the shapes they will occupy are not precisely known. It differs from them in that the agency for whom the plan is being made will also eventually control detailed design. Thus it can develop a long-range policy and rationally revise it as necessary. However abstract, long-range site planning occupies a natural interval in the scale of increasing area and time, and is not, like subdivision or professional specialization, an artificial separation. Nonetheless, it is difficult. It is even more so where the future is laid out for a group of diverse agents, as when a consortium of hospitals makes a site plan to govern the growth of a medical center. The characteristic problems of multiple developers and of long-range concern are here joined and compounded.

Long-range site design is preceded by studies of future function, which lie beyond the scope of this text. Indeed, long-range site planning is a halfway house between site and city planning. Preferred densities and land requirements are set, as is a generalized plan of use and circulation. But a guide to future form is also desirable. So it has been customary to make a site plan showing twenty-year building shapes of simplified mass. Future shifts will presumably be met by detailed adjustment. But such future building patterns are useless: no one can predict a building envelope over such a range of time, unless shapes are set by unchanging custom, or new functions can be kept behind false fronts. Sometimes these site plans are quickly abandoned. Sometimes they are maintained for a while, then slurred over, then forgotten. Occasionally, they are stoutly defended, until the strain of misplaced function becomes intolerable.

Yet while a general plan of use, density, and circulation will preserve the order of development, it will have only a secondary effect on its quality. Within this orderly framework, a skillful building designer can at best make his structure harmonious with its immediate neighbors. By chance, or by tradition, this repeated care can develop into a character of the whole. But it is rare to see a large-scale form or character created successfully in advance.

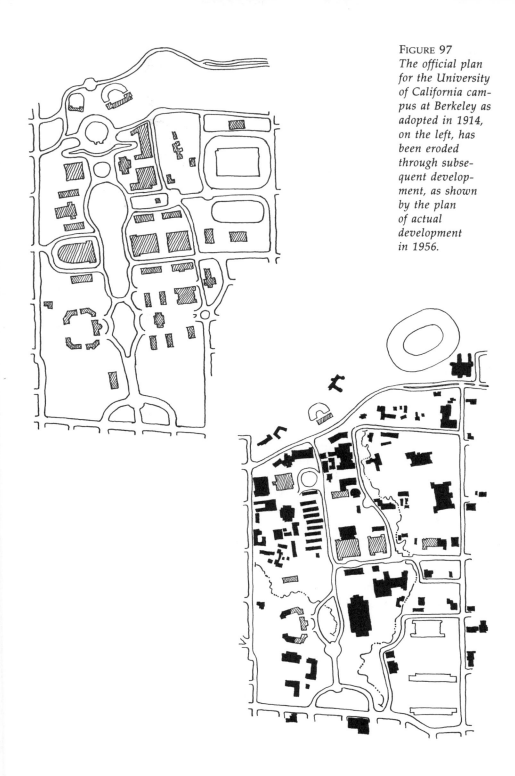

FIGURE 97
*The official plan
for the University
of California cam-
pus at Berkeley as
adopted in 1914,
on the left, has
been eroded
through subse-
quent develop-
ment, as shown
by the plan
of actual
development
in 1956.*

Future form

There are a number of ways of dealing with future form. As in a subdivision, the character of the path system may be set in advance. The sequence of major views may be provided for, the separate paths made identifiable by landscaping and detail, the whole network shaped into a legible structure. Selected species of trees can set the character of a road. Plant concentrations can mark the key paths and nodal points. At times, the road landscape may become the dominant impression, along which individual buildings will occur as incidents. Major spaces may be determined in advance of building construction by reserving open areas, setting building and height lines, and making mass plantings. Or instead of laying down the exact boundaries of these future spaces, one can prescribe a future spatial character, such as by recommending that development take the form of a continuous network of small courts, linked by short tunnels, and that the courts and tunnels are to have characteristic proportions, and characteristic uses at the ground level. New construction can be tested for conformity to this general but explicit pattern without mapping the future location of each court and tunnel. Continuities of this kind are the pleasure of many old towns, although tradition and technical limitation were the guides rather than an explicit rule.

The site planner must confine herself to that level of control which will confer character and continuity with a minimum of restricton and without unwanted side effects. Too often, detailed guidelines hamper function and creativity. They are ineffective for the desired purpose and all too effective for some unexpected one. The imagined and desired character—or perhaps the existing model that one is following—must be dissected to reveal its operative rules of continuity. Once extracted, those rules must be tested. This is done by devil's advocates, who try to produce the worst environment they can while literally following the rules, and next by an angelic host, who freely design varied and creative solutions to likely future problems, to see how far the rules will trip them up.

Therefore, instead of being an imaginary plan of future building envelopes, the long-range site plan should consist of a diagram of land use, circulation, landscaping, and major spaces, supplemented by a set of statements, patterns, rules, and illustrative details that will guide the form of future growth. Like any other long-range plan, this will be subject to intermittent revision.

Rules are essential elements of all three cases of disjunct site planning. They carry intent across the gap in the design process. But they are passive means, in contrast to the positive measures of design. Rules can be explicit, binding controls ("no building may extend more than 10 m above grade at its base") which are the clearest to follow, the most powerful, and the most galling. Binding controls are reserved for essential conditions that can be exactly specified, especially where the motives of a future builder are likely to run counter to those of the plan. When the rules cannot be put so explicitly, or where one is nervous about side effects and costs, or where the builder is likely to be in sympathy with the original ends, or at least indifferent to them, then the rules can simply be *guidelines*, recommended ways to achieve good form ("keep roof lines low and simple, following the contours of the ground"). Guidelines may only be advisory, or they may be the criteria by which projects will be reviewed and approved.

The rules can be specifications of expected performance. Rather than imposing an absolute height limit, a builder may be free to erect any structure that will not shade neighboring buildings more than so many hours per winter day. Performance criteria deal directly with effect and allow a variety of solution. But they may entail the testing of a long chain of consequences, from proposed form to predicted effect. It may also be difficult to be explicit about the desired performance. Requiring the planting of trees is much easier than specifying the visual quality to be gained thereby. Moreover, the actual performance will appear only later, after occupation, while the point of control occurs at the presentation of the design. Noise levels can be measured, but not until the factory is in operation. It is easier (not wiser) to exclude the factory. Thus, while preferring performance statements in principle, we use form criteria whenever performance is difficult to predict, specify, or test for, and when fixing form alone is not likely to have some serious side effect. Moreover, because of administrative simplicity, form standards may be best when performance is an immediate consequence of form, and the consequence is likely to be similar in all kinds of circumstances. Thus we prescribe a minimum grade for a paved parking lot rather than the speed with which water should flow over its surface or the frequency with which that lot may be permitted to be flooded. (And yet, remembering those initial reasons, an infrequently used lot in an arid climate can be built dead flat.) A sophisticated guideline escapes this dilemma between specifying either form or performance by prescribing a form and then stating its intended performance, adding that the form rule may be laid aside if the builder can show, by a careful analysis, that the desired performance will otherwise be achieved.

Use controls

Controls on use are commonly made and widely accepted since similar uses are presumed to have similar requirements for access and location, confer similar benefits or burdens on their neighbors, and have a characteristic appearance. The control may be expressed in terms of uses permitted or uses excluded. Useful as these rules may be, we have been too prone to purity: to large areas devoted only to residence or only to industry, for example, which may make it impossible for people to live near their work. Here we are both more effective and more flexible if we focus on performance: on the external nuisances that one use will impose on another. Limits can be set on the emission of light, noise, dust, vibration, or pollutants, beyond the lot boundary or on the traffic that will be generated. Prohibited noise levels can be specified in decibels, unacceptable lighting in lumens or the visibiity of the source, and so on. These rules will be more difficult to administer, but they go to the heart of the matter and apply to all uses. Use control can also *require* that certain activities be put in particular locations, as by demanding that the ground floor of any building in a dense urban zone be occupied by public commerce in order to keep the street level lively and to provide the services that people desire.

Density and building lines

Other types of control preserve more dimensions of freedom for subsequent builders. Density controls are a good example. They have a fundamental impact—technical, social, economic, even visual—and yet they allow a great diversity of form. The most effective way of expressing a density limit is the *floor area ratio*, that is, the total floor area of the building (adding all floor levels) divided by the ground area of its plot. Such ratios may run from 0.1 for very open areas, to as much as 20.0 for very dense areas, and have distinct effects on traffic, utility loads, street life, massing, public services, and so on. The floor area ratio (FAR) also goes under the name of "plot ratio" or "floor space index." The variance of name will at times cloak subtle differences about measuring the area of the plot or the built area of the structure.

Maximum building lines are often set, whether in the form of height limits or required setbacks. But if the objective is to control density or to ensure sunlight, then the former is better done directly and the latter by a performance standard that refers to shading. Building lines achieve a visual result or reserve an access or an area of ground for some future use, or provide for ventilation. Height limits and front setbacks are commonly used for visual effect and side yard setbacks for ventilation, fire safety, or emergency access. The side yard restriction may refer only to a single side, so that the two narrow strips on either side of a building can be consolidated into a wider, more useful, private space. Building lines can be varied, to define a public space or to produce an interesting street front. Occasionally, in a key location, it will be desirable to use a mandatory line, one that *requires* that a building come forward to a given line or that a common cornice height be maintained.

The designer may preserve important views by imposing a "view easement"—a two- or three-dimensional zone within which no permanent opaque object may intrude. She may control planting, as by requiring that certain areas be landscaped and maintained, or that trees over a certain size not be cut down, or that a minimum density of new trees be planted. The filling of wetlands or the stripping of topsoil can be outlawed. The volume of earthwork, which has such a powerful impact on the visible landscape and on its drainage, can be regulated by limiting the area of ground that is disturbed or the volume of earth displaced. She might prescribe the materials, colors, and textures of roofs and walls, or the general character of the fenestration. The shape of the roof is a subject for guidance. Other controls can refer to the quality of the details: signs, say, or fences. But as she inches closer to detailed form, she must be all the more cautious.

Controls are often designed for some secondary effect— a practice devious, usually wasteful, and at times hazardous. Developers may be required to install expensive improvements, for example, in order to slow down development, but this only raises housing costs. A minimum house size, justified on grounds of health, may really be intended to exclude low-income people. Many innocent devices are used, where direct exclusion is illegal. Even if the aim is innocuous, it is better to control an unwanted effect directly. All controls have their costs, and it is best to keep those costs in the open. Controls raise the price of development not only because they require more expensive materials or processes but because they limit options and impose delays. Costs

Costs of controls

must be balanced against the ends to be achieved. The more complicated the control, the greater the delay and uncertainty.

In reverse, a developer may be released from certain rules in return for providing some desirable use, space, or excellence of design. A public plaza at street level allows the builder to exceed the maximum floor area ratio. But watch out. You must be sure that the public cost of the added density (the additional traffic congestion, for example) is not greater than the amenity to be gained, and that the bonus received by the developer is both adequate to encourage him to make the plaza and yet not so lavish that the plaza might have been gained at far less public cost. In other words, it is difficult to equate plazas with congestion and risky to substitute inflexible control for a market adjustment. One might better allow the extra density in return for providing facilities to meet the extra congestion it will cause. Alternatively, provide plazas at direct public cost or simply require them of builders if they are sufficiently vital to the public welfare. Development control by bonus can have all the side effects of economic control by means of tax gimmicks.

Standards

Many controls are based on current standards, which are statements about desirable characteristics of the environment. We have national standards for pavement widths, pipe sizes, street lighting, fire egress, building spacing, ground slope, playground size, and many more. Some refer to form, some to the process of creating it, some to its subsequent performance. There are legal minimums, desirable optimums, current practices, and arbitrary standardizations that simply limit an unwanted variation in form, such as those that set screw threads. Standards are a necessity. Without them, decisions would be lost in a jungle of detail and uncertainty. With them, subsidiary questions can be handled summarily, and inexperienced participants will avoid major errors. Legally and psychologically, it is comforting to have an established way of separating right from wrong.

But contexts are ignored and side effects neglected in this sharp distinction of good and evil. Requiring two means of egress from apartments in tall buildings not only raises costs, which was foreseen, but makes it difficult for police to patrol interior hallways, which was not. The familiar apartment slab, with a stair tower at either end and its entrance and elevators in the center, is the child of this rule. Setting 15 m (50 ft) as the minimum right-of-way for any minor road makes housing expensive and gives many new

residential areas a barren look. Both rules are now nation-wide and have had an immense effect on the form of our housing. Other standards, reasonable enough in themselves, may have severe effects in combination. The synergistic result of standards about the minimum size of an efficient school, plus the space needed for customary athletics, plus the maximum allowable walking distance to that school, applied in a district of families with few children, is an empty open space surrounded by tower apartments.

Standards are set without thought for their side effects or are manufactured arbitrarily. They may be born as the personal opinion of some professional, repeated offhand as reasonable enough by others, then accepted as the best immediately available statement for some pressing legal purpose, and eventually codified across the nation. The connection to purpose is glossed over. For example, the relation of standard setbacks or lot frontages to health and welfare is by now obscure. A skilled site planner can often produce a better environment by violating standards. Yet standards are dangerous necessities.

In any case, one should habitually question the connection of form to performance and the relevance of performance to situation. Many standards would be more useful (but unhappily bulkier) if they stated the client and context to which they are relevant, as well as the purpose at which they are aimed. Since standards must be tested and revised repeatedly, the hypotheses that underlie them should be explicit somewhere. A little uneasiness could be salutary.

Controls and guidelines may refer to the process of development rather than solely to form or performance. Thus, approvals by regulating bodies may be required, for whom a set of specified drawings and statements must be produced. Public hearings are called for. Advisory guidelines may encourage a certain process of design, such as a preliminary analysis of the visual character of existing buildings in the vicinity, to be followed by an explicit demonstration of how that essential character is responded to.

Design review boards are a common control device, used where ends are difficult to specify explicitly and where it is important to allow for some unexpected situation. If the board is to have the power to accept or reject, then it must be furnished with guidelines to prevent it from acting arbitrarily. If carefully drawn, performance criteria can furnish those guidelines. Review boards with the power to deny should only be used in special situations, such as historic

Design review

345

or highly symbolic locations, where the consequences of poor development might be especially severe. Much depends on the skill of the reviewers, more on the presence of a staff who can advise builders from the earliest stages. Even a good staff and a capable review panel do not ensure success.

A less highly charged device is the board of review to which all designs must be submitted but which only has powers of persuasion and public discussion. On occasion, those powers can be effective enough. In addition to its original instructions, an advisory board may develop its own guidelines as it makes judgments on individual cases. It evolves a "common law" as it analyzes the quality of the accumulating development, extracting and codifying its locally specific nature. Incremental change is permitted, and character progressively intensified, without specifying character in advance.

Boards of review may be official public agencies, or may be set up by an institution or superdeveloper, or may be a local association of owners who take hold as they appear on the scene. Owner associations are now frequently used to exercise development controls but also to maintain and operate common facilities. Municipal governments can be jealous of these private powers or be concerned that they will not have the permanence to carry out their functions over a long period of time. The possibility of a loss of continuity must be provided for.

Working in built places

Site planning in a growing country, endowed with what seemed inexhaustible space, has traditionally been concerned with untouched sites. But the accumulation of structures, the slowing of growth, and the realization of resource limitations have shifted us toward the replanning of built ground. Our achievements there have not been brilliant and have often been marked by physical and social disruption. Designers who perform well on clear sites raise havoc in tight places. New issues, new difficulties, and new advantages appear.

The built site will usually be studded with structures and activities that still have social and economic utility. Likely, they will be so located as to block any clear geometric pattern. A designer trained to order things sweeps these nuisances aside or seals them off like lumps of foreign matter. The underground tangle of utilities, which follows its own perverse logic, is often too expensive to replace. The tough web of human relations, rights, and images is most intractable of all. Each special difficulty requires a special response, which costs time and money. Every decision disturbs someone, and the chaos of construction is a serious nuisance for all. Preconceived designs are compromised and brilliant effects precluded. A different definition of design quality is needed and a different strategy of working.

The reuse of built places has such obvious advantages that this reorientation of design cannot be evaded. Resources are conserved by reuse, although it is not always true that money costs are minimized. Given the efficiencies of scale and the organization of our construction industry, it may be cheaper to clear a site, discard all the old structures, and rebuild on a regular pattern than it is to patch and revise piecemeal.

But this financial calculation takes no account of resource depletion, social loss, personal anguish, or political resistance. Reuse in a settled region is supported by a web of services in place, not only of urban infrastructure and public facilities but the network of human relations and activities whose disruption and replacement is such a serious cost in any new settlement. Moreover, the environment finally resulting is likely to be richer and more inviting. The old buildings accommodate economically marginal but socially useful activities. Human associations have gathered about them. Much of the meaning and vitality of urban life rises from this sense of complex association—this visible evidence of social diversity and of historical development. Once a site is cleared, it normally takes years to establish a new use. Continuity is snapped off, and with it the possibility of imagining new uses for the demolished buildings. Just because of the special difficulties of rehabilitation, a successful solution is more likely to be of finer grain, more responsive, proper to that particular place. Since at least some of the future users are present (and if they are consulted), the solution will be better suited to their needs. Despite frequent disasters, some of the more interesting examples of site planning in this country are rehabilitations of an older urban fabric.

But people and their activities must be moved about in the rebuilding process. They suffer moving costs, the cutting of social and economic ties, and the loss of emotional associations. Sometimes, as when low-income people are forcibly removed to a remote site or the elderly shifted to a strange area, the move can literally be fatal. Occasionally, for a more resilient population, the move can be stimulating. The site designer must be concerned to minimize the dis-

Disruption and relocation

347

placement that his plans will bring about. As a first assumption, unless the existing population is changing rapidly or unless some public purpose intervenes, the new site plan should provide for the people already on the ground. Or they should only leave willingly as they are attracted to other locations. Thus, the plan must be sufficiently flexible and fine-grained that users can choose to remain or choose their moment of departure. The displacement plan is part of the site plan.

This plan may provide for temporary moves within its boundaries, so that present occupants can retain their social ties, even as they release land for renovation. To make this possible, the site work begins with vacant or abandoned land. The plan is linked to changes in the other areas to which the people will be moving. It may be possible to move groups of neighbors together so that the social matrix is not completely shattered. These considerations require a careful analysis of the existing occupants, even if they are to be totally removed.

Balancing interests

Lying behind this concern with present occupants is a more difficult issue, one endemic to planning and hardly soluble within the site planning domain: how are the interests of the occupants of the place, or of the neighbors of a place, to be balanced against more general public interests or against the interests of those who will later occupy that place? Should present suburbanites be allowed to exclude future migrants from the inner city? Should the Irish squatters have been driven out to make New York's Central Park? How seriously should present students be consulted about the design of dormitories when they will be gone before the buildings are completed? Site planners nibble at these questions when they consider staging, strive for future flexibility, and talk with existing residents.

Adjacent neighbors are always consulted, since they have continuing interests in the site that can sometimes be satisfied without compromising the plan. They may be concerned to preserve a view, provide a new public service, maintain a physical character (even without fixing the social rank of the new occupants), or ameliorate the traffic that the new development will unleash. They are likely, of course, to value what they have and resist replacement, and so someone must also advocate the interests of the eventual occupants.

Responding to context

How to respond to the existing physical context is another debated issue. New growth must respect its setting,

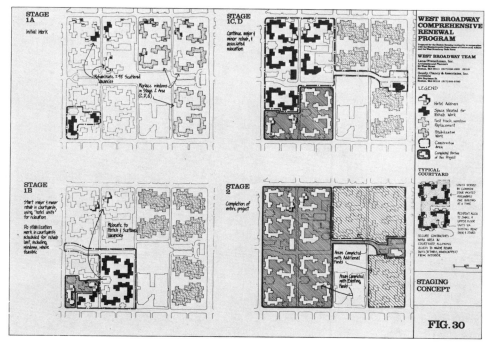

FIGURE 98 *The logistics of staging so that residents are moved only once was a major factor in the renewal of the West Broadway housing project in Boston.*

unless that is unpleasant or about to disappear. The occasional landmark may stand out, but most buildings are only backgrounds for the activities that enliven them. We look for an *integrated* townscape, a harmonious fabric of parts diverse in function and in age.

How to attain that integration? Designers who aim at it frequently miss. One accepted method begins with a checklist of building elements, each of which should be similar to those of existing buildings: setback, style, height, proportions, roof forms, color, materials, solid-to-void ratios, floor lines, directionality, use patterns and so on. Yet buildings that swallow all these prescriptions still sicken their neighbors, while others that break the rules may fit in surprisingly well. The only workable rule is to trust the eye and not a verbal checklist. Judge how the new structures will actually be seen, together with their older neighbors. Site design is still a craft, not a science of assembling parts.

Reference 11

349

FIGURE 99
The historic center of Delft has reached a fitting accommodation between old and new, residence and commerce, landscape and construction, and especially between motorist, cyclist and footman.

FIGURE 100
Recent buildings at Rice University echo the site patterns, building forms and materials of the original campus— without simply reproducing the old.

Certain elements *may* be critical in generating the character that one wants to reinforce: the skyline, perhaps; the texture of ornamental enrichment; the sense of scale; the type of activity on ground floors; certain familiar cultural symbols; a characteristic way of enclosing space; a play of light. But these key attributes are teased out by an attentive study of that particular place and tested by considering the real effect of any addition. The best test is a realistic simulation, displaying a proposal as it will actually be experienced and in its true context rather than as a remote object, framed in clouds and landscaping. Take a normal viewpoint for drawings. Add the new proposal to photographs of the existing situation or insert it into models of the context. But view the latter at street level and use sufficient detail to convey the actual character of the site. Some communities have written area guides for new development, which explain how physical continuity can be maintained. These guidelines have at times been inserted into, or even substituted for, conventional zoning codes. Until we are more skillful, such guidelines are better kept advisory, or at least quite flexible. Given an adequate review process, they might well be accumulated gradually, out of repeated experience with the actual juxtaposition of old and new, in the manner of the English common law.

Designers speak of "contextualism" and make a witty play on familiar symbols. But the links between environmental form and abstract ideas are extremely indirect and depend on slow cultural accumulations. Immediate visible form has a surer effect on the sense of continuity. Buildings should look and feel right in context, and this is best judged directly. It is more important to express the spirit of a particular place than the spirit of our time, since we are forced to respect the latter in any case.

Despite the current interest in context, social and economic pressures continue to make discontinuities. Large projects turn inward rather than outward. They emphasize their distinctiveness in order to isolate themselves from unfavorable conditions, or to corner some profitable market, or to expedite construction, or to exclude unwanted people. This is reinforced by the administrative procedures that divide a rebuilding process into bounded areas. We have indoor shopping malls, ringed by parking lots, exclusive office parks, residential "villages," walled compounds, hotels on the atrium plan, and luxury apartments perched high over parking garages. People may feel safer as they scurry from fort

Discontinuities

to fort, but they know less of the world around them, and the public landscape becomes blank and forbidding. The street degrades to a traffic channel. In reaction, site planners are concerned with recreating the vitality of the street, with use mix, with reknitting the urban fabric. They are motivated by an interest in the actual human experience of the city, by a concern for community and the public life, by a conception of the city as a common possession, by a delight in contact with different people, activities, and forms. In any case, site planning in built places always faces the question: what is the boundary of my concern, and how shall I treat it?

Site planning in built places is often fractionated. It is therefore tempting to employ a single large developer, who will do the entire project under a single umbrella. But this will homogenize process and product and lose much of that special quality latent in reuse. It squeezes out the small builder, who might be a local entrepreneur and who can respond more easily to local circumstance. It is also likely to squeeze out a mix of use or a mix of old and new, although large builders are becoming more sophisticated in dealing with diversity. Apparently the single builder will speed the process, but he may in fact retard it since he has monopolized the local market. The site designer who values context and diversity will push back against the constant pressure for large-scale, synoptic control. It has even been suggested that the scale of control should be set by deliberate public policy— as for example by an upper limit on the size of any sum given to any single group in a capital improvement budget, or by an upper lot size that could be sold to any one developer, or even by a legal limit on the value or size of any single piece of property that could be owned or built by a single entity.

Time and timing

Reference 58

The temporal context is as critical as the spatial one. Should we do something quite new, or imitate older forms, or preserve them, or strive to return them to some earlier state? Since we look at history as a staccato sequence of changeless periods, we acknowledge it by clinging to a chosen past, some charismatic period to be preserved in all its outward form. But history is a process of constant change, whose most important feature is its *continuity*, the way in which a long line of development links to the real and changing present. In this view, old forms are not things to be preserved but things to reuse and reshape in a way that sharpens our sense of continuity. Buildings should display the scars of former occupancy, grounds show the trace of former use. Special historic districts have their value, but it is more important to realize that *every* location has a history that warrants expression. Where were the former buildings, the former gathering places and pathways? What were the previous modes of living, and how did the present ones come to be? A shopping center in an old chocolate factory, or a community building in the home of a nineteenth-century feminist, has resonance in the present. Incremental plans have a natural advantage since a mix of old and new is always present. Yet even when the change must be convulsive, former traces can be built in.

The designer holds the same misapprehension of the change she is prescribing. There will be a brief mucking about while the project goes up, she thinks, but that will soon be over. Then it is all complete, and so it remains. In reality, the thing goes forward piecemeal, with halts and uncertainties. The cleared site, intended as the centerpiece of the plan, is for many years a vacant lot, which depresses the entire neighborhood. Activities leave because they are threatened with future displacement, and nothing takes their place. The street is torn up for a year, and shops wither on the vine. The new occupants who arrive first become vocal advocates of their own interests and take charge of the subsequent unfolding of the plan. The lengthy process of gathering financial and political resources requires a waiting period, which appears to be total abandonment, and this breaks the neighborhood spirit. The site plan must be judged for its impact at every stage, and the effects of timing and succession evaluated.

Temporary conditions must not become unwanted permanent ones. The designer considers how to encourage temporary use or landscaping of the space that is momentarily vacant. A street is completed, furnished, planted, and lined with market carts before the permanent fronting development arrives. Activities are incubated in temporary spaces to test their appropriateness for permanent quarters. Old warehouses on the Toronto waterfront took in small manufacturers and the Shipwright's Guild, which in those temporary locations proved themselves worthy of permanent homes. Engaging temporary uses took over the old market sheds at the abandonment of Les Halles in Paris. But if this temporary activity is successful, and the redevelopment agency not flexible enough to follow the new lead, then the ultimate clearance of the site may become still further complicated.

The site plan is a historical event, and so it must be planned.

Indeed, site plans for the temporary use of vacant sites and buildings may become more respectable. Some municipalities lease their vacant lands to local associations for temporary use as parks, gardens, or play lots. It must then be clear how such a lease can be revoked to allow a more permanent use. Impermanent parks and gardens, temporary uses that keep buildings occupied while they are in transition, the organization of festivals that prepare the way for something else, ways to plant ground that will only remain open for the time being, and shifting production yards or agriculture are useful elements of a dynamic settlement. We neglect many such opportunities in our worship of the fixed and the permanent.

Celebration of change

Especially on the built urban site, there is a good opportunity to celebrate the process of change. Uniforms, explanatory signs, and sidewalk video can explain what is occurring. Tours can be arranged at pauses in the work. An interpreter (just like a park guide) could be on hand to answer questions and to point out critical operations. Urban archaeology can uncover the past, volunteers can try their hand at it, and results could be communicated on the spot. Vice versa, when the ground is opened to lay foundations, residents might be allowed to deposit mementoes, for the delight of future archaeologists. The reasons for site planning decisions can be expounded, alternatives marked on the ground, illustrations of expected outcomes displayed and then retained for public comparison with the actual result. All stages in the work can be marked with festivals, not simply ground breaking and the cutting of a ribbon. Acting out the future can explore new possibilities. We can post views of a street as it was, at the same viewpoint, or display the implements of former activity on the premises of a similar current use. Such devices are not simply good public relations but an effective way of making change understandable. They help people to locate themselves in time and to play a more informed role in the social decisions that environmental change requires. Taking social advantage of the *process* of site planning is one of our unexploited resources. Its money cost is slight, but it will take management energy. Worse, it could expose an uncomfortable truth.

Site analysis

Since context and continuity are crucial in the built site and existing occupants so important, the designer makes a more prolonged analysis than she might do on open ground. Who lives in and uses the site and its surroundings? How do they use it, and what are their feelings about it? Is this group transient or stable? Who controls the place, and what are *their* motives? She talks with these people to evoke their images and values. She spends hours on the spot watching actual behavior: where people pass and congregate, the active and the vacant areas, the apparent misfits between environment and action, the character of celebration and display, where work is done, how children play, how things are maintained, the evidence of love and care, the favorite sitting spots. Even if all is swept away, present behavior must be accommodated somewhere and memories should be carried forward.

The physical environment will be a witness to this behavior. One looks for wear and upkeep, for symbols at the door or in front windows, for backyard wash and discards, for scattered toys or fences deliberately broken, for unplanned tracks across the lawn, for furniture or flowers set out, for signs of conflict or cooperation, for goods in shop windows, for the key community institutions. Most interesting, perhaps, are the signs of recent change. The site will have its special views, its particular texture of space and sound, its regularities of material, mass or ornament, a pattern of streets and public activity. There will be parks, landmark buildings, streets or street corners that are valuable to the community and whose presence should be enhanced. Boundary conditions and approaches must be observed so that the new design can be rewoven into the settled fabric. There may be wastelands that can be exploited or neglected amenities to be recaptured. Even in the most ordinary of places, the designer looks for hidden treasure, and sometimes finds it. The guiding rule is to extend what exists and works.

In the typical urban renewal scheme, but also in cases of fire or abandonment, the former occupants have been driven out, and to all appearances the site is empty. But no site is ever empty, and rarely is one completely abandoned. Most certainly it is not without a history. It has a topography, an ecology of plants and animals and human users, however furtive and weedy, an underground network of pipes and wires and foundations, a set of memories and meanings that living people attach to it, and many physical traces of past use. The apparently empty ground is observed as if it were a living place.

Since the initial anguish of clearance is now irreversible, the peculiar problem of such a site is its boundary. All around, there is an active settlement once directly tied to the site.

Empty sites

Here we are likely to design a "project," an island of new development that faces its old neighbors with blank walls or belts of parking. The demands of circulation and the abrupt shift of use, scale, and style of building make a gash hard to conceal. The gash is physical but also exists in the minds of neighbors. It has been reinforced by a long wait before the cleared site was rebuilt.

One obvious response is to shape the new project to imitate its surroundings or to grade from imitation at the edge to newness at the core, but that is hard to do. Better, existing streets are extended into the new fabric and their frontages continuously occupied. Disruptive uses such as parking are placed in the block interiors rather than along some boundary street. Shopping, or attractive public services, can be put at the edge, to create a common center rather than a division. Uses can be mixed in the new development and the scale of the parts be kept to that of the surrounding area. Preferably, clearance has been avoided until the last moment, and former activities have been retained as long as possible so that rebuilding is immediate. But the financial and political organization of large-scale building takes time, and activities are quite likely to flee under the threat of future clearance, leaving only a dead shell. Clear cutting in a city (or in a forest) is usually bad management. Selective clearance and incremental reuse leave fewer wounds. Still, there are times when clearance cannot be avoided.

Waste ground

The reclamation of some extensive region of waste ground or derelict structure is still another site planning opportunity. Such opportunities arise after the abandonment of rail yards, cattle yards, or large factories, in the reclamation of flood lands, waste disposal areas, or military reservations, on the sites of failed superprojects, or on land whose development has been blocked by long controversy, tangled ownership, or uses of low repute. Such areas are typically large, like a cleared renewal site, and like them may lie in a central urban location. But they are likely to be more isolated and were not preceded by any painful uprooting. They have a thinner history, or that history is more remote. Most often, they have a strong negative image: they are regarded as unpleasant and useless. Although they contain unrealized assets that can be exploited without disturbing existing use, they have two difficulties. One, since in the past they have been avoided, their access is poor. Roads pass them by, which is a psychological and a visual problem, as well as a functional one. A strategy of opening up is required, and this may entail costly initial expenditures for roads and main utilities.

Two, there is a popular image to expunge. This image can be persistent and will be reinforced where any initial development must contend with a larger adverse setting. If possible, use a strategy of growth from some favorable edge, in a manner that looks back toward the positive root and psychologically excludes the wasteland into which development is growing. To scatter new growth throughout the available ground, or to attempt to occupy all that ground at one stroke, can be fatal blunders. But some large-scale holding use, such as pasture or parking, may be possible, as well as temporary cosmetic improvements, such as supergraphics or the planting of groves of quick-growing trees. It may also be possible to plant users who do not share in the negative associations of the past, such as housing college students in a former red light district. Direct measures that attack the popular image are required: the organization of a festival or a public discussion of future possibilities.

The site may contain hidden booby traps: utility mains, massive foundations, toxic waste deposits, contaminated soils, buried streams, ancient rights of way. Neglected natural features can also be brought to light, picturesque derelict structures that can be reused in interesting ways, or forgotten history that can be celebrated. Gas Works Park in Seattle is a famous example of a derelict industrial plant converted into a remarkable pleasure ground; the history of its design is instructive.

Scarcity

The world's housing is largely built by small contractors or by residents themselves, without the blessings of architects or site planners and under conditions of great scarcity. Necessity revises priorities, and many principles of site planning seem at first irrelevant. We have often asked how ultimate users can participate in site planning. In the ordinary housing process the question is reversed: how can professionals participate? Are they of any use? We will argue that their skill is even more important in this situation, where the pressures are so desperate and the margins so narrow. But, to be useful, they must shed many preconceptions.

Demand at the lower end of the income scale is very variable—due to differences in class, culture, climate, family size, and position in the trajectory of economic development—and it is also inelastic. Some requirements may be nearly absolute, such as proximity to a source of casual labor.

FIGURE 101
Gasworks Park opens a formerly off-limits industrial world to the curiosity and imagination of Seattle's children.

But there is no financial reserve that can secure that urgent location if its price should rise. Inappropriate standards or mistakes in allocation can therefore have severe consequences. No planning decision is neutral. Factual data may be scarce and informants unaccustomed, or even from experience too fearful, to give direct answers to direct questions. Attending to actual behavior will therefore be all the more important.

The informal housing process

Despite this cultural diversity, there are a few things that may be said about this "informal" process of self-built or self-managed housing. The first is that such housing is itself a process of development. Housing improvement not only makes life more comfortable but is an essential strategy of economic and social advance. These are hopeful places, however chaotic and ugly they may appear. Site planning methods can support the process of advance once the priorities are understood.

In the usual case, when the family or individual first arrives in a region, they must find a room, however crowded, whose rent is very low, and which is close to kin and to some opportunity for employment. As the in-migrants establish themselves, they then seek a piece of land accessible to work, to the markets, and to public services such as schools and health services. They must obtain that land at low cost

358

and with secure tenure. Next they want certain basic utilities, a source of building materials, and a support network: friends and kin for whose labor they might barter, small contractors, short-term credit, advice. Later, priorities shift toward improving the size or quality of the house and the utilities that serve it and to finding ways of generating additional income on the lot, such as by keeping animals, opening a small store or workshop, or renting rooms. By that last move they may then aid others who are beginning the cycle. So priorities shift as people move along this trajectory, and they differ among different families. It is essential, then, that families be able to make their own choices—be able to spend their scarce funds on those items most important to them. Unwanted overimprovement must be avoided, and yet there should be opportunities for families to invest in further improvement if they choose. The families use their process of housing for shelter but also for generating income, for education, for social advance. Professional intervention should unleash this stream of construction, maintenance, use, and adaptation, not dam it up.

Reference 13

Land is the primary requirement: secure tenure of a plot that has good access and is so planned that eventually it can support the activities and structures that will be desired. New subdivisions must be laid out to augment this supply, whose scarcity is very often the most serious impediment to the self-managed housing process. Plots can be transferred to their owners at low prices, since the bedrock essential is simply raw land, a rational layout on the land, and secure land titles and clear rights-of-way. Elementary road and utility improvements are the next layer above bedrock, and they should initially be kept as simple as possible.

Lots

Small, narrow-fronted lots minimize the costs of roads, utilities, and raw land. To the designer, this will seem efficient. But the owner wants room to expand his house over the years, perhaps to establish a small shop or grow some of his food. His priority is to gain a generous plot at the beginning since it cannot later be expanded. In trade, he will wait for improvements until he can afford them. The proportion of frontage to depth, the minimum frontage, and the minimum lot size, which are interrelated numbers, are therefore critical. They will be tighter numbers than we are accustomed to, yet they will properly be more generous than those officially used in many developing countries.

If we assume the widely diffused minimum standard for shelter space of 5 sq m (54 sq ft) per person and a family

FIGURE 103
Squatters occupy a depleted quarry on the outskirts of Fez, Morocco. Their settlement pattern and housing contrasts sharply with the "official" housing project in the background.

of seven people, a two-story house with a fire break around it would require a lot of 70 sq m (750 sq ft). Even that would make a pit latrine impossible, as well as any substantial growth or the addition of any economic activity. As a rough rule of thumb, then, one might say that, while 70 sq m is an absolute minimum lot, 110 sq m (1200 sq ft) is a better floor. A range of sizes should be provided for different families, ranging upward from 110 or 150 sq m (1200 or 1600 sq ft). The latter begins to allow the addition of a workshop, or rented rooms, or provision for an extended family. Lot frontages should not be less than 6 or 7 m (20 ft), or, better, 9 or 10 m (30 or 35 ft). Ratios of frontage to depth can run from 1:1.5 to 1:4. Rectangular lots are best for easy registration and demarcation on the ground. But diversity is the key, to allow for all the variations of income, family composition, and modes of ownership or rental. As it is extended, the layout should allow the mix of lot sizes and locations to be varied according to demand.

Access is the second prerequisite for future development. Access Access is partly a function of the location of the subdivision with respect to jobs and public services and partly a function of the internal rights-of-way. These must be clearly defined and of adequate breadth and alignment, providing for immediate traffic and for the future. A common standard is that the collector streets, which connect minor streets to the major roads and on which any public transit will run, should form a connected network and have rights-of-way at least 10 m (35 ft) wide. The minor streets, which serve only to give access to the lots fronting on them, may be indirect or dead-ended and should be at least 6 m (20 ft) wide. But small groups of lots may front only on a footpath rather than on a street. These paths will range from a main through footway, capable of passing an occasional minitruck or emergency vehicle, with a 4 m (14 ft) right-of-way, down to a 2 or 3 m (6 or 10 ft) dead-end footway. But for the sake of later development, it is unwise to depend on paths that can never be upgraded to take a small motorized vehicle. That is, it is a mistake to use less than a 3 m (10 ft) right-of-way, or to include a turn which a small truck cannot negotiate at slow speed, or to employ a dead-end unless it is short and contains a turning space at its end. Room to park a future vehicle must be reserved on the lot, or in a local, semi-public open space. Looking farther ahead, however, knowing from sad experience how easily the car becomes a fatal weapon, these minor streets should not be overdesigned. Modest rights-of-way, indirect passage, and sharp but negotiable jogs or turns will preserve pedestrian dominance.

Access rights-of-way need not be open to vehicles from the start. At first, some may only be graded and paved as footpaths, with footbridges over the gullies. If good collector streets are laid down and if lots are within some reasonable distance of public transit on those routes (300 m or 1000 ft is typically cited as a maximum), as well as within reach of emergency vehicles or trucks supplying water or building materials (a distance often given as 75 m or 250 ft), then access to the lot may at first be confined to pedestrians, cycles, handcarts, and pack animals.

A range of road surfacings is available, from simple earth—cleared, scraped, and graded—through sand-clay, soil-cement, compacted gravel or rubble, asphalt seal, concrete, or asphaltic concrete. The collector streets, which carry the buses, trucks, and heavy traffic, must usually be paved or compacted in some fashion. But the minor ways begin at any point in this ladder of surfacings. The key considerations are that they be shaped to drain, that they be passable in all weathers, and that they can later rise from rung to rung: from bare earth to gravel to asphalt topping.

Upgrading

Even these generalizations may fail when one is engaged in upgrading an existing self-help housing area, in which small houses are jammed together in confusing ways. Upgrading may be more important than the creation of new subdivisions, since it is in the existing areas that the bulk of the population will be living and where the active housing process will be at its height. In this case, the key site planning activity is to find ways to demarcate the lots so that legal titles can be awarded, while providing definite rights-of-way for access and future utility extensions and while keeping the demolition or moving of structures to an absolute minimum. Under such conditions, the minimum standards for lots and for access will be revised downward. Even lots as small as 20 sq m (215 sq ft) may be acceptable, for example.

Utilities

The essential utilities are water, storm drainage, electricity, and the disposal of waste. Drinking water can, if necessary, be delivered by truck or be piped to community standpipes and hand carried to the house. Water piped to each lot is of course preferable, and in total cost over time is actually cheaper than truck delivery, although the initial cost is higher. Delivery to a standpipe is cheapest, if least convenient, and can provide for a subsequent extension of pipes to each house. Water consumption will thereby be restrained, but water-borne waste disposal cannot be employed, nor can irrigated agriculture be carried out on the lot unless there is a nonpotable water source at hand. Individual wells, springs, and nearby lakes or streams are potential sources of drinking water, but they are susceptible to contamination.

Surface drainage can run for short distances in the roads and paths but must soon be channeled or discharged into the natural stream courses. It can be carried in open surface channels, if it is not contaminated, or it may be directed onto gardens or into retention ponds. But if it is contaminated with sewage or builds up to a substantial volume before discharge, then it must be piped underground, with all the expensive inlets, manholes, and treatment plants that procedure entails. In small localities, drainage can be based on a five-year storm, or even on only a one-year storm, if residents are able to endure an occasional flood. Since roads and storm drainage can account for as much as two-thirds of the cost of a low-income subdivision, drainage must be carefully considered to avoid long channels or the invasion of sewage effluent. Major underground storm drains are large, expensive works and should be avoided if possible.

It is relatively cheap to bring electricity into a settlement if power is available. Like piped water, and quite unlike storm drainage, the distribution network is not demanding of space or alignment. At the same time, it is of great service. Along with water, then, it is one of the first utility networks to be acquired or to be pirated if it is not legally available. Telephone service is next in line, used for emergencies or to reach kin, but vital also for small stores and workshops.

Human wastes in the developed countries are discharged in water-borne systems. But these are too expensive for the developing world and too wasteful of water (and so they are with us). If we exclude the widespread custom of defecation on open ground, or directly into lakes or streams, and the uncertainties and hazards of dependence on a regular removal of night soil, then the remaining alternatives are the pit privy, the aqua privy, and the aerobic and anaerobic digesters. These devices were discussed in Chapter 8. The pit privy is simplest and cheapest, and quite acceptable if there is sufficient space on the lot to accommodate it, and if there is no danger of contamination due to soil conditions or the water table. Subject to that, the pit privy will often be the best solution, and that argues for lots sized to accommodate it.

Waste disposal

363

Where groundwater may become contaminated or lots are small, then the aqua privy is preferable. It is relatively modest in cost, safe, and free of nuisance. It produces a small flow of liquid effluent, which must be locally absorbed or dischaged into a low-capacity sewage system. The anaerobic and aerobic digesters are rather bulky and expensive and require that vegetable waste be added to the excreta to make a favorable environment for digestion. The anaerobic digester produces fertilizer and methane fuel but requires warmth and a safe way of storing and using the gas. The aerobic device produces a safe fertilizer, requires no water, controls odors and flies, and poses no risk to health nor danger of explosion. It can be put on a small lot. It is somewhat expensive, although cheaper than a water-borne system, and takes some care in its operation. Shared toilets rarely work, but where plots are extremely small it may sometimes be necessary to cluster individual toilets in a common location, giving each family (or each two families) their own locked cubicle. These can discharge into a single aqua privy or can justify a septic tank and drain field if sufficient water is available.

Human waste is the dangerous material, and its disposal has an important influence on the site plan. "Graywater," on the contrary (the liquid wastes unmixed with human excreta), can be absorbed in a garden, soakpit, or trench or allowed to run off in open street drains. Solid wastes are a nuisance, but less of a health danger, except perhaps for decomposing garbage. Truck access is the principal demand of solid waste disposal on the site plan, but wastes may also be carried off in small carts. Food waste can be composted for gardens, and other waste material can be recycled to form the basis of small local industries.

Management and control

To recapitulate, the base necessities in site layout for self-managed housing are the demarcation of lots of adequate size, the provision of good access (in terms of rights-of-way if nothing else), the supply of water and electricity, the provision (or canny avoidance) of storm drainage, and a wise choice of the waste disposal system. To that we must add the sites for necessary public services—schools, day care centers, and health clinics—to whose lack the low-income family is peculiarly vulnerable. Parks and other public open spaces will also be desirable but are unlikely to be maintained. If large, they will themselves be subject to invasion for housing. If open space is reserved for the future, it must be kept remote from access or be put to some active use, as for agriculture. But small open spaces for recreation or outdoor production may be allocated to, and controlled by, small groups of residents, if strong local assocations or kinship groups are a part of the culture. These spaces can be placed within a block, for example, or at the heads of culs-de-sac. An occasional widening of the street will provide a small place on which stores can locate, creating a social focus and giving some relief to the densely packed pattern that will develop. In any case, the access streets will be used for work and play, as extensions of the house.

Since public maintenance and control are likely to be weak, active management by neighbors should be encouraged. Formal controls should be as simple as possible: their enforcement oppresses both the official and the resident. A progressive increase of the density of occupation is to be expected and permitted—indeed encouraged—up to the capacity of streets and utilities. Use zoning need not be imposed except to prohibit activities that generate serious nuisances, such as very heavy traffic, dense smoke, or continuous nighttime noise (and even these activities may simply be excluded by the capacity of streets and lots). Residents must be able to establish small enterprises on their lots; this is a key to their economic advance. As far as possible, social diversity should be actively maintained and encouraged: by providing a diversity of lot shapes and utility services and a diversity of street access, and by the strategy by which lots are opened up for occupation. Coarse-grain spatial segregation of the lowest incomes removes them from work opportunities and also from the public services—the utilities, schools, and clinics—they need so desperately.

Sensuous quality is not beneath notice in these struggling communities, but it must be achieved by the simplest means: colors, trees, the direct expression of identity. We all have the same human senses, and poor people are even more exposed to their environment. Street trees may wither for lack of public responsibility, but the private yards in the poorest areas are often bright with flowers. Thus initial plantings might be made on private lots and the semi-public open spaces, where they will be tended, rather than in the streets. Plants can be chosen for food value as well as appearance. There is no need to separate the sense of a place from its other functions. Most of these settlements occur in severe climates: hot-arid or hot-humid. Shade, water, and air movement are important. Simple materials can be handsome. Pressed earth blocks, for example, are not only cheap

Sensuous quality

365

and serviceable but have a beautiful texture. Careful attention to the locality—terrain, soil, plants, the movement of water—not only avoids expensive adaptations but conserves the visual landscape in a way that large-scale development can rarely do. With all their mud, their dust and discomfort, these settlements, by their lively activity and powerful sense of personal care, are often far more visually engaging than the professionally planned project.

Appropriate technology

We think of high technology as evident progress, and yet low-resource technologies can be more truly progressive, in the correct sense of facilitating further development. We have employed many devices in our past that we now think primitive: dirt roads, dug wells, wind-driven pumps, pit privies, oil lamps, wood stoves, sod houses, adobe, squatters' shacks, foot warmers, thatched roofs, fieldstone fences, mule-drawn scrapers, sites laid out by strings and water levels. We forget why they were useful and have even forgotten the art of them: how to shape a firm dirt road, how to keep a privy clean. Even more foolishly, we may in our affluence romanticize them and fail to see that *some* advanced technologies are extremely useful when resources are scarce: piped water and electric power, for example; cement, glass, paper and sawn timber; buses, trucks, bicycles and bulldozers. Techniques do not have absolute value: their value depends on whether they are appropriate to present resources, culture, and stage of development. We should remember the old techniques; understand where new techniques are valuable and where destructive; and continue to create appropriate technologies (pressed earth blocks, aerobic digesters, solar cookers, closed-cycle fish farming). The developing world must learn to accept, reject, and shape those devices to fit their own ways of life. This also holds true for the intentional communities in the developed world, who are looking for a new way of life. A few groups—the Amish are one example—have shown us how to choose deliberately among available technologies in order to strengthen their chosen mode of living.

Just as we may burden the developing world with the technology of the developed world (that term carries the depressing implication that we have nowhere else to go), so we impose our rules on them. Our common standards—for road width, lot size, sanitation, or density— can be brutally inappropriate when applied in another context. They will block the normal housing process and generate black markets and bribery. Standards should change gradually,

366

along with increasing resources. Local residents are the best judges of their own values and should have the freedom to pick and choose among the improvements available. On the other hand, they may not be good judges of certain external effects for whose social cost they are not liable, such as downstream pollution or the breakdown of an electric power supply due to illegal tapping of the lines. Thus it is reasonable to reduce the standards that refer to the immediate living area and yet impose strict rules where that will prevent damage to a larger public.

Financial policy must be linked with site planning policy,   Finance
although that cannot be treated here in any depth. Incomes are not only low but irregular, and the margins of choice are narrow. To match this fluctuation and to increase the freedom of choice, any mandatory, regular payments should be kept extremely low. Normal mortgages, for example, can hardly be maintained. The initial cost of the lot must be held to rock bottom: it may be no more than raw land and surveying costs or be subsidized. It should be possible to pay off these sums at irregular intervals. Beyond that, there should be a broad array of improvement options, which can be taken on in small chunks and at times be accomplished by one's own labor or that of the local community. Small, short-term credits, easy to arrange, should be available, not only to the lot owners but also to small builders and to local producers and distributors of building materials. The production of simple building materials may be subsidized, or public outlets for them be set up, as yardsticks for price and quality. Planning, building, and management skills can be formally taught or passed informally through networks of kinship and acquaintance. The creation of a dense network of small suppliers and contractors is as crucial as the provision of public services and of developed land.

Speculation in land must be suppressed since it is a prime obstacle to an adequate supply. This may require a rationing of subdivided lots or granting them at first on leasehold until they have been developed and occupied. Capital gains or urbanization taxes may be assessed against those large holdings which are ripe for development and are being kept out of use until their market value soars. Taxation on the developed lots, however, should be keyed to the public services provided rather than to the improvements made by owners. Land-based taxation, so often advocated, may be especially appropriate in the less developed countries. Public ownership of the developable land, and its timely release for subdivision at nominal prices, will also keep the supply open. Squatter settlements and other self-managed areas have been considered as the poorest kind of housing, something to be severely regulated, and if possible abolished. On the contrary, they are the progressive response to crucial need.

Chapter *12*

Strategies

Plans imply agreements. Without the agreement of those with the power to make changes, and at least the passive assent of those who could stop them, plans remain on paper. To have an effect beyond that of an influential intellectual model, the process of site planning must follow a strategy: it must organize the analysis, programming, design, and implementation so that ideas and decisions are meshed.

A strategy includes many choices: how to define the problem, the particular design approach, the use of intuition or rationality, the response to uncertainty, the technique of learning, the degree of participation, the linking of form and management, the use of professionals, and the relation to the client and other decision makers. A good many of these decisions are in the usual case simply customary. But we have argued that such choices should be made explicitly.

In Chapter 1 we outlined the normal mode, and have developed it in subsequent chapters, while pointing out its limitations and indicating many of the variations that are possible. That classic model might be described as a well-bounded linear process. The problem is defined by the client, and the designer proceeds in an ordered sequence, from systematic analysis of site and users, to the preparation of a program, and then to designing a solution, using the design method that is personally most congenial. The schematic design, or perhaps a set of alternatives, is submitted to the client for review, and then the chosen or modified design is developed in detail. After a cost estimate and perhaps an environmental impact statement have been prepared, the necessary financing and official permits are acquired. Once they are acquired, the client, through contractual arrangements, proceeds to build under the watchful eye of the designer. The site is occupied, minor adjustments are made, and the designer moves on.

The client is clearly defined from the start, and other interests are represented through him. The internal decisions of designing are quite distinct from the external decisions of finance and legal control, which simply set the (often annoying) limits of the design. Rational techniques of prediction and evaluation are used wherever possible and are kept separate from questions of feeling, inspiration, and taste. Uncertainty is reduced, or assumed away. Designing and learning are two separate processes: one learns first (in school, by observation, or in research) and applies that to solutions later. Professionals are specialized by subject matter and generally control decisions within their area of specialization. They work in hierarchical teams. The focus of the design is the physical form of the site, which is controlled in as detailed a degree as is possible. Management and the particular use of the space are subsequent issues and will be handled by managers who arrive when the site is complete.

This is a caricature, as unfair as any other caricature, but closely based on normal practice and thus useful as a point of departure. By now it must be clear that we have been advocating a very different process, one that is cyclical and open rather than bounded, one that responds as the situation unfolds and is far more intimately connected to the network of social decisions within which the site plan is only one strand. We can summarize our point of view by noting how our strategy would differ from that normal model.

Other actors

The designer must realize that many other actors beyond the client and herself will influence the outcome of the plan. Financiers, neighbors, public officials, users, managers, and maintenance men will modify or even upset the original intentions. Although it cannot eliminate them, the planning process must be shaped to minimize these sudden upsets and blockages, to reduce unproductive backtracking and wasted resources. The key actors—those who will control the site and those who will suffer it—are brought in early and repeatedly so that their objectives and powers are recognized. The cost of a plan, its environmental impact, its influence on the current way of life, how it will be administered, are all considered from the beginning and not left to be faced at the end of the line.

Since these actors are numerous and often in conflict, to allow everyone an equal voice will prove impossible to manage. Who then shall participate and decide? In the ideal case, the user of a piece of ground would design it for himself, or it would be designed by a builder who was directly accountable to a small group of users holding the same clearly defined values. Then the professional designer would become a teacher, one who helps the users to analyze their own needs and create their own possibilities, and this book would become a source of information for people building their own places. Ongoing user management would be substituted for sporadic professional intervention. But even here the professional could not be self-effacing. He is responsible to reveal hidden needs and possibilities, to speak for the future and for users not yet present. Planners would still have to deal with care-taking situations, with problems of social exclusion, and with systems of large scale, broad use, or long life, where the users are necessarily numerous, transient, and hold conflicting values, or are not yet present to be consulted.

In any situation, however far from the ideal, the designer must at least be aware of the political decisions she makes when she accepts a client and decides whom she will consult. In every case, she will strive to increase the role of the user and to make the design and programming process explicit and open to the nonprofessional. She will build behavioral research into her work, look for ways to advance user control, support participatory action, advocate flexible forms and adaptive management. She expects that the original circle of interest will enlarge and that new requirements will come to light, and so her strategy will provide for recurrent shifts in problem definition. She looks ahead to the political and financial decisions that will be necessary to make her plan a reality and makes sure that the design process will connect into them. An open planning process can create a constituency that will safeguard the intentions of the plan long after the planner is gone.

The capable designer is not only aware that his plan is part of a larger set of social decisions but that it is only one event in a long history of site occupation. Instead of preparing a blueprint that will be executed in detail and then preserved immutable, he designs a form that will change in time: a plan that shows successive stages or proposes the form of change itself. Since the future is difficult to predict, he may, at one extreme, only prepare guidelines for future design,

Site history

a diagram without precise dimensions, perhaps illustrated by various schemes that might be possible within its rules. Or he may dispense even with this framework and deliberately defer all decisions about the site as a whole. Site planning then becomes a sequence of small decisions, responding to immediate needs and particular conditions. This works well where there is a powerful context—a strong natural landscape or built region—or where the user is the designer, acting in his own domain for his own inarticulate purposes—creating a fine garden or a traditional community. The risk to avoid is that one may be boxed in by previous decisions. Alexander's experiment at the University of Oregon is one example of this strategy, which shifted from site planning to the creation of a planning system. The Oregon campus was to have no master plan but be subject to an annual diagnosis and to a public debate about the allowable elementary patterns for components of the setting. Users could propose actual projects in conformity with those patterns, and budgeting was broken into increments that encouraged small projects.

Reference 2

The *structure plan* is a less radical response to this problem of future development and lies between the precise, staged plan, on the one hand, and reliance on incremental planning within a context or a pattern language, on the other. Structure plans fix the critical, long-term elements of a site and prescribe the desired character of various areas without specifying how this must be achieved. They deal with proposed activities, densities, major infrastructure and landscape character. A detailed plan of the first increment may be included, but subsequent local plans are left open to later choice as long as they take account of the given framework, meet the stated performance, and respond to the accumulation of past detailed decisions. Like the Oregon process, this also requires an institutional foundation since there must be design review to ensure respect for the framework, and there must be a way of modifying the framework from time to time to reflect changed conditions.

Whether he uses staged plans, increment plans, or structure plans, the designer is aware of his involvement in a historical process, as well as in a social one. His plans consist of changing forms. He is inured to uncertainty, makes continency plans for possible disturbances, and provides contingency allowances for shifts in demand: whether in the budget or the space provision or the infrastructure. Periodic monitoring is assumed so that if the shifts do not occur, the surplus allowances may be diverted to other purposes. Further, the designer provides for adaptability in his plans and for an adaptable management. The older towns whose environments we admire grew slowly, adapted gradually. Conventional methods of building were improved piecemeal in small ways. Our design freedom carries with it a need for increased social control if we are to avoid eroding the character of our environment.

"What is the problem?" is the question that sets off the planning process and continues to haunt it. Defining the problem means deciding who the client is and who the user, what the criteria for success will be, what resources can be used, what limits must be imposed, what type of solution is expected, and who should develop it. Thus the situation has already been analyzed in embryo, the values set, and the solution given. But the situation may have been misunderstood, the values may be wrong, the solution may be impossible. Or the imagined solution may be inappropriate: a social change or a shift in the budget or in activities may be what is needed rather than a site plan. The program or the budget or the place may be inadequate to meet the client's expectations. Ideally, the designer would completely redefine the problem at the very beginning, but complete redefinition requires infinite time. Moreover, all problems have a previous history and are predefined by a long process of accumulated experience.

The designer at least requires that the problem be explicitly set and will review it to guess whether it is solvable and to see that a solution would not run counter to his values and those of probable users. He is ready to derail the project by pointing out that no site plan is needed. He seeks to be involved as early as possible in problem definition, whereby he may propose new criteria or resources, suggest unanticipated types of solution, advocate the inclusion of a hidden client, or even create a client to match the proposals. Such a deep penetration of the problem-setting process is unusual, but at least the designer is careful to make his review and in his strategy to allow for a possible redefinition. Planning is a heuristic journey in which the direct path is often discovered along the way.

The previous chapters have stressed the need for internal cycling in the planning process, for carrying forward the various design tasks in parallel or in iterative alternation. Too much information is often gathered at the outset, without a framework for understanding what is needed. It takes time

Problem
definition

Cyclical
designing

to understand a problem, and repeated efforts at solution. Experienced designers have learned to begin with a brief reconnaissance of the site, the actors and their expectations, and then to proceed to an initial design which probes the problem. A brief, intensive "charette" with the key actors will uncover hopes, conflicts, constraints, and information gaps and point to possible avenues of solution. Data are then collected to test the competing ideas, and they are modified as this new information comes in. Design moves on to details or further possibilities, and more data are sought as they become crucial. Analysis and design are intertwined: each illuminates the other.

The same may be said of impact analysis—the documentation originally required as a factual base for public decisions, which considered the impact of the proposed project on the environment outside the project. This analysis is now progressively being enlarged to consider social impacts and the impacts on those who will inhabit a project, as well as those outside. Usually this procedure is accomplished at the end of the design process, prolonging the decision period and leading to sharp confrontations. But like data collection it should begin in the very first stages and parallel the continuous effort of design. Thus our checklist for data collection in Appendix G incorporates the typical impact questions. An impact review is conducted at each step of the design.

Predictions

Impact analysis is only one form of the predictions that must be made repeatedly along the way, whether openly and formally or as a series of intuitive hunches. "What will happen if I do this?" is always being asked, implicitly or explicitly. Even a modest site plan depends on a myriad of predictions: about use, the performance of materials, the effect on surroundings, the response of natural systems, the human meanings and values the site will acquire. A well-articulated program simplifies the review of those predictions since it focuses the discussion on how well the plan will satisfy the crucial agreed intentions. But ends and means cannot be disentangled. Trial plans may show that it is not possible to permit distant views and also maintain visual privacy, which forces a look at why both are sought and further predictions as to how future residents would value those two qualities. Designing is a learning process—about site possibilities, about trade-offs between objectives, about the risks in the predictions.

Predictions require a model of the situation. It may be a simple analogy: "A is like B that I know, and so it will work in the same way." It may be a mathematical model if the function is simple and the key criteria are quantitative. It may employ a scaled drawing or model, whether to predict visual form or the impact of sun or wind. But for many aspects, predictions will rest on experience and intuition, since effects are interactive and often subtle. Intuitive judgments are liable to bias, whether by the personal or class outlook of the judger, by her professional interests, or her emotional investment in the plan. Presumably neutral quantitative judgments can as easily be distorted by hidden assumptions. The best defense is the countervailing judgment of other professionals and laymen. Thus our emphasis on a program that is explicit about performance, and on an open design process that incorporates successive, multidisciplinary reviews. Quantitative evaluations of elements of the plan will be a useful support in a general review but can never supplant human judgments of complexity.

Decisions—open or hidden—are necessarily made throughout the planning process. They accumulate and mat together. Plan elements are constantly transformed but are historically connected, and a radical transformation requires tearing out whole chunks of the accumulated fabric. If left to a final review, this can be a painful and costly event and can leave a disfiguring scar. So there must be repeated consultations whether by continuous informal client participation, or by formal reviews of findings and alternatives, staged for multiple clients at regularly scheduled periods. Social decision must be brought along with design decision, and vice-versa. Communication

Communications must be developed between all those involved in the site design process and between them and clients, users, builders, and maintainers. That means not only an open and explicit process that nonspecialists can penetrate but changes in the organization of the design team, the use of strong programs, and the construction of new design languages. Design should not only in itself be a way of learning but should learn from its results. Site inhabitants, human and inhuman, have the nasty habit of behaving in unexpected ways, and effects imagined in the drafting room may fall flat in reality, or be seen quite differently by those on location. Thus site planning cannot be a task that terminates after the plan is made. Carrying design intentions forward to management, and actual outcomes back to the designer, are essential links in the learning chain. Postoccupancy evaluations are very informative, especially if based on the intended program. Unfortunately such feedback is not a normal part of the site planning process. Nor are programs and designs deliberately shaped as experiments from which to learn.

Management

Sites are subject to continuing management. Form, activity, services, and administrative controls can be modified together to maintain the level of performance. To take a simple example, the performance of a parking lot depends not only on its layout but also on the number and turnover of its users, their driving skill and expectations, the regulations and charges imposed, the maintenance, lighting, and policing of the lot, and the interactions of all of these. A parking lot design must take these things into account, by assumption or prediction or prescription. An on-the-spot manager, in close control and commanding a high flow of current information, can respond and maintain performance rapidly. But he is limited to incremental changes and cannot easily break out of a worsening situation. Moreover, performance may gradually drift in undesirable directions, without his being directly aware of it. Designers could find a role in the continuous support of management: designing new patterns in response to new needs or making experiments from which management can learn. Thus the designer might begin to see design as an organization of events in time as well as in space.

Environmental institutions

Behavior fluctuates, but two things tend to stabilize it: one is the spatial environment, the other the institutions that regularize the relations between persons. Both factors have long-term effects; both affect each other. The quality of a setting may be due as much to the nature of the decision process that brought it into being—or to who possesses it, or to what social relation it symbolizes—as to its spatial form. Environments change in response to underlying institutions, and environmental change has institutional side effects. The coupling is loose but substantial.

Occasionally the planner has a choice about how to organize the implementation of a plan. Where the project is unfamiliar or unprecedented in scale, or involves many clients, the planner may even have the opportunity to organize an entity for carrying it out. More often, he is asked for his advice, and at times, the client can be nudged in some direction, whether of decentralizing or of exercising more control. In many other cases, the institutional arrangements are fixed, and the challenge is to select a strategy for planning and communication that is matched to client capabilities. The designer must be aware of how the performance of his designs will be affected by the existing institutions, and what management changes his designs imply. He should recognize the opportunities for new institutions that can occur in creating new environments. Houses or grounds can be cooperatively owned or maintained, new schools become community schools, health care in a new town put on a group basis. Environment and institutions are patterns of long life. They have strategic effects on the quality of human life, and those effects are magnified when the two patterns are coordinated.

The site planning strategy we speak for, while it must be matched to the situation at hand, has some general characteristics: it is cyclical, with analysis, design, prediction, and decision done side by side; it defines and redefines the problem explicitly; it uses the internal and the external process as an occasion for learning; it meshes designing into the much broader network of social decision of which it is a part; it opens up the design process to the values and control of the actual user; it sees the site plan as a single event in a long historical chain; it coordinates management, behavior, and institutions with spatial form. It turns out to be more complex than we had admitted at our beginning and it may seem that we have brought the reader through far too many details to end in such uncertainties. Yet one must know the parts before one can play the game, and the purpose of the game is to provide human beings with places that support their daily lives, delight them, and let them grow.

Appendix *A*

Soils

Particles of soil are classified by their grain size:

Gravel: particles over 2mm in diameter
Sand: 0.05 to 2mm; the finest grains that are visible to the eye; having a gritty feel.
Silt 0.002 to 0.05 mm; the grains invisible but can be felt; smooth not gritty;
Clay: under 0.002 mm; smooth and floury or in stiff lumps when dry, plastic and sticky when wet

Soils are extremely variable mixtures of these particles. For agricultural purposes, these mixtures are grouped as shown in Figure 104. For engineering applications, a laboratory analysis is done by specialists and results in a quantitative description. But it is possible to make a rough identification of engineering type in the field. This rough estimate is useful in site reconnaissance and may be all that one needs to know for the siting of light structures. For this purpose, soils are divided into ten classes, which have significantly different engineering implications:

Reference 26

1. *Clean gravels:* in which the dominant constituent is gravel, and less than about 5 to 10% is silt or clay. These gravels may be further subdivided as being "well graded" or "poorly graded" according to whether the particle sizes fill the whole range from fine to coarse, or do not.
2. *Silty and clayey gravels:* mostly gravel, but with more than 10 to 12% silt or clay.

FIGURE 104
A three-coordinate
graph showing the
respective per-
centages of sand,
silt, and clay that
define the conven-
tional agricultural
classes of soil
texture.

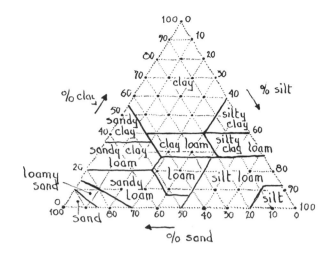

3. *Clean sands:* mostly sand and less than 5 to 10% silt or clay. These are also subdivided as well or poorly graded.

4. *Silty and clayey sands:* mostly sand, but with more than 10 to 12% silt or clay.

5. *Nonplastic silts:* inorganic silts or very fine sands, whose liquid limit is less than 50 (that is, which begin to flow like a liquid when containing less than 50% of water).

6. *Plastic silts:* inorganic silts with a liquid limit over 50.

7. *Organic silts:* silts with substantial organic matter and a liquid limit under 50.

8. *Nonplastic clays:* inorganic clays with a liquid limit under 50.

9. *Plastic and organic clays:* having a liquid limit over 50 and being either predominantly inorganic clay or a silt or clay with substantial organic matter.

10. *Peat and muck:* predominantly organic material, whether plant remains are visible (peat) or are invisible (muck).

Field
identification

These ten classes may be distinguished by the following field procedures:

Take a handful of soil, dry it, and spread it out on clean paper. If more than half the particles are visible to the naked eye, it is a sand or gravel. If this is difficult to determine even when the visible particles have been hand separated from the fine dust, then do the following: pulverize a dry sample, weigh it, cover it with 130 mm (5 in) of water in a transparent container, shake it thoroughly, let it settle for 30 seconds, and then pour off the water. Continue to do this until the water poured off is clean. The remaining residue is the sand and gravel, and its dry weight can be compared with the original dry weight of the sample.

In distinguishing a sand from a gravel, if more than half the coarse (visible) particles are over 6 mm (1/4 in), it is a gravel; if not, it is a sand. If less than 10% of the total soil sample is fine particles (invisible to the eye or poured off in the sedimentation test), then it is a clean sand or a clean gravel. If not, it is a silty or clayey sand or gravel. To distinguish a well-graded sand or gravel from a poorly graded one, simply look at the range of particle sizes to see if all sizes are represented, as opposed to there being significant gaps in the range of sizes.

We have now identified the soil if it belonged to one of the first four classes. But if it has proved not to be a sand or gravel, then two further tests are required. Both begin by picking out and discarding all the soil particles over about 0.5 mm (1/64 in) in size, that is, the coarser ones that would interfere with molding and working the soil, and by taking a sample that will make a pat of soil about 40 by 40 mm (1.5 by 1.5 in), and 15 mm (0.5 in) thick.

Dry-strength test: Wet the soil and mold it into a pat. Dry it thoroughly, take it between the thumbs and forefingers of both hands, and try to break it by pressure of the thumbs. If it cannot be broken or if it is broken only with great effort, snaps like a crisp cookie and cannot be powdered, then the soil is plastic clay. If it can be broken and powdered with some effort, it is an organic clay or a nonplastic clay. If it is broken and powdered easily or crumbles even as it is picked up, it is a plastic silt, an organic silt, or a nonplastic silt.

Thread test: Add just enough water to a pat of soil so that it can be molded without sticking to the hands. On a nonabsorptive surface (such as a piece of glass), roll it out into a thread about 3 mm (1/8 in) in diameter, then remold it into a ball. If it can be so remolded and the ball deformed again without cracking, it is a plastic clay. If it cannot be remolded into a ball, it is a plastic silt, or a plastic, organic silt or clay, or an organic silt. If it cannot even be rolled into a thread, it is a nonplastic silt. In the course of this test, the organic silts and clays, as well as peat and muck, will feel spongy to the fingers.

These two tests in part confirm each other and in part serve to separate each other's borderline cases—distinguishing a nonplastic from an organic clay, a plastic silt from an organic one, or a plastic from a nonplastic silt. The organic silts and clays not only feel spongy but tend to be darker in color. They have a musty odor if heated when wet. If one wants to distinguish a clayey sand or gravel from a silty one, the same thread test performed on the particles under 0.5 mm (1/64 in) will separate a clay from a silt, since clays can be remolded and silts cannot. Peat and muck are easily identifiable by their black or dark brown color, visible plant remains, very spongy feel, and immediate organic odor.

These four tests—the composition of visible particles by size, the dry strength, the behavior of a plastic thread, and the smell when heated—will distinguish the ten soil classes. In addition, there are other field indications, such as the spongy feel of organic soils and the soapy feel of plastic clay, which does not wash off easily and tends to stain. Between the teeth, sandy soils are hard and gritty. Silty ones are not gritty, but the grains can still be felt. Pulverized clay feels smooth and floury; a dry lump of it sticks when lightly touched by the tongue. The organic soils are dark, drab grays, browns, and blacks.

Engineering implications

Some of the implications of these soils for site planning are summarized in Figure 105. In general, gravel is a well-drained, stable material and bears heavy loads if it is well graded. Sand is also well drained and makes a good foundation if well graded, but it must be confined at the sides. Loose sands and gravels may settle initially under a load and therefore may need to be surcharged for a period before setting foundations on them. If they have appreciable fine material, they lose much of their good internal drainage. Fine sands or sand-silt mixtures may become "quick" when saturated and flow like a liquid.

Silt is stable when dry or damp, although it will compress under a load. It is treacherous and unstable when wet. Because it swells up and heaves badly when frozen, the foundations of roads and buildings must go deep enough to prevent this from happening or be strong or elastic enough to cope with it. The erosion of silt is likely to be severe. Loess, or wind-laid silt, is strong when dry and can maintain itself in a vertical face without slumping to a flatter angle.

Clay is stiff and cohesive when dry, and its reaction to frost is less extreme than that of silt. But it tends to be impervious and may slip, swell, or soften when wet. So it will often be a good bearing soil if it can be kept dry. Dull

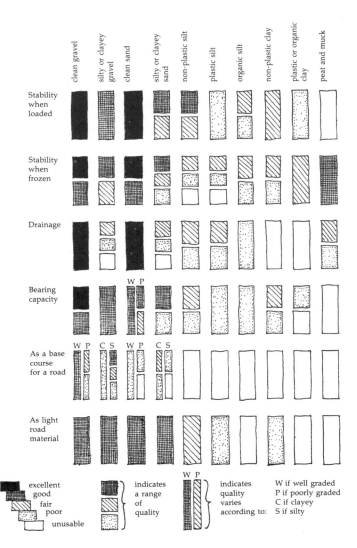

FIGURE 105
The engineering implications of soils: the variations between the ten basic engineering soil classes, in terms of such qualities as stability, bearing capacity, drainage, and their use in building roads.

gray-blue clays or mottled yellow or gray ones have very poor internal drainage. Thick layers of permeable soil, lying over an impervious clay layer on slopes over 10%, are liable to slip. Due to their expansion and slippage when wet, the plastic clays make special difficulties for foundations.

Peat and muck, and to some lesser extent the other organic soils, are very poor engineering materials, however good for growing things. They are elastic, weak, and have little cohesion. Normally they must simply be removed from the site unless the land will not be built on.

For foundations of light roads and buildings in undisturbed ground, the various sands and gravels are most likely to be suitable. Some of the nonplastic silts and clays are likely to be usable; the plastic and organic soils are suspect. Clays will swell, silts will heave with frost, and organic soils will compress under loads. Peat and muck are unusable. Bedrock can carry from 120 to 950 metric tons per sq m (10 to 80 tons per sq ft), as it varies from weathered formations to massive granites. Soils range downward from these capacities. Some presumptive values are given below, usable as first assumptions, prior to actual tests. Tests should be made for anything but the lightest of structures.

TABLE 6. PRESUMED BEARING CAPACITY OF SOILS

	metric tons/sq m *(U.S. tons/sq ft)*
Well graded, well compacted clayey sands and gravels	120 (10)
Gravels and gravelly sands, ranging from loose to well compacted	45–95 (4–8)
Coarse sands, from loose to well compacted	25–45 (2–4)
Fine, silty, or clayey sands, not well graded, from loose to well compacted	20–35 (1.5–3)
Homogeneous, nonplastic, inorganic clays, from soft to very stiff	5–45 (0.5–4)
Inorganic, nonplastic silts, from soft to very stiff	5–35 (0.5–3)

Foundations on fill are to be avoided, but if they are well compacted, the sands and gravels are acceptable, the others much less so.

The clean sands and gravels are very well drained and thus are usable for sewage drain fields. All other soil types must be checked for their absorptive capacity, but it is likely that other sands and gravels, as well as the inorganic silts, will be usable. The clays and the organic soils are not likely to be good for that purpose. Drain fields in fill should be avoided, but fills made of clean sands and gravels may serve.

The sands and gravels perform in varying degrees as a base course for permanent roads under a concrete or asphalt wearing surface. No other natural soil will do. To make a light road surface, the sands and gravels show marked hardening if stabilized by adding 3 to 5% of cement, by dry weight, in the upper 150 mm (6 in). The nonplastic silts can also be stabilized with 4 to 10% cement, and so can the plastic silts and nonplastic clays, but they will perform less well. Four to 10% of hydrated lime is the best additive for the clays and for the clayey sands and gravels.

Appendix *B*

Field Surveys

Making a simple map from a field survey is a useful skill. Surveying is the technique of transferring the locations of points, either from an abstract representation to the real environment (as in locating a planned highway or a lot line or a building on the ground), or, vice versa, from the real world to an abstraction (as in constructing a map). Both operations are based on the measurement of horizontal and vertical distances and angles. Such measurements are always in error, and much of the sophisticated craft of surveying is concerned with how much error is allowable and with controlling the survey's accuracy to lie within that allowable range. The choice of the points to be located and measured is a further judgment.

Reference 40

In making a reconnaissance map, however, we wish to create a useful representation of a real area, quickly, in the field, and with simple means. There are three strategies for doing this: to sketch the map by eye; to make a linear traverse, from which objects are located as offsets from the line; or to use a plane table. In each case, the horizontal, vertical and angular measurements can be accomplished by simple means, without the sophisticated instruments of professional surveying.

With some practice, horizontal distances of moderate scale can be estimated by eye with surprising accuracy if the intervening ground is fairly clear and yet not "empty" (as it is over a body of water, where the eye has few visual clues). The apparent sizes, at various distances, of certain

Lengths

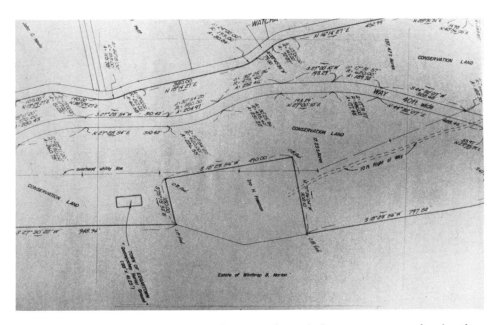

FIGURE 106 *A fragment of a typical property survey, showing the exact dimensions, directions, and locations of property lines, control points, and selected physical features.*

standard objects are memorized (the height of a man, or of a standard telephone pole, or the length of a football field, or of a host of common objects), and chains of these images are mentally overlaid on the ground before one. The ability to estimate distance is constantly useful and should be cultivated. Second, distance may be measured by pacing—often with an accuracy of 1:100 if an allowance is made for rough ground or slopes by a slight increase in the length of pace. The site planner should know the length of his normal stride by having counted, on several occasions, the number of strides he uses to cover a measured course.

Last, and of course most accurately, distance is measured with a 30 m (100 ft) steel tape. In using the tape, care must be taken to maintain its tension to prevent deep sagging and to make the measurements on the horizontal since slope distances are substantially longer. For that reason, on steep ground, the tape will have to be employed in short lengths, using a plumb bob to bring points on the ground up to the high end of the horizontal tape line.

The height of some vertical object can also be estimated by eye by piling up imaginary people or building stories, one above the other. But it is much more difficult to estimate the relative height of points in irregular terrain and almost impossible to do so over extended distances unless there are other clues such as the distant horizon or the level surface of a building floor or a body of water. It is easier to estimate heights when looking downhill, especially if the horizon is in sight, and a few tall references are visible. Then one can judge where the horizon would intersect the tall object and estimate the distance down from that intersection to the ground after subtracting one's eye height. But the best simple device for reading elevations with some accuracy is the pocket hand level, through which one sights on a distant object while also observing the reflected image of a bubble that indicates when the line of sight is level. Knowing one's eye height, one can identify points at the same elevation as that on which one stands. Or, if a graduated rod is held over some other point, one can determine its relative elevation, as long as the level line of sight does not soar over the rod or dig into the ground at its feet. Where this occurs, height is determined by going through a chain of intermediate points, no pair of which has a greater elevation difference than the height of the rod will allow. Without a rod and someone else to hold it, relative height can be measured by using an existing tall vertical reference on lower ground, as before, or by sighting from any lower beginning point forward to where the eye-level line intersects the ground; thence moving forward to that second point and repeating the operation until the final point is gained. The elevation difference is the multiple of one's eye height times the number of sightings, plus the final sighting as some fraction of eye height.

Angular measurement is almost impossible to measure by eye, although straight lines may be precisely extended simply by sighting over two low objects, such as stakes, or along the face of some vertical plane surface, such as a building wall. The location of various objects can then be approximated with reference to those extended lines. Moreover, a right angle may be laid out in the field, and its line extended by sighting, by remembering that in a right triangle the square of the hypotenuse is equal to the sum of the squares of the two opposite sides. The simplest case of this is the triangle whose three sides are in the proportion of 3:4:5. A

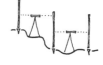

triangle of those proportions can be made out of wood as a sighting device, or one can be constructed with a measuring tape, looped around two pegs set on some line from which one wishes to erect the right angle.

For our purpose, however, the two best devices for angular measurement are the pocket compass or a piece of paper. The latter is the basis of the plane table technique, described below, but may also be used when sketching a map by eye. The sketch is simply held up close to the eye, and the directions to two different objects are drawn out freehand.

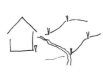

The pocket compass is constantly valuable in site reconnaissance since it not only records the orientation of objects to the cardinal directions (remembering to allow for magnetic declination) but can also be used for a quite accurate measurement of the angular difference between two lines of sight, by reference to the constant of magnetic north. A good pocket compass has a rotating sighting vane, a leveling bubble, and can be mounted on something stable, like a Jacob's staff (a 1.5 m or 5 ft stick). Indeed, a pocket compass, a hand level, a 30 m (100 foot) steel tape, a scale, pencil, and notebook or sketch pad, are all the essential equipment needed for making a good reconnaissance map.

Control points

In making any map, the strategy is to locate a few key points rather accurately and then to fill in adjoining detail. The key points are chosen because they are relatively distinct and easy to measure, are well distributed over the map area, and are the locations of important features or changes in the ground. They may be peaks or pits or breaks in the slope; they may be building or street corners; they may be changes in shorelines, riverlines, or the edge of a wood. Choosing these control points requires some thought and experience. They are mapped first, as accurately as time and equipment allow. When their relative locations seem correct, then the nearby detail can be drawn in, guided by those control points.

The traverse

In mapping by means of a *traverse*, or route of march, the important control points are chosen so that they can be occupied one after the other and so that all of the area to be mapped can be seen from one or another of these points. In particular, each successive point must be visible from the ones succeeding and following it. The string of points may be along a path that is a backbone of an area or along a boundary that encircles it. The directions between each point or "station" and the next are determined by forward compass sightings and confirmed by a "backsight" from each station to the preceding one. The difference in height of stations is read with the hand level, checking forward and backward, and making a connected chain of sightings if the rise or fall is too great. The distances between stations are paced off carefully—perhaps twice to make sure. Better, they are taped. If the traverse can be "closed" (brought around to its starting point), there is an opportunity to check the whole work, by determining the accumulated error, and to correct, or at least to distribute, that error.

While the traverse is being made, the local detail visible from each station is recorded by sketch or by direction and distance from the station point. Direction and distance may be estimated, or paced off and read with the compass. In addition, while measuring the distance from one station to another, further detail near the traverse route will be located by the point along the traverse line to which it is perpendicularly opposite, plus how far it is estimated to be from that line. The relative elevations of these details may be read with the hand level, or perhaps only the general shape of the land will be sketched in, supplemented by the elevations of a very few key points, such as ridgelines and rivers. Thus fairly extensive and broken areas may be mapped, with simple means and reasonable accuracy, even if the whole cannot be seen from any one location. In wooded country, it will be necessary to clear the traverse line so that one can see from one station to the next. The choice of the traverse stations is clearly a critical judgment. So is the choice of the detail to be sketched in and the accuracy with which it is to be located.

Another more graphic mapping method allows one to see the map as it develops in the field. It is most useful where one is interested in the detailed character of a piece of ground. This second method makes use of a *plane table* which is no more than a drawing board set up at some commanding location. Professional plane tables are set on tripods and can be independently leveled and swiveled about their centers. But any board will do, and it can be put on any firm support—even a kitchen stool—as long as it is made level, and, once set, will not be dislodged. Once made level and fixed in position, the station point is marked in the center of a sheet of paper fastened on the board, and a slender pin is pushed in at that point. A straightedge along which one can sight—properly a sighting alidade, but a ruler or any other straight piece of wood or metal will do—is then

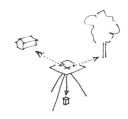

The plane table

laid against the pin and sighted on some feature of the site. A radial line from the pin toward the feature is lightly drawn on the paper, using the edge of the sighting stick as a guide. Meanwhile, the distance from station to feature has been measured by an assistant, by pacing or by tape. That distance can then be set off on the radial line drawn on the sheet, to the chosen scale of the map. If desired, the difference in height between feature and station can also be measured and noted on the map.

Thus one goes from feature to feature, the surveyor at the plane table recording the several directions, scaling off distances as reported, and using the hand level to determine relative elevations, while one or more assistants pace or tape the distances to the various features, hold up the leveling rods to be read by the mapper at the table, and report or record minor details not easily seen from the station. While locating each major feature by distance and direction, the mapper can also sketch in supplemental detail by eye. Thus the map grows before his eyes. He is immediately aware of gaps in his information or of gross errors.

He must be careful, however, not to disturb his board, which should be securely fastened to its support. The board must also be close to level (use the hand level as if it were a carpenter's level). The station point should command an extensive sweep of ground and preferably be higher than most of the other features to allow easy use of the hand level. However, if the features to be mapped are too far below the station, then it may be impossible to sight to them along the alidade which sits on the board, unless its ends have vertical extensions. The map is exposed, and so the work cannot be done in rain or snow. Therefore the method is useful in clear weather, when the ground is not too rugged, and when the entire site can be seen from one, or at the most a very few, stations. In the latter case, the successive viewing stations are graphically tied together by careful forward and back sights, just as in making a traverse.

Contours

In both mapping methods, the most difficult task is to indicate the contours of the ground, particularly if they are complicated. In professional surveying there are systematic and sophisticated techniques for doing this: by automated drafting based on aerial photographic stereo pairs or by careful leveling over a fine grid of ground points if great accuracy is necessary. In our case, the simplest method is to identify those key points where the slope of the ground changes in some marked way: the peaks, ridgelines, river edges, retaining walls, breaks of slope, and so on. When their several elevations have been recorded, then ticks representing the even levels chosen for the contours are located and numbered along the line between each nearby pair of points, as if the slope were uniform between those points. The contour ticks of equal elevation are now successively connected, in flowing shapes that visually correspond to the shape of the ground. Errors of shape soon become visible and are corrected by redrafting, checking the elevations of the control points involved, or by taking intermediate elevations. This immediate visual check is one of the advantages of the plane table method. In any case, plausible contour drafting requires practice. Often enough, a reconnaissance map will only record certain key elevations, while using "form lines"(unquantified contours) to indicate the general shape of the ground in the areas where that is important to show.

Rough field surveys of this kind may or may not be required of a site planner, depending on the quality of the base maps that are available. But personal site reconnaissance, and the freehand map sketching that usually accompanies it, will always be important. The freehand map uses the same strategies of measurement, control, and choice as does the plane table map or the measured traverse, even if its level of accuracy is much lower. Practice in field survey techniques is a foundation of the ability to make a good freehand map. It also allows the planner to understand maps and surveys in general: where they are true, and where they are false, and especially to what extent these apparently exact descriptions are yet necessarily *judgments*: arbitrary choices about errors to accept and things to be recorded, selected out of the buzzing confusion of the world.

Appendix C

Reading Aerial Photographs

Many designers are not accustomed to using aerial photographs for site analysis. The photos cover fragments of the site; they are hard to orient and match; they contain confusing, irrelevant detail; they have an unknown scale. They cannot easily be drawn on or traced over. The designer will prefer the clear, stable map, with its exact locations, fixed scale, and well-selected detail. Unaware of the compromises and judgments that map-making entails, he prefers these seeming certainties to the ambiguities of a representation that is a more direct reflection of reality. He does not

Reference 6

realize how rich a source the vertical aerial photograph is, and that with practice it can be read both as a general pattern, like a map, or for fine and up-to-date data, as a map can never be.

Vertical aerials are usually taken from an airplane flying at a constant elevation above the earth, as successive exposures along a series of straight, parallel lines of flight that cover the area to be mapped. The scale of the photographs, and thus the area covered by each shot, is determined by the height of the plane and the focal length of the camera. As nearly as possible, the camera points straight downward, and successive exposures are timed so that there is a substantial overlap between each picture—normally 60%. The parallel flight lines are sufficiently close to each other that the string of photos of one flight overlaps those of the adjacent flight by perhaps 50%. Thus each ground location is recorded in at least four different exposures, a redundancy that is essential to the control and interpretation of the images.

These photographs look as if they were pieces of a map, but they are not. They are *perspective* views, taken from a distant viewpoint, and therein lies their power and their difficulty. Scale is not uniform throughout the photo (since things are small or large as they are far or near from the lens), and directions and shapes are distorted, especially in hilly terrain. Adjacent photographs will not match each other along their edges. The only certainty is that all objects have been displaced relative to their true location on a map of uniform scale, precisely along that radial line which connects their photographic image with the point directly underneath the camera lens, or *nadir*. Points higher than the nadir are displaced away from it, and those lower are displaced toward it. Thus tall trees or buildings appear to lean away from the center of the picture. This regularity of the radial displacement is the key to the conversion of aerials into accurate maps.

For our purposes, assuming that the planner already has an adequate base map, the great value of these images lies in their display of detailed information, and second, in the ability they confer to read ground form and elevation. As a first step, the photo interpreter learns to lay out the overlapping photographs as they were taken in the flight pattern, matching them roughly, so that he can see his site as a whole and can locate the photo or photos that best record some part he is interested in. The flight and series numbers on the margin indicate sequence and adjacency. Individual photographs can be matched by "fanning" (quickly covering and exposing one photo with another that overlays it until the eye sees no jump in the corresponding detail).

Compiling photos

The complex variations of tone of the photographic image are the result of the degree to which the objects on the ground have reflected the incident light back into the camera lens. Gross features—such as buildings, roads, rivers, and woods—are easily identified, but far more can be seen with practice, including soil type, the nature of plant cover, building type and repair, minor paths, traces of occasional activity, traffic flow (vehicular or pedestrian), drainage, erosion or flooding, lot boundaries, small objects, and even some

FIGURE 107 *A vertical aerial photograph of a portion of Lexington, Massachusetts, illustrating the varied features that may be read from such a record. At top left is the date when the photo was taken; at top center and right are the numbers that identify the flight, the row, and the particular photo itself. The black half-arrows on the margins indicate the nadir, the point exactly in the center of view of the airborne camera at that moment. To find it, connect the bases of the concave arrow points, from side to side. The nadir lies at the intersection of those two lines.*

An industrial area lies on the left, a shopping center at the lower edge, single-family residences on the right, and a marsh and its meandering stream in the center. Roads and building shapes are obvious, but there is much more to see: bare-branched deciduous trees and dark evergreens (it is early spring), the old drainage and field lines of an agricultural past, swimming pools, used and unused paths, parked cars, buildings of various kinds, conditions, and stages of construction, the nested heaps of dumped fill, even the pattern of predominant turning movements in the intersection at lower left, made obvious by the tire marks on the pavement. Litter, vegetative cover, and ground disturbance are all visible. Since it is midday by the shadows, and the roads and parking lots are empty, this must be a Sunday or a holiday. The narrow line extending into the marsh is puzzling, until one sees the long shadows of three transmission towers. The detailed information that can be read from pattern, texture, tone, shape, size, shadows, and contexts is almost inexhaustible.

underground or underwater features, such as lake bottoms or the traces of ancient occupation. Detail is limited only by the quality of the incident light and the sensitivity and grain of the film. An aerial photo is an almost bottomless well of information, into which one dips as deeply as time and interest indicate. Photographs taken on different dates have the further advantage of recording changes.

Skill in interpretation and identification comes with practice, in which the site designer should have frequently indulged. Several good texts expound how identifications are made, with numerous examples. Clues for identification include shapes, patterns, textures, tones, shadows, and context. Having used such photographs frequently and having repeatedly compared the photographic image with the reality on the ground, the planner becomes skilled in reading them. Always use glossy, direct contact prints, since they will reveal even more detail under a magnifying lens. Photographic enlargements on cheap matte paper, on the other hand, may be useful as rough base maps on which field annotations or possible designs can be drawn.

Interpreting photos

Reference 93

The scale of the photograph is not uniform. But the average, approximate scale is the proportion of the focal length of the camera to the height of the camera above the ground, both of which are usually given (but must of course be expressed in the same units). Thus a series flown at 1500 m (6000 ft) and taken with a 150 mm (6 in) focal length camera will have an average scale of 1:12,000 (or 1 in equals 1000 ft). This average scale is sufficient for approximations. The scale is more accurate near the center of the photograph and along lines crossing near the nadir, since radial displacement is more marked at the edges. If focal length or flight elevation is not known, then the scale can be estimated by comparing the size of any particular image with its dimensions measured on the ground or from a map, or even as known from experience (the length of a truck or the standard distance between telephone poles). Once more, choose a length or an object close to or passing through the nadir.

Scale

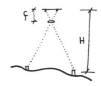

The individual photographs can be mounted together to form a composite *mosaic*, covering a large area of ground. Each photograph is overlapped on its predecessor in the flight line, and its overlapping edge is cut away to reveal the central area of the photo underneath. Where possible, the cut is made along some linear feature such as a road or lot line to make the lack of edge matching less obvious. As each photo is placed and glued to the previous one and as

Mosaics

each adjacent flight line is similarly matched to its neighbor, an extended composite is constructed, consisting of the central areas of the successive photos. Remember, however, that the whole mosaic becomes more and more distorted as it grows and is far from an accurate general map. Moreover, the set of prints has in the process been made unusable for stereovision, to be described below. Uncontrolled mosaics of this kind are often reproduced commercially. Look on them with suspicion.

It is possible by taking advantage of the fact of precise radial displacement to convert a string of overlapping photos into a controlled map of uniform scale if one knows at least one accurately measured length on the ground. Most map-making today is done from such photos, using sophisticated photogrammetric methods and automated equipment. One technique, the so-called radial method, can be accomplished with no more than tracing paper and ordinary drafting instruments. It is useful to know for those special cases where one has neither a good base map nor the photogrammetric support to make one. But the description is lengthy, and we will assume that the production of a controlled map of this kind is rarely required of a site planner.

Stereovision

Beyond the ability to collate aerial photos and to interpret their detailed features, the major data source for the site planner springs from the nature of stereovision. The human brain uses the two different images presented by the eyes for depth perception. Because of the position of the eyes in the face, each sees objects from two different sides. This variation of the image is mentally interpreted, very vividly, as variations in depth. Objects assume a solid form, and one thing appears to lie behind another. Since any two adjacent, overlapping, aerial photographs also see the world from two different viewpoints, this effect of stereovision can be simulated on a grand scale. By looking at one photo with the left eye and the adjacent one with the right, the two eyes are seemingly located at the two different camera stations. The result is what appears to be a marvelously detailed three-dimensional model of the ground below, in which height and ground form can be seen directly. This effect can be achieved by anyone who has reasonable vision in both eyes, and can, with practice, be achieved with the naked eyes alone. It is more convenient, however, to use a simple instrument called a pocket stereoscope: a small, inexpensive device consisting of two magnifying lenses, set in a folding frame, whose distance apart can be adjusted to fit the distance between the observer's two eyes.

The procedure is as follows: choose two overlapping photographs whose overlap covers the area to be studied. They should have been taken at the same time and elevation, but need not have been the two successive shots of a single flight line. Locate on each photo its nadir, which is at the crossing of the two lines indicated by the tick marks on the margin of the photo. Locate the nadir of each photo on its neighboring image, and, by "fanning," lay one photo over the other so that these two pairs of nadirs correspond. Now draw the photographs apart, along the line between their nadirs, so that the photo centers are about as far apart as your two eyes (about 6 cm. or 2.5 in). Tape one photo to the table, and fix the other temporarily with a weight. Illuminate both photos well, and see that the light falls on them in the same direction as do the shadows in the photographs. If the light cannot be moved, rotate the photos to achieve this.

Next, unfold the stereoviewer and move the lens separation to match your eye separation. Place the viewer over the two photos, parallel to the line between the nadir points, with each lens approximately over the center of the photo below it. Looking down through the viewer, one first sees an ambiguous and shifting double image because the eyes and brain are attempting to bring the two photographs into some stable, unified pattern. Focus your attention on one definite and easily recognizable detail, such as a building or a street corner, and, by slightly shifting and turning the photograph that is not fixed in place, bring that detail into correspondence with its double. Immediately the whole scene below will fall into focus, like a tiny relief model of exaggerated vertical dimensions. Ground slope and the height of structures become directly visible, details not previously apparent are now seen because they stand up from their background, and, to some extent, one can even see underneath things like trees, since the two views peep down, now on one side and now on the other, of the overhanging branches.

What is seen in this viewer is a relatively small area of the photo. The ground within the area of overlap of the two photographs (but not beyond it) can be searched by shifting the viewer and by occasionally making small adjustments in the orientation and separation of the unfixed photograph when the fused image seems to blur or tremble. Where the area of overlap is covered by the edge of the photograph on top, that edge can simply be bent upward out of the line

Sight lines

Measuring
heights

of sight, if care is taken not to crack the emulsion or to disturb the position of the unfixed photograph. A somewhat bulkier instrument, called a mirror stereoscope, allows the two photos to be fixed on the board at some distance from each other, so that any physical overlap is avoided. This makes it easier to scan the form of large areas. But the pocket instrument is better for detailed study, as well as being inexpensive and easy to carry. The whole technique is quickly learned and of constant use.

This stereo effect, which is directly related to the perspective nature of the aerial photograph and the radial displacement of its images, is the basis for the various photogrammetric techniques for producing contour maps with specialized equipment. This need not concern us here, except to know that it is possible to produce detailed contour maps by such means, at two- or even one-foot intervals, in relatively rapid time, and with only a few control measurements on the actual site.

There are two further manipulations of aerial stereopairs that may be useful to the designer. One is the determination of individual height differences and the other the investigation of sight lines. In the latter case, the planner may wish to know whether it is possible to see one location from another. To do this, pinpoint each location *exactly* on each of two overlapping stereopairs. On each photo, draw a fine white line between the two different points. Now observe the pair of photos under the viewer, as described for stereovision. In addition to seeing the ground in three-dimensional miniature, the observer will now see a floating white line, which seems to connect the two points in space. If the line soars above all obstacles instead of plunging through the ground or a barrier, then each point can be seen from the other.

The exact height of a building, or the elevation of a hill above a river below, or any other height differential between two points in the same overlap area can also be read in the office with simple means, although a very careful measurement is required. Choose two photographs showing both points, and mark the two locations *precisely* on each photograph by a fine pin prick. Locate and mark the nadir on each photo, as well as the nadir of the adjacent photo. Fix one photo down on the board and extend the line between its nadir and the photographic image of its neighbor's nadir. Fix the second photo down—at any convenient distance from the first that can be spanned by the measuring scales to be used—so that the line between its two nadir images falls exactly on the extended line of nadirs on the first photo. Measure as exactly as possible, using a finely graduated scale under a magnifying lens, the distance between the nadir images on each photo. The average of these two measurements is the "base distance" of the calculation and corresponds to the distance the airplane flew between the two exposures. Now measure—again as finely as possible—the distance between the images (one on one photo, one on the other) of one of the ground points whose difference of elevation is wanted. Next measure the distance between the two images of the other point. Unless these two points were at the same elevation, these two measured distances will differ, and that difference is called the "parallactic displacement." That displacement will remain the same regardless of how far apart the two photographs are placed on the board, and it is an exact function of the difference in height between the two real objects on the ground.

The difference in elevation can now be computed from the equation:

$$\frac{H - h}{H} = \frac{b}{b + p},$$

where h is the height difference that is wanted; H is the height of the airplane over the *lower* of the two points, in the same units as h; b is the base distance, and p the parallactic displacement. Both b and p are measured from the photographs, using the same units, but these need not be the units of h and H.

The method is simple to use and often accurate enough for site planning purposes. It is very convenient to have an office method for checking the height of a building or a hill or of the elevation of some terrain point that controls the local contours. However, the method depends on knowing the height of the airplane above the ground and on being able to identify exactly, on both photographs, the nadir points and the two locations whose height difference is to be read. At times, this is not possible. Accuracy depends on the accuracy of the measurement of the parallactic displacement, which is usually small. The error in calculating the height difference is to the height of the airplane, as the error in measuring the parallactic displacement is to the base distance. Thus, if the base distance were 150 mm (4 in) and the plane were flying at 600 m (2000 ft), and if the two measures that gave the parallactic displacement could be read to the nearest

0.25 mm (0.01 in) under a magnifying lens, then the height difference could be known to the nearest m (6 ft), since:

$$\left[\frac{0.25 \text{ mm}}{150 \text{ mm}} = \frac{1 \text{ m}}{600 \text{ m}}\right].$$

To summarize, the site designer should be addicted to using aerial stereopairs in any site analysis. As a minimum, he should be familiar with their nature; know how to obtain them collate and orient them; be able to interpret features on them and to compute their approximate scale; and finally know how to view them in stereovision, including the calculation of an occasional height or line of sight. Many other operations are possible with these images, including some that do not require sophisticated equipment, but they are usually beyond the call of ordinary site planning practice.

Remote sensing

We have focused on the use of the commonly available, black and white, vertical aerial photograph, taken on panchromatic film, which records reflected visible light plus some of the invisible ultraviolet and infrared. Color film may also be used but is less sensitive. Special infrared film, on the other hand, is quite useful, particularly for distinguishing vegetation types, detecting plant disease, or reading surface temperatures or heat emissions. Infrared images look strikingly different than the familiar panchromatic ones.

Other remote sensing systems are quite different from normal photography. The *line scanners* read the electromagnetic waves, at any chosen frequency, reflected from small units of ground area, which are rapidly scanned along a line perpendicular to the forward motion of the ongoing aircraft or satellite—much like the scanning of a television image. These readings are recorded on magnetic tape and can either be analyzed in a computer or be reconstituted into printed images. Contrasts between these digitized readings can be heightened and visual "noise" suppressed so that relevant information is made even more sharply visible. The frequencies read are chosen so that in combination they sharpen such features as vegetation character, water pollution, land use, and so on. The Landsat satellite, for example, reads four frequencies—two in the visible spectrum and two in the infrared. When these are combined, with a false color assigned to each, they make astonishingly beautiful images, which can be read with remarkable precision over extensive areas. They cannot be used stereoscopically, however, since they are continuous scans rather than successive, instantaneous views.

Side-looking radar is still another technique of remote sensing. It does not depend on reflected sunlight or on the emission of heat but sends out its own emissions and records their echo from the ground. The frequencies used are ones not normally emitted by earth features or interrupted by atmospheric conditions. Thus radar sensing can be conducted at night or through dense cloud cover. The direction, timing, and intensity of the ground echoes are read as the location and surface condition of the various features. The view is sideward—a high oblique—and so large areas can be covered from remote viewpoints. Resolution is relatively low, and objects can be hidden by intervening features. Thus these radar scans are more useful for the analysis of large or cloud-covered regions (or enemy territories at a distance) than for most site planning purposes.

Appendix **D**

Regional Climate

References 39, 48,
52, 60, 70

Any climate is complex and usually variable. The distribution of air temperature, relative humidity, and wind direction and force determine the effective temperature and its relation to the comfort zone. Precipitation indicates the need for shelter and drainage. The sun path and the hours of sunshine dictate the measures that must be taken to invite or ward off solar radiation. Other than the sun path, which is fixed for any latitude, these factors vary irregularly from place to place. Averages are useless. It is the *range* of conditions that counts, and especially the varying relations between these factors, through the seasons.

Figure 108 compares the key climatic information, in a condensed graphic form, for Boston, Massachusetts, and Phoenix, Arizona. For each month, the figure displays the distribution of temperature, the daily range of relative humidity, the precipitation, the hours of sunshine, and the typical patterns of wind direction and force. The differences are sharp and have important implications for site development. Lawns in Phoenix or massive masonry walls in Boston are equally absurd.

Boston

Boston is wet and windy: cold and damp in winter, hot and humid in summer, most pleasant in spring and fall. Its winds are lively and very variable, but unfortunately strongest in the cold months. Temperatures are usually below the comfort zone from October through May, but in those two transition months the effective temperatures are often high enough to be managed successfully by clothing and manipulation of the microclimate. In designing, one thinks first of the winter: orienting buildings and spaces to the low sun, avoiding frost pockets, sunless slopes and cold air floods, and using compact, tight, insulated, and steep-roofed structures. In midsummer, which can also be uncomfortable, one arranges for cross ventilation, invites the southwest breeze, avoids exposure to the hot afternoon sun in the west, shades a south wall with an overhang, and plants tall deciduous trees, which are open underneath, so that air passes beneath them and they cast shade only in summer. Rain and clouds are evenly distributed throughout the year. Winter days can be gloomy, and summer may see an occasional dry spell. Plants thrive but will need water at some critical moment late in summer. Mud, wet snow, and dampness are all to be reckoned with; and thus drainage, paving and ventilation are important. Wet and frozen ground means deep utilities and the attentive design of outdoor surfaces. Porches, arcades, and other outdoor shelters are useful if they do not darken building interiors. Orientation to the shifting sun is crucial, and sun traps extend outdoor activity in the spring and fall. It is a dynamic, stimulating environment, and a demanding one.

Phoenix is quite a different story. The climate is hot-arid, and one designs for the harsh summer. Temperatures are uncomfortably high for almost half the year, although they usually fall at night. Solar radiation is intense, and the sun shines during 85% of the daylight hours (rather than just over 50% in Boston). This is pleasant if one is in the shade and shielded from the glare. The abundant radiation can power solar energy devices, but in the summer months people and building interiors must be protected from it. This calls for permanent shading structures, thick insulated walls, ventilated double roofs, high ceilings, small windows, deep reveals, and vertical and horizontal louvers to shade the walls and openings. Sun pockets, where rays are reradiated from opposing surfaces—as in a narrow natural valley or a dense canyon of buildings—can be intolerable. Buildings may be sealed off during the day. Many structures use artificial air conditioning, but that wastes water and energy, discourages outdoor activity, and creates a jarring transition from inside to outside. Light-colored, reflective surfaces decrease the internal heat load but increase the external heat and glare. Large areas of unshaded pavement can be very unpleasant.

Phoenix

403

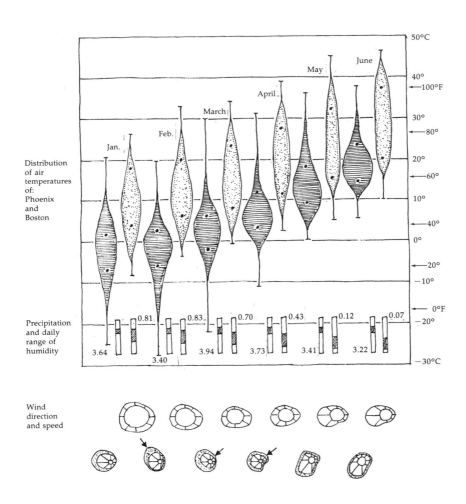

FIGURE 108 *A comparison of the average monthly climates of Boston, Mass., and Phoenix, Arizona, in regard to air temperatures, humidity, precipitation, winds, and sunlight.*

50°C

40°
←100°F

June

May
30°
←80°

April

March

20°
←60°

Jan.
Feb.

Distribution
of air
temperatures
of:
Phoenix
and
Boston

10°

←40°

0°

←20°
−10°

← 0°F
−20°

Precipitation
and daily
range of
humidity

0.81   0.83   0.70   0.43   0.12   0.07

3.64   3.94   3.73   3.41   3.22

3.40

−30°C

Wind
direction
and speed

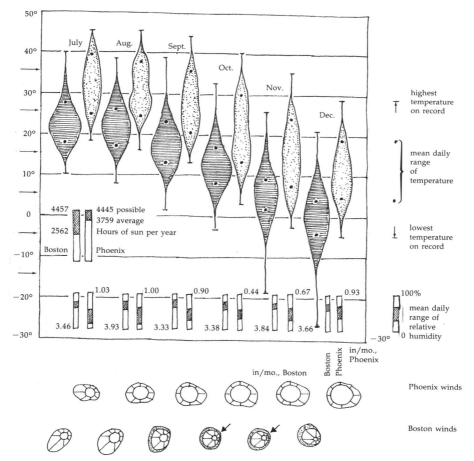

Distribution of winds: the length along any bearing; or
the diameter of the central circle, is proportionate to the
percent of time that the wind is of that direction and
speed.
Central circle: winds under 4 miles per hour.
Inner band: winds 4–16 miles per hour.
Outer shaded band: winds 16–32 miles per hour.
Arrow: winds over 32 miles per hour more than 0.5% of
time.

Nevertheless, there is a marked fall of temperature at night. The average daily range is about 19°C (34°F), as compared with Boston's 6°C (11°F). Outdoor evenings are attractive, even in summer, and massive wall materials and a diurnal opening and closing of openings can carry the night's coolness into the day's heat. A few feet below ground, the temperature is an even 21°C (70°F), summer and winter alike, so that dwellings set into the earth should be considered.

Winter, on the other hand, is very pleasant: sunny and calm, ideal outdoors. Enclosed courts catch the sun and shut out the cool winds. The winds are rather predictable: never violent as in Boston, but blowing from east or west with great regularity and only very moderate force, broken by substantial periods of calm. Unfortunately, this east-west pattern conflicts with the summer need to seal off the western wall. In the hottest periods, moreover, the hot dry wind may be something to avoid.

Irregularly, there are summer cloudbursts in scattered locations, but many months are almost rainless. Surface drainage can be primitive, which becomes quite apparent when a heavy storm does strike. The dry air tempers the heat, and evaporative cooling can be used. Fountains are a pleasant adjunct to any space. On the other hand, extensive irrigated agriculture around the city has modified its climate, moving it toward a less pleasant hot-humid condition, just as air pollution from the car has dulled its abundant sunshine. Water is precious here and must be conserved as well as celebrated. Extensive lawns and groves of trees are out of place, wasteful of water, and demand constant attention. Native desert plants are the appropriate landscape, although small, concentrated applications of water can produce a lush oasis.

These descriptions are familiar stories to Bostonians and Phoenicians. They call forth very different site planning responses, and the capable planner always consults these data when working in a new area. One can only be astonished at how frequently such elementary information is ignored.

Appendix *E*

Sun Angles

To make a sundial (whether for site analysis or just for the garden) or to analyze insolation by any other method, one must know how the sun angle varies with time. This variation is determined by latitude, season, and hour of the day. Tables of the direction and altitude of the sun, for some particular latitude, as it varies by hour and season, are often available. If they are not, sun angle may be calculated independently by means of the two following formulas, which are solved in sequence for each desired hour and season:

1) $\sin Al = \cos D \cos L \cos H + \sin D \sin L,$

and

2) $\sin Az = \dfrac{\cos D \sin H}{\cos Al}.$

In these two equations, we want to know: Al, or the altitude of the sun above the horizon, and Az, or the direction of the sun, measured as an azimuth angle east or west from the south (or from the north, if the site is in the southern hemisphere). We are given:

L, or the latitude of the place.

D, or the declination of the sun for the given date, above or below the celestial equator (which is the apparent sun path at the equinox, when day and night are of equal length). A northerly declination is positive (apparently above the equator) and a southerly one is negative (reversed in the southern hemisphere). While the declination for any date can be read from a solar ephemeris, all we need to know here is that D is zero at the equinox in fall and spring, + 23.5° at the summer solstice, and − 23.5° at the winter solstice.

and H, or the local hour angle of the sun, east or west of the noon meridian. Since 24 hours is a full circle, the sun traverses 15° in each hour. Thus H in our formula is zero at noon, 15° at 11 a.m. or 1 p.m., 30° at 10 a.m. or 2 p.m., and so on. This is local sun time, not standard time or daylight savings time. Standard time approximates local time but may differ by as much as 30 minutes, or more where the boundaries of time zones have been distorted.

In using these formulas, when negative angles occur (as in D in the winter) or angles over 90° (as H before 6 a.m. or after 6 p.m. in the summer), make use of the following identities:

$$\sin - 23.5° = -\sin 23.5°;$$
$$\cos -23.5° = +\cos 23.5°;$$
$$\sin 105 ° = + \cos 15°;$$
and $\cos 105 ° = -\sin 15°.$

Whenever the hour angle is over 90°, then the azimuth Az is also over 90°: the sun is north of east on a summer morning and north of west on a summer evening. Although an angle for Az that is less than 90° will always satisfy equation 2, so also will an angle over 90°, since $\sin a = \sin(180° - a)$. Therefore, in these late and early hours, before 6 a.m. and after 6 p.m., always use the larger angle—that is, subtract the angle gained from solving this second equation from 180° to get the true direction of the sun, measured from the south.

These formulas may be used for any place, time, and date. Thus one can make up one's own table for any given latitude, showing the altitude and azimuth of the sun for each hour of the day. Since the seasonal change is indicated by the change in the sun's declination D, and this changes with rough regularity, it is only necessary to calculate the sun angles for midwinter, midsummer, and the spring and fall equinox, and so indicate the range and midpoint of the sun positions. Other dates can be estimated between them. Since the movement of the sun is symmetrical during the day, sun angles need only be calculated for half the day in order to make a complete table. The sun's altitude is the same for the same hour angle, morning or afternoon, and the sun's azimuth will also have the same values, under-

TABLE 7. ALTITUDE AND AZIMUTH OF THE SUN, AT LATITUDE 42°N, TO NEAREST 0.5°

	Midsummer Solstice		Spring and Fall Equinox		Midwinter Solstice	
	Alt.	Azm.	Alt.	Azm.	Alt.	Azm.
noon	71.5°	0	48°	0	24.5°	0
11 a.m. or 1 p.m.	67.5°	38.5°	46°	22°	23°	15°
10 a.m. or 2 p.m.	59°	63°	40°	41°	19°	29°
9 a.m. or 3 p.m.	48.5°	78°	31.5°	56°	12.5°	41.5°
8 a.m. or 4 p.m.	37.5°	89.5°	22°	69°	4°	53°
7 a.m. or 5 p.m.	26.5°	99°	11°	80°	—	—
6 a.m. or 6 p.m.	15.5°	108°	0°	90°	—	—
5 a.m. or 7 p.m.	5°	117°	—	—	—	—

Note: the azimuth is east from south in the morning and west from south in the afternoon.

standing that it is east of south in the morning and south in the afternoon.

The construction of such a table (if not otherwise available) is well worth the effort for any site where insolation is crucial, and it will be of permanent value for designs at the same latitude. Table 7 is a sample, calculated for Lat. 42°N to the nearest 0.5 degree. These tables can be used for calculating overhangs, orienting buildings and solar collectors, locating shade-giving trees, and plotting sunlight and shadow in plan or section, at different hours and seasons. From them, one can also make a simple sundial for orienting a model for shadow-casting

The sundial is constructed as follows: On a card, locate a point 0 and draw a line NO, which will represent the north-south line. A vertical pin, of any convenient height P, will later be erected at 0. For any hour or season, the shadow of the top of the pin will fall along a line drawn from 0, whose angle from NO equals the azimuth of the sun from the south (since the direction of the shadow opposes that of its light source). The shadow line lies west of NO in the morning and east of it in the afternoon. Lay off a length x along this shadow line, outward from 0, such that:

Making a sundial

$$x = \frac{P}{tanAl},$$

where P is the height of the pin and Al is the altitude of the sun at that time. This is the same as $x = P \cdot tan(90° - Al)$ which is easier to use. The point so obtained is the tip of the pin's shadow, at that hour and season.

409

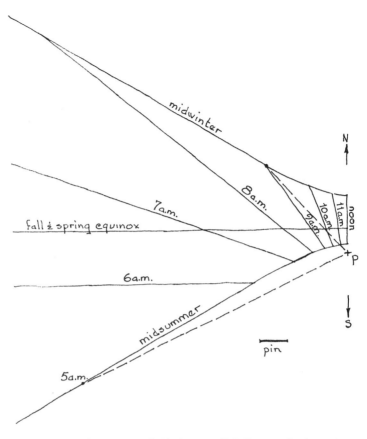

FIGURE 109 *The morning half of a sun dial diagram for latitude 42°N, constructed as described in the text from the altitude and azimuth tables for that latitude. The afternoon half is simply a symmetrical reflection of this, to the right of the north-pointing axis. When a pin of the length shown by the small bar is erected at point P, the diagram will serve as a sun dial if it is laid level and oriented to true north. Or, if it is attached to a model and pointed to model north, it can be used to orient that model to a light source so that the shadows on the model will simulate the shadows that would be cast in reality, at any chosen hour and season. The two dashed lines on the diagrams are examples that illustrate the length and direction of the pin's shadow, as it would be cast at 9 a.m. at the midwinter solstice (Dec. 21), or at 5 a.m. at the summer solstice (June 21). The diagram was constructed by laying out these successive shadows, and then connecting the paths of the shadow tips.*

This construction is repeated, to give a diagram of the form shown in Fig. 109, which has been drawn for the morning hours at 42°N Lat., using the angles given in Table 7 above. The season lines, which are the path of the shadow tip throughout the day at that season, and the hour lines, which are the location of the shadow tip at that hour during the various seasons, have been drawn by connecting the separate points for the particular hours and seasons. The hour lines turn out to be straight, and will converge on a common point below O. The seasonal line at the equinox is a straight line at right angles to the line NO, while the seasonal lines for the solstices are smooth parabolas. Due to these geometrical characteristics and to the symmetry of the whole, the entire diagram can be drawn if one knows only the sun angles for noon at the equinox, for 8 a.m. to noon at midwinter, and for 5 a.m. to noon at midsummer. This will require 14 separate calculations.

Having drawn the diagram, insert the vertical pin of proper height P at O. Place the dial flat on the model, with NO parallel to its north direction. Put the model in the sunlight and tilt it until the shadow of the pin's tip falls at the wanted intersection of hour and season lines. The sunlight is now falling on the model as it would do in reality at that hour, season, and latitude.

Appendix *F*

Noise

Noise is unwanted sound. While the power, pitch, and timing of sounds can be precisely described, their noisiness is a subjective quality. Thus the analysis and control of noise is marked by technical elegance and social confusion. Most work has been done on interior acoustics, yet the less easily controlled but increasingly pressing problem of outdoor noise is now receiving more attention. Environments with too little sound can be disturbing but are rare. Sound sources today are increasingly powerful and ubiquitous. The usual problem, then, is to find ways of reducing the sound level or its information content. The introduction or enhancement of desirable sound is usually neglected.

The loudness, or energy level, of a sound is measured in *decibels* (abbreviated dB). A decibel is a measure of the difference between the energy level of the pressure wave of which a sound consists and the energy level of some reference sound. To be exact, the decibel number is equal to ten times the logarithm to the base ten of the ratio between the sound in question and a reference sound. That reference sound is the one that is just barely audible to a good human ear, and so the decibel scale begins at 0 at the threshold of hearing and runs up to about 135 at the threshold of pain. Since it is logarithmic, each interval of 10 decibels indicates a level of sound energy ten times greater than before, an increase that the human ear distinguishes as being roughly twice as loud. So a noise that is 20 decibels louder than another one has 100 times the energy of the latter and may seem about

Reference 54

412

four times as loud. This logarithmic scale is made necessary by the amazing ability of the human ear to discriminate sounds that may vary in pressure by a ratio of as much as 10^{14}.

Some common sources and perceptions scale roughly as follows:

Decibels

- 0 threshold of hearing
- 10 rustle of leaves
- 20 inside a quiet country house; a soft whisper
- 30 inside a quiet city apartment
- 40 a quiet office
- 50 a noisy office; ambient noise of a normal kitchen; interference with sustained conversation
- 60 level of ordinary conversation; noise becomes intrusive
- 70 80 km/hr (50mph) auto at 15m (50 ft); difficult to talk on the telephone
- 80 busy city street; noise is clearly annoying
- 90 noisy kitchen; some possibility of hearing damage if there is long exposure
- 100 power mower; freight train close by; danger of hearing loss
- 110 pneumatic hammer; thunder close at hand
- 120 amplified rock music
- 130 jet airplane at 30m (100 ft)
- 135 threshold of pain

The individual perception of this scale is variable until we reach the levels of organic damage. Extremely loud sounds, or prolonged exposure at high levels, can cause deterioration of the auditory nerve and a loss of sensitivity to sounds in the 2000 to 8000 cycle range. This damage begins for most at continued exposures above 100dB but rarely occurs below 85 to 90dB. Below this, different ears have varying acuities for different frequencies, and, more important, culture, personality, and the task at hand will make the same noises agreeable or maddening. Some activities, such as sleep or quiet conversation, are very noise sensitive, others much less so. Culture, experience and expectations will shift the allowable limits. Sounds can be disagreeable as much because of their pitch, or their unexpected suddenness, or their contrast with background noise, or their information content (a distant scream, a malicious whisper, a subdued quarrel next door).

High-pitched noises and those that blanket the frequencies of human speech are more obnoxious. We can hear frequencies ranging from 20 to 20,000 cycles per second or 50 to 10,000 at low noise levels. Ordinary street noise ranges from 40 to 8000 cycles, while human speech is transmitted in the 100 to 3000 cycle range. Teaching is severely affected by excessive noise. In classrooms on one side of a public school in Manhattan, 70 m (230 ft) from the elevated and so receiving 89dB of noise, the reading levels of pupils lagged one year behind those of classmates on the other side of the school. Cushioning the rails reduced the noise to 81dB. The noise remained intrusive, but, within another year, reading levels reached those in the quieter classrooms. Our intensive use of energy imposes costs well beyond the dollars spent.

dBA, Ldn, and TA

It is difficult to predict the individual response to noise, but it is possible to say something about group response, that is, to set standards from experience as to what a typical community in a given culture will find tolerable. To make that prediction, however, the decibel scale must be modified in various ways, to approximate human perceptions more closely. First, noise levels in the middle frequencies, to which the human ear is more sensitive and which are more useful for communication, must be given greater weight. This produces the A-weighted scale (dBA), the one commonly used today. Second, since sound levels fluctuate continuously, there must be some way to measure the prevailing condition at any point. This is done by averaging the intensities over a 24-hour period, the so-called equivalent loudness, or Leq. More recently, this has been modified to give the day-night loudness, or Ldn, in which 10dB are arbitrarily added to all intensities occurring between 10 p.m. and 7 a.m., on the premise that noise is most likely to disrupt such activities as sleeping during these hours and most likely to stand out in contrast to normal levels (a cultural assumption, of course). In general, this measure has achieved the closest correlation with actual community reactions, and the standard maximums for noise in residential areas are expressed in Ldn.

Yet these average sound levels may seriously underestimate the disruption caused by noise, since irregular bursts of thunderous noise in an otherwise quiet region will produce low Ldn ratings, which are twenty-four hour averages. Near an airport, for example, where the problem is a series of brief but shattering noise events rather than continuous noise, average intensities may be close to meaningless. In this case, a better measure is "time above," which records the total number of minutes during which sound intensities rose above some particular level. 40 TA 65 would indicate a condition in which levels rose above 65dBA for a total elapsed time of 40 minutes in the 24 hours. While the TA measure is undoubtedly a better one in many situations, community standards have not yet been calibrated for it.

The U.S. Department of Housing and Urban Development has published a long list of typical activities, noting how they are normally affected at increasing levels of sound, by indicating at what point some interference arises, at what point the activity begins to be difficult to perform, and finally where it can no longer be performed "acceptably." In general, the lower bound for "some interference" ranges from Ldn 45 for such things as sleeping, conversation, teaching, theater, concerts, ceremonies, and technical work, to Ldn 65 for driving or working with equipment. Similarly, the "can no longer be performed" point ranges from Ldn 75 to 95 for those two classes of activities. Counting on some reduction of noise levels from outside to inside a normal building, HUD concludes that land subject to noise over Ldn 65 is unsuitable for residence unless special means of protection are used, and that land under Ldn 60 raises no problems for indoor activity and only moderate difficulties for outdoor use. The parallel Canadian agency (the Canadian Mortgage and Housing Corporation) sets stricter standards, even though they are expressed in Leq. They put 35 dBA as the maximum for the interior of sleeping rooms, 40 for other living areas, 45 for all other indoor spaces, and 55 for any outdoor residential use. Standard construction is then suitable for any land subject to no more than 55 dBA. Above this, special acoustical insulation of the house and exterior sound barriers can attentuate indoor and outdoor levels by as much as 20 dB more. Thus areas whose noise level is up to 75 dBA *may* be usable, if special precautions are taken, but no more. Swedish standards are much the same.

Existing noise levels are measured by meters that record the fluctuations in intensity as they vary over time. These meters can be moved about to sample the noise levels of an extended area, or fixed at locations for a period of time, giving either average intensities or the "time above" certain levels. If not continuous, a survey should record events both when noise is likely to be most severe (at the rush hour perhaps) and also most annoying (in the evening as people try to get to sleep). If desired, the actual timing of major

Noise standards

References 21, 79

Measuring noise

noise events can be recorded and can then be correlated with changes in traffic, movements of airplanes, and the like. Meter readings can also be compared with the impressions that people communicate in interviews or with the rate and fervor of complaints.

If no meters are at hand, a rough survey can be conducted without special equipment by two people of normal hearing and average voice. It is based on the fact that the point at which conversation just becomes impossible to understand is rather sharply defined. One person stands and reads something unfamiliar to both parties in a normal voice. The other gradually backs away and notes the distance at which he just no longer understands the gist of what is being read to him, that is, when he only catches a scattered word or two in a ten-second period. The trial is repeated, rotating reader and listener, and the distances averaged.

If the distance is over 20 m (65 ft), the noise level is less than 45 dBA and the site is good for housing and outdoor use. If it lies between 8 and 20 m (25 and 65 ft), the noise lies between 45 and 60 dBA, and so the location is acceptable for housing. Distances between 2 and 8 m (7 and 25 ft) indicate levels of 60 to 75 dBA, and the site can only be used for housing if the latter will have special insulation. Distances under 2 m (7 ft) mean levels over 75 dBA, and the location is simply unusable for residence.

Noise
propagation

The site planner, of course, is not primarily interested in measuring noise but in predicting and changing it. He wants to know what noise levels to expect when his project is in place. Then he usually wants to reduce it. The major generators of outdoor noise are our transportation vehicles, the principal consumers of outdoor energy: cars, trucks, trains, and airplanes. The ubiquitous source is the street, whose noise level varies directly with the quantity of flow, the proportion of trucks and other heavy vehicles, the speed limit, the steepness of the gradient, and the occasions for accelerating, decelerating, stopping and starting. Major intersections and steep grades used by trucks are particularly noisy. This noise is generated primarily at the contact between tires and the road surface and at the end of the exhaust pipe. There are complex tables available for estimating the noise levels that a road of given traffic will probably generate.

In free space, sound intensity decreases as the square of the distance from a point source, as the sound energy spreads out over the surface of an expanding sphere. Thus, each doubling of the distance means four times less energy, or a drop of about 6dB (since this is a logarithmic scale, and the log of four is approximately six). But for a linear source, such as a highway, which produces sound energy all along its length, the noise decreases only directly as the distance, meaning that each doubling of the distance causes a drop of only 3dB.

These attenuations are further affected by the ground surface, since if the sound is being transmitted close to the ground and that ground is acoustically reflective, then the otherwise regularly decreasing sound energy is continually replenished by the sound reflected from the nearby ground. Thus sound transmitted close to a predominantly hard (and therefore acoustically reflective) ground surface may decrease by only 3 dB for every doubling of distance, even from a point source. But if the ground is soft and planted with a thick mat of vegetation, it will absorb the incident energy, and propagation is like that in free space.

Thus it is unwise, in a noisy environment, to give a hard finish to walls or grounds or to arrange buildings in long rows or around closed courtyards since there the sound will reverberate between ground and walls. Acoustically non-reflective walls reduce noise levels, but it is difficult to make an artificial surface that is both weather proof and also sufficiently fine-textured to be an efficient sound absorber. On the ground, snow is effective to some degree (whence the apparent silence of a snow-bound landscape), and so is a fine-grained, relatively deep vegetative cover.

Noise levels within a normal building whose windows and doors are closed are typically 10 to 15 dB less than those just outside. Therefore summer noises are more critical than the sounds of winter, except in an air-conditioned nightmare. The special sealing of doors and windows, plus double and triple glazing and massive walls, may effect an additional drop of up to as much as 20 dB. This is expensive, and to be sealed off can be unpleasant for those inside. A wall at right angles to one facing a noise source may receive only one-half the sound energy received by the facing wall, or a decrease of 3 dB. A rear wall may receive as much as 15 dB less.

Sound waves are dispersed by air turbulence and carried off by the wind, so that distant sources seem to wax and wane as the breeze shifts, and areas upwind of noise generators are quieter. But that effect cannot be depended on. Undesirable noise can also be masked by the addition of desirable or random sound if the original noise is not too

Noise control

417

powerful. This tactic is more often used in indoor environments, but the sea, or a river, or even the steady hum of traffic can have that function outdoors. The waterfall in New York's Paley Park is a famous example of the deliberate and effective use of masking sound.

Most often, however, if the site planner cannot reduce the noise at its source (which is her most effective tactic), she will depend first on distance to reduce noise levels. So buildings and active outdoor areas are separated from each other, and from exterior noise sources. To prevent the transmission of speech, windows that open into different rooms are set no closer than 30 to 40 ft if face-to-face, or 6 to 10 ft on the same wall.

Noise barriers Distance failing, she erects a barrier to reduce the transmission of noise. Planted belts are of little use; they screen out only the high-pitched noise, and rather little of that. Three hundred m (1000 ft) of woodland, thick enough to limit visibility to 20 m (70 ft), will decrease noise in the 200 to 1000 cycle range by only 20 decibels more than would the open distance alone. To be effective, a barrier should be solid—without any holes or cracks—thick, and heavy, since it is the inertia of the obstacle that damps the sound. Its material should weigh at least 5 kg for each sq m (l lb per sq ft) of its surface, or even 10 kg per sq m (2 lb/sq ft) if one wants to achieve an attenuation of more than 10 dB. [Please note that this is a measure of the mass that lies behind each unit *area* of the wall's surface, and not the usual mass per unit volume. It can be achieved by increasing either or both density and thickness.] Furthermore, the barrier must interrupt the line of sight between source and receiver, since it is the extra distance that the sound must travel to surmount the obstacle that causes it to lose intensity. Thus a long, high, heavy wall or berm of earth, as close as possible either to the source or to the receiver, is most effective. If such a wall or berm is sufficiently dense and impervious and is very long (that is, it extends for more than ten times its distance from either the nearby source or the receiver, both to the left and to the right), then the additional attenuation it confers is approximately:

$$N = 5 + 4[10D]^{1/3}$$

where N is the additional attenuation in dB, due to the barrier, and D is the *additional* path length imposed on the traveling sound, in meters.

D is computed by drawing source, barrier, and receiver in section; giving source and receiver their proper height above the ground; then measuring or calculating both the straight line distance between the two and the shortest total path over the top of the barrier; and finally subtracting the straight line distance from that shortest indirect path.

$$D = a + b - c$$

In no case, however, can one expect to achieve an attenuation greater than 20 dB since refraction and reflection will defeat any further reduction unless the receiver is sealed off within a building. If the barrier does not extend both right and left more than ten times its distance to source or receiver, then the sound will pass around the end of the obstacle, and so the attenuation must be progressively reduced.

Appendix G

A Site and Impact Checklist

Early in a project it is useful to set down a list of site data that will be required in order to guide the collection of original and existing information. Such a list should be short at the beginning and lengthen as understanding of the site evolves. Too many data should not be gathered at first stages, not only to save energy for later investigations but also to avoid being drowned in partly irrelevant material.

Having said that, we present a list of data that is far too long for any project. At most, many of these topics would be handled sketchily. Use it as a checklist to decide what data need *not* be collected, as well as those that must.

It is customary to make an environmental impact study when project planning is complete, in the form of an indictment or a whitewash. We advocate that the impact study commence with the first gathering of site data. The impact analysis then develops as the design develops, and thus guides and is guided by it. In its final form, then, like the analysis of cost (which is what it is in a broader sense), it will contain no nasty surprises.

Like the site analysis, it should also be concise and pointed, covering the most critical subjects in depth, touching briefly on those whose impact is negligible. Its content largely overlaps the more general site analysis list since it is a schedule of information about those particular conditions which will have a primary effect on the neighbors of a project. In each subsection below, under the heading of "typical impact questions," we list the issues most likely to be crucial in environmental impact studies. Site and impact analysis should proceed together, and both should focus on essentials. Both contain negative and positive elements; neither determines a decision by themselves. Design, and then judgment, must be applied.

A. *General Site Context*
   (1) Geographic location, adjacent land use patterns, access system, nearby destinations and facilities, stability or change in development pattern.
   (2) Political jurisdictions, social structure of the locality, population change in surrounding areas.
   (3) Ecological and hydrographic system of the region.
   (4) Nature of the area economy, other proposals or projects nearby and their effects on the site.
Typical Impact Questions:
   Will important locations or resources become inaccessible to the general public?
   Will energy, water, food, or other scarce resources be depleted or degraded?
   Will the health or safety of the surrounding population be endangered?
   Will the project put an undue traffic load on its surroundings?
   Will surrounding political, social, or economic systems be disrupted?
   Will the project have a negative impact on existing businesses or institutions?
   Will its construction or maintenance lay undesirable financial burdens on the surrounding community?

B. *Physical Data, Site and Adjacent Land*
   (1) Geology and Soil:
      a. Underlying geology, rock character and depth, fault lines.
      b. Soil types and depth, value as an engineering material and as a plant medium, presence of hazardous chemicals or contaminants.
      c. Areas of fill or ledge, liability to slides or subsidence, capability for mining.
Typical Impact Questions:
   Are landslides, subsidence, or earthquakes likely to occur?
   Will the soil be contaminated?

Can the soil absorb likely wastes without damage?
Will the topsoil or its nutrient balance be lost?

(2) Water:

    a. Existing water bodies—variation and purity.

    b. Natural and man-made drainage channels—flow, capacity, purity.

    c. Surface drainage pattern—amount, directions, blockages, flood zones, undrained depressions, areas of continuing erosion.

    d. Water table—elevation and fluctuation, springs, flow directions, presence of deep aquifers.

    e. Water supply—location, quantity and quality.

Typical Impact Questions:

Will the purity, oxygen level, turbidity, or temperature of surface waters be affected?

Will siltation occur?

Can the drainage system accept the additional runoff?

Will lands be flooded, erosion be induced, or water bodies caused to fluctuate?

Will the water table rise or fall, affecting vegetation, basements, or foundations?

Will groundwater be contaminated, or the recharge or draw-down of aquifers be affected?

(3) Topography:

    a. Contours.

    b. Pattern of landforms—typology, slopes, circulation possibilities, access points, barriers, visibility.

    c. Unique features.

Typical Impact Question:

Will unique or valued landforms be damaged?

(4) Climate:

    a. Regional pattern of temperature, humidity, precipitation, sun angles, cloudiness, wind direction and speeds.

    b. Local microclimates: warm and cool slopes, wind deflection and local breeze, air drainage, shade, heat reflection and storage, plant indicators.

    c. Snowfall and snow drifting patterns.

    d. Ambient air quality, dust, smells, sound levels.

Typical Impact Questions:

Will the project cause general climatic changes, such as in regard to temperature, humidity, or wind speed?

Will local microclimates be affected adversely—by the deflection or funneling of wind, the shading or reflection of sunlight, the drying or humidifying of the air, the in-

*tensification of diurnal temperature ranges, or the drifting
of snow?*

*Will air pollution increase or dust or obnoxious odors be
generated?*

*Will the project increase or decrease disturbing noise
levels?*

Will the project cause any radiation or other toxic hazards?

(5) Ecology:

    a. Dominant plant and animal communities—their location and relative stability, self-regulation, and vulnerability.

    b. General pattern of plant cover, quality of wooded areas, wind firmness, regeneration potential.

    c. Specimen trees—their location, spread, species, elevation at base, whether unique or endangered, support system needed.

Typical Impact Questions:

Will important plant and animal communities be disrupted? Will it be difficult for them to relocate or to regenerate themselves?

*Will rare or endangered species be destroyed or pest species
increase?*

*Will the project cause eutrophication of water bodies or
algal blooms?*

*Will the plan remove significant agricultural uses or make
it difficult for them to be reestablished in the future?*

(6) Man-Made Structures

    a. Existing buildings: location, outline, floor elevations, type, condition, current use.

    b. Networks: roads, paths, rails, transit lines, sewers, water lines, gas, electricity, telephone, steam—their location, elevations, capacity, condition.

    c. Fences, walls, decks, other human modifications to the landscape.

Typical Impact Questions:

*Will present and planned roads and utilities serve the
site without adverse impacts on adjacent areas?*

Will the project require a substantial investment in surrounding roads and utilities?

*Can these new facilities be adequately maintained and
operated?*

Will new structures conflict with or damage existing ones?

(7) Sensory qualities:

    a. Character and relationship of visual spaces and sequences.

b. Viewpoints, vistas, focal points.

c. Quality and variation of light, sound, smell.

Typical Impact Questions:

Is the new landscape in character with the existing one?

Are existing views and focal points conserved and enhanced?

Are the new buildings compatible in character with the existing structures to be retained?

C. *Cultural Data, Site and Adjacent Land*

(1) Resident and using population:

a. Number, composition, pattern of change.

b. Social structure, ties, and institutions.

c. Economic status and role.

d. Organization, leadership, political participation.

Typical Impact Questions:

Will any of the existing population be relocated?

Will any segment of this population be disadvantaged?

Will present disadvantaged groups be aided?

How will existing jobs and businesses be affected?

Will the plan modify current lifestyles or cultural practices in undesirable ways?

Will existing institutions or social ties be disrupted?

(2) Behavior settings: nature, location, participants, rhythm, stability, conflicts.

Typical Impact Questions:

Will the plan destroy important patterns of use without replacing them?

Will new uses conflict with old ones or endanger safety?

Is future change and expansion provided for?

(3) Site values, rights, restraints:

a. Ownerships, easements and other rights.

b. Zoning and other regulations that influence site use and character.

c. Economic value and how it varies across the site.

d. Accepted "territories."

e. Political jurisdictions.

Typical Impact Questions:

Will the economic values of the site or its surroundings be depreciated or enhanced?

Will ownerships or customary "territories" be significantly disrupted?

(4) Past and future:

a. History of the site and its visible traces.

b. Public and private intentions for future use of site, conflicts.

Typical Impact Questions:

Are historic structures conserved?

Are archaeological sites and information conserved and developed?

Does the plan disrupt or facilitate current change?

Does it conflict with any existing plans for the future?

(5) Site character and images:

    a. Group and individual identification with aspects of the site.

    b. How the site is organized in people's minds.

    c. Meanings attached to the site, symbolic associations.

    d. Hopes, fears, wishes, preferences.

Typical Impact Questions:

Does the plan destroy or enhance group and individual identification with the site?

Does it disrupt or reinforce existing ways of mentally organizing the site?

Does it take account of the popular meanings and values of the site?

Is it in accord with the hopes, fears, and preferences of the users?

D. *Correlation of Data*

(1) Subdivisions of the site: areas of consistent structure, character, problems.

(2) Identification of key points, axes, areas best left undeveloped, areas where intensive development is possible.

(3) Ongoing changes, and those likely to occur without intervention—the dynamic aspect of the site.

(4) Ties to context—current and possible linkages, areas where consistent uses are desirable, patterns of movement to be preserved.

(5) Summary of significant problems and potentials, including a summary of the key positive and negative impacts of the proposal.

Appendix H

Costing

Through the course of a project, cost estimates will be required at varying levels of precision depending on the firmness of site plans. Detailed estimates are themselves costly to prepare and may not be needed for the decision at hand. Most site development projects require a sequence of cost estimates, progressively more detailed and dependable.

In deciding how much to pay for a site for residential development, for example, it may be sufficient to lump all costs together—"improvements will cost $8500 per residential lot, with five lots per acre"—based on averages from other recent projects. This is enough for back-of-the-envelope calculations. It runs the risk, of course, of being seriously inaccurate because of the special conditions of a site, but an experienced site planner will detect these and revise the average costs up or down.

Reference 82

Later, as first designs are being prepared, more detailed estimates will be called for. These may be tied to separate units of improvement but will still stop short of actually considering the work to be done in detail. Estimates will be made of the cost for roadways on the basis of the total length of each type of street, underground utilities on the basis of the cumulative lot frontages, and lot grading related to the number of housing sites. Such figures are normally arrived at by dividing total contract amounts (for road construction, underground utilities, grading, surveying, planning, etc.) by

Reference 80

the unit considered the best (or most easily measured) index of costs. Included in the unit cost is not only construction labor and materials but site preparation, the cost of working capital, supervision costs, overhead, profit and all other items for which the contractor must be reimbursed.

Estimates at this level of detail are useful to help in the selection of a planning approach and in establishing the timing and location of site construction. But their aggregated nature makes them insensitive to possible innovations, and they must be used with caution. As an example, the actual costs of one road network may be lower than another because it will require fewer areas with underground storm drainage, a fact that will be obscured by estimating the cost of storm drainage simply on the basis of the lineal feet of roadway.

Ultimately, a careful, detailed estimate of costs will need to be made, frequently as a basis for the decision to proceed to the construction contract stage. Where competitive bids will be asked for, this detailed cost estimate will serve as a check on the reasonableness of bids and will spare the client the embarrassment of calling for bids on a project that cannot be afforded. It may bring on adjustments in the plan before bids are called for. For the contractor or developer of a site, the final detailed cost estimate will allow a budget to be drawn up against which the construction process can be managed.

Detailed cost estimates are typically built up from elements that begin with the amount of material required and the hours of labor necessary to assemble and install a particular site component. Added together these are the *bare costs*. When the bare costs of all the components have been estimated, then come estimates for the project as a whole—cleanup at completion, repair of damages, providing electrical service to the site, fencing the construction area, building a construction shed, and other items that apply to the entire project rather than to any individual component. *Fees and permit costs* may be included under these *general conditions* or may be singled out if they are large and tied to particular construction items. This also applies to *sales taxes* on labor and materials and *property* or *ad valorum taxes* while construction is in progress. The contractor's *overhead* is a major additional element—the cost of his supervisory and office staff, vehicles, insurance, bonding, financing of working capital, and other general expenses to support his construction organization. When subcontractors are used, there may be a dual layer of overhead, although it may not greatly exceed the overhead of a single contractor. Where a system of construction management substitutes for a general contractor, each of the overhead items must be estimated separately. Finally, *contractor profit* must also be added, usually as a percentage of all other costs. It will reflect, among other things, the risks involved, the prevailing market for construction work, and the contractor's estimate of the difficulty of working for the sponsoring organization.

After an estimate of construction costs has been made, several other items must be added to arrive at an overall construction budget. There will be *professional fees* of various kinds: planners, architects, landscape architects, engineers, surveyors, lawyers (to draw up contracts), among others. A *contingency allowance* is generally essential to account for the unforeseen and to allow for errors in design or prediction. There will also be the cost to the client of *financing* the construction through its completion (as opposed to the working capital the contractor requires, which is generally included in his overhead).

Each of these elements will vary according to the project, its timing and the special difficulties posed. However, it is not uncommon for the additions to bare costs to lie within the following ranges of percentage:

TABLE 8.TYPICAL ADDITIONS TO BARE COSTS

General conditions	5–10%
Fees and permits	1–5%
Sales and other taxes	0–5%
Contractor's overhead	7–15%
Contractor's profit	0–15%
Professional fees	7–15%
Contingency allowance	5–10%
Construction financing	5–20%

When all of these additional items have been taken into account, the bare costs may represent as little as one-half of the construction budget. Nevertheless, they are the point of beginning for any estimate.

A number of cost estimating services publish annual unit cost figures, based on an analysis of many construction projects. Typically, these are organized by the sixteen categories of the Uniform Construction Index, a widely accepted set of divisions and subdivisions used for organizing specifications, product information, and contracts. There is some virtue in following this scheme from the beginning, since it corresponds to how most information is to be found and will allow comparison and updating of estimates.

428

In using standard unit cost figures, bear in mind that they are based on optimal construction conditions. Changes to any one of these can have a major effect. Typically, they assume a metropolitan location with an adequate supply of labor, an average-sized project, reasonable weather conditions (no winter construction), no exceptional building code requirements or serious local union restrictions, and new construction as opposed to alterations. In periods of rapid inflation, it is important to set the precise month of the cost estimates and to inflate future costs accordingly. Construction costs will also vary from city to city, and most sources provide indices to adjust cost estimates to fit the locale. Finally, the level of quality can have a major influence on costs. Tight tolerances, extreme attention to detail, constant supervision, and a high demand for uniformity can escalate costs and should be recognized when estimates are made.

Keeping within the construction budget may be the most pressing concern for the site planner, but she and her client are shortsighted if operating and maintenance costs are not also kept in mind. Data on future annual costs are more difficult to obtain. Even more problematic are the information necessary to make distinctions between alternatives. As an example, overland storm drainage systems generally cost less to build than systems of underground pipes, but this is partly offset by the higher annual maintenance costs of open channels. How much higher these costs are will depend on the quality of maintenance as well as the quality of initial construction—hence the difficulty of making the estimate.

Several construction cost services have begun providing annual unit cost data in computer-readable form, allowing automated estimates to be made rapidly. In the future many design and planning firms may subscribe to these services, supplementing their job cost files. But for large projects, professional cost estimating consultants are usually required. In some countries a separate profession has grown up to provide expertise in cost control; the field of quantity surveying in Great Britain is one example.

A good beginning in estimating operating and maintenance costs is to provide for the cost of replacing the facility after its useful life. If asphalt curbs typically last 10 years, concrete curbs 25 years and granite curbs 50 years, then their initial costs can be annualized for comparison. Routine maintenance costs also will not be equal and may be estimated from experience in the local area. For installations where operating costs are substantial—such as for garbage collection or for snow removal in northern climates—a very large differential in first costs may be justified by the significant annual economies of a more expensive proposal. It is sometimes economical to install vacuum garbage collection systems (if their cost of possible breakdown has been considered) instead of relying on site pickup, or to cover parking areas rather than remove snow from them each winter.

Cost is an allocating device, and it is hardly surprising that there are conflicts between construction and maintenance costs or between those costs and more intangible community costs. A cost estimate that includes ongoing maintenance and operation alongside of construction expenditures will expand the range of rational choice. But that choice also depends on the revenue side of the ledger, on how depreciation and taxes modify long-term expenditures, on the cost of money borrowed for construction and on how the burden of payment is distributed. Costing is but one part of the larger task of programming and managing a site.

Trees, Hedges, Ground Covers

The basic elements of a site are space and light and the land. We clothe and modify those elements with a variety of plants and artificial substances. Lengthy lists and descriptions of these may be found in other sources. Here we offer a condensed listing as a guide to subsequent search.

Reference 77

Mown grass is not the only planted ground cover and is too often used inappropriately, in deep shade, steep ground, or arid climates. There are a number of other covering plants available, each suitable for some particular situation. Many are evergreens or will tolerate shade or little water. Among the most useful are:

Ground covers

Ajuga reptans (Bugleweed) A dense ground cover, flat to the ground, which grows well in shade but not in sun. Blue, white, or red flowers on upright stalks in spring. Evergreen in mild climates and in protected areas. Needs watering, fertile soil, and weed control.

Arctostaphylus uva-ursi (Bearberry) A trailing shrub, turning reddish-brown in fall. Birds feed on the red berries. Grows in shade and in acid, sandy, low-fertility soil. Drought tolerant.

Convallaria majalis (Lily of the Valley) A graceful low plant with fragrant flowers and orange berries. Grows in full or partial shade but not in sun. Tolerates drought and poor soil and needs little maintenance.

Hedera helix (English Ivy) A trailing and climbing evergreen vine, whose broad flat leaves make a continuous cover. Grows in full sun or full or partial shade but is discolored by full exposure to winter sun. Ascends and covers walls and tree trunks. Drought tolerant but not hardy in the far north. Flowers inconspicuous, berries toxic.

Juniperus spp. (Ground Juniper) A dense, attractive evergreen cover requiring little maintenance. Needs full sun and well-drained soil but tolerates drought. Several varieties.

Liriope spicata (Lilyturf) A coarse, grass-like evergreen, six to twelve inches high, which needs little maintenance once established. It spreads slowly. Tolerates shade, drought, and low-fertility soil.

Lonicera japonica halliana (Hall's Japanese Honeysuckle) An exotic, aggressive, semi-evergreen vine, useful for covering large areas. Stems root as they run and must be restricted to prevent unwanted spread. Small yellow and white flowers in June, black berries in the fall, relished by the birds. Leaves turn brown in the fall. Tolerant of shade and drought.

Pachysandra terminalis (Japanese Spurge) A dense evergreen cover with large leaves and inconspicuous flowers and fruit. Grows in shade, not full sun. Needs watering and occasional fertilizer but defeats weeds. Clipping in spring stimulates new growth.

Vinca minor (Periwinkle) A nonaggressive evergreen shrub, six inches high, with glossy leaves and purple spring flowers. Grows in sun, shade, and low-fertility soil but not as weed resistant as *Pachysandra*.

Grasses

None of these ground covers will tolerate much traffic over them, however, and in a temperate climate, grass remains the surface of choice—where the ground is in full sun and will be walked on, where there is plentiful water, and when the turf can be properly maintained.There are dozens of useful varieties of grass, and seed mixes are chosen depending on whether a fine or a rough turf is wanted, whether the lawn is to be cut high or low, to have heavy or light traffic, to be in sun or partial shade, on soil rather wet or rather dry, acid or alkaline, in a warm or a cold climate. The best mown turf usually consists of red fescue (*festuca rubra*) and/or Kentucky bluegrass (*poa pratensis*). Fescue is a fine-leafed grass with densely matted roots, forming a complete cover within a year. It may temporarily go brown in a hot, dry summer. It is tolerant of shade and best suited to a well-drained soil.

Bluegrass, which does not like sandy ground, makes a very fine turf but requires fertility and much moisture. It germinates slowly and takes its time to become established. Both grasses are normally mixed with redtop (*agrostis alba*) or ryegrass (*lolium perenne*). These quick-growing grasses, which persist for only three or four years, hold the ground until the permanent cover is secure. Ryegrass produces a rapid effect, needs full sun, and grows best on fertile soil. Redtop, while also vigorous, tolerates poor soil and will not compete so severely as ryegrass with the permanent strain that it is protecting. Redtop is often used on badly disturbed ground. Some mix of these four grasses makes up most lawns in the temperate, humid climates.

In hot regions, the best wearing surface is Bermuda grass (*cynodon dactylon*), which withstands high heat and can grow on a wide range of soil. It wants full sun and occasional water but survives a drought by going dormant. This is a coarse-textured grass, which turns brown in cool weather, as well as in drought. It is an aggressive invader, difficult to restrain. There are further species that are useful in arid conditions, among them blue grama (*bouteloa gracilis*) and buffalo grass (*buchloe dactyloides*). Blue grama is a low-growing grass that adapts to a wide range of soil, while buffalo grass, which forms a dense, matted turf and is native to our western plains, needs a heavier soil, but can withstand long periods of drought. Beachgrass (*ammophila breviligulata*) is a tall grass that holds dry sandy areas, or builds up coastal dunes by trapping the wind-blown sand. It endures drought and grows in infertile ground, but an application of fertilizer will ensure a dense, enduring growth.

Perennial ryegrass and timothy (*phleum pratense*) are the favored species for grazing, as distinct from ornamental turf. Grass is usually seeded directly onto a prepared and fertilized layer of topsoil. Occasionally, with greater cost, it is established by transplanting the turf itself. On difficult ground, or where it is necessary to cover an extensive area with great speed, it can be seeded hydraulically, along with a liquid fertilizer.

In more heavily used areas, much of the ground surface must be covered with some inorganic material. The most common materials in an ascending order of cost are:

Earth itself is rarely thought suitable as an ultimate sur-facing yet often becomes so. Subject to erosion, likely to be dusty when dry and muddy when wet, under light use it can nevertheless be a proper choice, especially if well drained

Ground
surfaces

References 9, 16

or in an arid climate. A handsome material in its own right, it is soft to walk on and excellent for play. It can be stabilized with additions of sand, clay, cement, asphalt, or resins.

Gravel is the cheapest artificial surface, if we except untreated earth. It should be compacted, topped with stone dust, and edged with some solid material, such as brick. It requires substantial maintenance to keep it clean, level, and free of weeds. The base beneath the gravel is sometimes treated with herbicides or covered with a plastic film punctured by drain holes before the gravel is applied, to discourage weeds. The gravel may scatter onto surrounding areas. It will take moderate traffic. It is not pleasant for bare feet or for bicycle wheels, but it is handsome if well kept. Stepping stones may be set in it. It is difficult to clear snow from a gravel surface.

Asphalt is the automatic answer, since it is both cheap and practical. It is resilient, reasonably durable, can easily be shaped to fit the ground, and can be cut and patched as repairs or changes are needed. It will require occasional resurfacing and cannot take very heavy loads unless it is especially designed for that purpose. Alas, it looks terrible, and worse with age. Its appearance may be improved, at additional cost, by enclosing it within a network of harder pavings—bricks, stone, or strips of concrete—which also prevents breakage at the edge. Another mitigant is to top it with peastone.

Concrete is strong, durable, and of moderate initial cost. It requires very little maintenance, but it can crack or spall on the surface if it is not properly made. There must be expansion joints at intervals, which is also an opportunity for a change of material. Like asphalt, it is not very handsome in large expanses, but its color is lighter (if limited in range), and the surface can be well finished or given various textures.

Wood decking is occasionally used for special features outdoors and can make a beautiful surface, with many variations of design. But its life span is limited, it requires constant repair and maintenance, and must be carefully installed to resist rotting. Where it touches the ground, wood must be pressure treated with preservatives if it is to last more than a few seasons. The earlier use of end-grain wood block as a solid paving has now largely been discontinued, not for any lack of permanence but because it is dangerously slippery when wet.

Cement and asphalt pavers are small, interlocking units set on a sand base. They look well, although their color range is limited, and they wear well, although the edges of the asphalt pavers will crumble. They are easily maintained and can be reclaimed.

Brick and brick pavers include thin bricks for walks and full-depth ones for carriage-ways. For hard wear, they are set on edge. They are close in cost to the cement and asphalt pavers and wear well although they must be hard burned, and even then are subject to some frost damage. Where frosts occur, bricks and pavers are set on an asphalt base or on a concrete slab topped with a setting bed of sand. But if set in sand alone, the rain will reach the ground, which favors nearby plants. It is difficult to clear off the snow without chipping or dislodging bricks. People may stumble on them when they become uneven. But brick is one of the most handsome of outdoor surfaces, with a wide range of color. It can be laid in many interesting patterns.

Cellular concrete block, whose interstices are filled with earth and sown to grass, make a fairly expensive but attractive surface for extended pedestrian areas or for the parking of light vehicles. The grass must be watered and mowed, but it takes less care than a pure stand and will survive on slopes and under traffic in a way that grass alone would never do. It will not bear heavy vehicles, however, or even heavy foot traffic. A less expensive (and less well tested) variant for light foot and vehicle traffic is to embed galvanized wire mesh just at the ground surface before seeding and then allow the grass to grow over it.

Artificial turf is plastic grass on a neoprene mat, set in gravel or concrete. This is an expensive surface of permanent color, which from a distance looks rather like grass itself. It will take heavy pedestrian wear and is often used for sports fields. It is falling out of favor, since it has none of the resilience of real turf and causes injuries to athletes. There are other surfacings specialized for play, including *sand*, so delightful to mess in, *shredded bark*, also used for mulching planted beds, which is resilient to fall on but hard to maintain and to keep within its bounds, and various *rubber compounds*, which are quite expensive but excellent for heavy use as well as resilient underfoot.

Stone is the most expensive and the finest material of all—durable, handsome, with an enormous range of color, character and texture. Its availability varies from place to place. The various granites are the most permanent materials and have the strongest character. Bluestone is also useful, although it will not stand up to road salt. Limestone, marble, and slate are beautiful materials, but they do wear down. Many other local varieties of stone may be attractive. Stone can be laid in large finished blocks, or smaller setts, or even as rounded cobbles, although the last are difficult to walk on. A pattern of cobbles and smoother block will produce an interesting surface, which will guide the movement of people. Good stonework is expensive, not only for the cost of the material, but because it must be carefully installed.

Hedges Shrubs are used to create screens or solid masses of planting at the height of a human being. We list a gardener's dozen of the most useful ones, with notes on their mature height, their hardiness, their character, and their tolerance ($-20°$ refers to the average annual minimum *Fahrenheit* temperature that they will withstand, so that the temperature zones in Fig 110 may be used more easily. That figure, however, also gives the necessary conversions to Centigrade degrees).

Berberis thunbergi (Japanese barberry) 6 ft, $-20°F$, tolerant of shade and poor soil, thorny, can be a clipped hedge, foliage color in fall.

Buxus sempervivens (Boxwood) 25 ft, $-10°F$, evergreen, makes a fine clipped hedge, slow growing, shade tolerant.

Clethra alnifolia (Sweet pepperbush) 9 ft, $-35°F$, shade tolerant, fragrant flowers, moist soil.

Forsythia, 8 ft, $-20°F$, tolerant of soil and partial shade, pest free, yellow flowers early spring, arching, spreading habit.

Ilex crenata (Japanese holly) 20 ft, $-5°F$, evergreen, can be a clipped hedge.

Kalmia latifolia (Mountain laurel) 10 ft, $-20°F$, evergreen, showy flowers, shade tolerant, needs acid soil, leaves poisonous to cattle.

Ligustrum amurense (Amur privet) 15 ft, $-20°F$, soil and drought tolerant, much used for city hedges, numerous fine twigs can be clipped to desired width and height.

Pyracantha coccinea lalandi (Firethorn) 20 ft, $-20°F$, spiny branches, white flowers May, persistent orange fruit attracts birds, semi-evergreen, glossy, oval leaves, can be trimmed as a hedge, tolerant of soil, drought, and partial shade.

Rhamnus frangula (Buckthorn) 10 ft, $-40°F$ dark green, lustrous, very dense foliage, persistent until late fall. Can be pruned to desired height, a hedging plant brought in with the early European settlers. Tolerant of soil and drought.

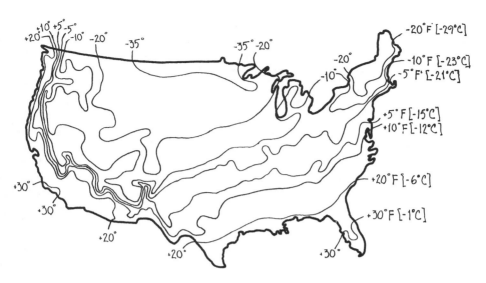

FIGURE 110 *Zones of the United States whose average annual minimum temperatures lie between the bounding temperature contours shown. This is a general guide for determining the hardiness of plants in the various zones.*

Rhododendron spp., mostly −5° to −10°F, the great flowering ornamentals; too many varieties to name and they include the azaleas; generally evergreen, requiring partial shade and moist acid soil. They range from 1 to 3 m (3 to 10 ft) in height.

Syringa vulgaris (Common lilac) up to 20 ft, −35°F, many varieties, soil tolerant, beautiful fragrant spring flowers, an old favorite.

Taxus cuspidata (Japanese yew) up to 20 ft, −20°F, fine dark evergreen foliage, shade and soil tolerant, pest free, slow growing, can be sheared, makes a fine clipped hedge.

Thuja occidentalis (Eastern arborvitae) 25ft, −30°F, dense native evergreen which can be sheared, but it grows to a 5 foot depth and makes a good screen in its natural form. Fairly tolerant of shade, drought, and soil.

Viburnum sieboldi (Siebold viburnum) 20 ft, −20°F, summer flowers and fall fruit, colorful stems. There are many other viburnums.

Trees

Finally, we list the most dependable trees for urban or suburban site development in the humid areas of the United States. In other areas, different species will be appropriate.

References 10, 45, 99, 100

Local knowledge should always be consulted. Even where suitable, a tree may not be obtainable, especially where commercial nurseries are lacking. Our list is a conservative one, restricted to particularly handsome and widely used trees that commonly reach at least 9 m (30 ft) in maturity and can be grown at least throughout the southern half of the United States, if not farther north. That is, they will withstand winter temperatures as low ,as 0°F. We have chosen trees of character suitable for major plantings rather than those best used as unique specimens. Most of them are not short-lived, nor are they prone to disease, nor do they require special maintenance. They are adapted to city or suburban living conditions. Planting need not be restricted to this conservative list, of course, but these are the finest of the common ornamentals, and any U.S. site planner should be familiar with their character and use.

For each tree, we list the botanical and the common name, the mature height in meters and (feet), and then the minimum average annual winter temperature that the species can withstand (in degrees *Fahrenheit* for the reasons given above, in our list of shrubs). Fig. 110 shows how these winter temperatures are distributed across the United States. This number therefore indicates the northern limit beyond which the tree should not be planted without special protection. After these numbers there may come three symbols: E when the tree is evergreen; C when it is tolerant of harsh urban growing conditions (air and soil pollution, dust, drought and heat); and T when it is relatively easy to transplant large specimens. Then follows a description of the visual character and preferred habitat of the species. The marginal sketch is a diagram of its outline, not drawn to scale.

Acer platanoides (Norway Maple) 15 m (50 ft); −40°F; CT. Broad, roundheaded, regular in form. Large, smooth medium green leaves, clear yellow in autumn, persistent in winter. Coarse texture, deep shade. Good street tree. Tolerates seashore conditions.

Acer saccharum (Sugar Maple) 23 m (75 ft); −30°F; T. Short trunk, upright branches, dense, compact, oval crown. Large deep-cut smooth dark green leaves, whiter beneath, turning brilliant yellow, orange, and scarlet in autumn. Wants moist, well-drained soil, pure air, full sun. A stately tree, finest of the maples. Source of maple syrup.

Ailanthus altissima (Tree of Heaven) 15 m (50 ft); −20°F; C. Coarsely branched, spreading open form, stark winter silhouette. Large, compound bright green leaves, coarse "tropical" texture, striped and dotted shade. Staminate flowers malodorous, but soon gone. Self-seeding, very vigorous, grows anywhere. Tolerates salt spray, wet, dry, or poor soil, partial shade. Smoke, dust, and disease resistant, the toughest city tree. Brittle, rapid growing and short-lived.

Catalpa speciosa (Northern Catalpa) 18 m (60 ft); −20°F; C. Pyramidal but irregular in outline. The thick, crooked, mostly horizontal branches are clearly visible. The large, long-stalked light green leaves are arranged in bursts on ridged branchlets. A heavy, plastic texture with many holes. Showy, spotted white flowers June and July. Long, slender, curving pods, persistent in winter, rattling in wind. Withstands heat and drought. Slow growing.

Cercidiphyllum japonicum (Katsura Tree) 18 m (60 ft); −25°F. Numerous upward-branching trunks, loose willowy outline. Becomes columnar if confined to single trunk. Leaves close to branches, fine texture. Foliage rosy in spring, blue-green in summer, yellow and scarlet in autumn. Rapid growth, pest and disease free. Wants rich moist soil and full sun.

Crataegus phaenopyrum (Washington Hawthorn) 9 m (30 ft); −20°F. Dense, upright, lustrous tree, finest of the hawthorns. Clusters of white flowers in early summer, foliage orange and scarlet in the fall, persistent bright red fruit in winter. Prefers well-drained soil, cold dry winters, full sun.

Eucalyptus camaldulensis rostrata (Longbeak Eucalyptus, Red Gum) 60 m (200 ft); +20°F; E. Grows only in extreme south or on west coast—an exception to our hardiness rule, listed here for its special usefulness. A tall, graceful, broad-leafed evergreen, whose narrow dark green leaves on pendulous reddish twigs sway with the wind. Flaking bark and aromatic wood. A good shade tree which needs space; difficult to transplant but spreading rapidly. Withstands extreme heat, drought, prolonged flooding, alkaline soil, and some frost. Insect free.

Fagus sylvatica (European Beech) 30 m (100 ft); −20°F, T. A massive, spreading tree; branches sweep the ground, forming a hollow within. Slow growing and needs growing room. A dense texture of dark green, small, thin, shining leaves, bronze and persistent in autumn. Can be trimmed as a hedge. Gray smooth bark like muscled skin, heavy trunk and branches. Long-lived: over 300 years. Needs rich, moist, well-drained soil, good sun. Relatively free from disease. Does not tolerate city conditions, or fill or compaction around the roots. Almost nothing can grow under it.

Fraxinus americana (White Ash) 24 m (80 ft); −35°F; C. Tall stem, long compact oval head of regular outline, stout ascending branches, well off the ground. Large pinnate leaves; a dense rich texture striped with light and shade. A stately tree. Deep purple or yellow in autumn. Seeds self vigorously. Grass grows well beneath it. Spray for oyster scale. Tolerates poor soil and city conditions.

Gingko biloba (Gingko) 30 m (100 ft); −25°F; CT. Tall, spiky, ungainly outline, becoming open and spreading in age, side branches diagonally erect. Fan-shaped leaves, leathery light green, pale yellow in autumn. Fruit malodorous, but pit is edible. Tolerant of soil if well-drained, of shade, and of severe city conditions. Pest free. An ancient, picturesque tree, perhaps the oldest surviving tree species.

Gleditsia triacanthus (Honey Locust) 30 m (100 ft); −25°F; CT. Round head, loose branching, lacy compound foliage, open underneath, light shade. Thorns and persistent long pods, but there are varieties without them. Leaves appear late in spring and drop early in fall. Tolerates the city, road salt, and poor soil. Relatively free of pests and diseases. Long-lived.

Ilex opaca (American Holly) 15 m (50 ft); −5°F; E. A full pyramidal tree, but can be trimmed for hedges. Stiff, glossy, dark green foliage, persistent throughout the year. Red berries in late fall and early winter. Wants a light, moist, well-drained soil, sun in summer but protection from winter sun and wind. Tolerates the seashore.

Liquidambar styraciflua (Sweet Gum) 30 m (100 ft); −20°F. This tall, broad, symmetrical pyramid needs space. Star-shaped leaves turn red, orange, and yellow in autumn. Fragrant sap. Tolerates seacoast conditions, sun or partial shade, and a wide range of soil. Free of pests and diseases.

Liriodendron tulipifera (Tulip Tree) 45 m (150ft); −20°F. An impressive tree of great height and rapid growth. Straight stem, short branches high from the ground, a rather oblong but open and irregular outline. Broad shining leaves, pale beneath, clear yellow in autumn. An open, spotted, trembling texture. Tulip-like flowers in June, greenish yellow with orange markings. Likes deep, rich moist soil. Deep-rooted and hard to transplant as a large specimen.

Magnolia grandiflora (Southern Magnolia) 30 m (100 ft); 0°F; CE. A tall, pyramidal straight-stemmed tree, spectacular for its giant white fragrant flowers and large lustrous evergreen leaves, rusty underneath. A stiff, coarse texture. Wants deep, rich, acid, moist but well-drained soil, plenty of summer sun, and, in the north, wind and winter shade protection. Roots easily damaged in transplanting.

Nyssa sylvatica (Tupelo, Sour Gum, Pepperidge, Beetlebung) 24 m (80 ft); −20°F. Erect, scraggly outline, short horizontal branches, rigid, crooked and twiggy, a bold winter outline. Rough dark bark. Leaves leathery, dark green, shining, turning flaming red in autumn. Fruit attracts birds. Roots are shallow and wind may uproot the tree if exposed. Difficult to transplant. Likes rich, acid, wet soil, full sun. Tolerates the seashore.

Pinus nigra (Austrian Pine) 24 m (80 ft); −30°F; E. Pyramidal when young, later flat-topped with spreading branches. Horizontal branches in whorls, beginning close to ground, yellow-brown scaly bark. Dense foliage on exterior, open within. Long, stiff, thick needles, dull dark green. A heavy, dark, somber tree. Good windscreen. Tolerates seashore and poor soil. Needs full sun. Transplant with care.

Pinus strobus (White Pine) 30 m (100 ft); −35°F; ET. A symmetrical pyramid at first, then tall and more rounded, and finally picturesque and wide-spreading in age. Horizontal, open branches, in regular whorls from a dark gray stem. Long fragrant soft green needles in massive horizontal planes; a softly shaded, sculptured texture. Ground beneath carpeted with brown needles and twisting roots. A majestic tree. Any well-drained moist soil, however infertile, but needs full sun. Intolerant of salt spray. Long-lived but can be pruned. Subject to weevil and to blister rust.

Pinus thunbergii (Japanese Black Pine) 15 m (50 ft); −10°F; ET. Dense and spreading, bright green needles, with crooked trunk and asymmetric head, in old age rugged and picturesque. Retains lower branches into middle age; good for screening and mass planting. Tolerant of salt spray, drought, and sandy soil. Most reliable evergreen for the coast.

Platanus acerifolia (Sycamore, Plane Tree), 27 m (90 ft); −15°F; T. Round head, spreading branches, upright stem, deep shade beneath. Mottled gray and creamy trunk. Dense foliage, large maple-like leaves, light green, a cheerful spotted play of light and shade. Rapid growth, transplants well, can be clipped, a common city tree. But subject to anthracnose and canker. Likes rich moist soil but will adjust. Tolerant of seashore but not of road salt.

Populus alba (White Poplar) 27 m (90 ft); −35°F; C. Wide-spreading open, rather irregular habit. The foliage— gray-green above, downy white below, and on a flexible stem—makes an interesting play of light in a breeze. Whitish gray bark. There is a columnar variety. Very rapid growth, but weak-wooded, and the roots penetrate everywhere. Used where other trees will not grow or as temporary fillers until better trees are established. Tolerates the city, the seashore, and wet or very dry ground.

Quercus alba (White Oak) 30 m (100 ft); −20°F. Broad ragged rounded crown, sturdy trunk and large, crooked, far-spreading branches, a strong skeleton. A mighty, slow-growing tree that needs great space and may live a thousand years. Rough, light gray bark. Deep-cut, bright green leaves, with paler undersides, turning russet and wine-red in autumn. Difficult to transplant, and so not often cultivated. Likes a dry, gravely, sandy soil, but will adapt. Tolerates the seashore, wants full sun. Subject to some pests and diseases.

Quercus borealis (Northern Red Oak) 23 m (75 ft); −20°F; C. An irregular, round-headed tree. The short, massive, ridged trunk divides into several stout branches fairly high off the ground. Finely cut leaves, medium dark green, turning dark red in autumn. A coarse, branchy texture. Grows rapidly, tolerates city conditions, and transplants more easily than the white oak, for which it is often substituted.

Quercus palustris (Pin Oak) 23 m (75 ft); −20°F; T. Stately, erect, and cylindrical. The numerous branches are upright toward the top, horizontal below, and down sweeping near the ground, making a tree that is as striking in winter as in summer leaf. Dense, deeply cut, shining green leaves, red in autumn. Not a street tree, since the lower branches block visibility. Best in moist soil that is not alkaline. Transplants well.

Quercus phellos (Willow Oak) 15 m (50 ft); −10°F; CT., Round-topped, dense ascending branches. Bark light red brown. Light green, long, narrow, willow-like leaves pale yellow in autumn. A fine-textured oak. Easy to transplant, a good street tree in southern cities.

Sophora japonica (Pagoda Tree) 21 m (70 ft); −20°F; CT. A compact, low, round head of graceful lacy outline, becoming like *Fraxinus* in age. Feathery, dark green pinnate leaves that take pruning well. A trembling, delicate texture. Large clusters of fragrant cream-colored flowers in August, yellow-green pods through the winter. Withstands city and seacoast conditions, road salt, poor soil, and heat. Pest and disease free. Rapid growth.

Tilia cordata (Little Leaf Linden) 21 m (70 ft); −30°F; CT. A tall, rounded pyramid, broad-based, dense and regular. Branches sweep to the ground, forming a darkly shaded cave beneath. Small bright green leaves, a fine dense texture. Abundant fragrant yellow flowers in early summer, attracting bees. A solid, handsome, formal shade tree. Needs moist soil and spraying for aphids and leaf-eating insects. Slow growth.

Tsuga canadensis (Canadian Hemlock) 27 m (90 ft); −35°F; E. Pyramidal but rather open outline, made by scattered, slender, often drooping branches persistent to the ground, on a tall stem. Ridged, red brown bark. Dense, fine, short needles, shining dark green above, light green below. A fine feathery texture, open at the edge, dark at the stem and on the ground below. Grows best in partial shade and moist well-drained soil on cool north slopes, but tolerates sun or full shade. Becomes dense under pruning, and is much used for hedges and mass plantings. Shallow roots, so tall trees may be blown down by wind. Intolerant of city conditions.

Ulmus americana (American Elm) 36 m (120 ft); −35°F; C. Stately, vase-shaped, high branching, symbol of old New England towns. It had no equal as an urban tree but is now disappearing because of two fatal diseases. In the hope that the diseases may be conquered, specimens should regularly be replanted, lest this elm become extinct.

Appendix *J*

Intersections

Reference 41

Traffic signals

Intersections are designed to ease conflicting maneuvers by reducing the confrontation or by separation in time or space. Conflicting maneuvers include merging, diverging, and crossing, and their danger is proportional to the relative speed of the approaching vehicles. The relative speed of two cars in a head-on collision is the sum of their individual speeds, while that of two vehicles going equally fast but merging into the same traffic stream from two slightly different directions is almost zero.

Traffic signals, by alternately stopping opposing movements, reduce the number of conflicts. Signals may be warranted when intersection volumes rise above 750 vehicles per hour, with at least one-quarter of the flow on the minor street. They may have a simple two-phase cycle, which alternately passes the traffic of one street and then the other, with a yellow warning interval between each change from green to red. Or they may be more elaborate, with three, four, or even more phases, to allow unhindered left turns. Total cycles are usually from 35 to 50 seconds long, and each intervening yellow interval is about 3 seconds. The capacity of an ideal controlled intersection could be computed by assuming that as many as 1000 vehicles can move through each lane during each hour of total green time, that is, excluding for each movement all red and yellow time (the stop and warning periods). But this is a high figure, attainable under optimum conditions, and does not allow for the effects

444

of heavy trucks, left-turn or pedestrian conflicts, or any stopping or parking at the crossing. Actual figures are closer to 300 to 600 vehicles per lane per hour of green.

Channelization, which is the separation of lanes by the use of islands and medians, does not reduce the number of conflicts but separates them in space and time so that only one conflict need be dealt with by the driver at any one moment. It allows drivers to wait for a favorable chance to conduct one maneuver without preventing other drivers from conducting other maneuvers. It also makes all maneuvers either a merging at low relative speeds, or a direct right-angled crossing, where the driver has better visibility and the conflict is of shorter duration than in an angled crossing. Channelization is often used in conjunction with traffic signals at major intersections. Even on minor streets, islands may be used to improve safety, to provide room for planting, or to allow an easier adjustment to a steep cross slope.

Channelization

The rotary is a device for converting all crossings into merging and diverging sequences, that is, into weaving operations, which are safer because of their low relative speeds. Since only one lane can weave at a time, the total capacity of a rotary is always less than can be gained with one lane of crossing flow around the circle. The length allowed for weaving is critical for capacity. Minimum weaving lengths are usually set at about 75 m (250 ft), but 250 m (820 ft) may be required for full single-lane capacity. The rotary will keep traffic moving smoothly only where flows do not exceed that single-lane level and where the circle can be made large enough to give ample weaving length. If drivers had better manners and always yielded to those already in the circle, large rotaries would carry more than most signalized crossings. But where the rotary is small or flow exceeds the capacity of a single weaving lane, traffic is likely to freeze. Rotaries consume tremendous areas of ground, and the enclosed circle is normally barren. Rotaries are also difficult for pedestrians to cross, except by bridges or tunnels. Thus the rotary pattern is no longer generally used.

Rotaries

Grade separations between vehicular roads are expensive, space demanding, confusing to the driver, and inflexible with regard to future change. They should be used only where necessary, that is, when a channelized intersection with signals cannot carry the load. A grade separation is often considered necessary when the flow on the major channel is over 3000 vehicles per hour or there are high turning volumes.

Grade separations

Intersection
analysis

One common type of grade-separated interchange is the cloverleaf, with its indirect left turns. Cloverleafs may be full or partial, depending on whether all possible turns are allowed. They take much space and are confusing in form, but the public is by now adjusted to them. Capacity is high, except with regard to the left turn, where no more than a single lane can diverge and speed is slow around the tight reverse turn.

If left-turns volumes are high, as for example where two urban freeways intersect, then a direct left-turn interchange will be used, which requires a complex and expensive structure. More than one lane can be pulled off, and in a direction that makes sense to the driver. Left-turning ramps may be provided for all left turns or only for particular ones.

Where only one channel is of major importance, it is common to use either a bridged rotary or a diamond intersection, in which conflicts are allowed on the secondary road but not on the major one. The diamond type, in particular, saves space in tight urban situations.

Many special types of grade separation are in use or can be developed. However complicated, they can be analyzed by tracing out each possible through or turning movement and by checking the capacity of each part of the intersection with expected flows in that direction. Special types for particular problems can best be developed by the use of movement diagrams, beginning with the expected pattern of heavy flows. Such diagrams explain the conflicts that must be dealt with. Colors can be used to separate levels diagrammatically and to indicate the bridging required, which is indicative of the total cost.

Rough scale drawings can then be used to check whether the intersection would be workable and to indicate the space required. The requirements that are most critical for the size and feasibility of a separated intersection are the maximum ramp grades, the minimum ramp radii, and the minimum lengths of acceleration and deceleration lanes. Maximum ramp grades are usually given as follows:

Up ramps, 4–6%
High volume up ramps, 3–4%
Down ramps, 8%.

Minimum ramp radii are the same as those for any traffic pavement and depend on design speed, which is usually set at 30 to 40 km per hour (20–25 mph). The required length of acceleration and deceleration lanes, including the entering taper, depends on the relative speed of traffic on the main road and on the ramp being entered or left. Given a ramp designed for 30 km per hour (20 mph), the required total lengths are:

TABLE 9. LENGTHS OF ACCELERATION AND DECELERATION LANES

Design speed of highway, km per hr	60	80	100
Length of deceleration lane and taper	75 m	100 m	120 m
Length of acceleration lane and taper	75 m	135 m	200 m

Design speed of highway, mph	40	50	60
Length of deceleration lane and taper	250 ft	350 ft	400 ft
Length of acceleration lane and taper	250 ft	450 ft	700 ft

The capacity of such complex intersections must be analyzed part by part: the through lanes, the turning lanes, and so on. Limits to capacity are likely to be met at the acceleration lanes, where turning traffic is merging back into through traffic. Here, if the maneuver is smoothly designed with an adequately long acceleration lane, total flow in the merging line may come up to 80 percent of full single-lane capacity. Where major flows are coming together, it may be possible to bring in two lanes instead of one, although merging cannot be effected for a long distance. In the extreme case, it is also possible to allow two, three, or even more separate lanes to merge or diverge simultaneously into or from an equal number of through lanes by using separate on or off ramps for each set of lanes. This is a complex, expensive solution.

Appendix **K**

Earthwork Computation

Here we describe four methods of computing the quantity of earthwork: by contour areas, by end areas, by the elevation of grid corners, and by the use of models.

Contour areas

The initial step in the first, or contour-area, method of calculation is to make an earthwork diagram on a copy of the grading plan. In this diagram, the new contours are brought out where they differ from the old, and the boundary lines of no-cut, no-fill are drawn. These boundaries are drawn by interconnecting the points where new contours rejoin the old ones and represent the boundaries between disturbed and undisturbed land or between areas of cut and those of fill. Along these lines, the new surface corresponds to the old one. Next, one shades the areas between old and new contours at each level, using one color or pattern for cut, and another for fill. The result is shown in Figure 111.

References 49, 94

Already, the diagram gives a good visual image of the amount and balance of cut and fill, since the volumes of earth to be moved are proportional to the sums of the shaded areas if one allows for overlap. Using this visual image alone, one can quickly resketch the new contours to get a better approximation of balance. The diagram also conveys the depth of cut and fill, since, where one shaded area almost touches the one above or below, the depth is almost one contour interval; where they overlap, the depth is just over the interval times the number of overlaps; and where they are widely spaced, the depths are shallow. Moreover, small regions of the earthwork diagram, when looked at downhill,

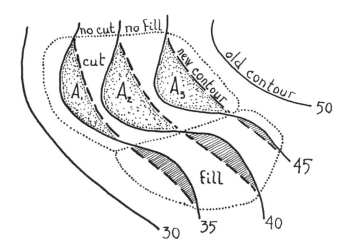

FIGURE 111 *A portion of a typical earthwork diagram, the first step in calculating the quantities of cut and fill by the contour-area method.*

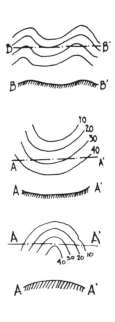

convey a somewhat exaggerated picture of how the ground would look in section, with the new grade line cutting through the old surface. However, when cuts or fills are several contour intervals deep, the shaded lenses overlap each other in multiple layers. For deep disturbances, then, this method can be confusing.

The diagram is valuable not only for visual inspection but also as a basis for quantity estimates. The estimate considers that each continuous cut or fill figure (the volume enclosed in the region indicated by one continuous no-cut, no-fill loop) is made up of a stack of solid figures, each composed of two parallel but irregular faces at the contour levels (the shaded areas in the diagram) separated vertically by the contour interval, and that this stack is concluded at top and bottom by a cone of earth where the cut or fill runs out to nothing. If we further assume that the volume of each internal solid figure is equal to the average area of its two horizontal faces, times the vertical distance between them (the contour interval), and that the volume of each concluding cone is equal to one-third the area of its base times *its* vertical height, and finally that this cone of cut or fill runs out about half the contour interval above or below the last shaded areas at top and bottom, then:

$$V = c \left(\frac{2}{3} A_1 + A_2 + \cdots + A_{n-1} + \frac{2}{3} A_n \right).$$

449

V is the volume, c the contour interval, and $A_1, \ldots, A_n$ are the series of shaded areas at each contour, running from top to bottom, within one continuous cut or fill figure. The shaded areas can be measured with a planimeter, using the map scale to express A and c in the same units. Given an accurate map, showing contour intervals of 0.5 m (1 ft) or less, and given careful drafting and careful use of the planimeter, this approximation will come within 5 to 10% of true values. Where the cuts and fills are extremely shallow and lie on gently sloping ground, however, the degree of error rises, since the shaded areas are far apart, and local irregularities may distort the calculation. By summing all the volumes in every region of cut, one can compare their total with a similar sum of sums for all the regions of fill, to see how close one is to total balance. Note that the percentage of loss or gain due to compaction must be applied to the sum of cut volumes at this step.

If the site is large, various groups of cut and fill regions can be compared to see if there is local balance, which would avoid long hauls. Where balance is lacking and this imbalance is not acceptable, the grading plan is reworked by redrawing the new contours in those regions where local balance is most sharply out, and the volumes for those regions are then recomputed. A few approximations will usually suffice to achieve the necessary balance, and meanwhile the entire topographic form has been kept under visual control.

End areas

The second, or end-area, method of calculation uses the same mathematical approximation for computing the sum of the volumes of the consecutive prismoids and cones, and is commonly used for a long, connected line of earthwork, as when grading for a road. But here the parallel faces are vertical rather than horizontal. Sections are drawn at regular intervals along a road center line, showing the new cross-section as applied to the existing ground. This is a two-dimensional representation of the cut and fill perpendicular to the center line at that point. Counting cut as positive and fill as negative and allowing for compaction, add the cut and fill areas at each section, average that sum with the corresponding sum at the next section, and multiply by the horizontal distance between sections (conventionally, one station or 100 feet). This gives a total volume of excess cut (positive) or excess fill (negative) between those sections. Where all the cross-sections are a standard distance apart, then the total excess cut or fill is the sum of the excess cut or fill area at each section times the standard interval between sections. This is a further simplification of the contour-area formula, since it is now assumed that:

$$V = c\left(A_1 + A_2 + \cdots + A_n\right),$$

which in principle overestimates at each end. But these continuous runs are long, so that errors at the ends are less important, and the stations are far apart, so that ground irregularities will generate greater errors.

If, instead of calculating the total balance, successive cuts and fills are progressively cumulated along the center line, a graph called a mass diagram can be drawn. This shows the surplus or deficit of soil that must be carried along if one were to begin cutting and filling at the very beginning of the road. Inflections (changes in upward or downward direction) in this mass diagram correspond to points on the road where cutting changes to filling, or vice versa, and the displacement of the line at the end of the graph is the total imbalance. More important, cut and fill are equal between any two locations defined by any horizontal line that cuts two points on the line of the mass diagram. The length of that horizontal line equals the maximum haul distance required to achieve that balance. Thus the mass diagram is useful for planning a strategy of earth moving in the field, as well as for adjusting the balance.

Calculations based on the elevations of grid corners— our third method—are appropriate for the volume of a borrow pit or a building excavation, as well as for more extensive regrading. The new surface is specified for construction by a regular grid of spot elevations rather than by a map of new contours. Calculation by grid corners is more accurate than the contour-area method and does not require the use of a planimeter. But continuous visual control while adjusting the grading surface is more difficult, and, without access to a computer, the successive approximations needed to achieve a balance are more laborious. The method is based on the assumption that a volume of earth of irregular depth but lying within the four vertical faces of a column based on a horizontal square is equal to the area of that square times the average depth of the four corners of the column.

An imaginary horizontal square grid is applied to the site or the excavation. For an extensive area, grid corners are often spaced at 30 m (100 ft) intervals, but the spacing can be as close as field data permit, if a more accurate result is required. The existing elevations of these corners are es-

Grid corners

451

tablished by field survey or by interpolation from a contour map. A trial proposed elevation is then set for each corner, and the resulting change of elevation at that corner is calculated—points of cut where the new elevation is below the old being positive, and points of fill negative. These differences must then be adjusted for compaction. For example, if the cut earth will eventually pack down to 95% of its original volume when replaced as fill, then all positive differences should be decreased by 5%.

The total balance of cut and fill can then be computed in the following way. In the diagram in the margin, if all the elevation differences at salient corners (which are part of only one grid square) are labeled c, those at the sides common to two squares are labeled s, those at reentrant corners common to three squares are called r, and those at the internal corners at the junctions of four squares are called i, then the excess cut or fill, V, is calculated by the equation:

$$V = \frac{x^2}{4}\left[\Sigma c + 2\ \Sigma s + 3\ \Sigma r + 4\ \Sigma i\right],$$

where x is the horizontal dimension of the side of each standard grid square. This total balance is positive if there is a surplus of cut, negative if there is a surplus of fill, and zero if there is a true balance. The total volumes of cut and fill, irrespective of balance, can be computed by separating the summation of positive and negative differences. Local balance can be identified by separating parts of the grid and treating them as if they were isolated figures. Since the general method assumes that the earth moved is a continuously varying set of square columns, all packed together, it miscalculates when the change in the ground is not continuous but abrupt, as at a retaining wall or the edge of a vertical pit. In that case, one must either make a special calculation for the squares concerned or must divide the volume along the line of discontinuity and calculate the divided elements as if they were isolated figures.

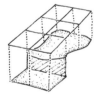

Balance is achieved by raising and lowering the various points and recomputing the whole, which may require three or four runs. This is laborious by hand but easily done by computer. It is a problem, however, to keep in mind the form of the whole surface as discrete points are pushed up or dropped. One means of doing so is to draw a series of sections through the grid corners, running along either the rows or the columns of this array. Locating and then connecting the existing and proposed elevations at each corner produces a profile of the old and the new ground along each particular row or column. If these profiles are placed one below the other, one gains a synoptic view of the whole. The proposed profiles are adjusted as balancing proceeds, and so the designer is made aware of the form of her trial surface as it shifts. But these successive views in one direction must eventually be checked by drawing the set of profiles in the orthogonal direction. Alternatively, computer graphics programs can be used to display the new contour maps that would result from each set of proposed grid corner elevations, or even display bird's eye views of the ground from different directions.

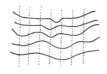

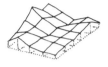

A simpler version of this method, used only for checking balance, neglects the differential effect of interior and exterior corners and is therefore appropriate to large areas or to situations where there is neither cut nor fill at any exterior edge or corner. In this case, the sum total of all the existing elevations at grid corners is compared to the total of all the new elevations as corrected for compaction. Equality indicates a balance, or balance may be achieved by adding or subtracting enough at the new elevations to make its total equal to the existing total.

The fourth general method of approximating balance is to model the existing ground surface in damp sand or plasticine. If the model surface is then changed without adding or subtracting material, it represents a new topography that can be achieved with a balance of cut and fill (although the compaction factor has been neglected). Alternatively, the volume of model material that was added or removed to make the new form is proportionate to the excess of fill or cut, at the model scale. Like the contour-area method, this is a way of simultaneously controlling form and balance, although its accuracy is only very approximate.

Approximation by model

But the new form must still be transformed into a contour drawing or a set of spot elevations, both for setting field controls and for adjustment to a precise balance. Unfortunately, setting elevations or making a contour drawing from a model is more difficult than the reverse. It involves measuring down from a grid suspended over the model terrain, or tracing the new contours with an accurate cantilever arm set to successive contour levels, or marking them out by submerging the model in a tank filled with successively higher water levels.

Lengthy computations for earth volume and balance are now largely done by computers, and it is unlikely that site planners will often have to make them in the future. It is more important that they understand the basis of those computations and that they be able to use simple methods where computers are unavailable or uneconomical or where they are giving the wrong answer. Most important of all, designers must be able to produce grading plans that approximate a balance or ones in which they are aware of the degree of imbalance. At the same time, they must keep control of the ground surface, since it is a crucial element of the design. It is for this reason that modeling and contour-area diagrams retain their usefulness.

Numbers

What follows is an extract of numerical standards, formulas, and normal quantities, taken from the text for ready reference. This summary may be convenient, but it is certainly misleading. These numbers are stripped of their context, that is, of the experience and reasoning that lies behind them and of warnings about when they are applicable and when they should be modified or discarded. It is dangerous to use standards without understanding these things. If uncertain, refer to the text.

Engineering characteristics of soil:

Particle size:

    gravel: over 2 mm in diameter

    sand: 0.05 to 2 mm

    silt: 0.002 to 0.05 mm

    clay: under 0.002 mm

Engineering classes:

Earthwork and foundations

	stability when loaded	drainage	as a base course for a paved road
clean gravel	excellent	excellent	fair-good
silty, clayey gravel	good	poor-good	poor-good
clean sand	excellent	excellent	poor
silty, clayey sand	fair-good	poor-good	poor-good
nonplastic silt	fair-good	poor-fair	unusable
plastic silt	poor	poor-fair	unusable

organic silt	poor-fair	poor	unusable
nonplastic clay	fair	unusable	unusable
plastic, organic clay	poor	unusable	unusable
peat, muck	unusable	poor-fair	unusable

Stabilization of light earth roads:

3 to 5% portland cement by dry weight, added to top 150 mm (6 in), if a gravel or sand,

4 to 10% cement, if a silt or a nonplastic clay,

4 to 10% hydrated lime, if a heavy clay or a clayey sand or gravel,

or: adjust the soil to make a sand-clay mix of approximately 10% clay, 15% silt, and 75% sand.

Bearing capacities, in metric tons per sq m (U.S. tons per sq ft):

bedrock, weathered to massive	120–950 (10–80)
well-graded and compacted clayey sand or gravel	120 (10)
gravel, gravelly sand, loose to compact	45–95 (4–8)
coarse sand, loose to compact	25–45 (2–4)
fine, silty, or clayey sand, not well graded, loose to compact	20–35 (1.5–3)
homogeneous, nonplastic, inorganic clay, soft to very stiff	5–45 (0.5–4)
inorganic nonplastic silt, soft to stiff	5–35 (0.5–3)

Slopes:

Min. grade for drainage, planted or broad paved areas: 1%

Min. grade for drainage, paved areas laid to exact elevation, or areas where temporary ponding is permissible: 0.5%

Min. grade at building perimeter: 2%

Min. grade, drainage swales and ditches: 2%

Max. grade, drainage swales and ditches: 10%

Max. grade of mown grassed areas: 25%

Max. grade of unmown planted banks: 50–60%

Max. grade with special ground covers: 100%

Angle of repose

loose, wet clay or silt: 30%

compact dry clay: 100%

wet sand: 80%

dry sand: 65%

cobbles: 70%

forested land: 70–100%

Apparently "flat" grades: 0 to 4%

Apparently "easy" grades: 4 to 10%

Apparently "steep" grades: over 10%

Earth machines:

	min. turning radius	*max. slope on which can operate*
bulldozer	3.5 to 6 m (12–20 ft)	85%
wheeled scraper	9 m (30 ft)	60% longitudinal, 25% transverse
power shovel	6 to 12 m (20–40 ft)	
dragline	12 to 25 m (40–85 ft)	

Earthwork computations:

Cut to fill ratios:

Resulting fill may exceed cut by as much as 15%, or cut may exceed resulting fill by as much as 10%.

Normal first estimate, cut will exceed fill by 5%.

Contour-area method:

$$V = c\left(\frac{2}{3}A_1 + A_2 + \cdots + A_{n-1} + \frac{2}{3}A_n\right).$$

End-area method:

$$V = c\left(A_1 + A_2 + \cdots + A_n\right).$$

Grid corner method:

$$V = \frac{x^2}{4}\left[\Sigma c + 2\,\Sigma s + 3\,\Sigma r + 4\,\Sigma i\right].$$

Dimensions:

Travel lane width, highway: 3.5 m (12 ft)

Travel lane width, residential street: 3 m (10 ft)

Curb parking lane width: 2.5 m (8 ft)

Planting strip, grass: 1 m (3 ft)

Roads and ways

457

Planting strip, trees: 2 m (6 ft)

Setback, poles from curb: 0.6 m (2 ft)

Width of normal sidewalk: 1 m (3 ft)

Width of collector walk: 2 m (6 ft)

Width of entrance walk: 0.8 m (2.5 ft)

Width of individual driveway: 2.5 m (8 ft)

Pavement, minor residential street: 8 m (26 ft)

Pavement, one-way residential street: 5.5 m (18 ft)

Travel way, light two-way track in park: 3 m (10 ft) with turnouts

Travel way, primary park road: 6 m (20 ft)

Bikeway in park: 1.5 to 2.5 m (5–8 ft)

Urban cycleway: 3.5 m (12 ft)

Min. vertical clearance for trucks: 4.5 m (14 ft)

Right-of-way, normal minor street: 15 m (50 ft)

Right-of-way, attainable minimum, normal minor street: 9 m (30 ft)

Right-of-way, collector street, low-cost development: 10 m (35 ft)

Right-of-way, minor street, low-cost development: 6 m (20 ft)

Right-of-way, foot access, negotiable by small vehicle: 3 m (10 ft)

Right-of-way, rail spur: 12 to 15 m (40–50 ft)

Vertical clearance, rail spur: 7.5 m (25 ft)

Truck loading dock, width: 3 m (10 ft)

Truck loading dock, depth of apron: 15 m (50 ft)

Truck loading dock, height: 1.25 m (4 ft)

Lengths and spacings:

Max. length of loop street: 500 m (1600 ft)

Max. length of cul-de-sac: 150 m (500 ft)

Max. length of block: 500 m (1600 ft)

Max. carrying distance, vehicle to door: varies upward from 15 m (50 ft)

Max. distance from supply or emergency vehicle to door, low-cost development: 75 m (250 ft)

Min. separation between driveway entrance and intersection: 15 m (50 ft)

Gradients:

Cross-sectional slope, concrete or bituminous: 2%

Cross-sectional slope, earth or gravel surface: 4%

Cross-sectional slope, paved walk: 2%

Min. longitudinal grade, paved road: 0.5%

Normal max. longitudinal grade: 10%

Normal max. longitudinal grade, no icing: 12%

Max. sustained grade a truck can mount: 17%

Max. sustained grade a car can mount in high gear: 7%

Max. grade of a highway, by design speed in km per hr:

20 kmph	12%
30	12%
40	11%
50	10%
60	9%
70	8%
80	7%
90	6%
100	5%
110	4%

Max. grade up ramp, grade-separated intersection	3 to 6%
Max. grade down ramp, grade-separated intersection	8%
Max. grade at on-grade intersection, for 12 m (40 ft) each way	4%
Max. grade parking lot	5%
Max. grade sidewalk	10%
Max. grade short pedestrian ramp	15%
Max. grade ramp for handicapped	8%
Gradient of stepped ramp	5 to 8%
Max. grade, public stairs	50%
Rule for exterior stairs: 2 risers plus one tread equals 70 cm.	
Max. grade, rail spur	1 or 2%

Curves, horizontal and vertical:

Min. radius of highway horizontal curves in meters, by design
speed in km per hour

20 kmph	25 m
30	30
40	50

50	80
60	120
70	170
80	230
90	290
100	370
110	460

Min. outside radius at end of cul-de-sac	12 m (40 ft)
Min. curb radius at shunt	6 m (20 ft)
Min. curb radius at driveway entrance	1 m (3 ft)
Curb radius at corner, minor street	3.5 m (12 ft)
Curb radius at corner, street carrying heavy trucks	9 to 12 m (30–40 ft)
Curb radius at corner, major intersection	15 m (50 ft)
Min. turning radius of a tractor-trailer	18 m (60 ft)
Min. radius, horizontal curve, rail spur	120 m (400 ft)

Min. length of vertical curve in meters, for each 1% grade change, by design speed in km per hr:

20 kmph	2.75 m
30	3
40	5
50	6.5
60	9
70	15
80	22
90	30
100	45
110	60

Intersections:

Max. deviance from perpendicular: 20°

Min. offset between T junctions: 40 m (130 ft)

Min. separation between arterial intersections: 250 m (800 ft)

Min. separation between freeway intersections: 1000 to 1500 m (3000–5000 ft)

Intersection flow warranting a channel or stop sign: 500 veh/hr

Intersection flow warranting a signal light: 750 veh/hr

Flow on one channel warranting a grade separation:
    3000 veh/hr

Capacities:

Theoretical capacity, single lane: 2000 veh/hr

Actual capacity, freeway lane: 1500–1800 veh/hr

Actual capacity, local street lane: 400–500 veh/hr

Actual capacity, congested street lane: 200–300 veh/hr

Capacity, signaled intersection, per lane per hour of
    green: 300–600 veh/hr

Unimpeded standing room: 1.2 sq m (12 sq ft)/person

Tolerable min. standing room in crowds: 0.65 sq m
    (7 sq ft)/person

Packed crowd: 0.3 sq m (3 sq ft)/person

Walkway flow in persons per minute per meter of width:

completely open	under 1.5
unimpeded walking	1.5 to 7
impeded walking	7 to 20
constrained walking	20 to 35
moderately congested	35 to 45
heavily congested	45 to 60
forced movement or at standstill	0 to 85

Parking:

Parking stall length: 6 m (20 ft)

Parking stall width: 2.5 to 2.75 m (8–9 ft)

Parking stall width for handicapped: 4 m (13 ft)

Parking stall dimensions for small cars: 2.5 by 5 m (8 by
    16 ft)

One-way aisle width, diagonal parking: 3.5 m (12 ft)

Two-way aisle width, perpendicular parking: 6 m (20 ft)

Total area of parking lot, per car: 23 to 40 sq m
    (250–400 sq ft)

Storm drainage: Utilities

Max. run of storm water in gutter: 250 to 300 m
    (800–1000 ft)

Max. run over unprepared surface: 150 m (500 ft)

Max. spacing between manholes: 100 to 150 m (350–500 ft)

Min. diameter, sewer draining street: 300 mm (12 in)

Min. diameter, sewer draining yard: 250 mm (10 in)

Min. slope of line, preliminary: 0.3%

Max. slope of culvert: 8 to 10%

Min. slope of culvert: 0.5%

Min. self-cleaning velocity: 600 mm (2 ft) per sec.

Max. velocity to prevent scouring: 3 m (10 ft) per sec.

Values of coefficient of runoff:

roofs, or asphalt or concrete pavements	0.9
macadam, compacted earth and gravel	0.7
impervious soil, plant cover	0.5
lawns, planted areas, normal soil	0.2
woods	0.1
residential development, 10 fam. per acre	0.3–0.5
residential development, 40 fam. per acre	0.5–0.7
dense urban commercial areas	0.7–0.9

Sanitary drainage:

Min. diameter, sewer main: 200 mm (8 in)

Min. diameter, house branch: 150 mm (6 in)

Min. slope of pipe, serving from 1 to 20 houses: 0.4 to 1.4%

Min. separation, drain field or privy from well: 30 m (100 ft)

Min. separation trickling filter from house: 100 m (350 ft)

Soil absorption rate, in liters per sq m (gals per sq ft) per day, by minutes required for water to fall 25 mm (1 in) in test pit:

time to fall 25 mm (1 in)	*absorption rate*
5 min or less	120 (2.5)
8	100 (2.0)
10	85 (1.7)
12	75 (1.5)
15	65 (1.3)
22	50 (1.0)

Min. separation of water table below bottom of privy pit   1.5 m (5 ft)

Min. capacity of aqua privy: 120 to 150 liters (26 to 33 gal) per person

Water supply:
Max. distance between valves in main line: 300 m (1000 ft)
Max. distance from hydrants to buildings: 100 m (350 ft)
Min. distance from hydrants to buildings: 7.5 m (25 ft)
Min. diameter water mains: 150 mm (6 in)
Min. delivered pressure: 1.4 kg/sq cm (20 lb/sq in)
Average demand, U.S. cities: 450 to 900 liters (100 to
    200 gal)/person/day

Lighting:
Standard mounting height, street lights: 9 m (30 ft)
Spacing between street lights: 45 to 60 m (150 to 200 ft)
Required average illumination, arterials: 10 lux (1 foot candle)
Required average illumination, local roads: 5 lux (0.5 foot
    candle)
Darkest areas not to fall below:
    40% of average on arterials
    10% of average on local roads

Mounting heights, walkway lights	3.5 m (12 ft)
Illumination of doorways, steps, and hiding places	up to 50 lux (5 foot candles)
Illumination of remainder of walkway	under 5 lux (0.5 foot candle)
Illumination of public parking garages	30 lux (3 foot candles)
Illumination of shopping center parking lots	10 lux (1 foot candle)

Other
Max. length of run, low-voltage line: 120 m (400 ft)
Normal spacing, electric power poles: 40 m (120 ft)
Width of easement for pole lines not on street: 2.5 m (8 ft)
Max. reach, truck to coal bin: 6 m (20 ft)
Max. reach, oil truck hose: 30 to 60 m (100 to 200 ft)

Bodily comfort: Climate
Max. temperature at which one can work without raising
    internal body temperature:
    in dry air: 65°C (150°F)
    in saturated air: 32°C (90°F)

Comfort range, inactive, in shade and in
light clothing, when humidity is   18° to 26°C
20 to 50%   (65° to 80°F)

Wind:
Wind speed is reduced up to 50% for a distance downwind
of 10 to 20 times shelterbelt height

Wind effects:

wind speed in m/sec (mph)	effects
2 (4.5)	wind felt on face
4 (9)	newspaper reading difficult; dust and paper raised; hair disarranged
6 (13)	begins to affect control of walking
8 (18)	clothing flaps; progress into wind slowed
10 (22)	difficult to use umbrella
12 (27)	difficult to walk steadily; unpleasant noise on ears
14 (31)	almost halted into wind; tottering downwind
16 (36)	difficulty with balance
18 (40)	grabbing at supports
20 (45)	people blown over
22 (50)	cannot stand

Equivalent wind speed = average wind speed times
(1 + 3T), where T is the root mean square of the instantaneous deviations from the average speed, divided
by the average speed. Or assume that equivalent speed
is 1.5 times average speed. Equivalent wind speed should
not exceed values given below for more than given percent of time:
In outdoor sitting areas: 4 m/sec (9 mph) over 20% of time
Where there are many pedestrians: 12 m/sec (27 mph) over
5% of time
Wherever there are people outdoors: 16 m/sec (36 mph)
over 0.1% of time

Insolation and sky exposure:
Altitude and azimuth of the sun at a given place and time:

$$\sin Al = \cos D \cos L \cos H + \sin D \sin L.$$

$$\sin Az = \frac{\cos D \sin H}{\cos Al}$$

where:

Al is sun altitude

Az is sun azimuth

D is declination of sun at the given date

H is local hour angle of sun

L is the latitude of the place

Shadow length on a sun dial:

$$x = P \tan (90° - Al)$$

where:

x is the shadow length

P is the height of the shadow-casting pin

Al is the altitude of the sun

Preferred max. visual obstruction of sky, from any principal residential window: no more than 30° above horizon

Albedos of surfaces:

fresh snow	0.9
bare dry sand	0.4 to 0.5
dry clay soil	0.2 to 0.3
meadows and fields	0.1 to 0.2
forests, dark cultivated soil	0.1
black asphalt, calm water	0.05

Decibel scale: Noise

quiet rustle of leaves: 10 dBA

soft whisper: 20–30 dBA

hum of small electric clock: 40 dBA

ambient noise, house kitchen or noisy office (speech interference begins): 50 dBA

light car traffic or normal conversation (noise begins to be annoying): 60 dBA

highway traffic at 15 m (50 ft): 70–80 dBA

subway, freight train, heavy truck at 15 m (50 ft) (hearing damage begins): 90–100 dBA

auto horn, pneumatic hammer: 110–120 dBA

military jet airplane: 130 dBA

Noise standards:

Preferred max. sound level outdoors: 55dBA

Preferred max. sound level indoors: 40dBA

Preferred max. sound level for sleeping or study: 35dBA

Zones unsuitable for housing:
  without special
  insulation of buildings   over 55 dBA or 65 Ldn
  with special insulation   over 75 dBA

Noise attenuation:

Min. spacing of openable windows, face to face: 9 to 12 m (30–40 ft)

Min. spacing of openable windows, separate rooms, same wall: 2 to 3 m (6–10 ft)

Decrease of noise from a point source, for every doubling of distance: 6 dBA

Decrease of noise from a linear source, for every doubling of distance: 3 dBA

Decrease of noise in a normal building, from outside to inside, with windows closed: 10 to 15dBA

Additional attenuation, in sealed, noise-insulated buildings: up to 20 dBA

Attenuation due to heavy wall or berm:

$$N = 5 + 4[10D]^{1/3}$$

where:

N is the additional attenuation in dB, and
D is the *additional* length of sound path imposed by the barrier in meters.

Housing

Densities:

| | FAR | families per hectare (per acre) | |
		net density	neighborhood density
single-family	up to 0.2	up to 20 (8)	up to 12 (5)
zero lot line detached	0.3	20–25 (8–10)	15(6)
two family detached	0.3	25–30 (10–12)	18 (7)
row houses	0.5	40–60 (16–24)	30 (12)
stacked townhouses	0.8	60–100 (25–40)	45 (18)
3 story walkup apts	1.0	100–115 (40–45)	50 (20)
6 story elevator apts	1.4	160–190 (65–75)	75 (30)
13 story elevator apts	1.8	215–240 (85–95)	100 (40)

Lot and structure dimensions:

Typical single-family lot frontage: 18 to 22 m (60–75 ft)

Typical single-family lot depth: 35 to 45 m (120–150 ft)

Min. lot frontage, low-cost development: 6 to 10 m (20–35 ft)

Min. lot size, low-cost development: 110 sq m (1200 sq ft)

Min. floor space in dwelling, international standard: 5 sq m (55 sq ft) per person

Min. dimensions of actively used private yard: 12 by 12 m (40 by 40 ft)

Min. dimensions of "outdoor room": 6 by 6 m (20 by 20 ft)

Min. spacing of eye-level windows, face to face: 18 m (60 ft)

Facility standards:

Max. distance to public transport, low-cost development: 300 m (1000 ft)

Swedish standards:

usable open space (i.e., not over 55 dBA, not over 50% grade, not less than one hour of equinoctial sun, and reachable without crossing a road)	100 sq m (1100 sq ft) within 50 m (165 ft) of door
max. distance to nursery school and supervised playground	300 m (1000 ft)
max. distance to school, public transport, and convenience store	500 m (1650 ft)

U.S. standards:

total area of playgrounds	0.5 hectare (1.2 acres)/1000 pop.
min. size of each playground	1.2 hectares (3 acres)
max. distance, playground to dwelling	800 m (2500 ft)
preferred max. distance, playground to dwelling	400 m (1200 ft)
total area of playlots, where no private yards	5 sq m (55 sq ft)/ child aged 2–6
min. size of site for elementary school and playground	2 hectares (5 acres)
area for neighborhood convenience shopping, including parking	0.25 hectares (0.6 acres)/1000 pop.

Parking spaces per dwelling unit:

suburban	2
normal	1.5
dense urban	0.5
elderly housing	0.3

| | Other uses | *Universities*:
Gross floor space per full-time student: 10 to 30 sq m (100–300 sq ft)
Floor area ratio: 0.3 to 2.0 |

Other uses   *Universities*:

Gross floor space per full-time student: 10 to 30 sq m (100–300 sq ft)

Floor area ratio: 0.3 to 2.0

Industrial districts:

Average size, U.S. districts: 120 hectares (300 acres)

Min. size, U.S. districts: 15 hectares (35 acres)

Floor area ratios, U.S.: 0.1 to 0.3

Floor area ratios, other countries: up to 0.8

Employee density, U.S.: 25 to 75 workers per hectare (10–30 per acre)

Employee density, other countries: up to 200 workers per hectare (80 per acre)

Parking spaces, per worker, U.S.: 0.8 to 1.0

Max. distance, parking to door: 300 m (1000 ft)

Block size: 120 to 300 m by 300 to 600 m (400–1000 ft by 1000–2000 ft)

Shopping centers:

Type of center	selling area in 000's of sq m (000's of sq ft)	site area in hectares (acres)	pop. served in 000's	radius of catchment area in minutes of driving time
neighborhood	4.5 (50)	1–2 (2.5–5)	10	5
community	9–27 (100–300)	4–12 (10–30)	40–50	10
regional	27–90 (300–1000)	20 (50) up	150 up	30

Interior mall width: 12 m (40 ft)

Interior mall, max. length: 120 m (400 ft)

Parking spaces per 100 sq m of selling area: 3 to 6 (3 to 5.5 per 1000 sq ft)

Max. distance of all parking to building entrance: 200 m (650 ft)

Max. distance of normal day parking to building entrance: 100 m (300 ft)

Miscellaneous   *Human scale*:

Max. range for detecting a human being with the unaided eye: 1200 m (4000 ft)

468

Normal distance for recognition of an individual: 25 m (80 ft)

Normal distance for reading facial expression: 12 m (40 ft)

Sense of direct personal relations occurs at: 1–3 m (3–10 ft)

Outdoor dimension that seems intimate: 12 m (40 ft)

Max. length of the smaller dimension of a successful large
outdoor enclosed space: 140 m (450 ft)

Aerial photos:

$$\text{Average scale} = \frac{f}{H}$$

where:

f is the focal length of the camera,

H is the height of the airplane above ground,

and f and H are in the same units.

Comparative height by parallactic displacement:

$$\frac{H - h}{H} = \frac{b}{b + p,}$$

where:

h is the height difference between the two points and

H is the height of the airplane over the lower of the
points

(h and H are in the same units);

b is the average base distance of the two photos, and

p is the parallactic displacement

(b and p are in the same units).

Typical additions to bare costs:

General conditions	5–10%
Fees and permits	1–5%
Sales and other taxes	0–5%
Contractor's overhead	7–15%
Contractor's profit	0–15%
Professional fees	7–15%
Contingency allowance	5–10%
Construction financing	5–20%

Bibliography

1. Alexander, Christopher, *et al.*, *A Pattern Language: Towns, Buildings, Construction*. New York, Oxford University Press, 1977.

   A fine compilation of patterns distilled from environments that support humane living.

2. Alexander, Christopher, *et al.*, *The Oregon Experiment*. New York, Oxford University Press, 1975.

   An experiment where patterns were substituted for a master plan, and users adopted roles usually reserved for professionals.

3. Appleyard, Donald, *Livable Streets*. Berkeley, University of California Press, 1981.

   Research and experiments on the use and meaning of local streets in Europe and the U.S.

4. Appleyard, Donald, Kevin Lynch, and John R. Myer, *The View From the Road*. Cambridge, MA, MIT Press, 1964.

   An early attempt to analyze the moving view.

5. Arens, Edward A. "Designing for an Acceptable Wind Environment," *Transportation Engineering Journal*, March 1981, pp. 127–141, and September 1981, pp. 595–596.

   A good discussion of design criteria and methods of analysis for wind effects in the outdoor environment.

6. Avery, T. Eugene, *Forester's Guide to Aerial Photo Interpretation*. U.S. Department of Agriculture Handbook #308, Washington, DC, Government Printing Office, 1969.

   An excellent brief discussion of the use of aerial photographs.

A guide to soil survey methods and soil capability assessment practices in the U.S., Canada and U.K. Identifies soil types likely to create problems for urban development.

27. De Chiara, Joseph, and Lee E. Koppelman, *Site Planning Standards*. New York, McGraw-Hill, 1978.

A compendium of conventional layouts, dimensions and standards for many site uses. Be mindful of the implicit values.

28. Dober, Richard P., *Campus Planning*. New York, Reinhold, 1964.

Still the standard reference on campus planning, with an international range of examples.

29. Dunne, Thomas, and Luna B. Leopold, *Water in Environmental Planning*. San Francisco, W.H. Freeman and Company, 1978.

A comprehensive text on hydrology, geomorphology and water quality, with emphasis on hazards posed to urban areas if water-related issues are neglected. See especially Chapter II, "Human Occupancy of Flood-Prone Lands."

30. Elliot, Michael, "Pulling the Pieces Together: Amalgamation in Environmental Impact Assessment, " *Environmental Impact Assessment Review*, vol. 2, no. 1, pp. 11–25.

Methods for reconciling and comparing impacts dimensioned in different ways.

31. Fairbrother, Nan, *New Lives, New Landscapes*. New York, Knopf, 1970.

Good sense, sharp observation, and useful ideas on the relation between environmental setting and contemporary changes in ways of life.

32. Fairbrother, Nan, *The Nature of Landscape Design: As an Art Form, a Craft, a Social Necessity*. New York, Knopf, 1974.

Full of opinions and ideas. Excellent illustrations.

33. Gill, Don, and Penelope Bonnett, *Nature in the Urban Landscape: A Study of Urban Ecosystems*. Baltimore, MD, York Press, 1973.

An excellent introduction to urban wildlife and its management.

34. Goodman, Paul and Percival, *Communitas*. New York, Vintage (paper), 1960 (orig. ed., 1947).

Insightful, if now dated, models for the design of settlements flowing directly from explicit values.

35. Gosling, David, *Design and Planning of Retail Systems*. London, Architectural Press, 1976.

A thorough discussion of the programming and design of shopping centers in Great Britain.

36. Grey, Gene W., and Frederick J. Deneke, *Urban Forestry*. New York, John Wiley and sons, 1978.

    A useful survey of the effects of urban vegetation on climate, runoff, air and soil quality. See especially Chapter 4, "Benefits of the Urban Forest."

37. Hackett, Brian, *Planting Design*. New York, McGraw-Hill, 1979.

    Use of plants, especially in large-scale, suburban or rural work, and primarily from the standpoint of ecology and U.S./British practice.

38. Hendler, Bruce, *Caring for the Land: Environmental Principles for Site Design and Review*. Planning Advisory Service report #328, American Planning Association 1977.

    Points to site arrangements that are consistent with the needs of a self-maintaining natural setting.

39. Heschong, Lisa, *Thermal Delight in Architecture*. Cambridge, MA, MIT Press, 1979.

    Explores how the thermal environment can reach beyond necessity into the sensory realms of delight, affection and sacredness.

40. Hewitt, Ralph, *Guide to Site Surveying*. London, Architectural Press, 1972.

    Surveying techniques used in construction and in the analysis of building sites.

41. Highway Research Board, *Highway Capacity Manual*. Washington, DC, National Academy of Sciences-National Research Council, 1965.

    The most broadly accepted standards for the design of roads and highways. But they greatly favor motorists over pedestrian safety, efficient flow over appearance or fitting the context, and heavy capital investment over minimal construction.

42. Hollister, Robert, and Tunney Lee, *Development Politics: Private Development and the Public Interest*. Washington, DC, Council of State Planning Agencies, 1979.

    An excellent example of "front-end" impact assessment applied to a large and contentious development project.

43. Hopkins, Lewis D., "Methods for Generating Land Suitability Maps: A Comparative Evaluation." *Journal of the American Institute of Planners*, October 1977 (v. 43, no. 4) pp. 386–400.

    Detailed techniques for scoring and aggregating the suitability of site areas for development. Useful for the initial analysis of large sites.

44. Hubbard, Henry V., and Theodora Kimball, *An Introduction to the Study of Landscape Design*. New York, Macmillan, 1917.

    A classic text, useful even today.

45. Hudak, Joseph, *Trees for Every Purpose*. New York, McGraw-Hill, 1980.

   An excellent, extended list of the ornamental trees with a thorough description of each.

46. Jenson, David, *Zero Lot Line Housing*. Washington, DC, Urban Land Institute, 1981.

   Technical details and examples of zero lot line housing especially useful in pointing to potential problems with this new housing form.

47. Kinnard, William N., Jr., and Stephen D. Messner, *Industrial Real Estate* (2nd Edition). Washington, DC, Society of Industrial Realtors, 1971.

   Still a classic brief text on industrial real estate.

48. Knowles, Ralph L., *Energy and Form*. Cambridge, MIT Press, 1974.

   An exploration of the shape and structure of buildings and settlements that are highly responsive to solar energy. The analyses of the form and energy characteristics of pueblos in Arizona and Colorado are especially interesting.

49. Kurt, Nathan, *Basic Site Engineering for Landscape Designers*. New York, MSS Information Corporation, 1973.

   A technical guide to topographic mapping, cut and fill analysis, roadway alignment design, and the design of site services. Written as a self-teaching text.

50. Lam, William M. C., *Perception and Lighting as Formgivers for Architecture*. New York, McGraw Hill, 1977.

   The design of lighting based on the nature of visual perception rather than on arbitrary industry standards. Many examples.

51. Land Design/Research Inc., *Cost Effective Site-Planning: Single Family Development*. Washington, DC, National Association of Homebuilders, 1976.

   An excellent exposition of site planning for higher density, less costly alternatives to the traditional single-family detached home.

52. Landsberg, Helmut E., *The Urban Climate*. New York, Academic Press, 1981.

   A thorough recent review.

53. Leveson, David, *Geology and the Urban Environment*. New York, Oxford University Press, 1980.

   A good general introduction.

54. Lipscomb, David M., and Arthur C. Taylor, *Noise Control: Handbook of Principles and Practices*. New York, Van Nostrand Reinhold, 1978.

   A thorough discussion of noise control techniques.

55. Lochmoeller, Donald C., *et al.*, *Industrial Development Handbook*. Washington, DC, Urban Land Institute, 1978.

The definitive handbook on the planning of areas for industrial development, illustrated with detailed case studies.

56. Lynch, Kevin, *Managing the Sense of a Region*. Cambridge, MA, MIT Press, 1976.

Designing and managing the urban environment to improve its sensuous quality.

57. Lynch, Kevin, *A Theory of Good City Form*. Cambridge, MA, MIT Press, 1981.

An attempt at stating the general criteria for a good physical environment.

58. Lynch, Kevin, *What Time Is This Place?* Cambridge, MA, MIT Press, 1972.

On how the environment might communicate the sense of past, present, and future.

59. Marsh, William M., *Landscape Planning*. Reading, MA, Addison-Wesley Publishing Company, 1983.

A compendium of techniques for analyzing environmental factors with many useful case examples of how they have been applied. Good treatment of microclimate, soils, watershed management and vegetation in urbanizing areas.

60. McClenon, Charles (ed.), *Landscape Planning for Energy Conservation*. Reston, VA, Environmental Design Press, 1977.

Ways to conserve energy through sensitive site planning. Excellent checklist and good case examples.

61. McKeever, J. R., *Shopping Center Development Handbook*. Washington, DC, Urban Land Institute, 1977.

The basic text on shopping center design.

62. McKeever, J. R., ed., *The Community Builders Handbook*. Washington, DC, Urban Land Institute, 1968.

A lengthy and practical treatise on large residential developments from the builder's point of view.

63. Melaniphy, John C., *Commercial and Industrial Condominiums*. Washington, DC, Urban land Institute, 1979.

A source book on organizing and planning mixed use, medical, and industrial condominiums.

64. Michelson, William M., *Behavioral Research Methods in Environmental Design*. Stroudsburg, PA, Dowden, Hutchinson and Ross, Holsted Press, 1975.

A good inventory of useful research techniques.

65. Newcomb, Robinson, and Max S. Wehrly, *Mobile Home Parks: Part II, An Analysis of Communities*. Washington, DC, Urban Land Institute, 1972.

Planning criteria for mobile home communities based on field surveys.

66. Odum, Eugene P., *Ecology*. New York, Holt, Rinehart & Winston, 1963.

An excellent brief summary of ecological theory.

67. O'Mara, W. Paul, and John A. Casazza, *Office Development Handbook*. Washington, DC, Urban Land Institute, 1982.

Standard reference source for developing office parks and suburban office buildings, including suggestions on site design criteria.

68. O'Mara, W. Paul, Frank H. Spink, Jr., and Alan Borat, *Residential Development Handbook*. Washington, DC, Urban Land Institute, 1980.

Widely used sourcebook on residential development practices, including site planning guidelines.

69. Perin, Constance, *Everything In Its Place*. Princeton, NJ, Princeton University Press, 1977.

The symbolic and social meaning of conventional site forms in residential areas in the United States as viewed by owners, regulators, and bankers.

70. Plumley, Harriet, "Design of Outdoor Urban Spaces for Thermal Comfort." In: *Proceedings: Metropolitan Physical Environment*, U.S. Forest Service General Technical Report NE-25, Upper Darby, PA, Northeastern Forest Experimental Station, 1977.

A good discussion of the subject.

71. Porteus, John Douglas, *Environment and Behavior: Planning and Everyday Urban Life*. Reading MA, Addison-Wesley Publishing Company, 1977.

The methods and concepts of psychologists and sociologists applied to environmental knowledge.

72. Pushkarev, Boris S., and J.M. Zupan, *The Pedestrian and the City*. Cambridge, MA, MIT Press.

An excellent detailed technical manual on calculating pedestrian capacity and demand in midtown Manhattan.

73. Rapaport, Amos, *Human Aspects of Urban Form: Towards a Man-Environment Approach to Urban Form and Design*. New York, Pergamon Press, 1977.

An extensive set of references on the ties between site arrangements and patterns of human occupancy.

74. Real Estate Research Corp., *Infill Development Strategies*. Washington, DC, Urban Land Institute and American Planning Association, 1982.

A thorough discussion of the problems and possibilities of infill housing in the U.S., with numerous examples.

75. Ridgeway, James, *Energy-Efficient Community Planning*. Emmaus, PA, The JG Press, Inc./The Elements, 1979.

Innovative approaches to community and housing design and management that seek to lower energy consumption. Interesting sample documents included that demonstrate how localities have mandated energy-sensitive development.

76. Ritter, Paul, *Planning for Man and Motor*. New York, Pergamon, 1964.

An exhaustive compilation of standards and examples for the planning of road and pedestrian systems.

77. Sasaki, Hideo, Charles W. Harris, and Nicholas T. Diner, eds., *Time-Saver Standards for Landscape Architecture: Design and Construction Data*. New York, McGraw-Hill (forthcoming).

Will be the standard reference.

78. Schon, Donald A., *The Reflective Practitioner*. New York, Basic Books, 1983.

A fine analysis of designers' internal methods and the nature of their knowledge.

79. Schultz, Theodore J., and Nancy M. McMahon, *Noise Assessment Guidelines*. Washington, DC, U.S. Government Printing office, August 1971.

Techniques and standards for assessing sonic environment of sites, especially for housing. Includes the simple walkaway test.

80. Shoemaker, Morrell M., ed., *The Building Estimator's Reference Book*. Chicago, Frank R. Walker Co., 1980.

A detailed source on methods for estimating costs.

81. Simonds, John O., *Landscape Architecture: The Shaping of Man's Natural Environment*. New York, McGraw-Hill, 1961.

Still one of the best manuals on landscape design. Particularly intersting in regard to pedestrian movement.

82. Simpson, B. J., *Site Costs in Housing Development*. London. Construction Press, 1983.

Comparative costs imposed by differing site conditions.

83. Smart, J. Eric, *et al.*, *Recreational Development Handbook*. Washington, DC, Urban Land Institute, 1981.

A compendium of information on the planning, development and management of recreational areas, ranging from large theme parks to amenities in residential areas.

84. Spirn, Anne Whiston, *The Granite Garden: Urban Nature and Human Design*. New York, Basic Books, 1984.

The city seen as a natural landscape and how it should therefore be shaped.

85. Stein, Clarence S., *Toward New Towns for America*. Cambridge, MA, MIT Press, 1966.

A full and honest description of the site planning and community development by Stein and Henry Wright, which comprised most of the innovative work in the United States in the twenties, thirties, and forties: Sunnyside, Chatham Village, Radburn, and Baldwin Hills.

86. Suttles, Gerald, *The Social Order of the Slum*. Chicago, University of Chicago Press, 1970.

A fine account of individuals, social structure, and place, all operating as a total system.

87. Tourbier, Joachim, and Richard Westmacott, *A Handbook of Measures to Protect Water Resources in Land Development*. Washington, DC, Urban Land Institute, 1981.

A good presentation of the management of storm water and water bodies.

88. Tuan, Yi-Fu, *Topophilia: A Study of Environmental Perception, Attitudes, and Values*. Englewood Cliffs, NJ, Prentice-Hall, Inc., 1974.

Illuminating discussion of the emotional bonds between people and places, with many fine examples.

89. Tuller, Stanton E., "Microclimate Variations In a Downtown Urban Environment," *Geografiska Annaler*, 1973 (vol, 55A, no. 3–4), pp. 123–128.

Excellent study of the effects of building surfaces and orientation on the microclimate of adjacent spaces in urban areas.

90. Urban Land Institute, *Residential Streets: Objectives, Principles, and Design Considerations*. Washington, DC, Urban Land Institute, 1974.

Street and subdivision planning for residential development.

91. Urban Research and Development Corporation, *Guidelines For Improving the Mobile Home Living Environment: Individual Sites, Mobile Home Parks and Subdivision*. Washington, DC, U.S. Department of Housing and Urban Development, Office of Policy Development and Research, 1977.

Exemplary site patterns and plans with an excellent analysis of the costs of improving livability beyond the routine.

92. Wainwright, A., *A Pictorial Guide to the Lakeland Fells*. 7 vols., 1955–66, Westmorland Gazette Ltd., Kendall, Westmorland, England.

A guide to the mountains of the English Lake District, whose careful descriptions and hand-drawn maps and views are a moving expression of a deep attachment to a landscape and a model of how to record it.

93. Way, Douglas S., *Terrain Analysis; a Guide to Site Selection Using Aerial Photographic Interpretation*. Stroudsburg, PA, Dowden, Hutchinson and Ross, 1973.

A useful text on how to interpret site characteristics from aerial photographs.

94. Weddle, A.E., *Landscape Techniques: Incorporating Techniques of Landscape Architecture*. London, Heinemann, 1979.

Informative essays on landscape construction methods.

95. White, Willo P., *Resources in Environment and Behavior*. Washington, D.C., American Psychological Association, 1979.

An annotated bibliography on the human use and meanings of the environment, along with contacts to those active in the field.

96. Whateley, Thomas, *Observations on Modern Gardening, Illustrated by Descriptions*. London, 1770.

Still insightful, especially on the subject of water in gardens.

97. Whyte, William Hollingsorth, *The Social Life of Small Urban Spaces*. Washington, DC, Conservation Foundation, 1980.

Careful studies of the actual use of streets and public open spaces in dense urban areas and guidelines for their design and management.

98. Wilbur Smith and Associates, *Parking Requirements for Shopping Centers: Summary Recommendations and Research Study Report*. Washington, DC, Urban Land Institute, 1981.

In-depth study of parking usage in a large range of types of shopping centers that can help in setting appropriate standards.

99. Wyman, Donald, *Trees for American Gardens*. New York, Macmillan, 1965.

The standard text on the varieties of U.S. ornamental trees.

100. Zion, Robert L., *Trees for Architecture and Landscape*. New York, Reinhold, 1968.

Detailed data on most of the principal ornamental tree species and their use in site planning. Magnificent illustrations.

List of Illustrations

Figure		Page
1	The Potiala, Lhasa	3
2	Frank Lloyd Wright's Millard House	4
3	The Isono-Kami Shrine, Japan	6
4	Street in Salem, Massachusetts	6
5	Existing conditions, Newtown Site	14
6	Planning issues, Newtown Site	15
7	Original scheme, Newtown Site	16
8	Site survey, Newtown Site	17
9	Landscape inventory, Newtown Site	18
10	Traffic access study, Newtown Site	19
11	Site character sketch, Newtown Site	20
12	Sketch design, Newtown Site	21
13	Site and building concept, Newtown Site	22
14	Detailed site design, Newtown Site	23
15	Grading and seeding plan, Newtown Site	24
16	Planting plan, Newtown Site	25
17	Site construction drawing, Newtown Site	26
18	Utility plan, Newtown Site	27
19	View of completed complex, Newtown Site	28
20	View of site, Newtown Site	28
21	Rural landscape, Sonoma County, California	31
22	An urban landscape	31
23	Succession of species	33
24	Soil survey, Yellow Medicine County, Minnesota	37
25	Geodetic survey, Bernardston, Massachusetts	44
26	Wind tunnel test for a tall building	56
27	Parc Guell, Barcelona	73
28	Neighborhood card players, Boston	75
29	Street of stairs, Lima	76
30	Courtyard, Clinton Prison, Dannemora, New York	76
31	Chatham Village, Pittsburgh	78
32	Steps to Whitby Abbey, England	83

33	*Street activity, Melbourne*	85
34	*Use of street details*	88, 89
35	*Children's imaginary worlds*	90
36	*Resident's sketch of street, San Francisco*	95
37	*Model for financial analysis*	111
38	*A financial pro forma*	120
39	*Critical path diagram*	121
40	*Envelope study for skyscraper*	122
41	*Sketch for the Coonley House*	140
42	*Sketch for Government Center, Boston*	140
43	*Garden at Sanzen-in Temple, Kyoto*	145
44	*Court garden at the Generalife, Granada, Spain*	146
45	*Garden at Villa Lante, Bagnaia, Italy*	147
46	*Grounds at Versailles, France*	148
47	*Garden at Ashburnham, England*	149
48	*Yard of the Dell Plain Place, Hammond, Indiana*	149
49	*Landscape of the Woodland Crematorium, Stockholm*	150
50	*Brazilian landscape*	150
51	*The El Pedregal Subdivision, Mexico City*	151
52	*Nolli's map of Rome*	155
53	*Piazza del Campo, Siena*	159
54	*Entrance into Dvortsovaya Square, Leningrad*	163
55	*Lane in old Cordoba, Spain*	164, 165
56	*Road near Naples, Italy*	166
57	*Stourhead, Wiltshire, England*	166
58	*Path in the Sento Gosho, Kyoto*	167
59	*Serpent Mound, Adams County, Ohio*	167
60	*Gardens of the Saiho-ji Temple, Kyoto*	171
61	*Ammonites in limestone wall*	175
62	*Courtyard of the Parroquia del Salvador, Sevilla, Spain*	175
63	*Machu Picchu, Peru*	175
64	*Courtyard in the Alhambra, Granada, Spain*	177
65	*Water garden at Villa d'Este, Italy*	178
66	*Riverwalk, San Antonio, Texas*	180
67	*Street in the Cyclades, Greece*	180
68	*Hampstead Heath, London*	184
69	*Majolica Cloister of Santa Chiara, Naples*	190
70	*Diagram of visual sequences along a highway*	191
71	*Woonerf, Delft, Holland*	204
72	*Plan of typical Dutch woonerf*	204
73	*Normal street cross-section*	207

74	*Circular curve for horizontal alignments*	213
75	*Parabolic curve for vertical alignments*	219
76	*Roadway contours*	232
77	*The townhouses of Beacon Hill, Boston, and Reston, Virginia*	254
78	*Original courts at Sunnyside, Queens, New York*	256
79	*Their conversion to private grounds*	256
80	*Baldwin Hills, Los Angeles*	258
81	*Manufactured homes*	275
82	*Infill housing in Woolloomooloo, Sydney*	286
83	*Washington Environmental Yard, Berkeley, California*	288
84	*Quincy School, Boston*	290
85	*Expansion of the Massachusetts Eye and Ear Hospital, Boston*	299
86	*Trinity College, Cambridge, England*	299
87	*The University of Virginia*	303
88	*Bourneville, England*	307
89	*Industrial Park*	309
90	*Wellesley Office Park, Wellesley, Massachusetts*	312
91	*Woodfield Mall, Schaumburg, Illinois*	315
92	*Burlington Mall, Burlington, Massachusetts*	319
93	*IDS Center, Minneapolis*	321
94	*Pedestrian Mall, Burlington, Vermont*	327
95	*Maria Luisa Park, Sevilla, Spain*	327
96	*Pioneer Square, Seattle*	331
97	*The University of California, Berkeley*	339
98	*West Broadway renewal program, Boston*	349
99	*Historic center of Delft, Holland*	350
100	*Additions to Rice University, Houston*	350
101	*Gasworks Park, Seattle*	358
102	*Self-help settlement, Lima*	360
103	*Housing invasion, Fez, Morocco*	360
104	*Graph of agricultural soil types*	380
105	*Engineering implications of soils*	383
106	*Typical property survey*	386
107	*Aerial photograph, Lexington, Massachusetts*	394
108	*Comparative climates—Boston and Phoenix*	404, 405
109	*Sun dial diagram*	410
110	*Minimum temperature zones for the United States*	437
111	*Earthwork diagram*	449

List of Tables

Table		Page
1	Wind effects	57
2	Walk capacities	210
3	Alignment standards	221
4	Soil absorption	241
5	Residential densities	253
6	Bearing capacities	384
7	Altitude and azimuth of sun at 42° N	409
8	Additions to bare costs	428
9	Lengths of acceleration and deceleration lanes	447

Illustration Credits

By Kevin Lynch: Figures 3, 27 (bottom), 32, 43, 54, 55, 56, 58, 60, 62, 68, 69, 70, 73, 74, 75, 76, 94, 95, 103, 105, 109, 111.

By Gary Hack: Figures 4, 46, 53, 65, 77 (top), 82, 96, 99.

By Others:

Figure 1 Martin Hürliman.

Figure 2 W. Albert Martin from *In the Nature of Materials* by Henry Russell Hitchcock, New York: Duell Sloan & Pearce, 1942.

Figures 5, 6, 7, 8, 9, 10, 11, 13, 14, 19, 20 Davis, Brody & Associates and Llewelyn-Davies Associates; Hanna/Olin.

Figure 12 Laurie Olin.

Figures 15, 16, 17 Hanna/Olin.

Figure 18 Day and Zimmerman.

Figure 21 Ansel Adams for Wells Fargo Bank American Trust Company.

Figure 22 Walker Evans.

Figure 23 U.S. Department of Agriculture, Forest Service.

Figure 24 U.S. Department of Agriculture, Soil Conservation Service.

Figure 25 U.S. Department of Interior.

Figure 26 Vaughn Winchell, Insight Studios, Somerville, MA.

Figure 27 Caryn Summer (top).

Figure 28 Nishan Bichajian.

Figure 29 John F. C. Turner.

Figure 30 Joshua Friewald, from *Institutional Buildings*, Louis G. Redstone, McGraw Hill.

Figure 31 Ogden Tanner, Architectural Forum.

Figure 33 Peter Downton.

Figure 34 Leon Lewandowski (left)
Al Grey et al, *People and Downtown*, Seattle: College of Architecture and Planning, 1970 (middle)
Walker Evans (right).

Figure 35 From *Planning with Children in Mind*, prepared by Suzanne deMonchaux, NSW Department of Environment and Planning, Australia, September, 1981.

Figure 36 Donald Appleyard.

Figure 37 *Real Estate Appraiser*, SREA, Chicago, Illinois.

Figure 38 Grenelle H. Bauer for Prof. Frank Jones, Department of Urban Studies, Massachusetts Institute of Technology.

Figure 39 From *Network-Based Management Systems*, by Russell Archibald and Richard Villoria, New York: John Wiley & Sons, 1967.

Figure 40 From *Architectural Visions: The Drawings of Hugh Ferriss*, New York: Witney Library of Design, 1980.

Figure 41 From *Drawings for a Living Architecture* by Frank Lloyd Wright, Horizon Press, 1959.

Figure 42 John R. Myer.

Figure 44 From *The Alhambra and the Generalife* by Mario Antequera, Granada, Spain: Ediciones Miguel Sanchez.

Figure 45 From *Italian Gardens* by Georgina Masson, New York: Harry N. Abrams, photo by author.

Figure 47 From *Capability Brown* by Dorothy Stroud, London: Country Life Ltd., 1950. Photo by Architectural Review.

Figure 48 From *Landscape Artist in America: The Life and Work of Jens Jensen*, Leonard Eaton, Chicago: University of Chicago Press, 1964.

Figure 49 From *The Architecture of Erik Asplund* by Stuart Wrede, Cambridge: The MIT Press, 1980. Photo by Sune Sundahl.

Figure 50 From *The Tropical Gardens of Burle Marx* by P. M. Bardi, New York: Van Nostrand Reinhold Co., 1964 and Amsterdam: Meulenhoff & Co. N. V.

Figure 51 From *The Architecture of Luis Barragan* by Emilio Ambasz, New York: The Museum of Modern Art. Photo by Armando Salas Portugal.

Figure 57 From *The English Garden* by Hyams and Smith. Photo by Edwin Smith.

Figure 59 Serpent Mound, Adams County, Ohio. Photo reproduced by permission of the Ohio Historical Society.

Figure 61 Nan Fairbrother.

Figure 63 Allyn Baum.

Figures 64, 66 Stephen Carr.

Figure 67 Dimitra Katochianos.

Figure 71 From *Livable Streets* by Donald Appleyard, Berkeley, University of California Press, 1981.

Figure 72 Royal Dutch Touring Club (bottom).

Figure 77 Rolf D. Weisse (Virginia).

Figure 78 From *Toward New Towns for America* by Clarence Stein, Litton Educational Publishing, Inc., 1957. Photo by Gottscho-Schleisner.

Figure 79 Michael Kwartler.

Figure 80 Fairchild Aerial Surveys.

Figure 81 Barry A. Berkus, from *Building Tomorrow* by Arthur D. Bernhardt, Cambridge: The MIT Press, 1980.

Figure 83 From *Children's Play Spaces* by Jacques Simon and Marguerite Rouard, Woodstock, New York: The Overlook Press, 1977.

Figure 84 From *Urban Design Case Studies* by Edward K. Carpenter, Washington, D.C.: R. C. Publications, 1979.

Figure 85 From *Hospital Planning Handbook*, R. W. Allen and I. Von Karolyi, New York: John Wiley & Sons, 1976.

Figure 86 Aerofilms Ltd.

Figure 87 University of Virginia.

Figure 88 From *The Bourneville Village Trust 1900–1955* by The Bourneviflle Village Trust, c. 1955.

Figures 89, 92 Julie Messervy.

Figure 90 Steve Rosenthal, Auburndale, Massachusetts.

Figure 91 From *Shopping Center Development Handbook* by James Ross McKeever, Washington, D.C.: The Urban Land Institute, 1977.

Figure 97 Long Range Development Plan for the Berkeley Campus, University of California, August 1956.

Figure 98 West Broadway Team; a joint venture of Lane, Frenchman and Associates, Inc., and Goody, Clancy and Associates, Inc.

Figure 100 Architectural Review, Feb. 1982; photo by Paul Hester.

Figure 101 Richard Haag, Landscape Architect.

Figure 102 John F. C. Turner.

Figure 104 *Soil Survey Manual*, U.S. Department of Agriculture.

Figure 106 Oyster-Watcha Midlands Assoc., Survey by Dean R. Swift.

Figure 107 Lockwood Keffer and Bartlett, Syosset, New York.

Figure 108 *Climates of the States*, U.S. Weather Bureau, and *House Beautiful Climate Control Guide*.

Figure 110 *The Yearbook of Agriculture, 1949*, U.S. Department of Agriculture.

Index

acceleration and deceleration of traffic, 447
access, 19, 75, 193–221
  systems, 193–197
acting out, 97
actions, initial, 137
activity
  classifying, 112
  diagram of, 85
  logs, 93
  management, 173
  pattern, 132
  in site design, 128
  and space, 158
  visible, 171–172
actors other than client and user, 370
adaptability
  of circulation systems, 206–207
  in hospital site planning, 297
  residential, 278
adaptation, 129
"add-ons," 10
air movement around buildings, 55
albedo, 49, 51
Alexander, Christopher, 130, 304, 372
Alhambra, 177
alignment
  in circulation systems, 197, 212–221
  standards, table of, 221
alternatives, 138, 139
  sequential, 141
altitude of the sun, 407, 409
ammonite wall (England), 175
apartments, 252
  high-rise, 281
  types of, 280–282
analogies as design method, 129–130, 131, 138, 143
analysis
  cluster, 120, 132
  content of, 82
angle of repose, 40, 456–457
angle, laying out a right, 387–388
archetypes, 132
archives, 81

Ashburnham (England), 149
Asplund, Gunnar, 150
Atlantic Richfield Company (ARCO) Research and Engineering Center (Pennsylvania), 13
audial quality, 62
automobiles, 266. See also roads; parking
  alternatives to,
  azimuth of the sun, 52–53, 407, 409

Baldwin Hills (Los Angeles), 258
bare costs, 427–428
  additions, to, 469
  base distance, 399
Barker, Roger, 84
Barragan, Luis, 151
Bath (England), 2
Beacon Hill (Boston), 254
behavior, 34–35
  assumptions about, 114
  circuits, 87
  selected, 87
  settings, 8, 34, 84–86, 112–113
bicycles, 211–212, 304
bids, 10
block, overcoming design, 137
bodily comfort, 463–464
bonuses, 344
Boston, climate of, 402–406, 404, 405
boundaries, 356
Bourneville (England), 307
Brown, Capability, 149
buildability, 334
building lines, 334, 342–343
building orientation, 266–268

California, University of (Berkeley), 339
  and continuity, 50
  growth predictions for, 302
  as learning place, 302
  organization, 300
  planning, 298–305
  plan over time, 339
  space requirements, 302

carrying capacity, 34
  of open spaces, 326
change, celebration of, 354
channelization of traffic, 445
Chatham Village (Pittsburgh), 78
checklist for continuity of character, 349
checklist, site and impact, 420–425
children's spaces, 268–270
choices
  forced, 96
  past, 81
  in site design, 369
circulation, 194–221
  adaptability of, 206
  and alignment, 197, 219–221
  cost of, 201
  effect on development, 201
  evaluation of, 206
  grain of, 198
  patterns, 132, 195–196
  in site design, 128
  social effects of, 202
  types of, 194–196
clay, 379–380, 381, 382, 383, 384
clearance, costs of, 347
clients, 3, 70, 141
climate, 47–59
  of Boston, 402–406, 404, 405
  in city, 57–58
  of Phoenix, 402–406, 404, 405
  and slope, 51–52
Clinton Prison (New York), 76
cloverleaf, 446
cluster analysis, 120, 132
comfort, bodily, 48
"common law" of design guidelines, 346
communication
  direct, 91
  by means of program, 108
  in site design, 375
community facilities
  and housing, 291
  management of, 291
compass, 388
competitions, design, 108, 142
complementaries in garden design,
  189
computers, 230, 429, 453
concept diagram, 22
condominiums, 257–258
conduction, 49–50, 51
congruence, 172
consequences, analysis of, 136
construction
  details, 26
  documents, 224
  process of, 223
context, 351
contingency allowances, 428

continuity, 350, 352
contour, 168–169, 390–391
  and grading, 231–232
  map, 169
  and street, 201
contract documents, 10
contractor overhead and profit,
  427–428
control
  of costs, 343
  points, 388
  process of, 345
  scale of, 352
  and use, 342
  and user, 77
convection, 50
cooperative housing, 259
Cordoba (Spain), 164
cordon line, 86
costs, 426–430
  bare, 427–428, 469
  consultants for, 429
  data in computer-readable form,
    429
  estimating, 9, 10, 427
  general, 427–428
  operating and maintenance, 429
  replacement, 429
  standard, 429
  types of, 79
  by types of improvement,
    426–427
critical path
  analysis, 120
  diagram, 121
culvert, 238
Cyclades (Greece), 180
cycleways, 211–212
cyclical designing, 373

data, permanence of, 66
decibels, 60, 412
decibel scale, 413, 414, 464–465
  weighted, 414
declination of the sun, 405
defile, 169
Delft (Holland), 350
Dell Plain Place (Indiana), 149
density
  controls, 342
  and housing types, 252–253, 466
design
  definition of, 9, 127–128
  framework, 192
  as learning process, 67–68, 374
  optimizing method of, 133–134
  processes of, 128–129
  review, 345
  teams, 142
detached houses, visual problems
  of, 274

developers, multiple, 336
descriptions, free, 94
discontinuity of character, 351
division by aspect, 132
drainage lines in site evaluation, 40
dry-strength test, 381
duplex, 275, 276

earth as site material, 174
earthwork, 225, 448–454
  computation by array of sections, 453
  computation by computer, 453–454
  computation by contour-area method, 448, 449–450, 457
  computation by end-area method, 450–451, 457
  computation by grid corner method, 451–452, 457
  computation by model use, 453
  and computers, 230, 453–454
  and cut and fill, 229–231
  diagrams of, 449, 451
  and grading, 225–226, 228
  and lines of no-cut no-fill, 448
  and machines, 227, 457
  and soil handling, 225
  standards, 455–457
ecology, 32–34, 182
  in open space planning, 326
electric power
  and distribution pattern, 245
  and power poles, 245, 463
elevation
  equation for, 399
  key points of, 390–391
El Pedrogal (Mexico), 151
empathy, 98
enclosure, 156–157
energy, 59
  and orientation, 266–267
envelope studies, 121, 122
environmental art, 188
environmental impact study, 124–125, 420–425
environment and quality of life, 12
ethnocentrism, 80
exotic plant material, 184
experiment, natural, 91
experiments in behavior, 90–91
exploring means of design, 136

factories, 310
false color in site photography, 400
fees, 427–428
fee-simple freehold, 255
fences, 185–186
Ferris, Hugh, 122

Fez (Morocco), 360
financial analysis, 111, 119–120, 120
fire stations, location of, 291
fit and user action, 74
flag lots, 273
flight patterns for aerial photography, 392–393
floor area ratio, 253, 303, 342
form
  guidelines for future, 340
  many-centered, 189
  sensible, 128, 132
  specification, 341
function
  essential, 134–135
  future, 338

gaming, 102
garages, 265
gas distribution, 247
Gas Works Park (Seattle), 357, 358
Generalife (Spain), 146
grading
  to control traffic, 445–446
  and earthwork, 225–229, 455–461
  plans, 24, 231–232
  of streets and sidewalks, 218
grain of circulation, 198
grasses as site material, 432–433
gravel, 379, 381, 383, 384
grid
  blocked, 196
  circulation pattern, 195–196
  repertory, 102
ground covers, 170–171, 431–433
ground form
  and circulation, 40
  and flow of water, 235
  representation of, 229
  and space, 163
ground surfacings, 433–436
ground textures, 170–171
growth predictions in campus planning, 302
guidelines, 341–345

habitability and user, 72
habitat, loss of, 34
Hampstead Heath (England), 184
hardiness, plant, 437
heating, central, 247–248
hedges, 436–437
height, estimation of, 387
hierarchy in site plan, 189
historic center, 350
history of site, 352–353, 371
homes associations, 257
hospital, site planning for, 297–298

hospitalization, experience of, 298
hour angle of the sun, 408
housing, 251–293, 295
  attached, 251
  categories of, 251–252
  and community facilities, 291
  and density, 252–253
  detached, 251
  and facility standards, 466–467
  and fit with context, 285
  hybrid, 252, 282
  infill, 283–284
  and lot and structure dimensions, 466
  rear lot, 276
  and recreation, 287
  and shopping, 285
  self-built, 76, 357–368, 360
    access, 361
    appropriate technology, 366
    dranage, 363
    finance, 367
    land tenure, 359
    lot form and size, 359
    management and control, 364–365
    process, 358
    sensuous quality, 365
    upgrading, 362
    utilities, 362
    waste disposal, 363
  and social-spatial relationship, 261
  standards, 466–467
  tenure, 253–260
human scale, 468

identity, residential, 278
images, 93
impact analysis, 374
  questions, 421–425
industrial districts, 306–311
  and control, 309
  isolation of, 311
  and land and utilities, 307
  layout of, 308
  and model village, 307
  and parking, 309
  and service facilities, 310
  standards, 308, 467
infrared photography, 398
infrastructure, 223
insolation and sky exposure, 464
institutional clusters, 305
institutions
  and environments, 376
  as neighbors, 296, 301
  site planning for, 295–297
  as symbolic settings, 301–302
interchanges, 200, 446
intersections, traffic, 444–447

interviews, 92, 99
inversion, 54
Isono-kami Shrine (Japan), 6

Jacob's staff, 388
Jensen, Jens, 149
justice and user, 77

Kahn, Albert, 305
Katsura Palace (Japan), 1
Kyoto (Japan), 145, 167

landforms, 39–43. See also ground form
Landsat satellite, 400
landscape, 153
  as symbolic medium, 173
languages of site planning, 192
latitude, 407
leasehold tenure, 260
lengths, estimation of, 385
Leningrad: Dvortsovaya Square, 163
levels, chain of, 387
  changes, 156
Lexington (Massachusetts), 394
light and building orientation, 270
  and space, 158–160
lighting, 246–247
  artificial, 160
  standards, 246–247, 463
Lima (Peru): self-built housing, 76, 360
linear patterns of circulation, 196–197
line scanners, 400
linkages in campus planning, 301
  in complex plans, 296, 298
literature, research, 82–83
Looking Backward, 325
loops in circulation systems, 197, 200
"lotsteading," 285

Machu Picchu (Peru), 175
maintenance, site, 183–184
maisonette, 279
malls. See shopping centers
management and performance, 116
manholes, 234
many-centered forms, 189
maps, 43–47
  base, 14, 43, 63
  contour, 43, 45, 169
  making, 385–391
  reading, 43
  reconnaissance, 385
  scale of, 43
  temperature zones, 437
  U.S. Geodetic Survey, 44

market analysis, 119
market share, 119
Marx, Burle, 150
Massachusetts Eye and Ear Hospital (Boston), *299*
materials, site, 174–190
matrix organization, 143
measurement, angular, 387
measurement by tape, 386
Melbourne (Australia), *85*
memories, 97
metaphor, as design tool, 128
microclimate, 58, 59
military crest, 169
mobile homes, 273–275
models in site planning, 96–97, 169, 411
modules, residential, 261, 262
  in site design, 131
Moore, Robin, 311
motion and space, 162

nadir, 393, 398
Naples (Italy), *166, 190*
neighborhoods, *95*, 291–293
neighbors, 348
noise, 60–62, 412–419
  attenuation, 61, 465
  barriers, 418–419
  control, 416–418
  day versus night, 414
  measurement of, 415–416
  measurement of, without instruments, 416
  propagation, 416–417
  standards, 415, 464–465
Nolli's map of Rome, *155*

observation
  direct, 83–84
  indirect, 80–81
  participant, 100
  self, 100–101
observer reactions, 102
office parks, 311–313, *312*
open space, 325–332, *327, 331*
  access to, 327
  approach and sequence, 329
  criteria for, 326
  as learning place, 330
  maintenance of, 332
  occupation rule of, 329
  openness of, 325
  pathways in, 329–330
  sense of territory, 328
  standards, 287
optimizing as design method, 133–134
Oregon, University of, experiment at, 372
orientation in temperate climate, 267

owner associations, 346
ownership, fee-simple, 255

package and program, 109–110
packager, 335
Paley Park (New York City), 418
parallactic displacement, 399
Parc Guell (Barcelona), *73*
park, pocket, 285, 331
parking, 216, 263–266
  on campus, 304
  curb, 265
  lots, 265
  standards, 461
Parroquia del Salvador (Spain), *175*
participant observation, 100
participation in design, 101, 304, 371
path, character of, 205
pattern and program, 116
pattern language, 130
patterns of residential modules, 262
Paul Revere Mall (Boston), *75*
peat and muck, 380, 383
pedestrian
  capacity of walkways for, 210
  grading for, 218
  flow, 209–211
perception of space, 154–157
perceptual organization, 189
performance
  and management, 116
  measure of, 115
  requirements, 113–114
  specifications, 341
Phoenix, climate of, 402–406, *404, 405*
photography, aerial, 46–47, 392–401, 468
  compiling, 393
  example, *394*
  flight patterns for, 392–393
  identifying features, 393–395
  measuring heights, 398
  mosaics, 395
  scale, 395
  sight lines, 398
  and stereovision, 396
photography by respondents, 47
photogrid, 47
Pioneer Square (Seattle), *331*
plan
  detailed, 10
  of existing landscape, *18*
  incremental, 372
  schematic, 9
plane table, 389–390
planning
  issues, diagram of, *15*

planning (continued)
  process, illustrated example of, 13, *14–28*
plant cover as indication of site conditions, 41–42
planting plan, *25*
plants
  exotic, 184
  habit of growth of, 181
  hardiness of, 181
  management of, 42
  as site material, 179–183
  and species mix, 185
  and stability and change, 182
  and succession, *33*, 42
  and texture, 181
play, *90*, 96–97
playgrounds, *288*, 289, 330–331
population and programming, 109
precedents, 81
precinct plans, 203
predictions, 97, 374
preferences, 94–96
prefabricated buildings, 336
privacy, 269–270
problem definition, 3, 5, 93, 135, 373
profit, 110–111, 428
programming, 107–126
  as communication, 108
  definition of, 107
  and design, 107
  elements of, 109, 115
  expression of, 108–109
  and front-end analysis, 118
  objectives of, 115
  process of, 117–125
  and prototype, 123
  and user involvement, 118
project evaluation and review technique (PERT), 120
proportion and scale, 157–158
prototypes, 104, 123, 129, 154
psychiatric methods in user analysis, 102

quad, 276
questionnaires, 99
Quincy School (Boston), *290*

radial patterns of circulation, 196
radiation, solar, 52
ramp grades, 446
reason and unreason in design, 137
recreation, 325
  and housing, 287
recreational use of streets and wastelands, 289, *290*, 291
relocation, 347, *349*
remote sensing, 400

rental housing, 260
repertory grid, 102
residential lot and structure dimensions, 466
Reston, Virginia, *254*
Rice University (Houston), *350*
ridge lines, 40
right-of-way, 212
Riverwalk (San Antonio, Texas), *180*
"roadability," 219
roads, 1. *See also* intersections; streets
  alignment of, 219–221
  capacities of, 461
  dimensions for, 457–461
  forward sight distance of, 220
  gradients of, 459
  horizontal and vertical curves of, 459–460
  imaginary drawing of, *191*
  intersection standards, 460–461
  lengths and spacing of, 458–459
rock as site material, 174
role playing, 98
Rome, Nolli's map of, *155*
rotary, 445
  bridged, 446
rowhouses, *78*, 277–280

Salem, Massachusetts, *6*
San Antonio, Texas, *180*
sand as site material, 380–381, 383–384
sanitary drainage, 239–243, 462–463
Sanzen-in (Japan), *145*
schools, 289, 298–305. *See also* campus planning
sea breeze, 54
security, 271
semantic differential, 96
semi-detached housing, 276
semiotics, 174
"sense of occasion," 174
sense of place and user, 72
sensed quality of place, 153
sensuous program, 192
Serpent Mound (Adams County, Ohio), *167*
sewage disposal
  non-water-borne systems, 241–243
  water-borne systems, 240
sewer, storm, 234–237
shade, 52
shadow casting on model, 411
shadows, simulation of, 53
shopping centers, 313–325
  changes in, 324–325

circulation in, 318
and community, 320
landscaping of, 318, *319*
layout of, 314
and malls, 315
and parking, 316–317
standards for, 467–468
types of, 313–314
shopping in relation to housing, 287
shopping streets, 320, 322
side-looking radar, 401
sidewalks as playgrounds, 289
Siena (Italy), *159*
sightlines, 161
signs as site material, 187–188
silt, 379–380, 382, 384
simulation, 94–96
single-family detached housing, 272–273
site
  abandoned, 355–356
  analysis, 5, 62–66, 354
  best use of, 65
  and building design, 335
  change, 30
  character, 42
  data, 63, 420
  identity, 30
  management, 11, 372
  and purpose, 29, 35
  reconnaissance, 46
  reputation of, 356–357
  scheme, *16*
  selection, 64–65
  sketches, *20, 21*
  visits, 98
site design, 272
  elements of, 127
  exploring means of, 136
  historic styles of, 154
  as linear process, 369
  strategy, 369–377
  when controls are lacking, 333
site plan
  context, 349
  detailed, *23*
  schematic, 139
  technical development of, 230
site planning
  definition, 1, 12
  in built places, 346, 352
  long-range, 338
  process of, 2, 13, *14–28*
  stages of, 11
slope, 40, 41
  and climate, 51–52
  standards for, 456–457
soils, 35–38, 379–384
  absorption rates of, 241

agricultural classification of, 35–36
bearing capacity of, 384
engineering characteristics of, 455–457
engineering classification of, 36
engineering implications of, 382, *383*
field identification of 380–382
field testing of, 36
particles of, 379
as plant medium, 36–38
surveys of, 37, *38*
texture, 380
social-spatial relationship of housing, 261
sound perception, 413
space
  and activity, 158
  connotations of, 161
  and ground form, 163
  and hearing and touch, 161
  and light, 158, 160
  and motion, 162–163
  perception of, 154–157
  and viewpoints, 161
specific heat, 50
"spirit of place," 5
standards
  noise, 60
  unforeseen effects of, 344–345
  for non-residential facilities, 285–286
  for open space, 287–289
steady-flow system, 195
stereoscope, pocket, 396
stereovision, 396–397
stimuli, distorted, 102
storm drainage, 234–239
  cost of, 233
  and pipe size, 237–238
  problems of, 238
  standards, 461–462
  and subsurface drains, 239
Stourhead (England), *166*
strategy of concentration, 190
street. *See also* intersections; roads
  behavior, 322–323
  capacities of, 217
  and contours, 201
  cross sections of, 207
  as design focus, 203
  detail, *88, 89*
  and forward sight distance, 214
  functions of, 202
  furniture, 186–187
  grades of, 218
  hierarchies of, 198
  horizontal alignment of, 212
  interchanges and terminals, 200

street (continued)
  and intersections, 215
  and lengths and endings, 215
  and the moving view, 205
  profiles, 218
  residential, 203
  and sidewalks, 209
  surface of, 208
  vertical alignment of, 217
street detail, use of, *88, 89*
structure plan, 372
subdivision, 333, 335
  criteria for, 335
subsurface problems, 39
succession, plant, *33*, 42
sun
  altitude and azimuth, 52–53, 407,
    409
  angles, 407–411
  equations, 407
sundial, 53
  diagram, *410*
  how to make a, 407–411
Sunnyside, New York, *256*
Suntop Homes (Ardmore, Penn-
    sylvania), 276
superblocks, 199, 292
supervision of construction, 10–11
surveillance, 271
surveys
  field, *17*, 385–391
  land, 45
  noise, 60
  personal, 64
  property, *386*
  quantity, 429
  systematic, 63
symbols and landscape, 173
synthesis, 64

Taliesin, 2
teenagers, 269
telephone lines, 247
temperature, effective, 48
  zones, minimum, 437
temporary use, 353–354
terminals, 200
terrain, 135
territory, sense of, 271
thematic apperception, 102
thread test, 381
thresholds and programming, 114
time, sense of, 174
timing and development, 353
"time above" sound measurement,
    415
topography, expressed by path-
    ways, 205
  and air movement, 54
townhouses, *254*, 277–280, *286*

townscape, 349
traces, 82
traffic
  acceleration and deceleration of,
    447
  channelization, 445
  count, 86
  hospital, 297
  signals, 444–445
transparency, 173
traverse, 388–389
trees, 437–443
Trinity College (England), *299*

Uniform Construction Index, 428
university, standards for planning,
    467
urban design, 336
use
  communal, 269
  controls, 342
  temporary, 353–354
  trial, of site, 113
user, 67–105
  and access, 75
  analysis, 75
    choice of method for, 102–105
    demographic, 69
    techniques for, 80–102
  and client, 68
  complex, 68
  and control, 77
  definition of, 67
  and fit, 74
  groups, 69–70
  and habitability, 72
  identifying, 68
  interests, 348
  and justice, 77
  selection, 70
  and sense of place, 72
  surrogate, 69
  voiceless or unknown, 68–69
utilities
  layout, *27*
  plans, 249–250
  standards for, 461–463

vandalism, 332
vehicles, low-speed, 212
ventilation, 267
Versailles, *148*
view and building orientation, 270
view easement, 343
Villa d'Este (Italy), *178*
Villa Lante (Italy), *147*
Virginia, University of, *303*
visual form of terrain, 41
visual sequences, 162–163

walls, as site material, *175,*
    185–186
Washington Environmental Yard
    (Berkeley, California), *288*
waste disposal, 248
  in self-help housing, 363–364
wastelands, *289, 290, 291,*
    355–356
water
  as site material, 176–179
  surface, 235
  table, 38–39
  supply standards, 463
water system, 243–245
  capacity of, 244
  layout of, 243–244
  and wells, 244–245
Wellesley Office Park (Massachu-
    setts), *312*
Whitby Abby (England), *83*
wildlife, 172
wind, 54–56
  breaks, 54–55
  table of effects, 57
  tunnels, 55, *56*
  speed, 56
Woodfield Mall (Illinois), *315*
Woodland Crematorium (Sweden),
    150
Woolloomooloo (Sydney, Aus-
    tralia), townhouses, *286*
woonerf, 199, 203, *204*
workplaces, 305–313
  and industrial districts, 306–311
  and office parks, 311–313
Wright, Frank Lloyd, 2, 4

yard, private, 269